50s Roadside Florida

Donald D. Spencer

Schiffer Publishing Ltd

4880 Lower Valley Road, Atglen, Pennsylvania 19310

Dedication

To my daughter, Sandra

Designed by Stephanie Daugherty
Type set in Bellevue/Swis721 BT/Swis721 BlkCn BT
ISBN: 978-0-7643-3364-4
Printed in China

Illustration and Photo Credits

This book is based mainly on the postcard, photo and memorabilia collection of the author, augmented by illustrations from Dover Publications, Inc., page 39 (top and bottom right) and photographs from the Florida State Photographic Archives, pages 32 (top right), 40 (right), 49 (bottom right), 59 (top left), 64 (right), 69 (bottom), 70 (center), 72 (left), 73 (top right), 79 (top left), 82 (bottom), 93 (bottom right), 95 (bottom right), 96 (bottom left), 101 (right), 107 (bottom left), 108 (top left).

Other Schiffer Books by Donald D. Spencer :

A History of the Alligator: Florida's Favorite Reptile
978-0-7643-3083-4, $24.99
St. Augustine, Florida: Past and Present
978-0-7643-3146-6, $24.99
Mid-Century Vegas: 1930s to 1960s
978-0-7643-3129-9, $39.99

Other Schiffer Books on Related Subjects:

Miami Memories: A Midcentury Journey
0-7643-2176-5, $16.95
Fort Lauderdale Memories: A Postcard History 1900-1960
978-0-7643-2828-2, $24.99

Schiffer Books are available at special discounts for bulk purchases for sales promotions or premiums. Special editions, including personalized covers, corporate imprints, and excerpts can be created in large quantities for special needs. For more information contact the publisher:

Schiffer Publishing Ltd.
4880 Lower Valley Road
Atglen, PA 19310
Phone: (610) 593-1777; Fax: (610) 593-2002
E-mail: Info@schifferbooks.com

For the largest selection of fine reference books on this and related subjects, please visit our web site at:

www.schifferbooks.com

We are always looking for people to write books on new and related subjects. If you have an idea for a book please contact us at the above address.

This book may be purchased from the publisher. Include $5.00 for shipping. Please try your bookstore first. You may write for a free catalog.

In Europe, Schiffer books are distributed by
Bushwood Books
6 Marksbury Ave.
Kew Gardens
Surrey TW9 4JF England
Phone: 44 (0) 20 8392 8585; Fax: 44 (0) 20 8392 9876
E-mail: info@bushwoodbooks.co.uk
Website: www.bushwoodbooks.co.uk

Contents

Section One: Preface

*F*lorida has been drawing tourists for over a century. After automobile travel became the norm after World War II, tourists began to swarm the open roads. Many of these tourists came to the Sunshine State to go to the beaches or visit other facilities—and they demanded a reason to stop along the way. With roadside attractions such as Marineland, Cypress Gardens, Weeki Wachee, and Silver Springs attracting visitors by the thousands, tourists found that Florida was loaded with a variety of interesting things to do. The roadside was speckled with citrus stands, beautiful gardens, alligator attractions, historical landmarks, unnatural oddities, famous homes, picturesque lighthouses, gaming facilities, museums, amusement parks, bird and animal zoos, bubbling springs, Seminole Indian villages, souvenir shops and other roadside diversions that reeled the tourists in for a short visit. *50s Roadside Florida* describes the attractions and curiosities that interested tourists during the "Golden Years of Florida Roadside Attractions," before today's theme parks became worldwide vacation destinations. All of the postcards are from the 1950s and most of them are valued between $2-$8.

Postcards and People

Postcards or Letters?

In the rapidly changing world of the 1900s, people found that they needed a way to communicate quickly. The time-consuming and cumbersome business of letter writing, which involved stationary and envelopes, was tiresome to a generation focusing on the patterns of a changing environment. The agitation for a single piece of card stock on which a hurried message might be written had become keen in many parts of the world. It didn't take long before the postcard became the chief means of communication. Picture postcards furnished people with a method of showing off strange and exotic places. No one had to say, "Wish You Were Here"—the postcard images made sure that you were.

Old postcards offer views of scenes both familiar and removed. They evoke memories of a happy time gone by, and, like family photographs, remind us of what's changed.

A postcard is better than a thousand words. The cards depict everything from small landmarks that no longer exist, to historical structures, to natural parks, to popular tourist attractions. And the large letter "Greetings from" state and city postcards are colorful reminders of each state or city a traveler has visited. The cards in this section represent some of the towns we'll be visiting on our roadside journey.

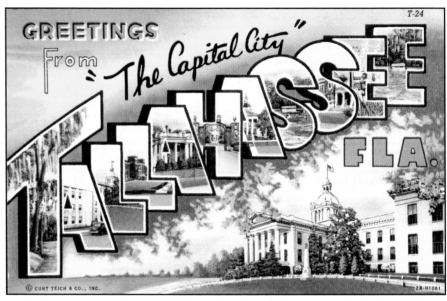

Introduction
1950s America

The Cold War between America and the Soviet Union ran through the 1950s. As the decade began, both countries had atomic bombs and the threat of a devastating nuclear war hung over the world, with thousands of Americans building bomb shelters in their backyards. It was the Hydrogen Age and people were frightened by the power of the H-Bomb—hence, the bomb shelter became a common sight in cities throughout the country. The Cold War with the Soviet Union created terrible tensions. Korea was supposed to be a short-term "police action," but it turned into a long and bitter war. Between the war's beginning in 1950 and its end in 1953, millions of civilians were hurt or killed. Even though the threat of a nuclear war hung over the world, for many people the international tension was balanced by home comfort. Particularly after 1955, they enjoyed high wages, large automobiles, and home comforts like vacuum cleaners and washing machines. Inventions familiar in the modern world made their first appearance. Teenagers chose their own fashions and music.

The 1950s also saw the new luxury of air-conditioning, suburban ranch-style homes in larger cities, dancing the mambo, ten-cent telephone calls and newspapers, three-cent stamps, and Cokes for a nickel.

Roadside Memories.

During the 1950s the population of the United States grew from 151.3 million to 179.3 million; the annual earning for the average employee was $2,992; in 1959 it was $4,743. A dozen oranges were 52¢ in 1950 and 75¢ in 1960; a loaf of bread was 14¢ in 1950 and 20¢ in 1959; and a pound of coffee in 1950 was 55¢, ten years later it was 75¢. Throughout the 1950s, African Americans experienced many hardships. Most good jobs were not open to them, and they still earned less money than whites. They often lived in dangerous and dirty parts of the city and were not allowed the same basic rights as white people.

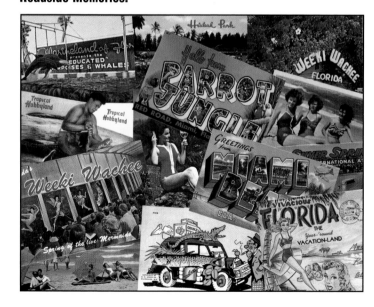

The top male singing stars of the 1950s were Eddie Fisher (Oh My Papa), Harry Belafonte (Jamaica Farewell), Perry Como, Mario Lanza, Tony Bennett, and Elvis Presley. The top female singers were Lena Horne, Julie London, Rosemary Clooney (Come On-a My House), Patti Page (Tennessee Waltz), Teresa Brewer (Music! Music! Music!), Peggy Lee (Fever), Jo Stafford (Shrimp Boats), Kay Starr (Wheel of Fortune), and Debbie Reynolds (Tammy).

The man who turned rock and roll into a national teenage religion was a 21-year-old Memphis truck driver named Elvis Presley. In the mid-1950s his single records Heartbreak Hotel, Don't Be Cruel and Love Me Tender each sold over a million copies. It wasn't long before he was being called the "King of Rock 'n' Roll." Presley died August 16, 1977.

America went crazy over TV. For many years families gathered in their homes every night to *listen* to their radios. They would listen to music, drama, the news, and comedy. Then, beginning in the early 1950s, families gathered in their homes every night to *watch* music, drama, the news, and comedy. Americans were fascinated with this latest provider of home entertainment.

Funnyman Milton Berle, known as "Mr. Television," kept millions glued to their TV sets on Tuesday nights for more than six years. Perhaps the zaniest and most popular show of the decade was "I Love Lucy," a spoof of married life starring movie actress Lucille Ball and her Cuban-born bandleader husband, Desi Arnaz. The show went on to lure an audience of 50 million viewers. Other popular TV shows were "Father Knows Best," "The Honeymooners," "Dobie Gillis," "The Phil Silvers Show," "Leave It To Beaver," "Ozzie and Harriet," "Burns and Allen Show," "Mr. Peepers," "Our Miss Brooks," "What's My Line," "Dragnet," and "Naked City." *TV Guide*, founded by media mogul Walter Annenberg in 1953, became one of the most widely read magazines in the country.

Marilyn Monroe (born Norma Jean Mortenson in 1926) was the reigning queen of American movies. Films such as "Gentlemen Prefer Blondes," "How to Marry a Millionaire," "The Seven-Year Itch," "Bus Stop," and "Some Like It Hot" made her a superstar and the "sex symbol" of the decade. She received 5,000 fan letters a week. Marilyn said, "It's nice to be included in people's fantasies."

Movie star James Dean became a symbol of the 1950s teenage rebel. He appeared in three very popular films. Dean will probably be remembered best as the "Rebel Without A Cause." His stardom was certain after starring in the film "East of Eden." Dean's last picture, "Giant," was released in 1956; he was in a fatal car accident on September 30, 1955.

A new commodity, 3-D glasses, was the rage for a while with 1950s movie audiences. Americans loved to see science fiction and horror film spring to life. The 3-D glasses changed the typical flat, two-dimensional image on the screen to appear in three-dimensions.

Popular books and authors of the 1950s were Grace Metalious (*Peyton Place*), Herman Wouk (*The Caine Mutiny*), James Jones (*From Here to Eternity*), J. D. Salinger (*The Catcher in the Rye*), and a tough-talking Brooklyn writer named Frank Morrison (Mickey) Spillane (author of several detective hero Mike Hammer mystery books). Fans devoured 27 million copies of Spillane's books like *Kiss Me, Deadly*. In 1954 writer Ernest Hemingway was awarded the Nobel Prize for *The Old Man and the Sea*. An entire generation of American children went Mad! *Mad Comics No. 1* went on sale in November 1952 and was a runaway hit. In 1953, the first issue of *Playboy* magazine, bearing a photograph of Marilyn Monroe on its cover, carried no date because its publisher, 27-year-old Hugh Hefner, was not sure there would be a second. The new magazine proved so successful that within three years it was outselling *Esquire*.

During the 1950s jet air travel became the ultimate luxury for those who could afford it. Many flight times were halved compared with those made by conventional aircraft. In 1954 Boeing introduced the Boeing 707 commercial passenger jet. Three years later a National Airlines Boeing 707 broke a speed record for cross-country passenger flight when it landed in Baltimore, Maryland from Seattle, Washington in just three hours and forty-eight minutes. The four-engine jet transport carried forty-two passengers and a crew of ten on the 2,330-mile trip. In January 1959 American Airlines was the first airline to offer same-day passenger service between New York and Los Angeles.

A powerful new electronic digital computer was released in 1951 by Remington Rand. It was UNIVAC (Universal Automatic Computer), the first such machine to be put on the market. Four years later International Business Machines (IBM) Corporation introduced the 700-line of computers. In 1953, Jonas Salk, an American physician and scientist, developed a vaccine for polio. In 1954, the U.S. Navy launched the world's first nuclear powered submarine. The *Nautilus* was 319 feet long and weighed 3,180 tons. Also in 1954, Ray Kroc of San Bernardino, California, a high-school dropout, came up with a newfangled stand for selling French fries, soda, and 15¢ hamburgers. Today it's a fast-food empire known as McDonald's.

Walt Disney realized his own dreams, as well as those of millions of children, when he opened his Disneyland theme park in July 1955. Disneyland proved so successful that the Disney Corporation went on to open three more theme parks; in Florida (1971), Tokyo (1983), and Paris (1992).

Hula-Hoops, plastic tubes formed into large rings, became popular. In 1958, millions of kids twirled them around their waists, arms, heads, and necks. In January 1959, Alaska was admitted as the 49th state and in August Hawaii became the 50th state. Also in 1959, Fidel Castro gained controlling power in Cuba and created hostile relations between Cuba and the United States, which still exists today.

Automobiles in the 1950s

The American passion for wheels reached its peak in the '50s. All across the country people were taking to the road. For the first time in years Americans had time on their hands and money to spend. So they added a new element to the American dream—the status symbol. And no other status symbol packed a bigger punch than the automobile. The car of the 1950s was big, powerful, and solid. No longer was a car just a means of transportation; it was freedom and luxury on wheels. Wrap around windshields increased visibility and huge tailfins were said to "add stability at high speeds." Some new cars looked like rockets. Seatbelts were introduced as extras. All-steel construction made cars stronger, and engines and transmissions were becoming more efficient. Prices varied. A new 1958 Dodge, with push button automatic transmission, cost about $2,500. People no longer had to stay in the same town where they grew up. They could see different cities and towns with ease.

The new ease of travel gave rise to the development of suburbs. A new youth culture was created around the car. Drive-in movies and diners became popular. During the '50s, kids started spending less time with their families and more time with friends. In one short decade, the housewives headquarters moved from the kitchen to the car. She might drop her husband off at the train station and then drive the kids to school and later pick them up. In between, she drove to the supermarket and the cleaners. By the end of the decade, the car was no longer a status symbol—it was a necessity. Roads were excellent, traffic was light, and gasoline was cheap (less than 10¢ a gallon).

In Retrospect

In summary, the America of the 1950s was enthralled by the novelty of television, but had not yet come to realize its full potential—good or bad. The fact that human events could be seen instantly as they happened—including wars, assassinations, the Olympics, and championship fights—made us see television as a window of the world. With its varied offerings of ballet, opera, drama, and scientific programs about the human body, space exploration, the environment, and life beneath the sea, television proved itself educational in a way no other medium ever could. It has also proved itself a wonderful babysitter, and a miracle of entertainment for the sick and the elderly, who might otherwise rarely hear the sound of another human voice.

The massive American automobiles of the 50s, although they looked like rocket-launchers, were built as family cars, perfect for weekend outings and vacations. As one Ford ad of the period put it, the car promised "freedom to come and go as we please in this country of ours." The car became a symbol of blissful escapism. By 1956 America owned three-quarters of all the cars in the world. The American car of the 1950s fanned the flames of the new industrial prosperity, created those rows of neat clapboard houses, and those miles of arrow-straight roadways, and gave America a mobility that was the envy of the world.

The Univac I was the first general-purpose digital computer offered as a commercial product. It was installed at the U.S. Census Bureau in 1951. Shortly after the Korean War started, the International Business Machines (IBM) Corporation announced its development of the IBM 701, and the first unit was delivered in early 1953. The IBM 650 was the most popular computer in the late 1950s. Other IBM computers delivered in the 1950s were the IBM 702, IBM 704, and IBM 709 computers.

The period from 1954 to 1959 was one of great expansion in the computer field. Many new designs were developed, but nearly all were based on the use of the vacuum tube. Computers built after 1959 used either transistor or microprocessor circuitry. A modern microcomputer can do more processing work in five minutes than the typical computer in the 1950s could do in a day. Today microcomputers are used in all aspects of our modern society.

Welcome to 1950s Florida

The 1950s began a new era...an age of affluence and awareness, of booming growth, but most important of all, an age of change that transformed the state forever from a charming Southern state into a growing competitor—a state with an exciting future.

Florida lost the corner grocery store and the neighborhood meat market in the 50s. Also lost were the milkman and his deliveries, the vegetable peddlers, the itinerant knife sharpener, the watermelon stands, and the local hand-dipped ice cream stores. In fact, Florida lost much of the charm that made it unique of all the southern states in America.

In the 50s, nationalism, patriotism, and even just causes would be challenged, and all those old "leftover beliefs" that had guided our lives in the 1940s were now obsolete.

The 1950s were a tranquil, upwardly time, but they led to upheaval and revolution when Third World nations, youth, women, and blacks emerged, each group demanding their right to be heard. Old was out; new was in. Long hair gave way to short; short skirts gave way to long. Black people began to demand civil rights. Women began to seek equality with men. Stand-up comedians joked irreverently about our political leaders. Youth began to accuse their middle-aged elders of making a mess of the world, and the middle-aged resented the youth's arrogance.

Veterans with college degrees earned on the G.I. Bill entered the work force with high goals. Young couples wanted everything: long, low houses and longer, lower cars, electrical appliances, kitchen gadgets, no-iron garments, and nylon stockings. Backyard barbecuing was a chief pastime of the 1950s, and in Florida, where weather favored outdoor fun almost year round, it became an institution.

Tourism is an industry where the customer comes to the product. In the 1950s it was the largest source of the state's primary income—about the same as the value added by manufacturing. Florida has much to offer—ideal winter climate, good accommodations and services, and many attractions. By the end of the 1950s, almost 13 million tourists arrived in Florida each year; there were around 400,000 available rooms for tourists and 16,000 restaurants. The state and its localities provided parks, camps, sports, races, festivals, and other attractions for visitors. Health and recreation facilities were everywhere. Almost all of Florida is fringed by beaches. Roadside attractions were located near all major cities and highways throughout the state.

"Taking In Everything"

Greetings from Florida. The State of Florida — Mecca for those who loved sunshine, water, and flowers — had several outstanding roadside attractions that were interesting, beautiful, and educational, and which appealed alike to the nature lover, the student, and the photographer.

Motoring Thru Palm Bordered
Orange Groves In Tropical Florida

1C-H1038

Driving through Orange Groves.
Many of the highways in Florida passed through orange groves that were located throughout central and southern Florida.

Florida Welcome Stations.
Tourist information houses located on main highways at the state line, officially greeting visitors with typical Florida welcome, free orange juice, and tourist information. Florida Welcome Stations were located on, among others, U.S. Highway 17 (near Yulee), U.S. 19 (near Monticello), U.S. 27 (near Havana), U.S. 41 (near Jennings), U.S. 90 (near Pensacola), U.S. 301 (near Hilliard), State Highway 231 (near Campbellton). Many Florida communities had regional Florida Welcome Stations that highlighted attractions in the local area.

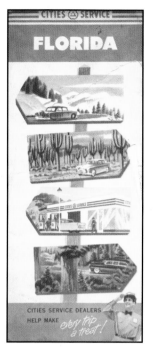

City Service Florida Map, 1950.
In the 1950s, tourists traveling the old road for pleasure relied on the service station road maps to find their way and help locate roadside attractions.

Florida Highway Patrol Guideline, 1953.

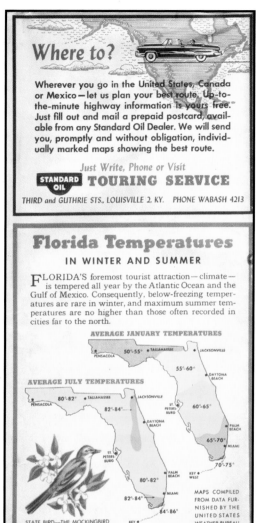

Florida Official Road Map.
Published by the State of Florida, this large 1953 road map listed attractions, national and state parks, rivers, highways, and roadside facilities.

Standard Oil Florida Map, 1955.
To help motorists plan enjoyable trips in Florida, gas stations gave away maps — like this Standard Oil pictorial guide — that described the highways and attractions; 77 of them were listed in this guide.

14

Roadside Businesses

In the 1950s Florida was one of America's favorite tourist destinations. It was a driver's delight, with roads that skirted some of the loveliest beaches in the world. Major highways linked cities that were brimming with things to see and do, and miles of roads and byways wandered through delightful small towns, cruised past some of the country's most historic sites, and looped through expanses of incredible beauty. Whether the tourist was interested in exploring a particular area or just looking for the pleasure that comes with discovering what was around the next bend, they found it along Florida's fabulous roadways.

Perhaps no other state in the country boasted such a diverse offering of roadside attractions and entertainment opportunities. Major attractions such as Silver Springs, Cypress Gardens, Weeki Wachee, and Marineland were complemented by smaller venues such as Gatorland, Monkey Jungle, Sea Zoo, and Tropical Hobbyland. There was something for everyone in the Sunshine State.

Hollywood movies, as well as magazine and newspaper articles, helped advertise many of Florida's attractions. Several Tarzan movies were filmed at Silver Springs and other Florida locations. "On An Island With You" and "Easy to Love" caused Americans to fall in love with Esther Williams and Cypress Gardens. The science-fiction classic "Creature from the Black Lagoon" was filmed in 1954 at Wakulla Springs and Tarpon Springs. "Moon Over Miami," a musical starring Betty Grable and Don Ameche, contained many glimpses of Miami, Cypress Gardens, and Silver Springs. In 1951, Cecil B. DeMille filmed his epic circus movie, "The Greatest Show On Earth," in Sarasota. Other popular movies that were filmed in Florida were "Lady Without A Passport," "Under the Gun," "Distant Drums," "The Barefoot Mailman," "Crosswinds," "The Miami Story," "Wind Across the Everglades," and "A Hole in the Head," with Frank Sinatra in a musical comedy set

TOP OF THE HILL GRILL AND CLUB FIESTA

U.S. HIGHWAY NO. 41 AND U.S. NO. 27A, WILLISTON, FLA.

in a Miami Beach hotel. The Hialeah Race Track appeared on the January 18, 1958 cover of the *New Yorker*, the imprimatur of elegance and taste.

In the 1950s, motels were located along all the major roadways in Florida. Many of the motels were built using the technique known as center-core construction, which involved single or multiple stories of rooms facing outside and set back-to-back along a central utility core. Bathrooms of every four rooms were grouped together, thus consolidating all the plumbing. Motel owners jazzed up their otherwise plain hostelries with neon trim and, most important, an attractive sign. The motels had parking, swimming pools, and signs with neon-edged palm trees, pink flamingos, or smiling suns.

Two-lane roadside businesses were run by families competing for the tourist dollar. Because the most important aspect is what is seen from the road, signs went up and facades began to change as

Roadside Gas Stations.
Service stations were located throughout the state to accommodate tourists driving on Florida highways.

highway speeds increased. Gradually the roadside became a wonderland of alluring oddities intent on calling attention to themselves. Billboards became not only a prime means to tout a product or an establishment, but also a source of distraction and entertainment for the entire family. Possibly the most memorable road signs of the two-lane blacktop were those produced by Burma Shave. These signs, spaced about one hundred feet apart, typically formed a series, with each sign in the series bearing one phrase of the complete message.

The external appearance of motels, restaurants, gas stations, and stores often contained a clever sigh, a fanciful name, or another gimmick to intrigue auto travelers. Log Cabin motels conveyed a trail-blazing spirit; tepee motels romanticized the West; and prefab roadside diners resembling train cars implied that the traveler who came in to eat had not stopped but was still moving. Florida relied on tropical and paradise-like themes such as palms, sunbursts, flamingoes, alligators, and pirates to beckon sojourners.

Scenically, motor touring in Florida had a unique charm in the 1950s. An infinite variety of scene, glimpses of lovely cypress-bordering lakes, and sweeping panoramas of the surf-washed Atlantic Ocean and Gulf of Mexico beaches. Orange Groves in blossom or in fruit, wide fields of green-carpeted with strawberries or gardens, and charming houses of the modified

Spanish type that Florida adapted from Cubans. Little farms and splendid estates at any turn in the road brought these into the tourist's ken. And over all was the enchantment of the tropics, the unfamiliar vegetation, the exotic bird life, and alligators, Florida's favorite reptile. Palm and pelican, hibiscus and heron, cypress and cormorant all combined to produce an effect both strange and charming.

Many of the side-of-the-road amusements were announced by billboards miles before they were approached. Many of the smaller attractions had to work hard to capture the traveler's attention. Catchy names, giant statutes, and signs that promised incredible things all enticed the tourist as sections of the Florida roadside came to resemble a carnival midway.

Early Florida roadside attractions were privately owned and often featured natural attractions such as springs or local flora and fauna. Thrill rides were reserved for the beach boardwalks at Jacksonville Beach, Daytona Beach, the traveling circus, or local fair. Families came to Florida for the tropical gardens and fantastic historical amusements and restorations. They came to have fun as well as to learn. The roadside attraction thrived. The climate meant year-round operation, and plenty of tourists traveled at a slow enough pace to take the time to pay and see.

Contrary to popular myth, theme parks dotted the state before Walt Disney World, but the theme was Florida. Prosperity's wake lifted not only the luxury yachts docked at Miami's Pier 5, but Evinrude bass boats on Lake Okeechobee and

REDLAND CAMP, 10 MILES SO. DAYTONA, 3 MILES NO. NEW SMYRNA, FLA.

glass-bottomed vessels at Silver Springs. Tourism sanctioned fun and profits in an era when consumption was replacing production as a national template. During the 1950s, tourism had changed remarkably little since the 1920s when the popularity of the automobile, the completion of major travel arteries, and national prosperity combined to promote vacations as a part of family life. Floods of tourists were drawn to Cypress Gardens, Marineland, Silver Springs, Weeki Wachee, Parrot Jungle, Monkey Jungle, St. Augustine Alligator Farm, Musa Isle, and numerous other attractions. Favorite adult tourist attractions were Hialeah Race Track, Gulfstream Park, Miami Jai-Alai Fronton, Derby Lane, Volusia County Kennel Club, and other pari-mutuel gaming facilities.

Perhaps one of the most spectacular stretches of highways in Florida was U.S. Highway 1 down the coast from the mainland to Key West, paralleling the famous overseas extension of the Florida East Coast Railroad. Motorists marveled at the unique sensation of traveling between the Gulf of Mexico on one hand and the Atlantic Ocean on the other, over the most interesting chain of islands in America.

Stuckey's and Texaco Gas Station.
Stuckey's and Texaco entered into a joint venture in the 1950s and both products were sold at Stuckey's roadside stores. This store, located on U.S. Highway 1 in Allendale, just south of Daytona Beach, was the typical store design in the 1950s.

DeLuxe Motel, Holly Hill, Florida

TREASURE VILLAGE TOURIST CAMP,
ST. PETERSBURG, FLORIDA

WHITE CITY MOTOR COURT DINING ROOM HOME COOKING

U. S. HIGHWAYS 301 and 1 . . . 6 Miles North of . . . HILLIARD, FLA.

THE FAMOUS EDGEWATER HOTEL AND COTTAGES

18 MILES SOUTH OF DAYTONA BEACH ON U. S. HIGHWAY NO. 1, EDGEWATER, FLORIDA

Roadside Motels and Cottages.

Motels and cottages were scattered throughout the state to accommodate the influx of tourists visiting Florida.

Tallahassee Motor Hotel

A Typical Cottage

A Typical Cottage

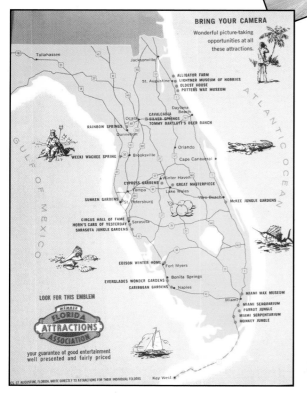

Florida Attractions Map, 1955.

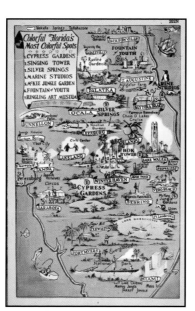

Howard Johnson's.

Howard Deering Johnson started this franchise idea, and his name became a marquee for many "Howard Johnson's" restaurants. By 1935 there were twenty-five Howard Johnson's in Massachusetts, and by 1940 there were more than one hundred along the Atlantic Coast from Massachusetts to Florida. Howard Johnson's pioneered the standard menu and décor for the new class of motorcar travelers and popularized one-stop shopping for a bed and meals.

As soon as travelers checked in, they felt as if they were home. The motel/restaurants usually had an orange roof that was topped by a white cupola with a weather vane featuring a pieman and his dog. The roadside signs were a large neon HOWARD JOHNSON'S in diagonal Art Deco letters. It was a promise of fun food that drew most people inside—grilled hot dogs and twenty-eight flavors of ice cream.

Roadside Restaurants.

During the salad days of the 1950s, Florida highways were a great smorgasbord of regional fare. All along the miles simmered a boundless brunch, an exciting variety of food and beverage that could be sampled at roadside diners, greasy spots, drive-in dinettes, truck stops, hot-dog stands, tourist attraction restaurants, and elaborate sit-down restaurants.

Attraction's Brochure, 1950s.

This brochure contained an attraction map, and a photograph and description of the following attractions: Alligator and Ostrich Farm, Bok Singing Towers, Cypress Gardens, Dupree Gardens, Everglades Reptile Gardens, Florida Wild Animal and Reptile Ranch, Gerbing Gardens, Highland Hammock, Lewis Plantation, Marineland, Monkey Jungle, Musa Isle, McKee Jungle Gardens, Oldest House, Old Sugar Mill, Oriental Gardens, Parrot Jungle, Rainbow Springs, Rainbow Tropical Gardens, Ravine Gardens, Ringling Art Museum, Ross Allen Reptile Institute, Sanlando Springs, Sarasota Jungle Gardens, Silver Springs, Sunken Gardens, Wakulla Springs, Wood Parade, and Zorayda Castle.

Map of Colorful Florida Attractions.

The Bowkers sent this card to the Phillips in Kalamazoo, Michigan from Fort Lauderdale in 1957: "Vacationing here in Florida. Weather has been ideal. We took a trip to the Keys, sure enjoyed it, it was an experience. Plan on stopping at Cypress Gardens on way home. Have taken quite a lot of pictures."

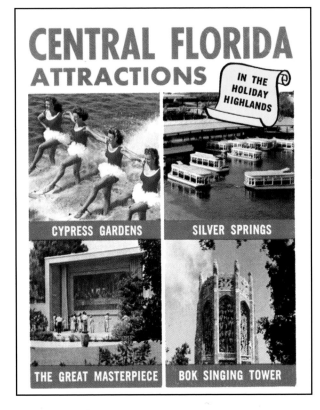

Nature's cameraland of moss-draped cypress, dense jungle growth, tropical plants and alligator dens in the Forest Primeval at the GREAT MASTERPIECE.

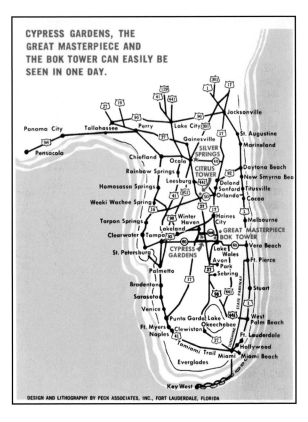

Top: Central Florida Attractions Brochure and Map, 1950s.

In 1950, there were 2.7 million people living in Florida. The state was rapidly growing. Many of last year's tourists became this year's resident. In 1949, more than five million passenger cars were manufactured and sold as fast as they could be made to a public eager for post-war luxury. By 1950 more than 44 million passenger cars were whizzing down the nation's highways. Many of these cars made their way to Florida's highways and its many attractions.

Bottom: Florida's Attractions Postcard Folder, 1955.

Highway 1 Road Sign.

U.S. Highway 1 stretches from the northern roads of Maine to the warm blue waters off Key West, Florida. Along its 2,468-mile journey, U.S. 1 passes through old faded towns of New England, through great Eastern cities, through the farms of the Old south, and through orange groves in Florida. U.S. Highway 1 was America's original main street and was the country's first designated highway.

U.S. Highway 1 enters Florida from Georgia about thirty miles from the Atlantic Ocean and, after crossing St. Johns River, emerges at St. Augustine to closely follow the East Coast all the way into Miami and through the islands in the Florida Keys to Key West. It connects all the coastal resorts, threading its way southward through dense moss-draped forests, again along picturesque palm-fringed shorelines, and often within plain sight of the broad Atlantic. Thirty miles below the Georgia line, U.S. Highway 1 meets two other mighty arterial highways, U.S. Highway 90 (Old Spanish Trail from California) and U.S. Highway 17 (Ocean Highway from Maine). U.S. Highway 1 sported one of the first official roadside welcome stations, built in 1951. The welcome canter offered maps, directions, clean restrooms, and, best of all, free Florida orange juice. U.S. Highway 1 was the primary connector of Florida's east coast from 1927 until the early 1970s. The 1950s were the Golden Age of U.S. Highway 1 Tourism Travel.

One of Andy Griffith's first successes as an entertainer was a comic monologue called "Number One Street," which told the tale of a rural family experiencing the wonders of the highway: "There was a sign that said, 'Free Picnic Table,' so naturally we stopped and got us one."

U.S. Highway 1 passes through the following Florida communities: Hilliard, Callahan, Jacksonville, St. Augustine, Ormond Beach, Daytona Beach, South Daytona, Port Orange, New Smyrna Beach, Titusville, Cocoa, Melbourne, Vero Beach, Fort Pierce, Stuart, Jupiter, Riviera Beach, West Palm Beach, Lake Worth, Delray Beach,

Florida's Main Street—U.S. Highway 1
& other Streets, Roads, and By-ways

Boca Raton, Pompano Beach, Fort Lauderdale, Dania, Hollywood, Miami, Coral Gables, Homestead, Key Largo, Islamorada, and Key West.

America's original Main Street was a poignant journey that sliced through Florida land and its history. St. Augustine, the oldest continuously occupied city in America, is a freeze-frame of the living history and geography of early America. Founded in 1565, the city is dotted with historical attractions throughout.

Other attractions located on or near U.S. Highway 1 include Africa U.S.A., Ancient America, Atomic Tunnel, Bongoland, Casper's Ostrich & Alligator Farm, Coral Castle, Dania Jai-Alai Fronton, Daytona Beach Jai-Alai Fronton, Daytona International Speedway, Gulfstream Park, Hemingway Home, Hollywood Kennel Club, Jupiter Lighthouse, Key West Aquarium, Lightner Museum, Marineland, McKee Jungle Gardens, Monkey Jungle, Museum

Beginning and End of U.S. Highway 1.
U.S. Highway 1 ran between Key West, Florida and Fort Kent, Maine.

Air View of Highway 1 in Miami.
In downtown Miami, U.S. Highway 1 was Biscayne Boulevard. This 1952 view shows beautiful Biscayne Bay, Biscayne Park, City Auditorium, Memorial Library, Bandshell, and the majestic hotels along this palm-studded boulevard.

of Speed, Oriental Gardens, Orchid Jungle, Palm Beach Kennel Club, Parrot Jungle, Parrots' Paradise, Ponce de Leon Inlet Lighthouse, Potter's Wax Museum, Rare Bird Farm, Ripley's Believe It Or Not, Sea Zoo, South Daytona Alligator Farm, Storyland, Theater of the Sea, Tomokie Fountain, Tropical Hobbyland, Venetian Pool, and Volusia County Kennel Club.

Florida's Overseas Highway

A magnificent 113-mile drive between the Atlantic Ocean and the Gulf of Mexico, Overseas Highway (U.S. Highway 1) links the islands of the Florida Keys. The roadway crosses forty-two bridges (the longest almost seven miles) along an ever-changing scene of turquoise waters and old-fashioned beach communities, bait shops, mom-and-pop seafood joints, tropical coconut palms, fiery orange Poinciana trees, twelve-foot tall crotons, marinas, and colorful tourist attractions.

The first "key" is Key Largo. Humphrey Bogart fans will recognize it as the namesake and setting of John Huston's moody 1948 film. Key Largo is also a major gateway to the only living coral reef in the continental United States. The next major key is Islamorada, the sport-fishing capital of the world, located about halfway between Miami and Key West. An interesting tourist attraction here was the "Theater of the Sea."

Marathon, located halfway between Key Largo and Key West, is one of the larger island communities. Big Pine Key, the largest of the Lower Keys leading to Key West, is home to the endangered Key deer (the smallest subspecies of the white-tailed deer). The National Key Deer Refuge, established in 1957, is located here. Deer sightings are more common at dusk and dawn. The Overseas Highway drive ends at Key West.

Though not quite in the tropics, Key West is to all appearances a tropical island. Lying low on a shimmering sea, it boasts homes with backyards lush with oleanders, hibiscus, frangipani, and mango trees. Its harbors are filled with battered fishing craft and handsome yachts. Key West is a small-town sort of place where narrow streets are lined with picket fences and lovely old frame houses. The cul-de-sac of the Overseas Highway, it is unlike any other city in the United States.

Four miles long from east to west and two miles in width, Key West provides more contrasts than one could dream up for any town. Men have both made and lost fortunes here, leaving legacies of fine, ornate houses along with quaint, weathered shanties. Closer to Havana, Cuba than to Miami, its residents are descendants of the English, Bahamian, Cuban, African, and myriad other folk who have found this tiny island to be an appealing home.

Numerous well-known writers and artists, most notably Ernest Hemingway, Tennessee Williams, and Elizabeth Bishop, have found Key West a place of inspiration. Hemingway wrote many of his best-known works in the second-story writing studio adjoining his Key West house.

Glorious Trip.
Mary sent this card of the Overseas Highway to Mrs. George Fry in Jamestown, New York in 1955: "From Naples to Key West today—a glorious trip. Tomorrow to Miami & then north reaching Cleveland, Ohio about Easter Sunday probably. Hope the weather in Jamestown is better. Spring in the north more exciting than in the south. I think."

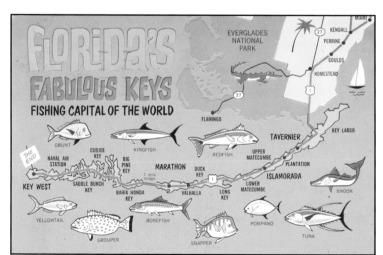

Map of the Overseas Highway.
This scenic route is of unbelievable beauty, combining the turquoise green and cobalt blue of the Gulf of Mexico on one side and the Atlantic Ocean on the other.

Overseas Highway to Key West.
Key West is the southernmost point of land—and city—in the United States. To reach it by land, the route is over the Overseas Highway, or the "Highway that goes to Sea." The longest span of over-water bridges in the world were contained in this highway, stretching 167 miles from Miami to Key West.

Beautiful Bahia Honda with Picnic Area.
"We went over to Key West about 160 mi from Miami. This is one of the bridges built on the ocean. We counted many on the way over the keys. Stayed there Wed. night & came back Thursday. Every minute has been busy so I haven't written before. It has been so warm since we got to Florida. I'd like to live here. Will tell you a lot when I get back." Mailed in Miami on April 21, 1956.

Seven Mile Bridge Over Pigeon Key.
In 1958 Mommy and Daddy sent this card to their daughter, Linda: "We're in Key West, Going Deep Sea fishing. We are going bring you two sometime." The island of Marathon is shown in the distance.

Major Florida Highways in the 1950s

In addition to U.S. Highway 1 the following major roadways networked throughout the state: U.S. Highways 17, 19, 27, 41, 90, 98, 301, and 441. State Highways A1A was the Atlantic Coast beach roadway. Several state highways connected the east coast with the gulf coast: 40, 50, 60, and 70.

U.S. Highway 17

The first Florida Welcome Center was built in 1946 on U.S. Highway 17. This highway passes through the communities of Yulee, Jacksonville, Green Cove Springs, Palatka, Crescent City, DeLeon Springs, DeLand, Sanford, Casselberry, Altamonte Springs, Orlando, Kissimmee, Haines City, Winter Haven, Bartow, Bowling Green, Arcadia, and Punta Gorda.

Roadside attractions along or near Highway 17 include Oriental Gardens, Ravine Gardens, Ponce de Leon Springs, Sanford Zoo, Senator, Gatorland, Kissimmee State Monument, Cypress Gardens, and Wonder House.

U.S. Highway 19

U.S. Highway 19 passes through the communities of Monticello, Perry, Cross City, Crystal River, Homosassa Springs, Tarpon Springs, Clearwater, and St. Petersburg.

Roadside attractions along or near Highway 19 include Weeki Wachee, Homosassa Springs, Florida Wild Animal and Reptile Ranch, and Million Dollar Pier.

U.S. Highway 27

U.S. Highway 27 passes through the communities of Havana, Tallahassee, Perry, High Springs, Williston, Ocala, Leesburg, Lake Wales, Lake Placid, Palmdale, Moore Haven, Clewiston, Hialeah, Miami Springs, and Miami.

Roadside attractions along or near Highway 27 include Florida State Museum, Devils Millhopper, Citrus Tower, Cypress Gardens, Bok Singing Tower, Great Masterpiece, Gatorama, and Hialeah Park.

U.S. Highway 41

U.S. Highway 41 passes through the communities of Jasper, White Springs, Lake City, High Springs, Archer, Williston, Dunnellon, Inverness, Floral City, Brooksville, Land O' Lakes, Tampa, Ruskin, Palmetto, Bradenton, Sarasota, Venice, Punta Gorda, Fort Myers, Estero, Naples, Ochopee, Miami, and Miami Beach. The southern part of Highway 41, from Tampa to Miami, is called the Tamiami Trail.

Roadside attractions along or near Highway 41 include Stephen Foster Memorial, Rainbow Springs, Weeki Wachee, Dupree Gardens, South Florida Museum, Cars of Yesterday, Ringling Museum of Art, Sarasota Jungle Gardens, Edison's Winter Home, Everglades Wonder Gardens, Everglades, Everglades National Park, and Ochopee Post Office.

U.S. Highway 90

U.S. Highway 90 passes through the communities of Pensacola, DeFuniak Springs, Marianna, Tallahassee, Monticello, Live Oak, Jacksonville, and Jacksonville Beach.

Roadside attractions along or near Highway 90 include Florida Caverns, Wakulla Springs, Stephen Foster Memorial, and Oriental Gardens.

U.S. Highway 98

U.S. Highway 98 passes through the communities of Pensacola, Fort Walton Beach, Destin, Panama City, Mexico Beach, Apalachicola, Perry, Cross City, Crystal River, Homosassa Springs, Brooksville, Dade City, Lakeland, Bartow, Sebring, Okeechobee, and West Palm Beach.

Roadside attractions along or near Highway 98 include John Gorrie State Museum, Wakulla Springs, Rainbow Springs, Weeki Wachee, Cypress Gardens, and Wonder House.

U.S. Highway 301

U.S. Highway 301 passes through the communities of Hilliard, Callahan, Starke, Hawthorne, Ocala, Belleview, Bushnell, Dade City, Zephyrhills, Tampa, and Palmetto.

Roadside attractions along or near Highway 301 include Florida Alligator Farm, Silver Springs, and Gamble Mansion.

Highway A1A Along the Atlantic Ocean.
This palm-lined highway (Indian River Drive) is between Jensen Beach and Stuart. The Atlantic Ocean is shown on the right.

U.S. Highway 441

U.S. Highway 441 passes through the communities of Lake City, High Springs, Gainesville, Ocala, Tavares, Mount Dora, Apopka, Altamonte Springs, Orlando, Kissimmee, St. Cloud, Okeechobee, West Palm Beach, Ft. Lauderdale, Hollywood, and Miami.

Roadside attractions along or near Highway 441 include Florida State Museum, Devils Millhopper, Silver Springs, Sanlando Springs, Gatorland, and Kissimmee States Memorial.

State Highway A1A

State Highway A1A parallels the east coast of Florida passing through the communities of Fernandina Beach, Jacksonville Beach, St. Augustine, St. Augustine Beach, Marineland, Flagler Beach, Ormond Beach, Daytona Beach, New Smyrna Beach, Cocoa Beach, Melbourne Beach, Vero Beach, Jensen Beach, Jupiter, Palm Beach, Delray Beach, Fort Lauderdale, Hollywood Beach, and Miami Beach.

Roadside attractions along or near Highway A1A include Fort Clinch, Gerbings Gardens, St. Augustine Alligator Farm, St. Augustine Lighthouse, Fort Matanzas National Monument, Marineland, Ponce de Leon Inlet Lighthouse, Cape Canaveral Spaceport, Jupiter Lighthouse, and Miami Beach Kennel Club.

State Highway 40

State Highway 40 ran from Yankeetown on the Gulf Coast eastward to Barberville and in the 1950s on to New Smyrna Beach. In the 1960s Highway 40 was extended from Barberville to Ormond Beach. Roadside attractions along this cross-state roadway include Rainbow Springs, Silver Springs, and Juniper Springs. Communities along the roadway include Dunnellon, Ocala, Astor Park, and Barberville.

State Road 50

State Road 50 connects Bayport on the Gulf of Mexico to Indian River City on the Indian River near Titusville. Communities along the roadway include Brookville, Groveland, Clermont, Orlando, and Christmas. Roadside attractions along Highway 50 include Weeki Wachee, Citrus Tower, Mead Botanical Gardens, and the Christmas Post Office.

State Highway 60

State Highway 60 connects Clearwater on the west coast of Florida with Vero Beach on the east coast. The roadway passes through Tampa, Bartow, Lake Wales, and Yeehaw Junction. Roadside attractions along this roadway include Wonder House, Bok Singing Tower, Great Masterpiece, Cypress Gardens, and McKee Jungle Gardens.

State Highway 70

State Highway 70 connects Bradenton on the west coast of Florida with Fort Pierce on the east coast, passing through Arcadia and Okeechobee.

A Peaceful Drive through Brooksville.
Many of Florida's U.S. and State Highways pass through picturesque small towns, such as Brooksville.

Highway A1A (Collins Avenue) in Miami Beach.
The busiest section of Highway A1A is Collins Avenue in Miami Beach. Luxury hotels line this highway for several miles.

Tamiami Trail

In the early days, there was no feasible means of transportation to make the area easily accessible. That is why the Tamiami Trail was so desperately needed. Unfortunately, the state had no money for the project. Barron G. Collier made a deal with the state that he would finance the building of the road through the area today known as Collier County if the state, in turn, would name a county after him. The east-west part of the Trail crosses the Florida Everglades, a remote tropical wilderness larger than the state of Delaware. This area consisted of a few widely scattered settlements and less than 1,200 people with no electric power, telephones, or telegraphs, and not a single mile of paved road.

The famed Tamiami Trail's name is compounded of the syllables from the names of its terminal cities, Tampa and Miami. The highway connects the Atlantic Ocean with the Gulf of Mexico, proceeding in long straight stretches across the Everglades, a primeval swampland. The highway also connects Fort Myers, Bonita Springs, and Naples with other cities along the Gulf coast.

Dade County tax assessor Captain J. F. Jaudon of Ochopee first conceived the idea for the trail and, in 1916, completed surveys of the route. Construction began in 1917, but proceeded slowly due to labor shortage during World War I. In 1923, a motorcade traveled over the proposed route to arouse public interest. The trail-blazing expedition of ten cars, twenty-three men, and two Indian guides left Ft. Myers on April 4, 1923. After a perilous three-week trip, during which they were reported lost several times, seven cars reached Miami, and the trail became the most discussed highway project in America. Smoothed and surfaced, the road was open to traffic on April 25, 1928 at a cost of $13,000,000. An immediate success, the highway helped to unite the lower east and west coasts of Florida. What once involved a two-day roundabout journey by automobile was now accomplished in little more than two hours.

Along the north side of the road runs the Tamiami Canal, a long ditch from which rock and mulch were taken to build the elevated roadbed. The canal side of the road is alive with birds, reptiles, and fishes. Sometimes raccoons, rabbits, turtles, alligators, and cottonmouth moccasin snakes can be seen.

Many Seminole Indian villages were scattered along the trail between Miami and Naples, hidden from view behind palisaded walls, above which rise the sun-bleached palmetto thatched roofs of the native houses. In front of each village was a shop in which Seminole Indian jackets and dresses, dolls, metal pins and buttons, air plants, miniature boats, postcards, and other native products were sold. Seminole women operated hand-operated sewing machines to produce many of the souvenir products.

The completion of the Tamiami Trail across the Everglades opened isolated Seminole Indian camps to the rapid tourist development of southwest Florida.

In the 1950s the Tamiami Trail was the southernmost 275 miles of U.S. Highway 41 from State Road 60 in Tampa to U.S. Highway 1 in Miami. The 165-mile north-south section extends to Naples, whereupon it becomes an east-west road crossing the Everglades before reaching Miami. The Tamiami Trail has been designated a National Scenic Byway by the United States Department of Transportation for its unique scenery in the Everglades and the Big Cypress Swamp.

Greetings from Tamiami Trail.
The Tamiami Trail starts in Tampa, crosses Manatee River, and passes through Bradenton, Sarasota, Venice, Punta Gorda, Fort Myers, Bonita Springs, and Naples, then through the Florida Everglades toward Miami. The Tamiami Trail officially opened April 25, 1928, linking Tampa to Miami via southwest Florida.
Key views on this postcard: **Upper left**—Memorial Pier Building and Yacht Basin, Bradenton; **Upper right**—Venice Street Scene; **Lower left**—Palm-lined First Street, Fort Myers; Lower center—Sarasota Lido; **Lower right**—Punta Gorda Bridge.

Crossing the Everglades.

Until the 1920s, getting from the west coast of Florida to the east coast took some doing. There was a road running from Tampa to Daytona Beach, but nothing south of there. Taking some old Seminole Indian trails, it was possible to cross from Fort Myers to Miami in less than a week if you could battle the mosquitoes, snakes, alligators, and other wildlife. The Seminole Indians built small shelters along the route where food could be stored to help travelers. Those who ran out could eat some of the Indian food and then replace it later at another shelter.

To publicize the idea of building the Tamiami Trail, some Ft. Myers citizens decided to stage a trail-blazing caravan from there to Miami. The 1923 Caravan consisted of one truck, seven Model T Fords, and a brand new Elcar. Thomas Edison and Henry Ford showed up to see the caravan off. The driver of the Elcar was the owner of the Elcar dealership in Fort Myers. He thought a successful crossing of the Everglades in his car would give the new model a boost. Unfortunately his car sank in the Everglades mire and, shortly thereafter, the dealership sank too. The truck also sank in the mire and may still be located there today.

Tamiami Trail Trivia

- The Tamiami Trail passes through seven counties. The longest and toughest stretch (76 miles or 28% of the road) was built across Collier County.

- A bonus system sped up construction from .7 miles to 1.1 miles per month. The record was two miles built in a month.

- Despite the heat, seven-foot-long rattlesnakes, and hazardous conditions, no lives were lost building the trail across Collier County.

- Explosives had to be hauled in by oxen. In rough spots, men shouldered the boxes of dynamite themselves and floundered neck-deep in water.

- Giant dredges followed the dynamiters, throwing up huge piles of rock from the canal that the dredges created.

- The 31-mile stretch from Carnestown to the Dade County line had to be blasted out of solid limerock and piled up again to form the roadbed.

- Seminole Indians proved invaluable as guides and were given free bus fare on the Trail until World War II.

- There have been reports of a 300-pound brown bear and Florida panther engaging motorists' automobiles.

- The average Trail worker earned about 20¢ per hour and literally lived on the job, in portable bunkhouses complete with cooks and rolling kitchens.

- The Seminole Indians built small shelters along the route where food could be stored to help travelers.

- Reports that work crews had struck quicksand in January 1925 sparked fears for a time that the road project would be abandoned.

- Work on the Tamiami Trail alone used up a railroad boxcar of dynamite every three weeks for three years.

- The Trail's first traffic accident occurred just hours after the road was officially opened when a dozy driver fell asleep at the wheel and flipped his car over.

- Saw mills and logging camps provided the lumber needed for buildings and bridges.

- The official flag of the Tamiami Trail is red with a white band running diagonally across, and the Trail insignia in the center.

- During the 1930s and 1940s many Seminole Indian villages were built along the Trail.

- Occasional service stations dot the Trail at sufficient intervals to meet all requirements of the average motorist.

The Buccaneer Trail

Orange Blossom Trail

The Buccaneer Trail, so named because pirates once used it, was a scenic drive/sightseeing trip near Jacksonville. The Buccaneer Trail was a section of U.S. Highway A1A between Fernandina Beach and St. Augustine. The trail, first opened for public use in 1950, operated as a toll facility and included a ferry trip across St. Johns River to Mayport. The Buccaneer Trail offered motorists a thrilling introduction to the wonderful vacationland of picturesque Florida.

Entering Florida from the north on the Orange Blossom Trail, the visitor to the Sunshine State crossed the famed Suwannee River at White Springs, then south through Lake City to Gainesville, home of the University of Florida, the state's largest educational institution. Next is Ocala with nearby Silver Springs, nature's underwater fairyland, seen through glass-bottomed boats and Ross Allen's Reptile Institute and Seminole Indian Village.

Further down the trail along orange and grapefruit groves is Leesburg, where fresh water fishing was at its best in the many lakes in this territory. Then Mount Dora, as its name implies, is a charming little resort located on a high bluff, overlooking Lake Dora. Then there's Plymouth, where one of Florida's largest citrus fruit packing and canning plants was located; Apopka, known for its large-mouth bass fishing, on to Orlando, Florida's largest inland city. Nearby is Sanlando Springs Tropical Park, with the state's finest fresh water for bathing.

Kissimmee, the Cow Capital of Florida, and on to Haines City with its rolling hills and miles and miles of citrus groves; here is where beautiful Cypress Gardens was nestled on the placid shores of Lake Eloise, perfumed by the gorgeous blossoms that flourished in this tropical wonderland the year 'round. Only a few miles south on this trail was Lake Wales, site of the world famous Bok Singing Tower and Bird Sanctuary.

The trail then takes the visitor to Sebring, home of Highlands Hammock State Park, nature's own wonderland of wild, tropical beauty. Still farther south lies Clewiston, the sugar land of Florida with the huge Sugar Mill of the United States Sugar Corporation, and on through the heart of the Florida Everglades to Miami, America's Tropical Winter Playground.

Buccaneer Trail Brochure.

Orange Blossom Trail Postcard Folder.

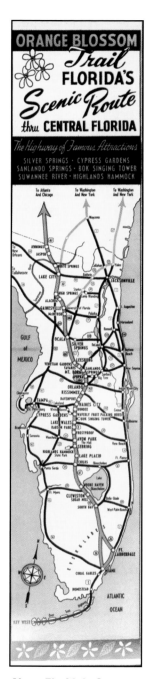

Along Florida's Orange Blossom Trail.

HARVESTING SUGAR CANE IN THE FLORIDA EVERGLADES

Along Florida's Orange Blossom Trail

Harvesting Sugar Cane in the Florida Everglades.
Sugar cane is harvested by hand in the Everglades. With a few deft strokes of a machete in the hands of an experienced cane cutter, the cane is ready for loading and hauling in field wagons to railroad cars that transported it to United States Sugar Corporation's huge sugar house at Clewiston.

Clewiston Sugar Mill.
Aerial view of the largest raw Sugar Mill in continental United States, owned and operated by United States Sugar Corporation in Clewiston, "America's Sweetest Town," showing the grounds surrounding the plant. Free tours were available daily during grinding season, November 1 to April 1.

Lighthouse Tour

With more than 1,800 miles of coastline, Florida has long been a natural beacon for lighthouses. The state's impressive collection includes some of the nation's oldest and tallest. Many invited visitors to step inside and climb their spiraling staircases to the top for the reward of a dazzling panoramic view.

The best way to see Florida's lighthouses was to hit the road. Spanning the coastal highway from St. Augustine to Pensacola was a popular tour.

- The first stop was the famous St. Augustine Lighthouse. Built in 1874, this 165-foot lighthouse is the state's oldest and most recognizable. Next, near Daytona Beach, came the 175-foot Ponce de Leon Inlet Lighthouse, the second-tallest lighthouse in the nation.

- Farther on down the Atlantic Coast stood the bright red, 125-foot Jupiter Inlet Lighthouse, the Hillsboro Lighthouse, and down near Miami, the 95-foot Cape Florida Lighthouse.

- The 86-foot Key West Lighthouse, located in Key West, was said to be the only lighthouse in the United States entirely within the city limits of a community. Tourists enjoyed taking the automobile ferry from Punta Rassa, near Fort Myers, to Sanibel Island to view the Sanibel Island Lighthouse and surrounding beach covered with thousands of seashells.

- Last but certainly not least was the 171-foot Pensacola Lighthouse. It was built in 1858 to guide navy warships in and out of the deep-water port and the U.S. Navy base that was established here in 1824.

Picturesque Lighthouse at Jupiter.
A guardian of the sea! It is one of the many picturesque lighthouses along the coast of Florida; the longest shoreline of any state in America. The historic Jupiter Inlet Lighthouse is one of eight major Florida coastal lights. No other location on the East Coast of the United States enjoys the international reputation for guiding ships throughout the centuries as the area now known as Jupiter. This location protrudes out into the Atlantic Ocean farther than any other point along the Florida coast. For this reason it has guided ships of all kinds since approximately 1550 to the present. Today, as was done by early New World explorers, ships consider this an important point when planning their routes to Central and South America.

The Jupiter Inlet Lighthouse, the oldest structure in Palm Beach County, has been in operation since 1860. The light was built on a hill that was later determined by archeologists to be an ancient Indian mound dating back to about 700 A.D. The lighthouse lens was designed and built in France by famed physicist, Augustin Jean Fresnel. Illumination was provided by oil lamps.

Pensacola Lighthouse.

The first lighthouse to be constructed on Florida's West Coast was in 1825 just after the U.S. Navy opened a deep-water base at Pensacola. A new massive brick structure was built in 1858 on the north side of the bay's entrance. Bombarded by Confederate forces during the Civil War and battered by countless storms over the years, the dauntless lighthouse survived and in the 1950s looked much like when it was built.

Ponce de Leon Inlet Lighthouse.

The Ponce de Leon Inlet Lighthouse, south of Daytona Beach, was the first lighthouse in Florida designated a National Historic Landmark. Standing 175 feet high, the 1887 lighthouse is the nation's tallest among those that remain on their original sites. The original lighthouse used a kerosene lamp to light the fixed Frensel lens. Its light could be spotted twenty miles out to sea.

Hillsboro Lighthouse.

The Hillsboro Lighthouse Tower is an octagonal, pyramidal, iron skeleton with a central stair cylinder. Designed by Lighthouse Engineers in Charleston, South Carolina in 1904, it was fabricated and assembled by Russel Wheel & Foundry of Detroit, Michigan, then disassembled and shipped by steamship to South Florida. J. H. Gardiner of New Orleans built the structure in Pompano Beach in 1906-1907, and the light was first lit in March 1907. It had the original second order bivalve (clamshell) Fresnel lens by Barbier, Benard & Turenne in Paris, France. The tower is 137-feet high and the total number of steps to the lantern room is 175.

Sanibel Island Lighthouse.

The Sanibel Island Lighthouse is perhaps the most photographed structure on the island. Built in 1884, it's located at the far eastern tip of Sanibel Island, and is a carbon copy of the Cape San Blas Lighthouse in the Florida Panhandle. The lighthouses on the Gulf Coast are far apart. The Sanibel Island Lighthouse is the last one heading south until Dry Tortugas in the Florida Keys, 130 miles away. In 1949, the 102-foot-tall lighthouse was automated with a modern light beacon.

When the Sanibel Island Lighthouse was built, Sanibel Island was nearly uninhabited, and the keeper and his family had 670 acres of land set aside for farming. Unfortunately, the sandy soil wasn't good for growing much of anything...except children. One lighthouse keeper who served there for twenty-two years had thirteen children. The grounds and beaches around the Sanibel Island Lighthouse are very lovely with white sand, sea grapes, and sea oats. Covered with shells, the beaches are popular for shelling and swimming.

30

Key West Lighthouse.
Although Key West's first lighthouse was built in 1825, a hurricane swept it away some twenty years later. A new conical stucco brick tower was built inland in 1847 to guide ships through the harbor. After climbing eighty-eight steps to the top, an excellent panoramic view was obtained of this flat little island. A huge Fresnel lens that cost $1 million back in the mid-nineteenth century is also located at the top. It's the only lighthouse in the United States entirely within the city limits of a community.

Cape Florida Lighthouse.
This historic station, near Miami, was established in 1825, and raised to ninety-five feet in 1855. The station was discontinued in 1878 when the new Fowey Rocks Light superseded it. The property was sold to private owners, and in the 1960s, it was incorporated into a state recreation area.

Anastasia Light House, St. Augustine, Florida 12

The Oldest City in the United States 60877

St. Augustine Lighthouse.
St. Augustine's Inlet to the sea was treacherous. Its shifting sands, called "crazy banks," were the dread of all who sailed to the ancient city. The St. Augustine Lighthouse, with its black and white spirals, was built in 1874, replacing the original coquina tower that was destroyed by the sea. This spiral-striped tower is an unforgettable landmark for visitors by land and sea. The light remains active and is visible from twenty miles away.

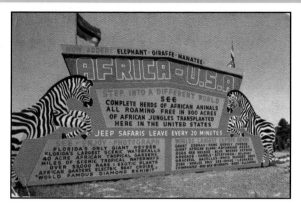

A

Africa U.S.A. to

Autorama

Africa U.S.A.

Africa-U.S.A.

Africa-U.S.A., based in Boca Raton, was Palm Beach County's first big animal attraction. Opening day of this African oriented theme park in February 1953 was filled with fanfare and hoopla as local dignitaries welcomed hundreds of new four-footed settlers to Boca Raton. Visitors to the park purchased tickets for an open-air train tour. The rubber-tired trains, some with canopy overhead, had a capacity of fifty persons in three cars. After boarding, the train started on the long safari through a lushly landscaped savanna with hundreds of African animals.

In addition to the wild animals, Africa-U.S.A. had a seven-acre lake, fed by the Zambezi Falls, a thirty-foot cascading waterfall that roared through eight hundred feet of flower-decked rapids, and the Watusi, a "natural" geyser, that blew its lid and sprayed water every hour and five minutes—and always when there was a boatload of people on the lake.

The Africa-U.S.A. attraction closed in September 1961 due to an infestation of African Red Ticks. Many of the animals had to be destroyed. John Peterson sold his remaining animals to various zoos and the land to real estate developers, who turned the property into Camino Gardens, an upscale housing development.

Masai Warrior in Jungle Town of Africa-U.S.A.

Visitors to Africa-U.S.A. were often intrigued by a tour of the pseudo-African village called Jungle Town, staffed by African Americans in African costumes. There, for 25¢ admission, chimpanzees put on a show for the patrons. In thatched jungle huts, concessions and a souvenir shop were also located.

Friendly Camels at Africa-U.S.A.

Shown are three of the twenty-three camels that were always seen in the same location at Africa-U.S.A. Many of the other animals were a bit more fickle, such as the ostriches, and could be seen almost anywhere on the 177-acre park.

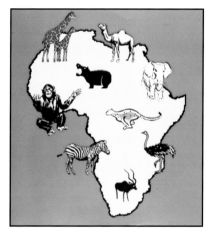

Wild Animals at Africa-U.S.A.

All the animals in Africa-U.S.A. were friendly vegetarians. There were no lions. The colorful African fowl and other non-carnivorous animals roamed freely. Many dipped in the rivers, several miles of which had been dredged throughout the jungle. The only potentially harmful animals, a pair of cheetahs, were restricted, and two elephants, lest they get too friendly, were chained so that they had plenty of roaming room, but where the tip of an outstretched trunk could not quite reach the train. Among the 250 wild animals at Africa-U.S.A. were a hippopotamus, eighty-one ostriches, twenty-three camels, thirteen giraffes, sixty-five zebras, two cheetahs, two elephants, three chimpanzees, fifty-five antelopes, and seventeen monkeys.

America's Smallest Post Office

From Storing Tools to Mail.

The nation's smallest post office is located on the Tamiami Trail (U.S. Highway 41) in Ochopee, thirty-five miles east of Naples and seventy miles west of Miami. Ochopee is the center of thousands of acres of tomato farms in the heart of the swamp country. It was the home of Captain J. F. Jaudon, who operated a sugar cane mill here and made the first survey of the Tamiami Trail. The town also had a small sawmill and several packing and canning plants. It was originally built in 1934 as a tool shed for the Gaunt tomato farm. The first post office was in the general store, but when it burned down in 1953, the postmaster began storing and sorting the mail in the tool shed. A short time later, the shed became Ochopee's official post office. The tiny structure measures only 10'6" in height, 8'4" in width, and 7'3" in length.

There is no hazard pay for working in this tiny outpost that serves as a lifeline to the world for the few people who live in the rugged but breathtaking Everglade scenery along the Tamiami Trail. No extra pay despite the mosquitoes that can turn body parts black in seconds and alligators, black bears, wild hogs, and other critters lurking just a few feet away in the grassy marsh. The post office is so small there is a plastic storage bin out back for outgoing mail. There isn't even a bathroom. The worker has to close and run down to a nearby business. The mail facility is a tough little structure, surviving Hurricane Donna in 1960 and Hurricane Andrew in 1992, two of the country's most disastrous storms. About three hundred residents in a three county area, mostly Indians, live in the post office's zip code, and their mail is delivered from this post office. The post office was listed in the 1975 edition of a *Ripley's Believe It Or Not* book. The small post office has been a popular tourist stop since 1953. It even has stacks of picture postcards for sale.

Ancient America

Ancient Indians Lived Here.

In 1953 Edmond G. Barnhill, a wealthy treasure hunter from Wisconsin, bought twenty-four acres of land containing ancient Indian burial and shell mounds and built a tourist attraction called Ancient America. The attraction, located on U.S. Highway 1 in Boca Raton, contained displays tunneled into the mounds, Indian artifacts, Spanish explorer artifacts, murals depicting Indian life in south Florida, pirate chests, shrunken heads, and at the entrance to the attraction, a thirty-foot long replica of a Spanish ship. The roadside attraction was not very popular and closed in 1958. Shown is Mick McKee standing in front of the Ancient America attraction.

Asolo Theater

From Italy to Sarasota.

The 300-seat Asolo Theater was built in Asolo, Italy in 1798 by Antonio Locatelli. It was dismantled in the 1930s and stored by Adolph Loewi of Venice. In 1937, Chick Austin saw it and, when he became Director of Ringling Museum of Art in 1946, arranged for its purchase. Asolo Theater opened in Sarasota in 1952. It was the only original Italian theater in America. This scene is from a Restoration play during the professional company's performing season. Seeing Asolo's production of "Amadeus" was like returning to the eighteenth century. The actors in their powdered wigs and satin breeches seemed at home in the little gem of a theater.

Atomic Tunnel

Home of the Walking Fish.
The Atomic Tunnel on U.S. Highway 1, seven miles south of Daytona Beach, was billed as "Florida's Biggest Little Attraction." It boasted an orchid room, parrots, piranhas, toucans, a monkey that posed for photographs, tropical gardens, Happy the Walking Fish, and a re-creation of a sixteenth century Turkish monk's living quarters. Everything was gathered around a circular tunnel housed in what was originally some type of Cold War concrete bomb shelter. Owner W. R. Johnson's Atomic Tunnel, which opened in the mid-1950s, was a popular roadside attraction until 1960. People wanted to see the man-eating piranhas, a sixteenth century Turkish monk's chamber, small mice that danced, and, of course, the walking fish.

Audubon House

Home of the Bird Watcher.
When famous artist and ornithologist John James Audubon visited Key West and the Dry Tortugas in 1832, he sighted and drew eighteen new species for his monumental *Birds of America* folio. Each day Audubon would explore the mangroves in search of native birds. It is believed that many of those detailed paintings were created in the garden of a house at 205 Whitehead Street in Key West—a beautiful old waterfront home built by Sea Captain John Geiger. In 1958 the house was restored, renamed the Audubon House, and opened to the public. Many original Audubon engravings and lithographs are on display. In the front yard stands the Geiger tree that appears in Audubon's painting of the white-crowned pigeon.

Autorama

Home of the Automobile.
The James Melton Autorama, on U.S. Highway 1 in Hypoluso, just south of West Palm Beach, opened in the 1950s. The Autorama traced the history of automobiles from the earliest days. Besides almost one hundred automobiles, the attraction displayed toys and music boxes. Other exhibits included the mural "America the Beautiful." Admission to the Autorama was $1.25. The attraction closed in 1961.

FLORIDA'S FUN-FILLED

St. Augustine Beach

NO BETTER PLACE CAN BE FOUND
TO HAVE FUN IN THE SUN THAN
THE WIDE WHITE SANDS OF
ST. AUGUSTINE BEACH.

*Just a minute from the Nation's Oldest
and most Historic Sights!*

B

Beaches to Busch Gardens

Beaches

Left: Frolicking on the Sand.
Going to the beach is a great American pastime. Whether for a vacation or just a day, Americans flock to Florida's shores in search of the inexplicable pleasure that comes with a stay by the water. Some come for serenity, others for action, and there are a hundred variations in between. Florida is a land of beaches flavored with a taste of the tropics. Sand covers 1,200 of the state's 8,462 miles of shoreline. Most of Florida's beaches lie on barrier islands, which, separated from the mainland, often enhance the beauty of these seaside locations. If someone says, "When you've seen one beach, you've seen them all," don't believe it, because it's not true in Florida. During the 1950s, it was almost impossible to experience Florida without taking advantage of the state's seaside beauty. The beaches have always been one of Florida's main attractions.

Right: Sun, Sand, and Water at Florida Beaches.
Sun worshipers dot the miles of Florida's golden sand. Sunning, picture taking, building sand castles, and splashing in the water were popular activities for residents and tourists in the 1950s.

FROLICKING ON THE SANDS OF MIAMI BEACH, FLORIDA

BEACH SCENE ALONG THE TROPICAL SHORES OF HOLLYWOOD-BY-THE-SEA, FLORIDA

S-107—Sun and Surf Bathing on the Gulf of Mexico At Pass-a-Grille Beach, Florida

Beach Racing

A Good Racing Course.

In 1947, when Bill France formed the National Association for Stock Car Auto Racing (NASCAR), sanctioned racing began on the oval racing course just south of Daytona Beach in Ponce Inlet. Consisting of a back stretch that went north on the hard beach sands, then turned (North Turn) onto State Highway A1A, and headed south toward the South Turn, which took it back toward the beach, this was a crude but useful oval-shaped track. Stock car and motorcycle races were run on this combination sand-and-asphalt track until the Daytona International Speedway opened in 1959. Visitors and racing fans stood along the roadway and in the sand dunes to watch these races. Racing fans came to these beach races from all over America.

Motorcycle Racing

Biscayne Kennel Club

Another Kind of Racing.

Sometimes called the "Sport of Queens," Greyhound Racing, or Dog Racing, involves the racing of greyhounds around an enclosed track in pursuit of an electrically controlled and propelled mechanical hare. The Biscayne Kennel Club opened in the Miami area in 1926. The $3 million facility could seat 5,000 fans with 440 box seats in the clubhouse. There were accommodations for 4,000 cars and the Grandstand had three levels. The Biscayne Kennel Club was located on Northwest 115th Street between Northeast Second Avenue and Northwest Seventh Avenue in Miami Shores. This popular dog-racing track attracted South Florida residents and tourists; it closed and was torn down in 1995.

Biscayne Fronton

"Jai Alai" (say Hi-Li) World's Fastest Sport, Biscayne Fronton, Miami, Florida

Biscayne Fronton.

Jai-Alai is similar to super-fast handball, played with a basket-like arm extension called a "cesta" to accelerate the speed and accuracy of the ball. Velocity and skillful handling of the ball require all players on the floor to be in constant motion. Pari-Mutuel betting was allowed on these games, which were played in a structure called a fronton. The Biscayne Fronton, located in Miami, opened in 1926. It was America's first Jai-Alai fronton. In the 1950s, in Florida, frontons were in Dania, Daytona Beach, Miami, Palm Beach, and Tampa. The Biscayne Fronton has a seating capacity of 5,909 and parking for 4,000 cars. Thousands of fans, South Florida residents, and tourists crowded into the fronton to enjoy Jai-Alai and bet on the games. The Biscayne Fronton was later renamed Miami Fronton.

Blue Spring

A Beautiful Spring.
A large sulfur spring of clear blue water, it flows via a short stream into St. Johns River. The water from the spring, located just west of Orange City, pours out of the ground at a rate of about 65,000 gallons a minute. A group of manatees annually migrate to the waters of this beautiful spring. Residents and tourists enjoy watching the giant manatees, also called sea cows, when they are in the spring.

Bok Singing Tower

The "Taj Mahal" of America.
The 205-foot tall Bok Singing Tower, dedicated February 1, 1929, is one of Florida's best-known and most lasting symbols. Designed by Milton B. Medary, the tower was constructed on the summit of Iron Mountain (elevation 324 feet) near Lake Wales. It was commissioned by Edward W. Bok as a gift to the American people and houses one of the world's finest carillons (more than seventy bells).

The Singing Tower is often called the "Taj Mahal" of America; it's built of Florida coquina rock and Georgia marble and is fifty-one feet in diameter at the base. The carillon bells vary in weight from just a few pounds to about eleven ton, and is one of the largest ever cast. The Bok Singing Tower is surrounded by forty-eight acres of beautifully landscaped grounds. Bok was a Dutch immigrant who came to this country at the age of six and would later become a Pulitzer Prize winning author and editor of the *Ladies' Home Journal.* On the right side of the tower, a brass door provides entry. Due to Florida fire codes, visitors are not allowed inside. The enchanting nature of the tower and surrounding gardens has always been a popular Florida attraction.

Above: Bok Singing Tower Booklet.
This 42-page postcard book describes the Mountain Lake Sanctuary and Singing Tower.

Braden Castle

Near Right: The Ruins.
Braden Castle was the home of Dr. J. A. Braden, for whom the surrounding Bradenton was named. It was constructed of tabby in 1845-51 on a 1,100-acre sugar plantation, and remained the home of Braden until 1864. For several years the Seminole Indians were troublesome, and Braden Castle often became a refuge for neighboring families when alarms were sounded. The last outbreak occurred in 1856 when Indians attacked the house while the Braden family was at supper. Although driven off, the raiders took with them the African American slaves, mules, and booty. The ruins were designated in the National Register of Historic Sites and attract tourists and history buffs.

Bongoland

Land of Pre-Historic Animals.
In 1948 Manny D. Lawrence opened Bongoland just a few blocks west of U.S. Highway 1 in Port Orange. Bongoland was one of the first Southern attractions to take visitors back 150,000,000 years where they could see strange prehistoric animals reproduced authentically in natural size. Lawrence constructed several life-size concrete dinosaurs and displayed a trained baboon named Bongo at the entrance. Bongoland evolved into a primitive theme park, with a replica of a Seminole Indian village, historic sugar mill ruins, and a collection of concrete dinosaur statues—all within a primitive jungle setting. The attraction had a train that was converted from an old truck to haul visitors around, but was never very crowded, which may be why it closed in 1952. The concrete dinosaurs can still be seen at the Sugar Mill Botanical Gardens. Shown is the front view of a plant-eating Stegosaurus and a side view of a Triceratops, another plant-eating dinosaur.

Busch Gardens

A Tropical Garden.
Busch Gardens opened in Tampa in 1959 primarily as a tropical garden with exotic birds and small animals adjacent to the Anheuser-Busch brewery. Admission to the attraction was free. It included the Stairway to the Stars, which led to a brewery tour and the famous Hospitality House overlooking a lagoon, where complimentary beer was served. It was Florida's most attended attraction. In the following years the small attraction grew into a major theme park with a world-class Wild Animal Park, monorail, thrilling carnival-like rides, and an African village.

C

Cape Canaveral to Cypress Knee Museum

Cape Canaveral Spaceport

Cape Canaveral Spaceport.
During the 1950s, Brevard County, home of Cape Canaveral, was the fastest growing county in the United States. This fantastic growth can be attributed a large part to the establishment of Cape Canaveral as America's launching area for rockets and missiles.
In 1958 with the creation of the National Aeronautics and Space Administration (NASA), manned weather space flights, deep space probes, and weather and communication satellites, massive missile systems became part of the launching activity that occurred in the Cape Canaveral area. Over the years, millions of residents and visitors have witnessed space launches from sites along U.S. Highway 1, Highway A1A, Indian River, Banana River, and area beaches. Space launches have become a huge Florida activity and attraction.

The Race to Space.
On October 4, 1957, the Soviet Union's *Sputnik I* satellite could be seen clearly in the night sky. At about twenty-three inches wide and 185 pounds, it glided overhead like a shooting star. In the following month, the Soviet Union launched the 1,120-pound *Sputnik II* satellite that carried a dog named Laika. America didn't have a successful space launch until January 31, 1958 when *Explorer I* became the country's first artificial satellite to circle the globe. On March 17, 1958, the U.S. launched the *Vanguard I* from Cape Canaveral. The *Vanguard II* a 22-pound satellite was launched February 17, 1959. The race to space had begun and it became a race between the United States and the Soviet Union, competing to achieve the next historic space "first." We have gone from simple satellites like Sputnik, Explorer, and Vanguard to complex communications satellites that now circle the globe, providing a network of worldwide communication. We have witnessed the journey of robot probes to faraway planets, landed American astronauts on the Moon, and built a Space Station, complete with shuttling vehicles that carry astronauts and cosmonauts into space. This magnificent view of the Earth was photographed from the Apollo 17 lunar module *Challenger* during the final lunar landing mission in the Apollo program.

First Missile Launch from Cape Canaveral.
On July 24, 1950, a German V-2 rocket, similar to those that bombed London in World War II, was placed on a concrete slab and topped with a smaller rocket called an Army WAC Corporal. The combination was given the inelegant name *Bumper*. The rocket was serviced from a painter's scaffold, and the control center consisted of an old tarpaper bathhouse protected by sandbags. Although *Bumper* traveled only ten miles, the firing was hailed as a success.

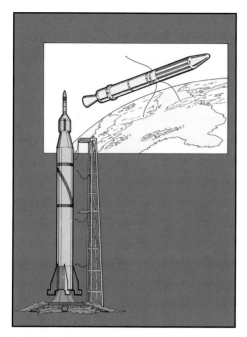

Above: First U.S. Earth Satellite.

On January 31, 1958, the U. S. Army launched *Explorer I* into orbit atop a Jupiter-C/Juno1 rocket. *Explorer I* was a cylindrical device, 6.5 feet long, weighing 30 pounds. At its highest altitude, its orbit reached 1,580 miles. Its instruments confirmed the existence of the Van Allen belt, a layer of natural radiation encircling Earth at a height of 600 miles. *Explorer I* completed 58,000 orbits and reentered Earth's atmosphere March 31, 1970.

Near Right: Vanguard I Satellite.

On March 17, 1958, the U.S. Navy successfully orbited America's second satellite, *Vanguard I.* The satellite was a 3.5-pound sphere, six inches in diameter. The launch booster consisted of a Viking rocket first stage, an Aerobee second stage, and the Vanguard third stage for a combined total thrust of 28,000 pounds. *Vanguard I* continued to orbit and transmit data for seven years. Its most important discovery was that the Earth was slightly pear-shaped with the narrow end toward the North Pole. The Vanguard program continued with other satellites through 1959.

Thor Leaving the Launch Pad.

The first Thor long-range ballistic missile was launched at Cape Canaveral January 25, 1957. Thor, a 65-foot tall, 110,000 pound ballistic missile with a range of 1,700 miles, exploded in a tremendous fireball. However, many of the missile launches in the pioneering 1950s were less than perfect. It was not until the fifth vehicle that Thor scored a completely successful flight and then went on to score a creditable record during forty-nine launches at the Cape. The Thor missile was an important member of America's missile arsenal.

Above left: Redstone Being Fueled.

The first Army Redstone missile was launched August 20, 1953. Shown is the Redstone, which was test-flown over the Air Force Missile Test Center's range, being fueled at the Cape Canaveral launching site. The gantry service tower standing beside the missile was used in pre-flight preparations.

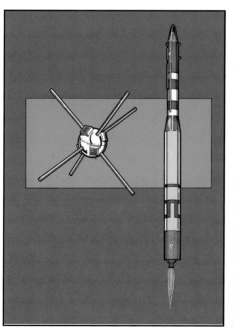

Above Right: First Missile Launch.

Launching of First Bomarc Missile, Cape Canaveral, September 10, 1952.

Near Left: First Titan Launch.

The Air Force Titan I, a two-stage ninety-foot tall, ten-foot diameter missile that weighed more than 220,000 pounds, was first launched at Cape Canaveral February 6, 1959.

Caribbean Gardens

Carriage Cavalcade

Exotic toucans are among the hundreds of rare birds and waterfowl that roam freely in this beautiful sanctuary.

Midway thru the Gardens, the friendly atmosphere of our Pavilion Restaurant invites you to relax and enjoy luncheon.

Feed the birds at Caribbean Gardens, Naples, Florida

Caribbean Gardens.

Famed botanist Dr. Henry Nehrling founded the Naples Gardens in 1919. The gardens were his dream tropical gardens where rare plants from all over the world could grow. Nehrling expanded his collection to over 3,000 plant species. But after his death in 1929, his gardens grew wild and untended for the next two decades. Julius Fleischman, grandson of the man who pioneered Fleischmann yeast, acquired the gardens, restored the site, added birds, lakes, and plants, and in 1954, opened it as Caribbean Gardens. In 1964, after Fleischmann's death, world traveler and expedition leader Colonel Lawrence "Jungle Larry" Tetzlaff and his wife, Nancy "Safari Jane" Tetzlaff, relocated their collection of rare and endangered animals to the gardens and renamed the place Jungle Larry's Safari. It closed after thirty years in 1994, and at the same time, the location reverted to Caribbean Gardens.

Carriage Cavalcade.

The Carriage Cavalcade, located across State Highway 40 from the entrance to Silver Springs, opened in 1953. It was a museum of antique coaches and cars. On display were almost one hundred coaches and carriages of early America, the same vehicles that put America on wheels and started the momentum that has carried this country up the road to progress. It was a collection of rare old motor driven vehicles, steam, electric, and gasoline, whose persistent chugging finally gave birth to the multi-powered motorcars of today. The Carriage Cavalcade presented this transformation from the earliest horse drawn cart, the first horseless carriage, to the more modern car of the 1920s, which fathered our present day vehicles. The antiques were housed in a 33,000 square foot building. Mannequins, dressed in the attire of the 1800s and the early automobile age were used to recreate typical scenes of the past. A very popular feature of the Carriage Cavalcade was the stage or sightseeing coach for an old fashioned ride through the grounds in the area. In 1963 this attraction was renamed Early American Museum.

Cars of Yesterday

Horn's Cars of Yesterday.
In 1953, brothers Herbert and Robert Horn opened Horn's Cars of Yesterday on U.S. Highway 41 in Sarasota. Over seventy antique and classic automobiles, along with a variety of antique music boxes and arcade games were housed in a building with a "Gay Nineties" atmosphere. Sold to Walter Belim in the 1960s, he enlarged the collection and today the attraction is called the Sarasota Classic Car Museum.

Casper's Ostrich & Alligator Farm

Gators and Ostriches.
This attraction, located two miles north of St. Augustine on U.S. Highway 1, contained a large and interesting collection of ostriches, rare birds, alligators, crocodiles, and reptiles. Casper's opened as a roadside attraction in 1946. William Casper's Farm was always in the shadow of the established St. Augustine Alligator Farm on nearby Anastasia Island. Casper's never achieved the popularity of its neighbor despite being located on heavily traveled U.S. Highway 1. Casper's was the only alligator and ostrich farm with an ostrich racetrack. Ostriches were raised and trained at Casper's for racing. Ostrich sulky races were held daily on the 125-mile track.

Castillo de San Marcos

Christmas Post Office

Left: Receiving Holiday Mail.
Christmas, a little town on Highway 50 west of Titusville and east of Orlando, receives much mail during Yule-tide holidays, canceling thousands of letters through the postal system. Since 1942, when people throughout Florida started sending cards and packages to World War II servicemen overseas, people have been coming to this small post office to have their mail stamped with the Christmas postmark. Today over 300,000 pieces of mail are stamped with that postmark during the holiday season.

Above: Oldest Fort in the U.S.
An attack by the English in 1670 solidified Spanish resolve to better fortify St. Augustine. Groundbreaking for the fort took place in 1672, with the basic structure completed by 1696. Constructed of massive blocks of coquina stone quarried nearby, the fort was built by Cuban engineers including Ignacio Daza. Skilled stone masons from Havana, slaves, and Indians participated in its construction. With its twelve-foot thick walls, encircling moat, dependable water supply, and latrine flushed by tidal action, the entire, 1,500 residents of St. Augustine found refuge here in times of trouble. The coquina structure measures 324 x 311 feet. There are twenty-nine casemates and two rooms within the Castillo. Castillo cannons commanded the harbor's entrance.
Castillo de San Marcos was built to protect the Spanish settlements and Spanish treasure fleets. The Castillo survived two major sieges and was never captured by an enemy during battle. The fort has walls twenty-one feet high, a moat that surrounded it, bastions on the corners, heavy casemates, dungeons, and subterranean passages. The Castillo took twenty-three years to build and cost more than 138,000 pesos ($218,360). The design of the fort is "stellar." It has a square central courtyard with a series of storage rooms around it with diamond-shaped bastions at each corner. The Castillo de San Marcos was the most attended attraction in St. Augustine and one of the most popular attractions in Florida.

Circus Hall of Fame

The World of Circus.
The Circus Hall of Fame, located on U.S. Highway 41 north of the Ringling Art Museum in Sarasota, opened in 1956. This attraction introduced visitors to the world of the circus. Visitors could watch the puppets that were from countries all over the world and inspect the model circus trains, posters, photographs, wagons, or any of the thousands of exhibits on display. The last of the Ringling Bros. and Barnum & Bailey ticket wagons was on display. It was used when the "Greatest Show on Earth" played under the Big Top. The Circus Hall of Fame presented live professional circus acts daily in an indoor arena and attracted around 80,000 visitors a year until 1979, when the land, which was leased, was sold and the attraction was forced to close. A group from Peru, Indiana, acquired the collection for $450,000 and relocated the facility to their town, expanding its scope and size.

Circus Winter Quarters

Wintering in Sunny Sarasota.
The Ringling Circus occupied a unique place in American culture. Governors and community leaders sat in guest boxes at Ringling Circus premiers while, in Washington, D.C., John Ringling personally escorted President and Mrs. Coolidge to their seats. The Ringling Bros. and Barnum & Bailey Circus Winter Quarters attracted thousands of visitors, including Ernest Hemingway, Cecil B. DeMille, Betty Davis, and Prince Rainier. John Ringling was recognized around the world. He was tall, elegantly dressed, soft spoken, and reputedly one of the richest men in the country. During the winter months, the circus settles down to the busy months of preparation and rehearsing for the next season, and many members of the circus family

became home folk until the following April. The Ringling Circus spent its winter months under Sarasota's warm sunny skies. Here new equipment and tents were built, repairs were made, new acts were rehearsed, and the public could see the circus getting ready for the next season. Since 1927, when John Ringling moved the Ringling Circus Winter Quarters from Bridgeport, Connecticut to town, the circus has been of a major importance to Sarasota's economic base. Initially, the move provided hundreds of jobs building the complex, but the Ringling Winter Quarters were a perennial bonanza to the community as a tourist attraction, bringing visitors from all over the world. Tourists were fascinated by the colorful activity and the skills of circus performers, whose rehearsals were often open to visitors, and marveled at the exotic animals.

Elephant and Clown at Ringling Bros. and Barnum & Bailey Winter Quarters

Gargantua, Feature Attraction at Ringling Bros. and Barnum & Bailey Winter Quarters, Sarasota, Fla.

Citrus Fruit Stands and Tower

Above and Near Right: Citrus Tower.
This ten-story structure north of Clermont on the Orange Blossom Trail (U.S. Highway 27) was constructed in 1956 when orange groves were abundant in the area. Visitors enjoyed viewing the hundreds of large citrus groves that surrounded the tower. Only a half hour drive from Orlando, the landmark tower is very near the geographic center of the state. The structure contains five million pounds of concrete in 149,000 pounds of reinforcing steel. From the glassed-in observation deck in this two hundred-foot tall tower, visitors could see thirty-five miles to the horizon. In 1959, visitors could take a land and water tour of the citrus groves and lakes around the tower in a World War II-like amphibious vehicle called "The Ducks." Today the citrus groves have been replaced with shopping centers and housing developments. The tower remains as a monument to the citrus industry that once occupied this area of Florida.

Far Right: Citrus Fruit Stands.
Hundreds of thousands of citrus fruit trees wound eastward from Pinellas and Hillsborough counties on the Gulf Coast, around the lakes of Polk, Orange, and Lake counties, and extended on the east coast from Daytona Beach almost to the southernmost tip of the state. U.S. Routes 1, 17, 27, 41, 92 and 441 sliced through the checkerboard-patterned groves and led to the citrus town centers of Winter Haven, Orlando, Leesburg, Tampa, Clearwater, Lakeland, and Vero Beach. The Florida Citrus Museum, situated in Winter Haven's Florida Citrus Building, recounted the history of citrus in America. Visitors enjoyed stopping at the orange groves, picking oranges in the groves, and purchasing citrus products to ship home. Roadside citrus stands were located along all the major highways in Florida.

The Box of Oranges I Promised you from the Sunshine State, Florida

153N

GREETINGS from FLORIDA

FLORIDA ORANGES

Coral Castle

Above: Coral Castle.

Painstakingly carved out of more than 1,000 tons of coral, this remarkable structure was erected by Latvian-born Edward Leedskalnin as a symbol of his unrequited love; he devoted twenty-five years of his life completing it. Among the castles many fascinations are hand-made furniture, solar-heated bathtubs, and a nine-ton swinging gate—all sculptured from coral. Claiming that he knew the secrets of the Egyptian pyramid-builders, the one hundred-pound Leedskalnin never divulged the means by which he himself transported the massive pieces of coral. Coral Castle is located on U.S. Highway 1, twenty-five miles south of Miami.

Cypress Gardens

Swampland to Beautiful Garden.

Richard "Dick" Pope is the genius who first saw a beautiful garden to which millions would flock, in the wild moss-hung cypress swamp bordering—and even marching out into Lake Eloise—Winter Haven. He bought acres of swamp and native tangled jungle; then he built the gardens—Cypress Gardens. On January 2, 1936, the *Swami of the Swamp* opened Cypress Gardens to 136 customers who paid twenty-five cents admission. By 1950, the Cypress Garden Gift Shop sold more Kodak film than any retail center in America. Pope hired eight fulltime photographers simply to help guests load and shoot film. *Life* magazine called Cypress Gardens "A Photographer's Paradise." In addition to the Gardens, there was a water ski show featuring some of America's best water skiers. Dick, and his wife Julie, created a fairyland of flowers for over a million visitors a year to enjoy. The graceful palm trees and lofty trunks of the tall cypress trees provide a cathedral-like corridor for the trails through the Gardens, while the winding waterways rival those of far off lands. The Popes assembled rare and exotic plants and flowers from the four corners of the globe. Over the years many movies and television shows have been filmed at Cypress Gardens.

Water Ski Capital of the World.

Florida Cypress Gardens, surrounded by many sparkling, spring-fed lakes, was the acknowledged "Water Ski Capital of the World." The sport grew and blossomed into the most exhilarating and fastest outdoor sport in the world. Dick Pope's wife, Julie, put on the first water ski show at Cypress Gardens to entertain World War II soldiers from a nearby military base. The water skiing performers were the Popes' children, Dick Pope, Jr. and Adrienne, and some of their school friends. The following Sunday over eight hundred soldiers from the military base arrived, donated gas for the towboat, and watched the second show. From that time on, Cypress Gardens presented four water ski shows a day, day after day, year after year...a thrilling sight to behold. Kite and barefoot skiing were invented here. The beautiful water skiing Aquamaids has thrilled thousands of audiences with national skiing champions performing thrilling stunts and jumps.

4 EXCITING WATER SKI SHOWS DAILY AT FLORIDA'S

CYPRESS GARDENS

Cypress Gardens Magazine Ad.

America's Tropical Wonderland.
A bouquet of floral beauty abounds in every corner of Cypress Gardens. Whether visitors walked through or rode the quiet electric boats, they sensed an atmosphere of serenity and peacefulness, unequally anywhere. The international language of flowers was spoken fluently at Cypress Gardens. Electric boats took visitors through winding, flower-bordered lagoons. Adding charm and more beauty to the Gardens were lovely models in antebellum dresses reminiscent of the Old South. Some 8,000 varieties of plants, gathered from seventy-five countries, are landscaped on over two hundred acres. The lovely models in antebellum dresses strolled through the azaleas, gardenias, camellias, bougainvillea, crotons, bromeliads, and other colorful flora, where they were viewed and photographed by visitors.

Cypress Knee Museum

Above and Top Right: Esther Williams' Swimming Pool.
A swimming pool in the shape of Florida was built at Cypress Gardens in 1953 for the MGM water-musical film spectacular, "Easy to Love," starring Esther Williams, Tony Martin, Cyd Charisse, and Van Johnson. Other Esther Williams movies filmed at Cypress Gardens included "Million Dollar Mermaid" and "Dangerous When Wet." The pool projected out into Lake Eloise.

The Cypress Tree—A Signature Species.
Cypress trees are one of the south landscape's signature species and can be found throughout Florida. They form dome-shaped regiments in many low, wet areas. Cypress trees have tall, straight trunks and fluted bases, which provide stability in wet soil. The trees are perhaps best known for their wide-spreading systems of shallow roots with odd-shaped, protruding "knees." The Thomas Gaskins Cypress Tree Museum, located on U.S. Highway 27 in Palmdale, featured a collection of cypress knees fashioned from the roots of age-old swamp cypress trees. There was a scenic swamp walk and swamp-buggy tours. Admission to the museum was $1. Visitors were attracted to the unusual shaped knees and were able to purchase polished knee souvenirs. The museum was open between the 1930s and 2000 and had many "Burma Shave-style" signs that lined Highway 27 for several miles north and south of the attraction. One of the interesting hand-lettered road signs read, "Lady, If He Won't Stop, Hit Him On The Head With Shoe." Shown is Tom Gaskins with one of his unusual cypress knees.

Dania Jai-Alai Fronton

Daytona Beach Boardwalk

Dania Jai-Alai Players.
Jai-Alai is a fast-paced betting sport. According to *Guinness Book of World Records,* it's the fastest ballgame in the world, with its rock-hard *pelota* traveling up to 180 mph. Each game is short and fast, lasting only about ten minutes. Two players face off in a court, trying to hurl a small hard ball against the front wall of the court with so much speed and spin the opponent cannot catch or return it before the second bounce. Each player retrieves and throws the ball with a scoop-shaped *cesta*. The winner stays on the court to meet the next player in rotation.

Above: Dania Jai-Alai Fronton.
In 1953 flamboyant, former circus owner, Roy McAndrews built a Jai-Alai Fronton in Dania (Miami's closest neighbor to the north) just east of Federal Highway (U.S. Highway 1) between Ft. Lauderdale and Hollywood. The Dania Fronton was the second Jai-Alai Fronton built in the United States. The fronton is home to international Jai-Alai superstars making wild catches, climbing the walls in the world's fastest ball game. The Dania Jai-Alai Fronton was an immediate success and proved the point that the more frontons available, the more people would flock to them.

Right: Daytona Beach Boardwalk.
The Boardwalk, located along the Atlantic Ocean in Daytona Beach, was built in the late 1930s by the Works Progress Administration (WPA). This carnival-like attraction was very popular with tourists and locals throughout the 1950s-1970s. Many of the Boardwalk structures, including the Bandshell, Clock Tower, tourist shops, and amusements were built of coquina stone. The Boardwalk also had a long fishing pier and dancing pavilion that reached out into the Atlantic. The Ferris Wheel and other amusements at the Boardwalk were razed a few years ago.

Daytona Beach Jai-Alai Fronton

Daytona Beach Jai-Alai Players.
They call Jai-Alai the fastest game on two feet, and it's one of the oldest ball games in the world. The game is played in a large arena called a fronton. Jai-Alai (pronounced hi-li) originated in the Pyrenees Mountains of northern Spain during the fifteenth century. Daytona Beach's fronton opened in 1959, allowing thousands of excited spectators to view Jai-Alai players in action.

Daytona Beach Jai-Alai Fronton.
The Daytona Beach Jai-Alai Fronton opened in 1959 as the Volusia Jai-Alai Fronton. The fronton was located on Highway 92 across from the Volusia County Kennel Club and the Daytona International Speedway. It had a seating capacity of 4,353. The fronton closed following the April 14, 1988 strike of Jai-Alai players.

Daytona International Speedway

Daytona International Speedway.
Daytona Beach and racing are almost synonymous. Since the early 1900s, Daytona Beach has hosted car races that began on the beach and grew into the Daytona International Speedway. Known as the "World Center of Racing," the speedway hosts NASCAR, sports car, motorcycle, and go-kart races; the better known of them is the Daytona 500. Now a very large motor-sports complex, the speedway was built in 1959. Fans come from all over the world to attend races at this 2.5-mile speedway.

Deer Ranch

Many Types of Deer.
Tommy Bartlett's Deer Ranch was
established in 1954 by well known
television host, Tommy Bartlett. Visitors
could walk among and feed deer, and tour
a dense swamp-like subtropical jungle in a
jeep-pulled trailer vehicle. The Deer Ranch,
in East Park of Silver Springs, had one of
the most complete collections of deer in
the world. Deer from all over the world were
featured. The entire ranch was surrounded
by a backdrop of natural Florida jungle,
truly an appropriate surrounding for these
fleet-footed creatures of the forest. Colors
of the different types of deer included
black, brown, red, spotted, and snow white.
In addition to deer, the ranch also had
mountain sheep and goats with beautifully
arched horns. It closed in 1975, with many
of its inhabitants incorporated into other
Silver Springs attractions.

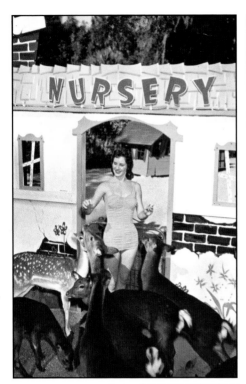

"THE TWO DEARS", AT OCALA SPRINGS, FLA. IN THE "KINGDOM OF THE SUN".   105284

Derby Lane

Racing Greyhounds.

Packed grandstand and "railbirds" watch thrilling greyhound races at "Derby Lane," historic home of the St. Petersburg Kennel Club that opened in 1925 in St. Petersburg. Tourists and residents enjoyed watching this major winter sports attraction in the Sunshine City. Release of the starting gate put the greyhounds in action.

Perfect Break at "Derby Lane", St. Petersburg, Fla. "The Sunshine City" P-144

S-142—First Turn Thrill in Greyhound Racing at "Derby Lane" St. Petersburg, Florida

B-1—Monument Marking De Soto's Landing, Bradenton, Fla.

DeSoto National Memorial

Commemorating an Early Explorer.

The DeSoto National Memorial on Highway 64, five miles west of U.S. Highway 41 in Bradenton, contains thirty acres and was authorized in 1948 to commemorate the May 1539 Florida landing of Spanish explorer Hernando DeSoto. He arrived with an army of over six hundred soldiers in the Tampa Bay area in nine ships laden with supplies, 220 horses, a herd of pigs, war dogs, cannon, matchlock muskets, armor, tools, and rations. They were executing the order of King Charles V to sail to Florida and "conquer, populate, and pacify" the land. The expedition did not yield the gold and treasure these men sought. Instead, they marched from one village to the next, taking food and enslaving the native people to use as guides and porters. Hundreds of lives were lost on this calamitous four-year, 4,000-mile journey. The DeSoto expedition would change the face of the American Southeast forever, and cause Spain to reevaluate her role in the New World. Ultimately, it was the first-hand accounts of survivors, describing the native cultures and the richness of the land, that became the journey's enduring legacy. The visitor center contained exhibits to help tourists interpret the DeSoto expedition. Visitors could also attend living history demonstrations or walk the nature trail through a Florida coastal landscape similar to the one encountered by Spanish conquistadors almost five hundred years ago.

Devil's Millhopper

A Large Sinkhole.

The Devil's Millhopper, located northwest of downtown Gainesville, is a sinkhole that opened when an underground cavern collapsed. The sinkhole ranges from 120 to 500 feet deep, and was formed between 14,000 and 20,000 years ago. Visitors climbed down into the large hole to hear the sounds of trickling streams and cascading waterfalls, and view tiny caves in the wall of the rainforest-like environment.

The Devils Mill Hopper. Near Gainesville, Fla.

Dry Tortugas

Home to Birds and Turtles.

Sixty-eight miles west of Key West, the seven tiny coral and sand islands of the Dry Tortugas are home to rare migratory birds and a wealth of marine life. Spanish explorer Ponce de Leon came across the islands in 1513 and named them "Las Tortugas" because of the large number of turtles that occupied the land. Later sailors renamed them the Dry Tortugas, as a warning, because there was no fresh water on the islands. In 1832 famous artist and ornithologist, John James Audubon, spent several days observing and painting some of the more than two hundred species of birds nesting there.

Dry Tortugas became a national monument in 1935. Visitors to Key West took either a boat or small seaplane to visit these islands. In 1992 the Dry Tortugas were designated a national park. Shown here is the only entrance and exit of Fort Jefferson located on the Garden Key island. *(More information about Fort Jefferson can be found in the "I" section.)*

D. K. 1—Old Fort Jefferson on Dry Tortugas, near Key West, Fla.

The Blossom Center of Florida

DUPREE GARDENS

OPEN FROM NOV. 1 TO JULY 1

TAMPA *Florida*

Moss-Festooned Lagoon at Dupree Gardens

102 - Mirror Pool in Dupree Gardens

Dupree Gardens

Florida's Blossom Center.
Dupree Gardens opened on U.S. Highway 41 about twenty-five miles north of Tampa in 1940. This attraction covered twenty acres of a vast nine hundred-acre estate owned by Tampa attorney J. Williams Dupree. It was a fairyland with flowers everywhere—millions upon millions of blossoms tucked into shaded nooks, along winding pathways, and in artistically arranged beds. Rustic bridges, quiet pools, the tinkling sound of a waterfall, and soft music coming from singing birdhouses in the trees lent enchantment to the scene. Dupree Gardens closed in 1954 and the land was used for residential development.

E
Eastern Garden Aquarium to the Everglades

Eastern Garden Aquarium

Eastern Garden Aquarium.
The Eastern Garden Aquarium on U.S. Highway 1, five miles south of Miami, was at the time the world's largest aquarium attraction. Twenty-five years of research in breeding tropical fish helped build this huge aquarium. With more than five hundred tanks displaying the Sea Horse, fighting fish from Siam, and many rare tropical fish from jungle streams of the world, this interesting and educational attraction opened in the early 1950s. Visitors especially enjoyed seeing thousands of baby fish emerging from eggs and mated pairs caring for their young. It was a sight that attracted visitors from faraway distances.

M6—Discus or Pompadour Fish (Symphysodon Discus)
Located at Eastern Garden Aquarium
U. S. #1, South of Miami, Fla.

M.108—See Breeding Angel Fish at
Eastern Garden Aquarium
5 Miles from South Miami, Florida

Edison's Winter Home

Edison Home Brochure.

No single American has matched the creativity of Thomas Edison. The inventor registered 1,093 patents, including seventy-five in 1882 alone, with 141 for batteries, 150 for improvements to the telegraph, and 389 for electric power and light. Edison not only developed his own ideas, he also improved those of others, including the telephone of Alexander Graham Bell. A shrewd businessman, he perfected a workable light bulb and then a meter to charge customers for the electricity they used. His Edison General Electric Company, founded in 1890, employed more than 7,000 people. The press dubbed him "The Wizard;" however, Edison never pretended that inventing was easy. "Genius is one percent inspiration and ninety-nine percent perspiration" is one of his best-known sayings. The $40,000 he made from inventing the stock market ticker-tape machine in 1871 freed him to become a full-time inventor.

Thomas Edison Winter Home.

Thomas Alva Edison found health and happiness in building a Queen Anne-style winter home and garden on the banks of the Caloosahatchee River in Fort Myers. Seminole Lodge, as his home was named, lies literally buried in a jungle of rare tropical shrubs, trees, and other plants. Two houses connected by a breezeway comprised the lodge—the family home section and the Edison Guest House. The Edisons and their visitors used the kitchen and dining room in the Guest House. Among the guests at Seminole Lodge were Henry Ford, President Herbert Hoover, Harvey Firestone, and Charles Lindbergh. Seminole Lodge was designed by Edison and built in sections in Fairfield, Maine in 1885. The sections were then transported to Fort Myers by four sailing schooners and erected in 1886. Circling the homes are large overhanging porches, which, combined with French doors on the first floor, provide a cool breeze through the home at all times. Electric chandeliers, "electroliers," were designed by Edison, hand-made of brass in his own workshop. The Edison house is the main attraction in Fort Myers.

Thomas Edison's Home, Fort Myers, Florida   106

58

Everglades

Everglades National Park

The Everglades.
From the air, it seems a vast, mysterious world of land and water at whose edge civilization suddenly stops, a place where no one dwells. From the highway, it appears as an endless prairie above which birds fly in winter and clouds build into towering summer storms. A shining expanse of sawgrass evokes the Indian name for the Everglades, Pa-hay-okee or "Grassy Water." The vast, thick river

of grass stretches across the Everglades, drawing its life from the fresh water below it. Sawgrass is not really grass at all, but a sedge-one of earth's oldest plant species. In the Everglades, life teems, water flows, and creatures struggle for survival in miraculous cycles that have repeated themselves over and over since prehistoric times.
The Everglades chief resident is the American alligator. Like dark, greenish-black, lifeless logs, they often lie basking motionless on the sunny banks of water holes or sometimes beside the road. Of particular importance is the alligator's role as the "Keeper of the Everglades." Getting ready for the region's annual dry season, the alligator prepares its own water reservoirs by cleaning out large holes, dissolved cavities in the limestone bed of the Everglades. As the rains decrease, these "gator holes" become important oases for all wildlife. Fish, turtles, snails, and other freshwater creatures seek refuge in the pools. Here many will survive until the rains return. Tourists that took the Tamiami Trail east of Naples, toward Miami, drove through the Everglades and saw Seminole Indian villages and souvenir stands, air boat rides, lots of alligators lying beside the roadway, many flying birds, and America's smallest post office at Ochopee.

Wood Ibis Rookery in Everglades National Park

Everglades National Park.
Everglades National Park comprises over 1.5 million acres and was established in 1947 to preserve a unique subtropical wilderness with extensive fresh and saltwater areas, open prairies, and mangrove forests. It's located across the southern tip of Florida. There is no other park like it in the world. Inhabitants such as wood storks, roseate spoonbills, green sea turtles, alligators, crocodiles, bald eagles, deer, and other animals and birds can be seen by walking the trails, canoeing or kayaking the waters, and exploring with park rangers. Entrances to the park lie just southwest of U.S. Highway 1 in Homestead and south of the Tamiami Trail (U.S. Highway 41) in Everglades City.

Everglades Wonder Gardens

Crocodiles and Alligators.
In 1937 brothers Bill and Lester Piper opened the Everglades Reptile Gardens along the Tamiami Trail (U.S. Highway 41) in Bonita Springs, twenty-three miles south of Ft. Myers. After World War II, the attraction was known as Everglades Wonder Gardens. The Piper brothers had one of the biggest alligator and

crocodile collections in Florida, and were especially proud of their crocodile pool, which included thirty-two crocodiles in one enclosure. Dynamite, a 14'3" long crocodile, was king of the pool. In a separate pen was Big Joe, a twelve-foot long bad crocodile that killed seven other crocodiles in a few months time in 1949. The alligator pool was full of large gators, scores of them ten- to fourteen-feet long, many caught by the Pipers themselves in the nearby Imperial River. The attraction is still open and is owned by Lester's grandson, David Piper, Jr.

A Resting Crocodile.
In the 1950s this roadside attraction had an All-Florida exhibit with 2,000 alligators, crocodiles, snakes, animals, and birds that taught visitors about life in the mysterious Everglades.

F
Fairchild Garden to Fountain of Youth

Fairchild Tropical Botanic Garden

Top Left: A Botanical Garden.
The Fairchild Tropical Garden, located on eighty-three acres at 10901 Old Cutler Road in Coral Gables, opened in 1938. It was one of the world's most noted botanical gardens with extensive collections of rare tropical plants including palms, flowering trees, and vines. David Fairchild spent thirty-seven years collecting plants from all over the world that would live in south Florida.

Bottom Left: Fishing.
Florida's fine fishing waters contain more than six hundred varieties of fish. First choice with fresh water fishermen is the giant largemouth bass. Salt-water anglers pit their skills against such spectacular performers as sailfish or the silver tarpon. Florida is a fisherman's paradise with 2,750,000 acres of fresh water within its boundaries and 8,426 miles of tidal coastline plus easy access to the limitless Atlantic Ocean and the Gulf of Mexico. Nearly every town in Florida truthfully advertises that it is the center of a great fishing area. The popularity of Florida fishing is not entirely due to the tremendous numbers of fish that inhabit these waters, but rather to the varied species that are available.

Flamingo Groves & Gardens

An Orange, Anyone?
It was fun to take pictures at the Flamingo Orange Groves and Tropical Botanical Gardens in Ft. Lauderdale. Here visitors found over three hundred different kinds of tropical fruit trees, shrubs, vines, and, of course, oranges. The orange groves, one of the largest in Southeast Florida, had more than seventy-six kinds of oranges and other citrus fruit. Visitors were always welcome.

Florida Alligator Farm

Near Left: A Popular Attraction.
The Florida Alligator Farm, located six miles north of Callahan on U.S. Highway 1, had a free zoo, picnic area, snack bar, souvenir shop, gas, and over 150 animals and reptiles. This roadside attraction was open from the late 1940s through 1960.

Florida Caverns

Shelter for Native Americans.
The caverns are located near Marianna in the Florida Panhandle. Native Americans used the caverns for shelter for thousands of years. Hanging stalactites and standing stalagmites are features of these electrically lighted caverns. The cave, covering an area of nearly two acres, and the park has been open to the public since 1942. Equal in beauty to such famous sites as Mammoth Cave and Carlsbad Caverns, the caves at Florida Caverns contain dazzling formation of stalactites, stalagmites, soda straw columns, draperies, flowstones, and rimstones. A tour of the caverns begins about sixty feet beneath the surface of the ground. Today the Florida Caverns are a Florida State Park.

Florida Reptile Land

A Free Zoo.
Florida Reptile Land on U.S. Highway 98, eighteen miles south of Perry, was a free zoo with over one hundred different kinds of animals from all parts of the world. This roadside attraction also sold gas, candy, pecans, milk shakes, orange juice, hot dogs, and tropical jellies.

Florida State Museum

Displaying Natural History.
Located in Gainesville, Florida State Museum contained an extensive ornithological collection, other natural history exhibits, and archaeological historical displays. In 1970 this collection formed the basis of the Florida Museum of Natural History, located in a modern, part-underground architectural designed building on the campus of the University of Florida.

Florida Wild Animal Ranch

Flamingos in Tropical Florida

Florida Wild Animal and Reptile Ranch.
This seven-acre attraction, at North 4th Street and 48th Avenue in St. Petersburg, had a variety of animals on display, featured trained animal acts, and offered rides on elephants. There were herds of alligators and crocodiles, beautiful birds in a tropical setting, strange wild animals, and rattlesnakes in action. The attraction opened in 1937 and closed in 1959. Shown are pink flamingoes at the ranch.

Fort Barrancas and Fort San Carlos

Historic Fort San Carlos and Fort Barrancas, Pensacola, Fla.

Fort Barrancas and Fort San Carlos.

Historic Fort San Carlos (shown in the lower right corner) was built by Spanish General Andreas de Arriola in 1669 to guard the entrance to Pensacola Bay and protect the settlement he established around the fort. During the wars of the eighteenth century between England, France, and Spain, the old fort changed hands many times. Fort Barrancas (top left corner) was erected by the United States between 1839 and 1844 to protect the harbor during the many tumultuous battles of Pensacola's illustrious past, as this strategic coastal site was a focal point. Barranca is a Spanish word for a bluff. The fort was designed to defend the Pensacola harbor with a cross fire from Santa Rosa Island where Fort Pickens had been erected in the sand dunes a few years earlier. Fort Barrancas was built immediately north of the Spanish Fort San Carlos. The two forts are connected by an underground tunnel. The 65-acre fort sites later became part of the Pansacola Naval Air Station, and today, the forts are operated by the National Park Service.

Fort Caroline National Memorial

A French Settlement.

Fort Caroline National Memorial was authorized in 1950 to commemorate the historic French settlement of La Caroline. The park comprises 139 acres and is located in northeastern Florida between U.S. Highway 1 and Highway A1A, east of Jacksonville. In June 1564, an expedition of three hundred French Huguenots (Protestants) anchored their three small ships in Florida's St. Johns River. Along the southern bank they established a colony named La Caroline in honor of King Charles IX of France. The colony included a triangular earth-and-wood fort. The intent was to establish a French presence in the New World and provide a Huguenot haven from the religious wars in France. In 1565 Spanish conquistador Pedro Menendez and his soldiers established St. Augustine, the oldest settlement in Florida, and destroyed the French fort and removed the French settlers from the New World. A model of the French fort is located at the memorial.

Fort Clinch

A Historical Site.

An aerial view shows the remains of Fort Clinch, three miles from Fernandina Beach, east of Jacksonville. An outstanding historical site, especially for students and Civil War and fort buffs, the fort, located on the north end of Amelia Island, began in 1847 just two years after Florida became the twenty-seventh state. After the first year of the Civil War, the Union seized and occupied it.

Fort Matanzas National Monument

Defending St. Augustine.
Fort Matanzas National Monument comprised nearly three hundred acres and was established in 1924 to preserve the most important auxiliary defense of St. Augustine and a unique specimen of a vanished style of military architecture and engineering. Once decayed and crumbling, this old landmark bears mute testimony of that historic period when the Spaniards heroically struggled to defend St. Augustine against the invader. Militant English colonists were a constant menace and the fort was primarily built to repel a possible attack from that "back door" quarter between the years 1740-1742. Just inside Matanzas Inlet, on Rattlesnake Island, it is eighteen miles south of the Castillo de San Marcos and St. Augustine. Fort Matanzas guarded the "back door" to St. Augustine.

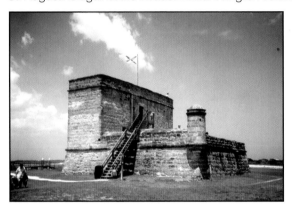

Fort Pickens

Coastal Fortification.
Construction of this coastal fortification began in 1829 and was completed in 1833. The seven-acre, five-sided structure was named after General Andrew Pickens, a Revolutionary War hero. Gun emplacements for more than one hundred cannons were mounted within and on top of its walls, which were constructed of locally-made brick. Fort Pickens became important during the Mexican (1845-1848) and the Civil wars, but otherwise it was lightly garrisoned. The fort was held by Union forces throughout the Civil War, contributing to Confederates' withdrawal from Pensacola in 1862; it also served as a military prison until 1868. From 1886 until 1888, Geronimo and other Chiricahua Apache Indians were held as prisoners there, but by 1934 it was obsolete. Fort Pickens was then used as a training facility, especially during the early days of World War II, but by 1947 it was abandoned. The fort became part of Gulf Islands National Seashore in 1972 and is administered by the National Park Service. It's located at 1801 Gulf Breeze Parkway in Gulf Breeze, near Pensacola.

Fort Zachary Taylor

Air View Showing Fort Zachary Taylor in Key West.
Construction of Fort Zachary Taylor began in 1845 as part of a chain of forts designed to protect Florida's coastline, but its primary objective was to guard the strategic port of Key West. Named shortly after President Zachary Taylor died in 1850, the three-story fort was completed in 1866, having remained in Union hands throughout the Civil War. Its five-foot thick walls rose fifty feet above the water, and the three-mile range of the fort's cannons at one point held 299 Confederate ships in Key West's harbor. Shaped like a trapezoid, the structure originally was located 1,000 feet offshore, but silt and dredge fill over the years have caused the fort to become landlocked. Technological advances in weaponry during the Civil War made the fort and its 198 guns obsolete. By the end of the Spanish-American War, the walls were reduced to one-story to accommodate new guns. The fort became a National Historic Landmark in 1973.

Fountain of Youth

Where Christian Indian Burials Were First Discovered.
The popular Fountain of Youth Park was located north of the Castillo de San Marcos in St. Augustine. Entrance to the park was located on Myrtle Street off San Marco Avenue (U.S. Highway A1A). Important archaeological discoveries at the park include the first Christian Indian burials in North America with Mission Period interments: Timucua Indian hut foundations and relics; artifacts indicating Timucua Indian habitation for more than 1,000-years prior to Ponce de Leon's arrival; and evidence that Menendez' colony occupied the site during the sixteenth century.
The park has a prehistoric Indian spring that still flows.

G

Gamble Mansion to Gulfstream Park

Gamble Mansion

Gamble Mansion.
Constructed in 1844 in Ellenton, northeast of Bradenton, of tabby and red brick, the mansion was surrounded by a large sugar plantation that employed about three hundred slaves. The two-story mansion had thick walls, shuttered windows, and wide double verandas on three sides, supported by eighteen columns. Cypress and oak were fashioned into immense beams, windows and doors, wide plank flooring, banisters, and paneling. This was the oldest building on Florida's west coast and the state's greatest Confederate shrine. Steeped in legend and tradition, it now stands in its original glory as a historic reminder of the Civil War days. Flags of the Confederacy, pictures of military heroes, and similar relics are on exhibit in the mansion. Today the Gamble Plantation State Historic site is designated the Judah P. Benjamin Confederate Memorial because of its connection with the dramatic events at the close of the Civil War. Moreover, it's a memorial to the way of life swept away by war.

Gatorland Booklet.
A twenty-two-page, 1950s pictorial booklet, it gave readers an excellent description of alligators.

Gatorama

Near left: An Alligator Attraction.
Gatorama, located on U.S. Highway 27 in Palmdale, was one of Florida's first roadside alligator attractions and reminded one of a tropical jungle. About 3,000 alligators and 250 crocodiles lurked about in this out-of-the-way property a few miles east of Fort Myers and west of Lake Okeechobee. Giant oak trees and palm trees covered the fifteen-acre attraction. Monkeys, bobcats, raccoons, peacocks, ducks, and geese also called Gatorama home. Cecil Clemons opened this attraction in 1957. The star attraction at Gatorama was Goliath, a fourteen-foot, forty-year-old crocodile. Other boarders at Gatorama were Salty, a fourteen-foot saltwater crocodile; Rambo, a thirteen-foot alligator; and Mighty Mike, another thirteen-foot gator. Today this roadside attraction is owned and run by Allen and Patty Register; their family members purchased Gatorama in 1986.

Gatorland

Middle Left: World's Largest Alligator Farm.
Owen Godwin opened Gatorland on U.S. Highway 441 between Orlando and Kissimmee in 1948. This roadside alligator attraction, originally named "Snake Village and Alligator Farm," started with a handful of alligators and a few huts and pens made from cypress poles and thatched roofs. By 1954, the sixteen-acre park was renamed Gatorland and displayed thousands of alligators. The subtropical setting and climate at Gatorland were ideal for raising alligators. Breeding pens, baby alligator nurseries, and rearing ponds were located throughout the park. Bridges and walkways were designed to permit visitors an opportunity to observe and study the fascinating life of the alligator. In 1962, Frank Godwin, son of the founder, designed the signature icon of Gatorland: gaping jaws of a huge concrete and steel alligator head entranceway. Gatorland has grown to be one of the largest and most popular alligator attractions in Florida. Today, Gatorland occupies 110 acres.

Gatorland Brochure.

64

Gerbings Gardens

Below: Beautiful Camellias.
Gerbings Gardens, north of Fernandina Beach at Yulee, has the largest collection of camellias in Florida with over five hundred varieties. Imagine an eight hundred-foot-long camellia windbreak planted entirely with the Sara Frost variety and in full bloom in March. Picture an amphitheatre shaped terrace planted with 25,000 azaleas, or an 1,800-foot walk backed with dogwood-Tung oil-red bud and azalea. Visualize a four-acre sunken garden planted with azaleas, roses, perennials, and thousands of bulbs. All this against a background of ageless Live Oaks draped with Spanish Moss, Southern Magnolias, Pines, Red Cedars, Water Oaks, Bay Hickories, and other trees. The garden is now a residential neighborhood.

Goofy Golf

Goofy Golf.
Goofy Golf, the classic roadside attraction, was built in 1959 in Panama City Beach. The builder of this attraction, Lee Koplin, created other miniature golf courses in other locations including Ft. Walton Beach and Pensacola. The Panama City attraction contained a variety of attention getting obstacles for golf putters: rocket ship, mechanized alligator, windmill, giant monkey, octopus, castle, monster, Buddha, Easter Island statue, and other unusual structures. The colorful Goofy Golf was a popular attraction for visitors from nearby Alabama and Georgia.

The Great Masterpiece,
near the Bok Singing Tower Lake Wales, Fla.

Bartholomew   Peter   Thomas   Phillip
James the Younger   John   Jesus   James the Elder   Matthew   Thaddeus
    Andrew   Judas   Simon

THE GREAT MASTERPIECE
Mosaic Reproduction of Leonardo da Vinci's Great Masterpiece — Lake Wales, Florida

Great Masterpiece

Above: Mosaic of da Vinci's Masterpiece.
The Great Masterpiece, a mosaic of Leonardo da Vinci's *Last Supper*, was located off U.S. Highway 27, north of Lake Wales. In 1952, European artists painfully crafted the mosaic over a two-year period: 300,000 pieces in over 10,000 color hues came together to form the whole. Lush vegetation surrounded the mosaic's housing, which was little more than a large outdoor wall with a pull curtain. Several rows of benches under palm trees provided a place for visitors to gaze. During the 1950s, the Great Masterpiece, coupled with Cypress Gardens and the Bok Singing Tower, were coined "The Big Three" attractions of central Florida. Expanded in the 1960s, the Great Masterpiece attraction closed in the late 1970s.

Gulfarium

Near Left: Performing Dolphins.
Gulfarium, located in Fort Walton Beach in the Florida Panhandle, opened in 1955. The performing dolphins were the stars of the main tank at the Gulfarium. Other animal attractions were sea lion shows and a dolphin interaction program. The mission of the attraction is to provide an entertaining experience while inspiring people of all ages to learn more about the marine world around them.

GULFARIUM

D. C. 257—*Gulfstream Park Race Track, showing Walking Ring, between Miami and Hollywood, Fla.*

Gulfstream Park

Horse Racing Track.

Gulfstream Park on U.S. Highway 1 in Hallandale, north of Miami, opened February 1, 1939, drawing 18,000 fans—the biggest turnout ever to watch horse racing in Florida up to that time. After World War II, South Florida started to grow. Gulfstream Park grew with it. The track went on to overtake Hialeah as Florida's most successful horse race track. In 1952 a clubhouse was built and Grandstand seating expanded. The following year the purse for the *Florida Derby* increased to $100,000—the first stakes event so richly endowed in Florida. When the horses were racing at Gulfstream, fans, many of them visitors to the Sunshine State, flocked to the track to place their bets.

Harness Horse Racing

Above: Harness Horse Racing.

Ben White Raceway at Orlando was the world's largest winter training center for trotters and pacers. About 550 Standard bred horses were quartered there each winter. The raceway, located in city-owned Fairview Park, three miles from downtown Orlando, had three training tracks plus harness racing. Visitors were welcome to attend the morning training sessions and races.

H
Harness Horse Racing to House of Refuge
Hemingway Home

A Great Author's Home.

Key West was once a pirates' base, but was taken over and developed by the U.S. Navy in 1822. Later it became fashionable with the louche and the literary, its most celebrated residents being Tennessee Williams and Ernest Hemingway. Hemingway drank regularly and, doubtless, heavily, at Sloppy Joe's Bar, formerly Captain Tony's Saloon. Hemingway wrote many of his best-known works in the second-story writing studio adjoining his house at 907 Whitehead Street in Key West, including *Death in the Afternoon, For Whom the Bell Tolls, The Green Hills of Africa, The Snows of Kilimanjaro, The Old man and the Sea, To Have and Have Not,* and *The Fifth Column. For Whom the Bell Tolls* and *The Old Man and the Sea*, were both made into memorable movies; the latter in 1958, starring Spencer Tracy as the eponymous Old man. Mary Hemingway, the author's fourth wife, had a small part as a tourist. Hemingway and his wife lived in this old coral-rock house from 1931 until the end of their marriage in 1940. Through this marvelous house and luxuriant grounds roamed sleek six-toed cats, said to be descendants of Hemingway's own.

Hialeah Race Track

More Horse Racing.

Hialeah Race Track opened January 15, 1925 in Hialeah, a small town near the eastern Everglades and Miami. By the 1950s, the racetrack was a place of beauty. Hialeah was known for its vine-covered grandstand, royal palm-lined clubhouse entrance, 550 pink flamingoes, large electrically operated totalizator, and beautifully landscaped areas. Drawing top horses, jockeys, and trainers, Hialeah also attracted the glitterati of society, entertainment, sports, and politics. During

the 1950s, Hialeah was the popular Florida racetrack of the decade. Today the gates of Hialeah Race Track are closed and thoroughbred horse racing at this once beautiful track is no more.

Highlands Hammock

Highlands Hammock State Park, Sebring, Florida

Left: State Park.
The 7,596-acre Highlands Hammock State Park, four miles west of Sebring, has an open-air amphitheater, boardwalk, campground, museum, picnic tables, recreation hall, tram tours, biking and horse trails, and ranger station. The cypress swamp trails boardwalk shows off one of the park's many habitats. The park has been described as three of the outstanding natural parks in the nation. Here lush plant growth and native wild life have been made conveniently accessible.

Homosassa Springs

Left: A Giant Fish Bowl.
Located on U.S. Highway 19 between Crystal River and Weeki Wachee Springs, seventy-five miles north of Tampa, in the 1930s, the springs were used as a local swimming hole. In 1940, outdoor sports writer David Newell opened the springs as Nature's Giant Fish Bowl. Newell built an underwater walkway so visitors could view both fresh and salt-water fish through portholes. This natural attraction was home to many types of wild and tame animals and was a popular tourist attraction throughout the 1950s. Six million gallons of water flow from the springs each hour, forming the Homosassa River that flows into the Gulf of Mexico. Its name was eventually changed to Homosassa Springs after Chicago businessman Bruce Norris purchased the property. Today visitors can see hundreds of alligators basking in the sun or thrashing wildly about in the water in pursuit of a food item. Feeding time is a photographer's delight as the scaly reptiles actually leap for their dinner.

Hollywood Kennel Club

Above: The Greyhounds Are Still Running.
On December 12, 1934, Hollywood Kennel Club opened on U.S. Highway 1 in Hollywood, Florida. In 1940, with the growth of Greyhound Racing, a clubhouse was added to the Grandstand. One of the greatest attractions of greyhound racing is that it could be seen by fans from start to finish. The racing oval is only about a quarter-mile, compared to horse racing's one-mile track. The greyhounds are still running at this busy Highway 1 track; however, it has a new name, Mardi Gras Gaming.

House of Refuge

A Safe Haven.
In the 1870s Florida's coast was so remote the U.S. Government constructed Houses of Refuge where shipwrecked sailors could find safe haven. Gilbert's Bar House of Refuge, on Hutchinson Island near Stuart, is the only remaining structure. The shelter opened December 1, 1876, under the care of keeper Fred Whitehead, who patrolled the beaches for the state during storms and lived in the structure for a salary of $40 a month. The house had four ground-floor rooms: bedroom, dining room, kitchen, and living room. The second floor contained an open dormitory for rescued sailors. The house sheltered shipwreck survivors for nearly seventy years. The house served through the Spanish-American War, World War I, and World War II before being deactivated in 1945. In 1955 the House of Refuge was turned into a popular museum.

I-J
Inaccessible Ft. Jefferson to Jupiter Springs

Inaccessible Fort Jefferson

Inside Ruins of Fort Jefferson Dry Tortugas, Key West, Florida

Fort Jefferson.
The six-sided Fort Jefferson on Garden Key in Dry Tortugas, sixty-eight miles west of Key West, is the largest of the massive brick fortifications built during the nineteenth century for the defense of the American coast. Fort Jefferson became part of the National Park System in 1935. The fort is accessible only by (a 2.5-hour) boat or (a sixty-minute) seaplane from Key West. This is the hardest one to get to, but one of the most interesting historic attractions in Florida. Inside Fort Jefferson, down its labyrinth of gloomy corridors, visitors can envision the tragedy of Dr. Samuel Mudd, sentenced there as punishment for having set the broken leg of John Wilkes Booth, performing heroic work during a yellow fever epidemic among the garrison and prisoners, and pardoned too late to do him any good. Fort Jefferson is now a National Monument.

Indian Museum

Seminole Museum, 1958.
A small Seminole Indian Museum located in Dania, north of Miami and south of Fort Lauderdale, in 1966 the Dania Indian Reservation was renamed the Hollywood Indian Reservation. Today a large museum, village, and casinos are located there.

Jacksonville Beach Boardwalk

Along the Boardwalk.
During the 1950s, residents and tourists of northeast Florida enjoyed amusement attractions, the boardwalk, and water activities at Jacksonville Beach, a coastal city east of Jacksonville.

"Cooling-Off" at Jacksonville Beach along the Boardwalk

B-23—Fun-Packed Jacksonville Beach Fla.

SEMINOLE MUSEUM WALK IN

Japanese Gardens

Japanese Garden at Eagles Nest.
This view shows a Pagoda in the Japanese Garden at Eagles Nest in Belleair, near Clearwater. Pagodas, which first served as lookout on Japanese estates, are now for the most part set up in gardens as ornaments. Eagles Nest, opened in 1936, was later renamed Marine Gardens, and closed permanently in 1962.

John Gorrie State Museum

PAGODA, JAPANESE GARDEN, EAGLES NEST,

CLEARWATER·BELLEAIR, FLA.

John Gorrie Museum.
Located on 6th Street, one block east of U.S. Highway 98 in Apalachicola, the museum proudly highlights the life of Dr. John Gorrie. Concern for his yellow fever patients motivated the young physician to invent a method for cooling their rooms. He became a pioneer in the field of air conditioning and refrigeration, inventing a machine that made ice, and receiving the first U.S. Patent for mechanical refrigeration in 1851. A replica of his ice-making machine is on display at the museum. Gorrie died in 1855, unable to market his invention and witness the far-reaching effects of his discovery.

near Ocala, Fla.

O-3 Juniper Springs near Ocala, Fla.

Juniper Springs

An Ocala, Florida Attraction.
Juniper Springs on State Highway 40, east of Ocala, is the center of the Ocala National Forest. The springs are a popular attraction for swimming, nature trails, and picnicking.

K-L
Kapok Tree Inn to Long Beach Resort

Kapok Tree Inn

An International Tourist Destination.
Opened in Clearwater in 1958, the Inn was known more for its lavish décor than its menu. It was an international tourist destination, complete with souvenir and gift shops. The restaurant's massive dining rooms featured classical columns, imported statues, Victorian fountains, antique paintings, and sparkling chandeliers, all tastefully accented with vines and tropical plants. And, as if that were not enough, the entire restaurant was surrounded by fantastic formal gardens that guests could stroll with a drink before or after dinner. A large Kapok Tree, over 150 years old stood at the entrance as a perpetual invitation to their guests. Unfortunately the restaurant closed in 1991.

Key West Aquarium

DK-11—Municipal Aquarium
Key West, Florida

The First Open-Air Aquarium.
Built by the Works Project Administration (WPA), the Key West Aquarium has been delighting visitors since 1934. That means it predated the opening of U.S. Highway 1 into the city. It was the first visitors' attraction built in the Florida Keys. Here visitors saw live coral, sea turtles, starfish, sharks, moray eels, barracuda, tarpon, parrotfish, grouper, octopuses, sting rays, and little purple Portuguese man o' war with their trailing stingers. The facility was the first open-air aquarium in the United States. Brilliantly colored tropical fishes were on display in tanks, lighted and heated by the sun, through which salt water was pumped.

Killiarn Gardens

Killearn Gardens, Tallahassee, Florida

A Beautifully Landscaped Garden.
Located 5.5 miles north of Tallahassee on U.S. Highway 319 is 307 acres of beautifully landscaped gardens featuring camellias, azaleas, and other flowering trees and shrubs. In 1953 the property was donated to the State of Florida and renamed Alfred B. Maclay Gardens State Park in honor of the gardens' developer.

Kissimmee States Monument

A Show of Unity.
The Monument of States in downtown Kissimmee is an irregular quadrilateral step-pyramid of twenty-one tiers. In 1942, Dr. Charles W. Bressler-Pettis wrote letters to every governor and President Franklin Roosevelt asking them to send him rocks or fossils as a symbol of unity in the early days of World War II. Marble, agate, quartz, petrified wood, sandstone, part of a meteor, and alabaster are just a few of the rocks and fossils sent to the doctor, who was president of the All States Tourist Club. In 1943, the specimens were mortared into the odd-shaped fifty-foot tall pyramid. The stones represent every state, plus twenty-one countries. Tourists were drawn to this oddball, one-of-a-kind architectural curiosity that is now owned by the city.

Lewis Plantation

"The True South."
Visitors could see an old turpentine still and plantation showing the south's oldest industry and the African American life that surrounded it. In this beautiful old-time atmosphere were also modern cottages and a colonial dining room. This attraction represented plantation slave life and was opened from 1936 to 1960 on U.S. Highway 41 south of Brooksville. Pearce Lewis, the white owner of the plantation, was able to attract African-Americans to live at the plantation and play the demeaning roles because they sometimes had no other place to live.

Lightner Museum

Showcasing Victorian Memorabilia.
In 1947, wealthy Chicago publisher Otto C. Lightner purchased the former Alcazar Hotel for $150,000, ending his search for a location to house his extensive collection of Victorian memorabilia, including pottery, stained glass, musical instruments, paintings, crystal bowls, and just about everything else he could collect on his world travels. In 1950 Lightner bequeathed the building and his extravagant collection to the City of St. Augustine. A million dollar restoration project returned the structure to a grand illustrious architectural treasure. Lightner Museum boasts hundreds of collections, numbering more than 20,000 individual items and making it one of the most preeminent museums on Florida's east coast. There are three floors of exhibits catering to all kinds of interests.

Lightner Museum stands in the center of St. Augustine as a reminder of the Gilded Era. The architectural vision of Henry M. Flagler and the many collections of Otto Lightner bring to life a simpler time when there were fewer distractions to prevent people from enjoying the finer things of life. The former hotel was added to the National Register of Historic Places in 1971. In the north courtyard is a statue of Pedro Menendez, erected in 1972. It was a gift from Aviles, Spain, and the garden was dedicated as the Parque de Menendez in 1979. Today a portion of the old Alcazar Hotel houses the St. Augustine City Hall.

S.A.14—The Municipal Lightner Museum of Hobbies, St. Augustine, Fla.

Long Beach Resort

Greetings from Long Beach.
U.S. Highway 98, along the Gulf of Mexico, began to boom after World War II, and one of the first attractions was the Long Beach Resort, eight miles west of Panama City. The beach here was the biggest attraction for tourists, who mainly came from the neighboring states of Alabama and Georgia. Many people called this area the "Redneck Riviera" because most of the area's tourist base came from other parts of the South, whereas the "classier" beaches of Florida's other coastlines generally attracted what was considered to be a more sophisticated, affluent clientele from northern states.

A 1950s advertisement for Long Beach Resort stated that it is an ideal vacation spot. It had cottages, resort motel, hotel, supermarket, restaurant, Florida's largest skating rink, amusement park, and the "World's Most Beautiful Bathing Beach." Over the years the sun-and-fun spots at Panama City Beach, Fort Walton Beach, and Pensacola Beach became known as Florida's Miracle Strip. The beach cities in the Florida Panhandle now attract millions of visitors, many of whom probably come from the northern states.

Greetings from LONG BEACH RESORT PANAMA CITY, FLA.

Maine Monument

Maine Monument to New Smyrna Sugar Mill

Manatee Springs

Swimming and Snorkeling.
Manatee Springs State Park, off U.S. Highway 19 on State Highway 320 near Chiefland, opened in 1955. The park has the first-magnitude Manatee Springs, attracting swimmers, snorkelers, and divers.William Bartram named the spring two hundred years ago. The springhead is one hundred-feet across and forty-five-feet deep. A 1,200-foot spring run discharges into Suwannee River, flowing twenty-three miles into the Gulf of Mexico.

Marineland

Florida's Giant Fish Bowl.
Humans have enjoyed watching fish in aquariums since ancient times, but not until the late 1930s was it possible to stand a few inches from the predatory tiger shark, the vicious barracuda, or the malicious moray eel and watch them together in surroundings like those of their natural habitat. Marineland, the world's first Oceanarium, opened as Marine Studios on U.S. Highway A1A between Daytona Beach and St. Augustine June 23, 1938. Marineland gave visitors an up-close view of life under the sea and an opportunity for filmmakers to use the tanks for underwater movie scenes. The tanks were carefully planned and maintained to approximate conditions of marine life in the open sea; 10,000 fish lived in the scientifically designed Oceanarium, not separately as in aquariums, but together in two huge tanks connected by a flume. The tanks were an eleven-foot circular and eighteen-foot rectangular habitat with two hundred portholes below the water's surface. Through these portholes along the sides

and beneath these giant "fish bowls," the scientists and visitors could observe the drama of undersea life. Added to these huge tanks was a Porpoise Stadium, where "educated" porpoises demonstrated their amazing achievements. Marineland has greatly increased the public's knowledge of marine life. Its walled-in pools, refreshed daily with five million gallons of seawater, represent an approximation of the ocean itself; winter temperature in the tropical tank is a constant 70 degrees F.

Maine Monument.
The U.S. Battleship *Maine* visited Key West many times before its final departure on January 25, 1898. Its goodwill visit to Havana, Cuba ended February 15, 1898 with a mighty explosion. Many of the dead and injured were brought back to Key West. Since some of the dead were buried here, the citizens of Key West dedicated a monument to these victims on December 15, 1898. Because the sinking brought about the Spanish-American War, the ship remained partially submerged in Havana Harbor for twelve years. The *Maine* was later floated and towed to deep water off the Cuban coast, where it was laid to rest. The *Maine* Monument is located in the Key West Cemetery, at Angela and Margaret streets. Due to the rocky geology of the island, many of the stone-encased caskets in this cemetery rest above ground. The Key West Cemetery contains many interesting and sometimes comical headstones. Two of them are, "I Told You I Was Sick" and "At Least I Know Where He's Sleeping Tonight."

Star Performers at Marineland.

Porpoises were the most popular performers with the public, and Porpoise feeding time at Marineland was a major attraction. In addition to learning to accept food from an attendant's hand in the water, the creatures learned to leap high into the air to take the fish from the outstretched hand. Porpoises are natural clowns and love to perform. The mammals seem to walk on water as thrashing tails propel them up to the feeder's hand. Friendly by nature, the porpoises gauge their jumps so as to hurt no one. But visitors standing too close sometimes receive showers of sparkling seawater.

Near Left: Marineland Booklets.

Pictorial booklets describing the Marineland facilities and its many occupants; porpoises, sharks, green turtles, groupers, seahorses, octopus, angelfish, dragon fish, barracuda, sawfish, stingray, eels, amberjack, tarpon, hogfish, cobia, dolphin, mullet, channel bass, red snapper, triggerfish, parrotfish, yellowtail, and many more.

Martello Towers

Below: Fortfying Fort Taylor.

At the beginning of the Civil War, the government fortified Key West with two Martello Towers to protect Fort Zachary Taylor from Confederate attack. Fort Taylor, lying at the entrance to Key West harbor, was begun in 1845, but the Martello Towers were not begun until 1862. The purpose of the towers, East Martello and West Martello, was to fortify Fort Taylor from an attack by land from the rear. The two towers were identical in plan and consisted of an outer wall of casemates that was designed to carry ten-inch Rodman smoothbore cannons. Within the walls was a tower, a square brick affair with gun slits and cannon firing positions in which there were eight-inch Columbiad cannons. Four rifled Parrot guns were to be mounted on top of the towers. The towers were built of brick with arched casemate batteries to the sea and a center tower and galleries, or storerooms, on the landside. In 1866 orders were received to suspend work on the towers. They were never completed or armed because the structures proved obsolete when the new rifled artillery came into use during the Civil War. In 1944 the towers were declared surplus by the government and turned over to Monroe County. The West Martello Tower was in rundown condition for many years. The East Martello Tower was converted into a museum.

McKee Jungle Gardens and Sunken Treasure Museum

A Tropical Wonderland.

Arthur G. McKee and Waldo E. Sexton opened McKee Jungle Gardens in 1932 on U.S. Highway 1, three miles south of Vero Beach. This eighty-acre attraction drew 100,000 visitors a year to see the native and exotic plants, ponds, waterfall, an aviary, a cathedral of three hundred palms planted in rows, deer, parrots, monkeys, and alligators. Located here was the largest variety of water lilies in the United States, deep blue and fairy pink, golden and white, and blood-red beauties that bloomed night and day the whole year round. Also were rare plants, shrubs and trees, robust towering palms, brightly blooming shrubs, a dense palm and oak forest, over-hanging live oak trees filled with orchids and air plants. The park thrived until competition from the major Orlando theme parks caused it to close in 1976. Most of the grounds were turned into condominiums and a golf course. Fortunately eighteen acres were preserved and restored, and a smaller version of the gardens opened as McKee Botanical Gardens in 2001.

Martello Towers. Old Union Fort, Key West, Florida 3

FF-44 An "Old Timer" in McKee Jungle Gardens, Florida

V-4—Florida, the Tropical Wonderland McKee Jungle Gardens Vero Beach

McKee's Sunken Treasure Museum.

In 1952 treasure diver Arthur McKee, Jr. opened McKee's Sunken Treasure Museum on U.S. Highway 1 in Plantation Key, between Tavernier and Islamorada. McKee, an ex-Navy diver, had previously found the remains of the 1733 lost Spanish fleet and filled his museum with artifacts, including cannons, ballast, and silver coins that he found. He found so many bars of silver that it gained him the name of "Silver Bar McKee" and he was often referred to as "the father of modern treasure diving." The museum was a replica of an old Spanish fortress. The name McKee's Museum was later changed to Treasure Village.

DIRECTLY ON U. S. 1 — VERO BEACH, FLORIDA

McKEE JUNGLE GARDENS

Florida's Tropical Paradise

POPULAR TOURIST ATTRACTION SINCE 1932

McKEE JUNGLE GARDENS

ON THE DIXIE HIGHWAY – U. S. Nº 1
THREE MILES SOUTH OF
VERO BEACH, FLORIDA

O-108 Entrance to the Mead Botanical Garden, Orlando-Winter Park, Fla.

Mead Botanical Gardens

Top Left: Garden of Plants.
Lying between Orlando and Winter Park is a fifty-five-acre tract of land that was developed into the Mead Botanical Gardens. This botanical garden opened in 1940 in honor of Dr. Theodore L. Meade, a Central Florida horticulturist who died in 1936. Dr. Meade specialized in tropical and subtropical plants, especially orchids.

Miami Beach Dog Track

M-60 AERIAL VIEW OF MIAMI BEACH, FLORIDA

MIAMI BEACH DOG TRACK IN FOREGROUND   7A-H1243

Breaking from Starting Box at Miami Beach Dog Track, Florida 91

Miami Beach Kennel Club.
Noted sports promoter Tex Richard built the Miami Beach Kennel Club in 1929 just prior to his death. The architectural masterpiece was patterned after a Spanish mission. Lapped by the Atlantic Ocean's blue rippling waves, it was set like a jewel amid gently swaying palms at the entrance to Miami's harbor. The track presented a picture of beauty and charm—a fitting background for the "Sport of Queens." For many years ladies attired in fine dresses and gloves and men in suits and ties relaxed with a cocktail in the glass enclosed Clubhouse or enjoyed the sea air from the Grandstand. Other entertainments enticed patrons elsewhere over the years and the Kennel Club fell on hard times. The dog track, with its private three hundred-foot beach, was torn down as part of assembling the land for the original South Shore redevelopment project and faded into history. The South Point Towers now stands on the site.

78

Miami Seaquarium

Ocean Life Displayed.

Located on Rickenbracker Causeway, Key Biscayne, in Miami, was a water attraction where visitors observed a fabulous collection of ocean life in its natural habitat through rows of large glass windows. There were thrilling shows and marine life exhibits: high-jumping porpoise took fish from a feeder's mouth, Seaquarium workers hand-fed colorful tropical fish, loggerhead turtles, moray eels, and other fish. Today the thirty-eight-acre attraction has been enlarged and has many new borders, including Lolita, the killer whale; TV's Flipper; and Salty the Sea Lion.

Miami Serpentarium

Left: A Snake Park.
In 1948 William Haast opened Miami Serpentarium on U.S. Highway 1, twelve miles south of Miami. It became a very popular attraction where visitors could see snakes and other reptiles of the world exhibited in their natural habitat as well as tour a research laboratory. The Serpentarium featured one of the largest collections of snakes in the world. The laboratory conducted invaluable studies in snake venom research. The attraction, which had a huge cobra statue along the roadside to draw driver's attention, closed in 1984.

The Million Dollar Pier, St. Petersburg, Florida. "The Sunshine City".

Million Dollar Pier

Above: A Popular Social Center.
The Million Dollar Pier, extending a half-mile into Tampa Bay at St. Petersburg, opened to the public in 1926. It was the areas most popular social center where residents and visitors enjoyed entertainment, dances in the ballroom, eating in the restaurant, fishing, picnics, bridge parties, gift shops, and watching small sailboats skimming over the placid waters, as pelicans dove for fish, or begged from winter visitors. The building on the pier was replaced with the present inverted pyramid building in 1972.

DC-280—Iguana, Lizard of South America
Miami Serpentarium, Just Below Kendall, Fla.
12 Miles South of Miami

Taking Life Easy at Monkey Jungle, South of Miami, Florida.

Chimpanzee at Monkey Jungle near Miami, FLa.

Monkey Jungle Near Miami, Fla., Where Humans are Caged and Monkeys Run Wild

Monkey Jungle

"Monkey-ing" Around.
Twenty-two miles south of Miami, just off U. S. Highway 1, was a sight unmatched this side of Singapore. Racing through the jungle branches, hundreds of monkeys ran wild. It was the humans who were caged. Visitors walked in a tunnel of chicken wire extending into the tangle of trees. As the roadside sign said back on the highway: See the Monkey Jungle, YOU are caged, the monkeys RUN WILD. Joseph and Grace DuMond opened Monkey Jungle, a nineteen-acre attraction, in 1935. It has one of America's most complete collections of monkeys and apes, ranging from tiny marmoset to gorillas. Visitors enjoyed the view of the beauty of monkeys running free and experiencing first-hand the primates' lifestyle. They also saw crab-eating macaques swimming for treats in their pond.

MUSA ISLE SEMINOLE INDIAN VILLAGE

ALLIGATOR WRESTLING BY SEMINOLE INDIAN

MUSA ISLE SEMINOLE INDIAN VILLAGE

ENTRANCE
MUSA ISLE INDIAN VILLAGE
Now Serving Our Famous Refreshing
TROPICAL FRUIT PUNCH

MUSA ISLE
Home of The
SEMINOLE INDIANS

Musa Isle Indian Village

Home of the Seminole Indians.

The Musa Isle Indian Village was located along the Miami River at Northwest 25th Avenue and 16th Street in Miami at the site of a Seminole Indian Trading Post that was established around 1900. In 1922 Bert Lasher opened the attraction in 1933 William Osceola and Allan Davis took over the five-acre attraction. Musa Isle became one of Miami's most popular tourist attractions. As visitors entered the grounds they were in a tropical beauty spot of tropical foliage of every kind from the towering royal palms to the lowly cacti. There were daily exhibitions of alligator wrestling, tours through a Seminole Indian Village, displays of Indian handwork, and reptile and bird exhibits. The Musa Isle attraction closed in 1964.

Museum of Speed

Speed on Display.
Bill Tuthill, one of the original organizers of NASCAR, opened the Museum of Speed on U.S. Highway 1 just south of Daytona Beach in 1954. The Museum of Speed was a popular attraction for motorcar enthusiasts in town for the auto beach races and after 1958, races at the Daytona International Speedway. The museum was the home of *Bluebird V,* Sir Malcom Campbell's record-breaking racecar. Powered by a 2500-hp Rolls Royce engine, *Bluebird V* the fastest vehicle ever to run on the beach racecourse at Daytona Beach.

Museum of the Sea & Indian

Native American History.
Located on U.S. Highway 98, east of Destin, the museum opened in 1959 and offered a wide array of exhibits depicting the history of Native Americans from North and South America. It was a typical 1950s low-tech roadside attraction with small cages for animals, dioramas with mounted animals, and Indian artifacts. Marine life and a zoo were also part of the museum. The attraction was destroyed by hurricane in 1995.

Turtle Mound at Sunrise on the Indian River near New Smyrna Beach, Fla.

Native American Mound

Above: Turtle Shell Mound.

In prehistoric times the Timucua Indians inhabited the entire northeast Florida area and were builders of large shell mounds. The fifty-foot high Turtle Mound south of Daytona Beach was known as far back as 1564 and for years it was marked on ship's maps as an aid to navigation. It is the largest Indian mound in the state. Visitors can climb to the top of the mound via a walkway. The mound was built of discarded oyster shells, which may be seen lying all over the mound.

New Smyrna Sugar Mill Ruins

Right: A Historical Exhibit.

In 1830 New York merchants William Depeyster and Henry N. Cruger built a plantation and a Sugar Mill in New Smyrna, south of Daytona Beach, to process the sugar cane of nearby plantations. The Sugar Mill and plantation had a very brief life. On Christmas Day in 1835, a band of about one hundred Seminole Indians attacked and destroyed the Sugar Mill and plantation buildings. The ruins of this old Sugar Mill became a wonderful historical exhibit opened to the public.

84

O
Oldest Drug Store to Ormond Art Museum

Oldest Drug Store

From A Store to A Museum.
T. W. Speissigger and Sons entered the pharmacy business in 1875. Their St. Augustine drugstore opened in 1887, and carried medicine, miletries, and tobacco. The business was later converted into the Old Drug Store Museum.

Oldest House

Oldest House in the Oldest City.
The Gonzalez-Alvarez House, known at the "Oldest House" is the area's oldest surviving Spanish colonial house. For more than three centuries the site at 16 South Francis Street in St. Augustine has been occupied by St. Augustinians. Beginning about 1650, successions of thatched wooden structures were their homes. A coquina stone house was built soon after the English burned St. Augustine in 1702, and originally was a one-story rectangle with two rooms. As times changed during the Spanish, British and American occupations, a wooden second story, an off-street porch, and other features were added. Tomas Gonzalez y Hernandez, an artilleryman at the Castillo de San Marcos, and his family were the next occupants of the house. A Spaniard, Geronimo Alvarez, bought the house in 1790; he and his descendants lived there for about one hundred years. Notable features of the interior include low ceilings, huge fireplaces, crushed coquina floors in the old section, and hand-hewn cedar beams. The Oldest House became part of a museum complex owned and operated by the St. Augustine Historical Society. The society restored the structure to its late eighteenth century glory days. Only the roof was completely replaced. The remainder of the house was restored and renovated. The rooms were furnished with Spanish treasures from the 1600s and 1700s many of which pay tribute to the owners.

Oldest Store Museum

An Old-Time General Store.
From the 1880s forward this St. Augustine building housed the store of C. F. Hamblen, which by 1908 was Florida's third-largest hardware store. Hamlen later moved and during the 1910s the building was used as a warehouse and garage. The building was eventually transformed into the Oldest Store Museum. There were more than 100,000 items of old general store merchandise on display, including guns, toys, old farm equipment, tools, notions, clothing, early automobile relics, high-wheeled bicycles, butter churns, corsets, sunbonnets, and cracker barrel. The old time general store's shelves were stocked high with calico, derby and straw hats, high-topped shoes, food items and patent medicines from the 1890s. Out front was a cigar store Indian, a high-wheeled bicycle, an old roasted-peanut wagon, a steam tractor, and a 1927 Model-T Ford. This was the kind of store of our fathers, grandfathers, and other residents of that time visited to have their teeth pulled, get a haircut, or spectacles fitted. The museum made visitors realize how far we have come since the days of grandpa's red underwear and the Gibson Girl corset. Most of the items in the store were actually found in the attic of the old store's warehouse. It was here that the first pharmaceutical license in the nation was issued.

Oldest Wooden Schoolhouse

A 200-Year-Old Homestead.
Originally a small homestead, America's oldest wooden schoolhouse first appeared on St. Augustine's tax rolls in 1716. The schoolmaster lived upstairs with his family and used the ground floor as a classroom. Boys and girls were taught in the same classroom, making the St. Augustine school the first in the nation to go coed. Located near the City Gate, the Oldest Schoolhouse is a surviving expression of another time. Built over two hundred years ago, while Florida was under the rule of Spain, it was constructed of red cedar and cypress and put together with wooden pegs and handmade nails.

Old Jail

The Oldest Surviving Government Building in St. Johns County.
St. Augustine's Old Jail, completed in 1891 and built with funds provided by railroad magnate Henry M. Flagler, housed prisoners for over sixty years. One of the surviving nineteenth century jails. Here, the early sheriff, Joe Perry, and his wife Lou, lived and worked for $2 a day. The building, which held up to seventy-two prisoners, served the county until 1953. It was later opened to the public as a historical attraction. Visitors to the Old Jail can imagine themselves being processed as an inmate in 1908. The Old Jail is one of the very few surviving nineteenth century incarceration facilities in the state and is the oldest government building in St. Johns County. Visitors learn about justice and punishment when Florida was America's southernmost frontier.

Old Jail, St. Augustine, Florida

Old Sugar Mill

Right: Sugar Mill Gardens.
Patrick Dean, who was granted 995 acres by the Spanish government in 1804, established the first sugar mill at Port Orange, south of Daytona Beach. The plantation changed hands twice before it was burned down in 1836 during the Second Seminole War. It was rebuilt in 1846 by John Marchall, who converted the refining process to steam. These nineteenth century sugar mill are probably the most complete and best-preserved ruins of their kind in America. The old English Sugar Mill ruins have machinery still intact because the mill operated up through the Civil War and almost to the 1900s. Next to

Lost Mission and Olde English Sugar Mill

3 Miles South of Daytona Beach, Florida

the Sugar Mill ruins is the Confederate Oak, a huge live oak tree so named because of the many Confederate soldiers who rested their weary bones under its spreading branches. The property later became the site of an amusement park called Bongoland, and still later a beautiful garden, called Sugar Mill Gardens, with roses, blooming magnolias, wandering ivy, bromeliads, ferns, and several trails. In 1963 the property became a Volusia County public park and ten years later the park was placed on the National Register of Historic Places. In 1988 the property became a horticultural garden called the Sugar Mill Botanical Gardens, where visitors can still see the Sugar Mill ruins, the concrete dinosaurs, the Confederate Oak, a sugar cane grinding mill, and a wide variety of beautiful Florida flora. Visitors have always been able to tour the gardens for free.

Orchid Jungle

Left: Blooming Orchids.
The 19.5-acre Orchid Jungle opened on U.S. Highway 1 in Homestead in 1923. This roadside attraction displayed thousands of blooming orchids hanging from live oak, pigeon plum and gumbo-limbo trees. In 1992 Hurricane Andrew damaged Orchid Jungle and in 1994 the attraction was closed.

Sugar Mill Gardens

PORT ORANGE, FLORIDA
OPEN FREE TO THE PUBLIC
FROM 9:00 A. M. TO 5:00 P. M. DAILY

THE ORIENTAL GARDENS

15 THE ORIENTAL GARDENS — JACKSONVILLE, FLORIDA

FLORIDA'S ORIENTAL GARDENS

RECOMMENDED AAA ATTRACTION

JACKSONVILLE, FLORIDA

Oriental Gardens

A "Triple A" Recommended Attraction.

Formerly an eighteen-acre private estate, Oriental Gardens, located on the banks of the St. Johns River, two miles South of downtown Jacksonville, was an early 1900s attraction of tropical and subtropical flowers, shrubs and trees, and an entrancing Sunken Garden with small lakes and streams, bridges, fountains and numerous Asiatic ornaments. Visitors could enjoy quiet, restful strolls along side mirror-like lagoons under the cool shade of towering Oak, Cypress, Pine and other stately trees. These gardens were the most popular tourist attraction in Jacksonville from 1937 until it closed in 1954. Oriental arches, stone lanterns, a summer house and numerous other ornaments, together with Asiatic plantings, created an atmosphere of Oriental beauty. The citrus groves at the Oriental Gardens were the nearest spot to downtown Jacksonville where visitors could see orange trees in fruit and bloom.

Ormond Memorial Art Museum and Gardens

Ormond War Memorial Gardens, Ormond Beach, Fla. — K-48-D-9

Ormond Memorial Art Museum and Gardens.

A tropical paradise, complete with peaceful ponds, shaded stone walking paths, and tinkling waterfalls is located in Ormond Beach, a small city north of Daytona Beach. The Ormond Memorial Art Museum and Gardens opened in 1946 as a living monument to the creativity of humankind and in honor of World War II veterans who fought to protect the ideal of freedom. The museum housed paintings of Canadian painter Malcolm Fraser and other collections of artwork from resident and international artists. The gardens attracted nature lovers, bird watchers and other visitors. Sago palms, ferns, Chinese fan palms, bamboo, banana trees, and flowering plants lined the paths throughout the gardens.

Parrot Jungle

Palm Beach Kennel Club

Above: A Racing Track.
The Palm Beach Kennel Club opened in 1932 in West Palm Beach at the corner of Belvedere Road and Congress Avenue. The greyhounds were running throughout the 1950s; today, the track is still open with a year-round racing schedule.

Hello from Parrot Jungle.
Austrian born Franz Scherr opened the Parrot Jungle in 1936 on twenty acres of hammock land south of Miami. Here in a natural Florida jungle of huge cypress trees, cocoplum, native rubber trees, and countless other tropical trees, plants, and shrubs native to the Everglades, was located one of the largest collections of Parrot type birds in the world. Hundreds of brilliant macaws were free to fly at will, live and breed as they would in their native land, yet were tame and could be fed by hand. Some were trained to pose for pictures on the visitors shoulder; others to perform tricks at hourly shows. Rare cockatoos, pheasants, peafowl, ducks, and cranes, also found these surroundings a paradise. In addition to the natural jungle a large flamingo lake and hibiscus garden was a sight in itself. The Parrot Jungle was extremely popular, however, the attraction moved to a new nineteen-acre site on Watson Island in 2003 and had a new name, Parrot Jungle Island. This new $47-million park had over 1,100 tropical birds, 2,000 varieties of plants and flowers, trained bird shows, and exotic birds flying in natural habitats.

PARROT JUNGLE, MIAMI, FLORIDA

Entrance to the Parrot Jungle, Red Road, Miami, Fla.

DC-86—Parrot Jungle, Red Road, Miami, Fla.

90

Ormond Tropical Gardens,
Near Daytona Beach, Fla.

Parrots Paradise

Parrots Paradise.
The twelve-acre Ormond Tropical Gardens, one of Florida's outstanding all-year show places, started operating around 1930. It included a zoo with monkeys, birds, lambs, an ox and *Bambi,* the fawn featured in the movie, "The Yearling." The gardens closed after World War II. In 1956, this beautifully landscaped Ormond Beach location operated as Parrots Paradise and continued exhibiting beautiful rare birds in a tropical setting until the 1970s.

Ponce de Leon Springs

Remembering Ponce de Leon.
This structure welcomes visitors to Ponce de Leon Springs, a major tourist attraction on U.S. Highway 17 in DeLeon Springs, just north of DeLand. The statues of Ponce de Leon and the girl are symbolic of the historic background and glamour of the gardens. Ponce de Leon Springs was once a popular winter resort destination and during the 1950s it became a tourist attraction with swimming, boat tours, beautiful landscaped gardens and a water circus that included a water skiing elephant. The springs became a State Park in 1982.

Historic Ponce de Leon Springs
De Leon Springs, Fla.

Potter's Wax Museum

Potter's Wax Museum.
In 1949 George L. Potter opened the Potter's Wax Museum on the first floor of the Plaza Hotel building on King Street in downtown St. Augustine. It was the oldest wax museum in Florida. On display were wax figures of well-known individuals from history, politics, entertainment, science, and other areas. Later the Wax Museum relocated to a new King Street location, a few doors west of the Plaza Hotel building.

BIBLICAL FIGURES DISPLAYED AT POTTER'S WAX MUSEUM
ST. AUGUSTINE, FLORIDA

Far Left: Museum Brochure.
In the tradition of Madam Tussaud's internationally famous Wax Museum, George L. Potter brought to life great figures of ancient and modern history, religious leaders, poets, musicians, artists, writers, explorers, philosophers, kings, queens, presidents, premiers, generals, entertainers, and sport figures. Visitors could see everyone from Babe Ruth to George Washington, George Bernard Shaw to Winston Churchill.

92

Prince of Peace Memorial

Seeing How and Where Christ Lived.
The Prince of Peace Memorial, located beside the entrance to Silver Springs, housed thirteen handsomely designed, three-dimensional scenes depicting the Life of Christ. These works of art represented a lifetime of work and research. Beyond their obviously inspirational qualities, the scenes were interesting for the faithful and accurate re-creating of the actual scenes where Christ lived and conducted His work, the kinds of clothing, agricultural tools, plants and shrubbery in His world. Ten miniature chapels housed the scenes.

Quaint Wigwam Village

Orlando's Largest Motel.
Wigwam Village, advertised as Orlando's largest motel, was located on the Orange Blossom Trail (U.S. Highway 441). This unusual motel had thirty guest wigwams and a main wigwam, fifty feet tall with a forty-foot base diameter. The guest wigwams were about thirty feet tall and had a twenty-foot base diameter. The wigwams were styled after Plains Indians' homes and arranged in a horseshoe shape. Though not unique, Wigwam Village was a popular Orlando attraction. Guests were served citrus fruit and juices from trees in their own Wigwam Grove that bordered the village. Their gift shop sold genuine Indian-made jewelry and handiwork. Wigwam Village, part of a small chain of similar motels based in Kentucky, set up its tepee in Orlando in 1948 and replaced with a Days Inn Motel in 1973.

Rainbow Springs

A Beauty Spot.
Rainbow Springs was an intriguing beauty spot in natural surroundings located on U.S. Highway 41, three miles north of Dunnellon. Underwater boats, specially designed, show colorful aquatic plants, marine life, and geological formations. It opened in 1937 on a four hundred-acre tract surrounding the spring. During a jungle boat tour on the Rainbow River, an overflow from the springs, visitors could see the underwater world as schools of freshwater fish swam past the portholes. Magnolias, redbud, dogwood, and azaleas grew around the giant springs, which gushed 659 million gallons of water daily. In 1971 a monorail was added and a year later the springs was designated as a National Natural Landmark. The beautiful clear-water attraction operated until 1974 as a pre-Disney wonder. Later six hundred acres, including the area once occupied by Rainbow Springs, was acquired by the state to form the Rainbow Springs State Park.

R
Rainbow Springs to Ross Allen

Rainbow Springs,
As Seen from Terrace of Rustic Rainbow Lodge
Near Dunnellon, Fla.

Rainbow Tropical Gardens

Near Left: Walking through Loveliness.
In 1940, architect C. O. Miller opened Rainbow Tropical Gardens on U.S. Highway 1 south of West Palm Beach. The attraction was a mile of winding walks through fascinating loveliness, unsurpassed examples of bougainvillea, rare tropical plants and trees; also animal life and a half-mile boat trip. The attraction was floodlit at night. Rainbow Tropical Gardens closed in 1959.

T. C. 7. Flamingos
Will Eat from Your Hand
At Miami's Rare Bird Farm
Miami, Fla.

DC.284—Huge Ostriches at Miami's
Rare Bird Farm

DC.154 White Cockatoos
At Miami's Colorful Rare Bird Farm
© CURT TEICH & CO., INC.

Rare Bird Farm

Home of Ostriches and Flamingos.
In 1938 A. V. Freeman and G. F. Yessler opened the Rare Bird Farm on U.S. Highway 1 in Kendall, ten miles south of Miami. This seven-acre attraction had over 1,500-feathered creatures in a setting of landscaped gardens, pools, and fruit groves. Flamingoes would eat from your hand! Parrots would pose on your shoulder for the camera. Ostriches seven feet tall! Monkeys had their private island. The Red Flamingo, one of the most ornamental birds, is a native of tropical South America. It was successfully bred and raised in protected flocks at the Rare Bird Farm. This popular attraction closed in 1967.

P-3 RUSTIC WATER-WHEEL AND SUSPENSION BRIDGE, RAVINE GARDENS, PALATKA, FLA.

4A-H2029

Ravine Gardens

Left: Florida's Only Natural Ravine.
Three quarters of a million dollars blended into the hillsides of the eighty-five acres of Florida's only natural ravine, ranging in depth from seventy to 120 feet. Ravine Gardens, located in Palatka, had the largest single collection of azaleas in the world, 95,000 including sixty-four of the known seventy-two varieties, all that will live in Florida's outdoor climate. The ravine had 11,000 palm trees and over 250,000 million ornamental plants. The plantings were considered at the time to be the largest collection of flowers of these types in the world. The visitor is greeted at the entrance by a sixty-four-foot obelisk. The monument is dedicated to President Franklin Roosevelt and flanked by the Court of States monuments. The partnership between Mother Nature and three hundred workmen created one of Florida's hidden treasures.

Rawling's Home

Bottom Right: An Author's Home.
The home of Marjorie Kinnan Rawlings, located off County Road 325 in Cross Creek just south of Gainesville, is a notable example of the Cracker style of architecture, derived from a variety of influences to suit the climate and available technology of the rural South. Rawlings was the author of many major literary works, including *The Yearling*, which received the 1939 Pulitzer Prize for fiction, and the books *Golden Apples, South Moon Under, Cross Creek, The Secret River, When The Whippoorwill*, and *Jacob's Ladder*. Rawlings divided her time between a home in St. Augustine and this home in Cross Creek. The Marjorie Kinnan Rawlings House was designated a National Historic Landmark in 1970.

P-2 MINIATURE FLORIDA PENINSULA, RAVINE GARDENS, PALATKA, FLA.

4A-H2030

Ringling Art Museum

An Extensive Art Collection.

John Ringling created the John and Mable Ringling Art Museum, located at 5401 Bayshore Road in Sarasota, in 1927-1930 for the people of Florida. After making millions through his far-flung business enterprises, Ringling built an art collection of over six hundred paintings, numerous statues, and decorative arts, including approximately twenty-seven tapestries. Ringling and his wife, Mable, assembled their amazing collection between 1924 and 1931. The Art Museum opened for public viewing in 1930 and has become one of Sarasota's most popular attractions.

Ringling Museum of the American Circus

Documenting the History of the Circus.

In 1948 the Ringling Museum of the American Circus opened in Sarasota. It was the first museum of its kind to document the rich history of the circus. The museum contained rare handbills and art prints, circus paper, performing props, posters, wardrobe, as well as all types of circus equipment, including carved parade wagons. Sarasota became known as "Florida's circus city" because the Winter Quarters of the Ringling Bros. and Barnum & Bailey Circus was located here. The Ringling Museum was an additional circus attraction that brought visitors to the city.

Ripley's Believe It Or Not Museum

Believing It...Or Not.

Ripley's Believe It Or Not! of St. Augustine is the original Believe It Or Not! The St. Augustine's Ripley's featured more than 750 exhibits to fascinate, delight, and entertain people of all ages. There was a gigantic Ferris wheel, the world's largest moving erector model containing 19, 507 pieces standing 21.3 feet tall and Beauregard, a six-legged cow that lived fourteen years with two extra legs growing from its back. Robert Ripley's life was an unbelievable adventure. For more than forty years, he explored the uncanny and witnessed the amazing. During his career, he visited 198 countries collecting oddities that would later create the fabulous world of Ripley's Believe It Or Not!

Milking Rattlesnake,
Ross Allen's Reptile Institute,
Silver Springs, Fla.

PHOTO BY SAM ANDRE "PIC MAGAZINE"

6B-H2593

Ross Allen's Reptile Institute

A Reptilian Collection.
Ross Allen's Florida Reptile Institute was one of Florida's most unusual attractions. It housed one of the finest collections of live poisonous snakes, reptiles and wild animals in the country. Visitor were given a tour of the Institute which included demonstration-lectures in which the lecturer entered various pens and cages with animals, handled them, discussed their habits, habitats, and other characteristics. A highlight of this tour was the demonstration-lecture staged in the poisonous snake pen. Rattlesnakes were "milked" for venom. Ross Allen's collection of Florida reptiles numbered some 2,000 snakes, alligators, crocodiles, and turtles. Allen, a kind of Frank Buck of the Florida woods and Everglades, captured many of his specimen. During World War II, Ross Allen's Reptile Institute supplied ninety percent of the venoms used by the Army and Navy doctors, most of it for producing antivenin for treatment of snake bit. The reptile institute was one of Ripley's "Believe It Or Nots."

Alligators at Ross Allen's Reptile Institute.
Big George, 14'7" of alligator, charges his keeper, Ross Allen at his Reptile Institute at Silver Springs. Mrs. Allen, a capable photographer, took the photo for this postcard. Allen deliberately invaded the alligator's home territory to study

its defense reaction. This postcard view is untouched and unfaked. Big George is not kidding! Years of experience taught Allen exactly how close he could get to a charging alligator. Visitors to the Reptile Institute never got this close to charging gators, however, they could see several large alligators and watch an alligator wrestling show.

98

Ross Allen's Seminole Village

A Seminole Settlement.
Ross Allen's Seminole Village, located at Silver Springs, was an authentic village built in 1935 by Seminole Indians, who then occupied it for many years. During the 1950s the Seminoles lived at the village only a few months each year. Visitors could browse in an unusual gift shop of authentic Seminole handiwork.

Silver Springs. Seminole Settlement. Florida

238

INSTITUTE, SILVER SPRINGS

S

Sanford Zoo to Sunshine Springs

Sanford Zoo

Above: Monkey Island.

In 1923 the Sanford Zoo started with a collection of donated animals held by the Sanford Fire Department. In 1941, the Municipal Zoo was relocated to new facilities in downtown Sanford along the shore of Lake Monroe. The zoo remained here until 1975 when the Central Florida Zoological Park opened a short distance to the west on U.S. Highway 17-92. Shown is a 1957 view of Monkey Island at the Sanford Zoo.

Sanlando Springs

Right: A Recreation Attraction.

Sanlando Springs Tropical Park was a popular recreation attraction on U.S. Highway 17 in Altamonte Springs, just north of Orlando. The beautiful park, landscaped with tropical plantings, had two clear, sulphur springs with an even temperature of seventy-two degrees the year round. Special aquatic programs featuring prominent personalities were also performed. One popular show involved professional log rollers who dazzled crowds with a variety of acts twice a day. Walkways through picturesque gardens surrounded the springs. Residents and tourists in the Central Florida area enjoyed cooling off in this beautiful water attraction.

SARASOTA JUNGLE GARDENS

SARASOTA·FLORIDA

Sarasota Jungle Gardens

Tropical Birds in Beautiful Scenery.

In the early 1930s, newspaperman David B. Lindsay, purchased ten acres of swamp and, with nurseryman Pearson Conrad, brought in thousands of plants from all over the world to create the Sarasota Jungle Gardens. Admission fees were instituted in 1936 and it began to be promoted as a tourist destination. Areas of the park included Gardens of Christ, Tiki Garden, and a number of open lagoons. The notable plants at this attraction included Florida's largest Norfolk Island pine, a rare Australian nut tree, a Peruvian apple cactus, strangler figs, royal palms, and a bunya–bunya tree. Sarasota Jungle Gardens name accurately describes itself. The attraction featured tropical birds, reptiles and mammals, some of which starred in daily educational shows. The Sarasota Jungle Gardens, located at 3701 Bayshore Road in Sarasota, was a ten-acre extravaganza of lush tropical growth, waterfowl, and beautiful sculpture. The Gardens have become recognized as one of the truly great ornamental tropical plant exhibits of the world.

SARASOTA JUNGLE GARDENS

TROPICAL BIRDS IN FLORIDA'S MOST BEAUTIFUL SCENERY

UNCAGED FLAMINGOS, cranes, swans, peacocks, wild ducks and macaws mingle with visitors amid 4,000 varieties of exotic plants. A paradise for garden enthusiasts, bird lovers, camera fans and children. 1½ Mi. N. of downtown Sarasota on U.S. 41.

See Listing Page 52

Variety in Sarasota Jungle Gardens S25

SarasotaKennel Club

A Dog Racing Track.
Located at 5400 Bradenton Road in Sarasota, the club has been open since 1929. The Collins family has been operating the track since 1944. Jerry Collins lived a full and adventurous life. In addition to being a successful dog track owner, he spent time as a state legislature, a motorcycle stunt rider, and a policeman.

Sarasota Reptile Farm and Zoo

A Place of Reptiles.
In the mid-1930s, one of Sarasota's most colorful characters, Texas Jim Mitchell, opened the Sarasota Reptile Farm and Zoo on Fruitville Road, two miles east of downtown Sarasota. The attraction featured many animals including alligators, snakes, monkeys, and birds. Shown is Mitchell teasing a gator while O. F. Vischer, a newspaperman from Toledo, Ohio, looks on with interest. After approximately thirty years of operation it closed in 1965.

Sea Zoo

The Sea Cow-one of the many unusual attractions at Sea Zoo - So. Daytona, Fla.

Sea Zoo.
The Sea Zoo, located two miles south of Daytona Beach in South Daytona, was originally the Marine Life Laboratory founded in 1949 by M.S. Bangs and Stephen Loughman. In 1951, with the addition of Dr. Perry Sperber, a partnership was formed creating Sea Zoo. The nine-acre roadside attraction on Ridgewood Avenue (U.S. Highway 1) became a popular stop for tourists. It expanded during the 1950s to include alligator wrestling, a snake pit, porpoise show and tropical bird display.

FAMOUS SEA-ZOO FLORIDA'S GREATEST OCEANIC SHOW!

SEA ZOO

WORLD'S ONLY CONTINUOUS SEA CIRCUS
ON U.S. HIGHWAY NO. 1

Two Miles South of Daytona Beach Florida, At The Sign Of The Jumping Porpoise.

Continuous Entertainment At
The Sea Zoo

Featuring . . .
- The World's only educated Sea Cows
- Personality Porpoises
- Professional Performing Sea Lions
- Wrestling Gators

Supported by a cast of . . . Playful Otters . . . Giant Ancient Sea Turtles . . . Colorfully Plumed Marine Birds . . . Venemous Reptiles . . . All-Stars of TV . . . Radio . . . Press and LIFE. Conducted by the Southlands Finest Trainer, Guides . . . Captains Bill Walsh and Jack Pitts.

Don't Leave Florida Until You Have Seen The Best—The World's Only SEA CIRCUS

Seminole Indian Villages

M19 A SEMINOLE INDIAN VILLAGE IN THE FLORIDA EVERGLADES

SCENE ALONG THE TAMIAMI TRAIL NEAR MIAMI   PHOTO BY CHARLES C. EBBETS

Along Tamiami Trail in the Florida Everglades

Seeing How Indians Lived.

After the Tamiami Trail (U.S. Highway 41) was built, many of the Seminole Indians living in the Everglades moved to, and built their villages and camps along this modern highway. In roadside stands and concessions, they displayed their handicraft products; dolls, handbags, beautifully designed jackets, capes, and dresses were all for sale to tourists. Almost every Seminole Indian camp along the Tamiami Trail was a sightseeing concession where, for an admission fee, the tourist could enter and inspect the village. As an added attraction, a high-walled pen of alligators was shown nearby. Permission was usually granted to tourists for taking snapshots, but generally the Indians remained aloof from the visitors. Reserved and quiet, they spoke only when directly addressed. Only after many, many visits could a white man expect to win their confidence and friendship. A few of the Seminole Indian families owned land. For the most part, Seminoles along the Tamiami Trail were squatters, literally and legally. They were subject to eviction anytime at the whim of the landowner, but the nature of the property was such that few owners ever evoked such rights. Many other Seminoles lived in isolated camps in the Everglades, far removed from the Trail or other highways. These Indians had less contact with the outside but they did visit with other clan members living on reservations and along the Tamiami Trail.

Senator, The

Oldest Cypress Tree.

The Big Cypress Tree, located in Big Tree Park on U.S. Highway 17—midway between Orlando and Sanford—is the oldest and largest Cypress tree in the world, and largest tree east of the Rockies. The height before it was damaged in a 1926 hurricane was 165 feet. The tree is now 127 feet tall, has a 17.5-foot diameter, a circumference of forty-seven feet, and is over 3,500 years old. The Forest Department used an instrument called "Increment Borer" to accurately determine the age of the Big Cypress Tree. The Big Cypress Tree is often called "The Old Senator" or "The Senator." Seminole Indians and early traders used the Big Cypress Tree as a landmark.

The "Big Tree" Oldest Cypress in The U.S. 3500 Yrs old - 127 Ft High 47 Ft in Circumference 17.5 Ft in Diameter - On U.S. 17 and 92 Between Sanford And Orlando Fla.

Silver Springs

Greetings from Silver Springs.
Located seven miles east of Ocala, Silver Springs was one of the oldest, most beautiful, and most popular tourist attractions in the state. Visitors from all over the globe have come to marvel at and enjoy the springs. The springs have a flow of 550 million gallons of water each day and are the source of the Silver River, an important tributary of the Ocklawaha River (which feeds the St. Johns River, the major river in Florida.) The flora and fauna along the banks of Silver Springs and the Silver River provide a spectacle—weird, wondrous, and magical—to be remembered as one of the great experiences in a lifetime.

Map of Silver Springs.

Below: Glass-Bottom Boats at Silver Springs.
Known also as Florida's underwater fairyland, Silver Springs is really a subterranean river springing from the earth through a vast cavern 65 feet wide, twelve feet high at its mouth, and lying fifty feet below the surface of the circular basin that forms the head of the springs and the source of Silver River. Silver Springs flagship attraction was (and still is) its glass-bottom boats. A fellow by the name of Hullam Jones created the glass-bottom boat at Silver Springs in 1878. By installing a glass-viewing box on the flat bottom of a dugout canoe, Jones created a window to an underwater world teeming with life.

Jungle Cruise on Tropical Silver River at Florida's Silver Springs

Above: Jungle Cruise on the Silver River.
Another way to travel the waterways at Silver Springs was to take a three-hour Jungle Cruise trip on the Silver River. During the 1950s the cruise went down the seven-mile river to a stopping place at the intersection of the Silver and Ocklawaha rivers. During the cruise the boat Captain would point out the flora and fauna on the river and then stop to feed the wild monkeys. In later years the Jungle Cruise was a much shorter trip over a manmade canal and only a short part of the Silver River.

SS32   YEAR ROUND BATHING AT FLORIDA'S FAMED SILVER SPRINGS

Under Water "Clear as Air" at Silver Springs, Florida

Left: Year Round Bathing at Silver Springs.
The sender of this postcard wrote: "Have just taken the glass-bottom boat trip and it was wonderful. Wish you could have seen all the fish."

Above: Silver Springs Brochures.

Left: Underwater Acting at Silver Springs.
Silver Springs became a favorite location for filmmakers around the 1950s. Some of the well-known movies that were shot at Silver Springs included the six original *Tarzan* movies, starring Johnny Weissmuller; *The Yearling* starring Gregory Peck and Jane Wyman; *Distant Drums* (1951); *Jupiter's Darling* (1955); *Creature of the Black Lagoon* (1953); *Revenge of the Creature* (1955) and *The Creature Walks Among Us* (1956). In addition, more than one hundred episodes of the 1950s television series "Sea Hunt," starring Lloyd Bridges, was shot there. Silver Springs has established a reputation as a key underwater filming location for feature films, documentaries and television commercials.

K131—ALLIGATOR FARM, TROPICAL PARK, DAYTONA BEACH, FLORIDA

R. H. LESESNE PHOTO

South Daytona Alligator Farm

A Jungle Beauty Spot.
This native jungle beauty spot on U.S. Highway 1 in South Daytona, south of
Daytona Beach, was home to a large collection of alligators, crocodiles, ostriches,
monkeys, and birds. It was at one time called the Daytona Beach Alligator Farm.

Spanish Village

A Spanish Settlement.
An eighteenth century Spanish Village replica was built at Pensacola Beach
in 1959 to commemorate the 400th anniversary of Pensacola's founding.
The buildings were furnished with early 1700s furniture and accessories, and
occupied by Spanish re-enactors in period costumes. Tourists were attracted to
this historical village. The village closed in 1968.

108

St. Augustine Alligator Farm

Seeing the Gators.

In the early 1890s Everett C. Whitney developed a small souvenir shop called the Burning Spring Museum on South Beach (later St. Augustine Beach). In 1893 he, along with George Reddington and Felix Fire, opened the South Beach Alligator Farm next to the museum. Whitney ended his association with the Alligator Farm in 1903. (It was later renamed the St. Augustine Alligator Farm.) Reddington became the sole owner in the early 1930s, though Fire continued to work there until his retirement. By 1910 the Alligator Farm had become an established Florida attraction. A 1916 St. Augustine guide publication said that it contained thousands of reptiles.

In 1937 Reddington sold the Farm to W. I. Drysdale and F. Charles Usina. Hard-working and aggressive businessmen, Drysdale and Usina promoted the facility locally and nationally, capitalizing on the public's fascination with alligators. In 1937 they constructed a new "Mission Style" main building containing offices, a gift shop, a taxidermy shop, and the entrance to the Farm. The attraction drew passengers from the Clyde Steamship Line in Jacksonville and soldiers from a nearby Army base in Starke. These visitors came from all parts of the nation and they consequently spread far and wide word about the museum with all the alligators. During the 1950s, the St. Augustine Alligator Farm was one of the major animal attractions in Florida—and it's still popular today.

St. Augustine Alligator Farm Brochure.

Stephen Foster Memorial

Honoring A Great Composer.

High up in North Florida and way down on the Suwannee River at White Springs is Florida's famed Stephen Foster Memorial—the state's most visited non-commercial attraction. Developed as Florida's tribute to the nation's great composer, whose masterpiece, "Old Folks At Home" (or "Suwannee River") is the state song. The beautifully wooded, landscaped 243-acre park opened in 1950 and offered interesting things to see and do for the entire family. Stephen Collins Foster died in Belleview Hospital, New York City, on January 13, 1864, but the memory of what he gave in music to Florida and the Nation shall live forever. The Memorial, located on the banks of the quiet flowing Suwannee, lends a peaceful charm, where beauty of the river and its wooded banks blend with the wistful and enchanting melodies of Stephen Foster. Admission was free.

North View of Museum, Stephen Foster Memorial on the Suwannee River — Florida   W-3

Stephen Foster Memorial

A NATIONAL SHRINE
"Way down upon the Suwannee River"

WHITE SPRINGS, FLORIDA

The beauty of the river and its wooded banks blend with Foster's music to make this spot a "must" to Americans and world travellers.

Sponsored by

THE STATE OF FLORIDA

DF.80—Enchanting Storyland, Florida

Storyland

A Land of Make Believe.

Storyland was a fantasyland of make believe, located on U.S. Highway 1, in Pompano Beach. This attraction, opened on November 25, 1955, was designed as an amusement park for children. It was long before Disney came to Florida, a land of multi-colored plaster buildings designed to fulfill kid's fantasies as it emptied their parent's wallets. Visitors crossed a wooden "drawbridge" to what looked from the road like a castle with minarets. This attraction was destroyed by Hurricane Cleo in 1964. Nothing remains of Storyland except a few postcards, photographs, and memories.

S-154 "FOUNTAIN OF YOUTH"
ST. PETERSBURG, FLA., "THE SUNSHINE CITY"

St. Petersburg's Fountain of Youth

A Spring of Health Benefits.

St. Petersburg's Fountain of Youth began in 1889 when mining industrialist Edwin H. Tomlinson dug the well when he built a long pier at the foot of Third Avenue S. out into the bay. Dr. Jesse F. Conrad bought the property in 1909, created an arched entryway to the pier out of willow branches, and turned it into a tourist attraction, which evoked Spanish explorer Ponce de Leon in marketing the well's sulphur water for its purported health benefits. Tourists and residents visited the fountain until the early 1970s, when it closed. The sender of this card wrote, "Dear Friend—well Frank if you could drink water from this fountain of youth for two weeks you would be full of PEP and feel and look as young as any shown at the fountain. Looking forward to seeing you soon."

89—Beach and Pool at Sulphur Springs, Near Tampa, Florida

Sulphur Springs

A Popular Recreation Area.

Located on the Hillsborough River, north of downtown Tampa, was a popular community and recreational area throughout the early 1900s. In 1900, Dr. J. H. Mills opened the Sulphur Springs recreational area, which included a swimming pool, a dance pavilion, a Ferris wheel, a toboggan water slide, a high diving platform, and an arcade. The Sulphur Springs recreational area eventually became part of Tampa and the popular facility was Tampa's version of Coney Island.

St. Petersburg's SUNKEN GARDENS

305 18TH AVENUE NORTH
ST. PETERSBURG, FLORIDA

5-114—Entrance to Beautiful Sunken Gardens, St. Petersburg, Fla., "The Sunshine City"

Sunken Gardens

A Retreat from Urban Life.

George Turner opened Sunken Gardens in 1935 not far from downtown St. Petersburg. A thick wall of tropical vegetation sealed off the gardens from the surrounding urban flurry, as visitors found an entirely different world that lied, at its lowest point, a full fifteen feet below street level. The gardens' winding paths, stream-spanning bridge, quiet lagoons, and cascading waterfalls lent a strong sense of the tropics. Thousands of tropical plants and trees grew among a canopy of magnificent live oak trees. One also encountered wildlife in a walk-through aviary of exotic birds and in the enclosures alongside the garden trails. Visitors saw pink flamingoes, spoonbills, rainbow-colored macaws, and alligators. There were more than 5,000 varieties of plants and flowers in Sunken Gardens. One of Florida's most popular attractions during the 1950s, it was later owned by the city of St. Petersburg.

Sunshine Park Race Track

Horse Racing.
Tampa Downs was centrally located in the Tampa Bay area in Oldsmar. The horse-racing track had its inaugural meting in 1926. During World War II the U.S. Army built barracks and turned the track into a jungle warfare training center. In 1947 the track opened as Sunshine Park with a new tote board, electric starting gate, and photo finish camera. Sportswriter Grantland Rice called the track the "Santa Anita of the South." In 1953 a new $300,000 Clubhouse was built. In 1966 the track was renamed Florida Downs and Turf Club. In 1980 the track was renamed Tampa Bay Downs.

Sunshine Springs & Gardens

Sunshine Sally and Pretty Aquabelles.
In 1955, on Proctor Road just east of Sarasota was the attraction known as Sunshine Springs and Gardens. Twenty acres of landscaped tropical gardens were viewed from swan boats traveling along a series of canals. On a four hundred-acre artificial lake were water ski shows featuring female "aquabelles" and a trained elephant called "Sunshine Sally." Trained by 37-year-old Baptiste Schreiber, formerly of the Ringling Circus, the 1,200-pound Sally glided across the water on specially designed pontoons. Dixie Graves (now Grubbs), in a revealing Ocelot-print swimsuit would often ride atop the elephant. Dixie, who was featured in a 1956 *Life* magazine photo spread highlighting Florida tourism said Sally wasn't really nuts about performing and would often rock back and forth on her skies. The opening was impressive. Featured guests included Ringling Circus vice president, Henry Ringling North, Academy award winning writer Budd Schulberg ("On the Waterfront"), nationally known artist Ben Stahl, and local congressman James Haley. The new attraction was a new star in the crown of Sarasota and Florida. But, even a water-skiing elephant couldn't keep the attraction open. Sunshine Springs and Gardens closed in 1959. Today, a public park occupies part of the land where Sally, the Aquabelles, and Aquaboys performed.

Horse Racing at Sunshine Park, Oldsmar

T

Tampa Jai-Alai Fronton to Tropical Park

Tampa Jai-Alai Fronton

Below: A Popular 1950s Attraction.
The Tampa Jai-Alai Fronton, located on Dale Mabry Highway in Tampa, opened in 1953. The fronton had a seating capacity of 3,882 and parking for up to 3,500 cars. The Tampa fronton closed on July 4, 1998. The structure was destroyed and the location became a parking lot.

Theater of the Sea

Right: Jumping Dolphins.
Located on U.S. Highway 1 on Windley Key, north of Islamorada in the Florida Keys, it opened in 1946 as the second oldest marine mammal facility in the world. Its natural saltwater lagoon was originally a 1907 railroad quarry that supplied rock for Henry Flagler's famous railroad, which opened the Keys to the rest of the country in the early 1900s. When Theater of the Sea opened, the lagoon became the home to bottlenose dolphins, California sea lions, sea turtle, tropical and game fish, sharks, stingrays, and other forms of marine life. The seventeen tropically landscaped acres also included exotic birds and crocodilians.

114

"BUTTONS" Leaves the Water
THEATER OF THE SEA - 73 Miles South of Miami

"JEANNIE" taking fish from guide's mouth.
THEATER OF THE SEA - 73 MILES SOUTH OF MIAMI

Tomokie Fountain

Chief Tomokie.

The statue of Chief Tomokie, located beside the intersection of the Tomoka and Halifax Rivers, was fashioned by artist Fred Dana Marsh in 1957 with clay dredged from the Tomoka River. The statue, which stands above a reflecting pool of water, is forty-five feet tall. A story about the statue was created for tourists. The topless figure at the center of the edifice is the Indian maiden Oleeta, depicted in the act of skewering Tomokie (the figure on top) with an arrow for the sacrilege of drinking the Water of Life from the Sacred Cup (that is the object in Tomokie's hand shaped like a champagne glass). The robust, orange Amazon who slew him would in turn, be killed with a poisoned arrow as she reclaimed the Sacred Cup. In 2002 two tourists vandalized the statue and ran off with Oleeta's head. The statue is located in Tomoka State Park.

Tropical Hobbyland

Right: Scenes of Inidan Life.

The Seminole Indian Village at Tropical Hobbyland, located at Northwest 27th Avenue and 15th Street in Miami, opened in 1938. These thatched huts, with the exception of being fireproofed, were exact replicas of a typical Seminole village in the Everglades. The thatched roof shed tropical showers, and the open construction was very practical for a tropical climate. Tropical Hobbyland remained a popular Seminole Indian attraction until it closed in 1966.

Seminole Family Group.

Here is the immediate family of Sam Willis, Chief of the Seminole Indians, at Tropical Hobbyland Indian Village. Standing by the totem pole is his son, Jackie, one of the daring young braves who gave exhibitions of alligator wrestling there.

Seminole Handicraft at Tropical Hobbyland.

Seminole women were noted for their intricate needlework. Here, observed by the next generation, Mama Willie demonstrates use of her hand-operated sewing machine. She is the wife of Chief Sam Willie of the Tropical Hobbyland Indian Village.

Below: Seminole Children at Tropical Hobbyland.

Shown are a curious mixture of the old and new Seminole Indian youngsters at Tropical Hobbyland. While being trained in the ancient arts and skills of their forefathers, these kids also got a formal education in the nearby public schools.

Seminole Indian Huts, Tropical Hobbyland, Miami, Florida

Seminole Family Group, Tropical Hobbyland, Miami, Fla.

M.166—Seminole Children at Tropical Hobbyland

Tropical Park

STAIRWAY TO GRANDSTAND, TROPICAL PARK

Horse Racing to Equestrian Center.

Bill Dwyer and Frank Bruen opened Tropical Park December 26, 1931. This thoroughbred horse-racing track was located just off Bird Road in Coral Gables, south of Miami. In the mid-1930s America's most notorious mobsters, Al Capone and his henchmen, started running Tropical Park and gave the race track a tawdry reputation and added nothing to Miami's glamour. Eventually the mobsters were forced to sell their ownership in Tropical Park to honest men. World War II caused the track to close. Horse racing continued at Tropical Park from 1949 until it closed in 1972. Today, Tropical Park is an Equestrian Center where equestrian shows are held.

U-V
Unconventional Spook Hill to Volusia County Kennel Club

Unconventional Spook Hill

Is It Really Spooky?

Spook Hill was a gravity-defying hill in Lake Wales, near Orlando, the Bok Singing Tower, and Cypress Gardens, where you can park your car at the bottom and it will roll uphill. It is such a popular place for curiosity seekers that the city put up direction signs showing how to get to the hill. A sign also explains how to experience Spook Hill: Stop your car on the white line painted on the street, place in neutral, and watch as the car rolls up the hill. Of course, the lay of the terrain around Spook Hill is responsible for the illusion, but people have enjoyed the mysterious hill for years.

Venetian Pool

"Venetian Pool," Coral Gables

Coral Gables' Famous Attraction.

The Venetian Pool, Coral Gables most famous tourist attraction, was an irregularly shaped, artistic freshwater pool that was designed to transform an unsightly coral rock pit into a spot of beauty. With vine-covered trellises, aged coral buildings, a waterfall, sand beach, many palm trees, and other plants, the pool is the object of thousands of visitors and camera fans each year.

Vizcaya

M-281 VILLA VISCAYA, MIAMI, FLORIDA

Vizcaya Museum and Gardens.

This impressive example of Italian Renaissance style architecture began in 1914, took eight years to complete and cost $18 million. Constructed as a winter residence for International Harvester heir James Deering, the museum's thirty-four-room house is a vast collection of fifteenth to nineteenth century furniture, textiles, and sculpture. The villa's ten acres of formal gardens were designed as an extension of the villa and combine the elements of sixteenth and seventeenth century Italian hill gardens with seventeenth century French gardens. An ornate stone barge, anchored in front of the mansion, serves as a decorative breakwater for Biscayne Bay. Vizcaya is located on U.S. Highway 1, south of downtown Miami and north of Homestead.

Volusia County Kennel Club

Nightly crowd at the Volusia County Kennel Club Dog Track. Daytona Beach, Florida

Where Greyhound Racing Began.

Volusia County voters approved the Volusia County Kennel Club in a referendum August 28, 1947. The track, dubbed the "pooch saucer" by sports writer Bernard Kahn, introduced the sport of greyhound racing to Daytona Beach. Opening night in 1948 drew 32,695 paid onlookers. Bettors wagered $53,708 on the ten races. This popular dog track was located on Highway 92 near where the Daytona International Speedway and Volusia Jai-Alai Fronton were built in 1959. The track later changed its name to Daytona Beach Kennel Club. In 2008 the Kennel Club moved to a new facility a short distance from Highway 92.

W

Wakulla Springs to Wrecker's Museum

Wakulla Springs

Above: Cruising and Lodging at the Springs.
In 1937 railroad magnate Edward Ball developed beautiful Wakulla Springs into a tourist attraction with a Spanish-style lodge, underwater boats, and jungle cruise boats. Wakulla Springs is the largest and deepest spring in the world. Each day, over 252 million gallons of water surge out of this 225-foot deep spring from a single fissure. The springs became a Florida State Park in 1986. It has been designated a Natural Nature landmark and listed on the National Register of Historic Places. Wakulla Springs is located fifteen miles south of Tallahassee.

Top Left: Wakulla Springs Jungle Cruise.
Boat and tourists return from a sightseeing jungle cruise on the Wakulla River.

Right: Underwater Boat at Wakulla Springs.
Tourists were able to view underwater scenes from a glass-bottom boat. One was this picnick that occurred ten feet underwater. This scene was taken from Grantland Rice Sportlight "Shooting Mermaids." Parts of the movies "The Creature from the Black Lagoon" and "The Creature Walks Among Us" were filmed here in 1953 and 1956.

T-26—Picnicking Under Water at Wakulla Springs

Warm Mineral Springs

"..... the Real Fountain of Youth."

Warm Mineral Springs, located on U.S. Highway 41 just south of Venice, is known for its free-flowing artesian spring, which fills a sinkhole with healthy mineral water at a temperature of eighty-seven degrees. About 10,000 years ago, during the Paleo-Indian Period, animals such as mammoths and giant sloths gathered around the springs. Native American hunters also frequented the area. Bones and bone tools have been preserved in a debris cone 150 feet below the surface. In 1953, an underwater explorer diving in the springs discovered stalactites and stalagmites below the water's surface, indicating that the site was for a very long time a dry cave. A 1960 report by Royal and Clark indicated that a partly burned log and human skeleton remains found by scuba divers was dated about 8050 B.C. In 1972, underwater archaeologist Carl J. Clausen made dives at the site and found two fragments of human skeletal material which radiocarbon-dated to 8000 B.C., confirming colonel William Royal's report. The spring is rich in minerals and has a distinctive sulfur smell. More than 9 million gallons of water flow through the spring daily, and the mineral content is the highest in the country and the third highest in the world. The warm waters can help provide relief for aching muscles, skin conditions, sinusitis and many other health conditions. More than 65,000 people every year visit the spring to relax and enjoy the water's healing powers. In 1977 the National Register of Historic Places listed it as a significant site.

Webb's City

Florida's Greatest Showplace.

In 1925 James Earl "Doc" Webb opened Webb City in St. Petersburg. Starting out with a small building 17 x 28 feet, by the 1950s Webb City was seventy-two individual stores in a single shopping area. Famous writers and celebrities acclaimed it the nation's outstanding showplace. As described in the 1957 sixteen-page booklet shown here, there were four different types of places to eat: a cafeteria, the world's largest fountain and luncheonette, a delicatessen sandwich bar, and a take-home snack shack, and the stores were open day and night. Visitors could fill their car's tank with gasoline at 3¢ a gallon less than the competition. Webb City had parking for 2,000 cars, 2,000 employees, and served 60,000 customers daily. The sales were over $30 million in 1958. Webb City was by far the largest one-stop shopping center on Florida's West Coast! Shopping here was more fun than going to a circus. In fact, Webb City featured entertainment with star acts from the Ringling Bros. Circus. Doc Webb didn't care about money—he wanted customers. And customers he got; they came for the two-cent breakfast, and the five-cent-a-pack cigarettes. Webb City closed in 1974.

Weeki Wachee Springs

City of Mermaids.
Weeki Wachee, a city and theme park, is located on U.S. Highway 19 at one of Florida's great natural springs on the Gulf of Mexico north of Tampa. The city calls itself the "City of Mermaids." This is a fitting title since mermaids have been performing here and delighting audiences for more than sixty years. In 1947, Newton Perry, an ex-Navy frogman who had purchased the land a year earlier, presented the first live underwater Mermaid show to the public. American Broadcasting Company (ABC) took over Weeki Wachee Spring in 1959 and, for the next twenty years, expanded and improved the Mermaid program. The operation of the springs changed hands again, however, all owners have continued the tradition of improving the main attraction begun by Newton Perry—the Mermaid Show. Guests sit below the spring's surface and watch mermaids perform. The performers do musical numbers such as *Tribute to America* and *The Little Mermaid*. The remarkable mermaids even eat and drink underwater of the 137-foot deep spring. Today the theater seats five hundred people and is embedded in the side of the spring fourteen feet below the surface. It is the only show of its kind in the world.

Thirsty Mermaid.
This 1950s Mermaid is having a refreshing underwater drink.

123

Welcome to the Weeki Wachee Show.
The beautiful underwater Mermaids perform in the crystal clear waters at Weeki Wachee Springs while the brochure advertises their performance of "Adagio," Weeki Wachee's trademark.

Wonder House

Top Left: House of Gadgets.
In the early 1920s Conrad Schuck, a Pittsburgh physician, and his family came to Bartow and started building a four-story mansion of rock with many unusual features that were far ahead of their time. Schuck worked on the house for forty years, but never moved in. The house became the subject of a *Coronet* magazine article in the 1930s, and when "Ripley's Believe It or Not" called it the Wonder House, the name stuck. When conducting tours, Schuck enjoyed the reactions to his gadgetry and items placed in the house. The unfinished Wonder House was open to the public until 1963, when Schuck was forced to sell it.

Wood Parade

Top Right: Seeing How Wood Can Be Art.
The Earl Gresh Wood Parade, located at 4th Street North, in St. Petersburg, was the only wood museum in the world (1940-1959). It depicted people's use of wood as a medium of expression and necessity, since primitive times including wooden pocketbooks, belts, pins, and novelties. Unusual and interesting, visitors could see wood carvers at work. The Wood Parade was one of the most popular attractions in St. Petersburg.

World's Only Rattlesnake Cannery

Welcome to Rattlesnake, Fla.
In the 1930s the community known as Rattlesnake was located at the east end of the Gandy Bridge between Tampa and St. Petersburg. This section of Florida was populated with Eastern Diamondback Rattlesnakes. George End, a Connecticut Yankee who owned a rattlesnake cannery in Arcadia, relocated his "novelty" business to Rattlesnake where he had more exposure to tourists visiting Tampa and St. Petersburg. He converted an old gas station to his needs and opened "Geo. K. Ends Original Rattlesnake Headquarters." George canned the meat and made novelties from the remainder of the rattlesnake: billfolds, belts, shoes, purses, tobacco pouches, watch straps, rings, charms, hat bands, and other rattlesnake related items. The meat was canned and sold as "Genuine Diamondback Rattlesnake with Supreme Sauce," for $1.25 per tin container. George hired brave locals to catch the rattlesnakes from the immediate area. By 1939 George had talked the federal government into establishing a post office at his Rattlesnake Headquarters. Many tourists and residents of the area were repeat customers to see George's display of rattlesnakes, purchase snake related items and sample rattlesnake meat. After George's death, his widow, Jennie, sold the business and built a small wooden building, just west of the original location, to house the Rattlesnake post office. The last day of business for the post office was May 31, 1954. Rattlesnake was later annexed to Tampa and now is just an interesting memory. How did George die? Of course, by a rattlesnake bite.

Wrecker's Museum

**Near Right:
Oldest House in Key West.**
The Oldest House in Key West, built around 1829, was home to Captain Francis B. Watlington and his family from the 1830s to the 1930s. Watlington was a professional wrecker who salvaged cargo from sunken ships. Tourists are attracted to the old house, which contains displays of Key West wreckers.

X-Z

X marks the Spot to Zorayda Castle

X marks the Spot

Florida's Shell Island.
An island along the Gulf Coast, near Fort Myers, is the SPOT in Florida where residents and visitors go to collect shells. Sanibel Island is notable for the number and variety of sea shells on its beaches. Every tide and storm washes ashore thousands of specimens of some three hundred varieties.

Yesteryear's Attractions

Remembering Past Attractions.
Florida has been drawing tourists for over a century with natural and man-made attractions. Some of these attractions still exist; however, many of them had only a short life and disappeared even before 1950. Some of these closed attractions were Florida Alligator Farm, Florida Ostrich Farm, Miami Beach Aquarium, Orlando's Spouting Well, Palm Beach's Florida Alligator Farm, and Vedder Museum. Shown is Dixieland Park, an amusement park in Jacksonville that opened in 1907 and closed a few years later. This riverfront park featured an arena of over four hundred wild animals, including eighty-seven lions, elephants, and camels.

Dixieland Park at night
Jacksonville, Fla.

Zorayda Castle

World Famous Moorish Palace.

Villa Zorayda, a vine-covered coquina and concrete structure of Moorish design, was trimmed in bright red, blue, and yellow, the Moorish colors. The house was erected in 1883 by Boston architect Franklin W. Smith, who based his design on a portion of the famed Alhambra Castle, in Spain. Smith had a large collection of inlaid and elaborately carved Oriental pieces, ancient Egyptian hangings, valuable rugs, ancient firearms, and many Oriental items. In 1913 Abraham S. Mussallem purchased the Villa Zorayda, adding his collection of valuable and rare furnishings obtained while serving as Egyptian consulate. From 1922 to 1925 Villa Zorayda was used as the Zorayda Club, a nightclub and gambling casino. The club closed when Florida outlawed gambling. Since 1936 the Mussallem family operated the building as a tourist attraction, Zorayda Castle. The flamboyant architectural building houses a collection of priceless relics that are world famed. On display was the Sacred Cat Rug, over 2,300 years old, found in the casket of a mummy in the Valley of the Kings along the Nile River. The rug was made from the hair of prehistoric cats that roamed the Nile. Also shown was the Harem Quarters, the place where the Sultan kept his wives.

Bibliography & Reading Suggestions

Blashfield, Jean F. and Cima Star. *Awesome Almanac: Florida*. Walworth, Wisconsin: B & B Publishing, 1994.

Breslauer, Ken. *Roadside Paradise: The Golden Age of Florida's Tourist Attractions 1929-71*. St. Petersburg, Florida: RetroFlorida, Inc., 2000.

Butcher, Russell D. *Guide to National Parks: Southeast Region*. Washington, D.C.: National Parks and Conservation Association, 1999.

Butko, Brian and Sara Butko. *Roadside Attractions*. Mechanicsburg, Pennsylvania: Stackpole Books, 2007.

Carlson, Charlie. *Weird Florida: Your Travel Guide to Florida's Local Legends and Best Kept Secrets*. New York, New York: Barnes & Noble Publishing, 2005.

Genovese, Peter. *Roadside Florida*. Mechanicsburg, Pennsylvania: Stackpole Books, 2006.

Gittner, Cory H. *Miami's Parrot Jungle and Gardens*. Gainesville, Florida: University Press of Florida, 2000.

Grimes, David and Tom Recnel. *Florida Curiosities*. Guilford, Connecticut: Globe Pequot Press, 2003.

Hatton, Hap. *Tropical Splendor: An Architectural History of Florida*. New York, New York: Alfred A. Knopf, 1987.

Hiller, Herbert L. *Highway A1A: Florida At the Edge*. Gainesville, Florida: University Press of Florida, 2005.

Hollis, Tim. *Dixie Before Disney: 100 Years of Roadside Fun*. Jackson, Mississippi: University Press of Mississippi, 1999.

Florida's Miracle Strip. Jackson, Mississippi: University Press of Mississippi, 2004.

Glass Bottom Boats & Mermaid Tails. Mechanicsburg, Pennsylvania: Stackpole Books, 2006.

Selling the Sunshine State. Gainesville, Florida: University Press of Florida, 2008.

Jakle, John A., Keith A. Sculle, and Jefferson S. Rogers. *The Motel in America*. Baltimore, Maryland: Johns Hopkins University Press, 1996.

Kirby, Doug, Ken Smith and Mike Wilkins. *The New Roadside America*. New York, New York: Simon & Schuster, 1992.

Kleinberg, Eliot. *Historical Traveler's Guide to Florida*. Sarasota, Florida: Pineapple Press, 2006.

Leslie, Candace and Ann Boese. *Florida Keys & Everglades*. Berkeley, California: Ulysses Press, 2008.

Liebs, Chester H. *Main Street to Miracle Mile: American Roadside Architecture*. Baltimore, Maryland: Johns Hopkins University Press, 1995.

Margolies, John. *Fun Along the Road*. Boston, Massachusetts: Little, Brown and Company, 1998.

Martin, Richard A. *Eternal Spring*. St. Petersburg, Florida: Great Outdoors Press, 1966.

Monroe, Gary and Bruce Mozen. *Silver Springs*. Gainesville, Florida: University Press of Florida, 2008.

Pelland, Maryan and Dan Pelland. *Weeki Wachee Springs*. Charleston, South Carolina: Arcadia Publishing, 2006.

Peterson, Eric. *Roadside America: Landmark Tourist Attractions*. Lincolnwood, Illinois: Publications International, Ltd., 2004.

Pinkas, Lilly. *Fairchild Tropical Garden*. Miami, Florida: Hallmark Press, 1996.

Rajtar, Steve. *Historic Photos of Florida Tourist Attractions*. Nashville, Tennessee: Turner Publishing Company, 2008.

Sandler, Corey. *Miami With Fort Lauderdale and Key West*. New York, New York: McGraw-Hill, 2001.

Scott, David L. and Kay W. Scott. *Guide to the National Park Areas: Eastern States*. Old Saybrook, Connecticut: Globe Pequot Press, 1999.

Shaffer, Michael and Andrew Fleming. *Bathroom Book of Florida Trivia: Weird, Wacky and Wild*. Blue Bike Books, 2007.

Sinclair, Mick. *Drive Around Florida*. Peterborough, United Kingdom: Thomas Cook Publishing, 2005.

Spencer, Donald D. *Early Florida Attractions On Old Postcards*. Ormond Beach, Florida: Camelot Publishing Company, 2001.

Summerlin, Cathy and Vernon Summerlin. *Traveling Florida*. Winston-Salem, North Carolina, John F. Blair, Publisher, 2002.

Vickers, Lu and Sara Dionne. *Weeki Wachee: City of Mermaids*. Gainesville, Florida: University Press of Florida, 2007.

Index

Contemporary Australian Garden Design

Contemporary Australian Garden Design

Secrets of leading garden designers revealed

JOHN PATRICK AND JENNY WADE

ABC
Books

For μ who encouraged her family to be enthusiastic, inquisitive and to do things.
With thanks for years of encouragement.
John Patrick

I lovingly dedicate my part in this book to Ruby, Eliza and Nelson, who bring me
inspiration, joy and fulfilment beyond measure.
Jenny Wade

Published by ABC Books for the
AUSTRALIAN BROADCASTING CORPORATION
GPO Box 9994 Sydney NSW 2001

First published in November 2008

ISBN 978 07333 23027

Cover by Nada Backovic and Judi Rowe, Agave Creative Group
Internal design by Nada Backovic. Page design and layout by Judi Rowe, Agave Creative Group
Colour reproduction by Graphic Print Group, Adelaide
Printed and bound by SNP Leefing, China

Contents

Foreword

While there are many books about Australian gardens, *Contemporary Australian Garden Design* does something unique: it captures the essence of contemporary Australian residential garden design through its profiles of twenty leading Australian designers and the gardens they have designed. Of particular relevance to the home gardener are the design tips that accompany each chapter and provide practical advice on various principles and elements of garden design.

A garden can give great pleasure to the person who is its caretaker. I am always impressed by seeing people in their gardens and hearing what they have to say about them: 'This tree was planted for Harrison's second birthday,' or 'This plant is in memorial to . . .' Gardens can take on many meanings through their shape, the plants used, environmental attitudes, artworks and family responses. I remember in Tasmania seeing a very elderly couple in their garden littered with big old used television sets, which had their tubes replaced by plants. The couple in that scene were having a gentle kiss. It was that kiss in the garden that made the setting so complete.

Most gardens cater for a specific need, whether it's the imperatives of the human spirit or a creature's right to exist. Making a garden is a creative act; one that is guided by, and encourages, the evolution of this spirit. It can be an act of great sensitivity, or one of great arrogance. In this sense, the making of a garden can be a gift, and I believe that this sensibility is one directed by forces outside of ourselves.

As we make our gardens, we must never lose that sense of knowing our place in the universe that a garden provides, and the consequent sense of security that we feel in a garden.

For many, gardens are a place of refuge where they can retreat and feel at home. This sense of feeling at home in your garden comes through in this book through the profiles and voices of Australian gardeners and the garden designers' attitudes to making their gardens.

Gardens need design anchors to help build them; without them they seem to drift and float. John Patrick and Jenny Wade have succeeded in putting together stories that explore the spirit of garden-making and give us the design anchors to create our own gardens. Design brief, site analysis, design response, planting design and design tips are all included.

The authors have also been able to keep a finger on the pulse of contemporary garden design. I believe that the stories in *Contemporary Australian Garden Design* help create the future of garden-making and offer inspiration for the way forward for Australian garden design.

Jim Sinatra AAS BLA MLA FAILA

Introduction

As a country that has a relatively short tradition of designed gardens, Australia may be said to be still developing its own garden style. Throughout the years since European settlement, the roles and appearances of gardens have been in a constant state of flux because what we have required from them has continually changed. We have, too, become more understanding of our environment, so that earlier attitudes to gardening that developed from traditional European precedents have now been modified to reflect our own gardening environment.

For the earliest gardeners in Australia, survival was critical. Crops and fruit took pride of place in the garden. Water was hard won and was used to secure vital food for survival rather than securing beauty from ornamental plants. As confidence and a sense of security within the settlers' new environment took hold, a passion for ornamental plants soon followed, especially among ladies for whom the decorative plant material of home offered a welcome feeling of security, a sense of nostalgia and, no doubt, a few regrets for family and land left behind.

Practicality brought with it a degree of austerity in garden design. Practical straight-edged beds—easily accessed for crop gathering, tending and watering—dominated,

yielding to a more decorative form of garden only as the settlers' toe-hold in the landscape became secure. Then the influence of John Claudius Loudon and his gardenesque design principles pervaded garden design as his books were included in many a settler's library.

The transition from survival gardens to display would have occurred at different times in different places. Wherever the pioneer wave moved, new survival gardens were created, leaving behind a more secure community for whom decorative gardening became a possibility.

Gardening for decoration and display is a product of wealth and time. Without the security of income and available time, gardening remains about productivity and securing food. For those who established wealth, ornamental gardening—with its attendant pleasures of strolling—became the norm, whereas for those with less income, productive gardening remained a priority.

Changes in social and economic conditions also had an impact. During periods of economic recession, and especially through the Great Depression, the use of the garden as a place to grow vegetables was important. World Wars also had a role in focusing the skills of many gardeners, though perhaps less in Australia than in Britain, where the need to produce vegetables from home gardens during both major wars had a significant impact upon gardening trends.

Fiona Brockhoff's design for this coastal garden on Melbourne's Mornington Peninsula extends into the nature strip and intergrates the garden with its setting.

Early professional designers

Development of public gardens, especially in the capital cities but also in regional towns, brought forth professional designers who, with differing degrees of skill, implemented parks and botanic gardens as recreational spaces for the community. Their development was a further indication of the spread of civilisation. Wealthy patrons employed the most outstanding of these designers to lay-out their own gardens, some with great success, for example Guilfoyle at Mawallok and Banongil and later Charles Bogue Luffman at Killamont, Wyuna.

The age of the professional garden designer was dawning, for those with adequate money at least, though for the vast majority, garden design remained self directed and, while it often left much to be desired in terms of sophistication, it often lacked nothing in terms of creativity and imagination, though as today, standards and interests varied. Front gardens provided an image, a setting for a house that contributed to the neighborhood. Here full vent was given to colourful planting, ornamental fences and gates and a sense of pride in property. To the rear, fruit and vegetables (it was never done to display these in public) prospered alongside service areas that contained items such as a clothesline and incinerator. Surprisingly, while a lawn was essential, little of the rest of the garden was given to paving or other features we now consider essential for outdoor living. Perhaps when efforts completing and maintaining the garden were over there was no time for rest and recreation!

Social status played a large part in the development of gardens. For the wealthy, grass tennis courts and a croquet lawn, cutting gardens as well as fruit and vegetables and an ornamental garden might all have been found on a property. It is likely that many poor didn't garden at all.

In Australia there is a surprisingly diverse list of garden designers who worked in different parts of the country, their practice limited in extent by the practicalities of travel. Many were nurseryman who put their knowledge of plants to good use. An example is William Sangster who, working from nurseries in South Yarra and Mount Macedon, supplied plants to many of the large estate gardens of Victoria in the late nineteenth century. These plants now grace the skylines of numerous gardens as mature trees.

The first Australian garden designer who truly captivated the broader Australian imagination, and in fact continues to do so, was Edna Walling. Greatly influenced by European design, including the work of Edwin Lutyens and Gertrude Jekyll but also, and importantly, the work of Renaissance Italian designers, she provided garden designs to many of Melbourne's most prestigious families, blending formal structure with intricate and romantic planting schemes.

Her style varied from garden to garden. At Marwarra in the Dandenongs it was formal and structured, using masonry to good account to provide dramatic steps and retaining walls. In her village at Bickleigh Vale she looked generally to more plant–orientated design solutions, albeit with attractive and strategically placed low walls to create seating terraces and courtyards.

Walling was able to increase her popularity and awareness of her work by writing regular contributions for *Australian Home Beautiful*, where she could discuss her designs and the plants she used. Passing years saw other designers join her in Melbourne: Olive Mellor, Joan Jones, Emily Gibson and a little later, Ellis Stones, Grace Fraser and John Stevens. The establishment of the Australian Institute of Landscape Architects in 1966 saw the development of a professional body aiming to represent the interests of professional designers. The existence of this institution and the growth in the number of designers were testament to an increased demand for garden designers. Not all of this was for residential design. New demands were coming from government agencies for the design of roads and airports, parks and other public sites but, in parallel, the post-war years saw a rising expectation that home gardens would be designed.

A greater focus was placed upon landscaping new housing developments. Ellis Stones worked with Merchant Builders in the design of estates, including Elliston, named to honour his achievements.

Recognition that gardens provided an invaluable adjunct to the Australian lifestyle began to grow and with it the involvement of professionally trained designers who brought to their work a background in, and understanding of, international design trends. Australia's earliest landscape architects had trained in north-east England at the University of Durham, younger designers looked to the USA while, as demand grew, home-based courses provided increasing numbers of graduates. As demands for public sector landscape design grew, few landscape architects worked on residential garden design, generally preferring to work on a larger canvas.

There were always exceptions and many well established landscape architectural practitioners became involved in residential design, including, for example, Bruce McKenzie. In general the growth in residential garden design took place among those graduating from horticultural courses. Burnley College in Melbourne was a focus. Among its graduates, Rick Eckersley and Robert Boyle were pioneers of a more contemporary approach to design.

International exemplars

A growth in interest in gardens in Australia, or more specifically, professionally designed gardens for the broad community, lagged behind that of other parts of the world during the years after the Second World War. In Britain, followers of the Jekyll/Lutyens partnership provided professional design that was perhaps somewhat conservative. Percy Cane developed an extensive practice, while others like Russell Page began to establish a more international practice, originally basing himself in England but proceeding to Europe to meet an increasing market. Given that he worked through a broad range of climate zones, it is not surprising that his work found acceptance in Australia and that his book *The Education of a Gardener* became a bible to many of the more aware gardeners in Australia.

With the arrival of John Brookes and his books *The Room Outside* and *The Small Garden*, there came a new sense of the opportunities that the garden provided. Brookes' designs were suited to small urban gardens as well as larger properties. He offered sophistication for those with restricted budgets and limited space. They brought to everyman the sense that they could enjoy the benefits that a garden bestowed without owning vast estates. In many ways Brookes' title *The Room Outside* reflected an earlier book emanating from California, Thomas Church's *Gardens Are for People*. It was Church who, in the years following the Second World War, developed gardens in California that responded to the expectations of migrants leaving east-coast USA to enjoy a hedonistic lifestyle in sun-baked California. Church's gardens brought together all the essential items of an outdoor lifestyle—pool, patio, pergola, carport, vegetable garden and service elements—to create gardens that were accessible, affordable and enjoyable, largely without the owner needing to have an interest in gardening. The new gardening lifestyle was about the pleasure that a garden could offer to life outside, rather than the pleasure to be had in growing plants! Church responded to the desire to have a life of pleasure and in doing so brought gardens to the attention of home-owning masses. From Palm Springs to Sonoma County, houses of the 50s and 60s enjoyed the benefits of gardens in a way that had not occurred before.

The influence and impact of John Brookes can hardly be over-estimated. In a series of books that influenced later authors he developed simple directions for design through a variety of examples, mostly derived from his own work, that resonated with home owners worldwide. He increased this influence through lecture tours that brought him to wider audiences in the UK, USA, Japan and eventually, Australia.

A sense of the increasing interest in gardens can be gauged by the number of books published about gardens. In the years following the Second World War in Australia, Edna Walling published a series of immensely popular gardening books. Ellis Stones followed. Then in the 1970s came a succession of books that described the use and suitability of Australian native plants in garden design. Little of note had been written to describe how Australia's native flora could be harnessed for use in gardens since these plants had been considered as a novelty by nineteenth-century Australian gardening pioneers. Luffman had proposed their use for the new Australian capital, and had used them at the Metropolitan Golf Course, Oakleigh, to create what Edna Walling had called 'probably the finest essay in the use of Australian native plants in a planting scheme'. Burley Griffin saw value in their use; not only in Canberra but at Castlecrag and in Melbourne too, but it was not until Edna Walling wrote her visionary book *The Australian Roadside* that the true value of Australian native plants began to be recognised.

Perhaps Glen Wilson's *Garden Design with Australian Native Plants* was the pioneering work that focused broad attention on the potential of Australian plants for garden use. His analysis of the foliage forms of the grevillea species was a remarkable assessment of the potential value of Australia's flora to garden design.

The 1970s in Australia were dominated by an increasing sense of discovery of the country's native flora. Many books were written that described the benefits and values of the use of native flora, with educator and environmentalist Thistle Harris at the vanguard. Sadly, some of the enthusiasm for native flora was misplaced. A lack of discernment and discrimination about which plants were truly worthy of garden inclusion meant that the broader public, to whom the idea of native gardens had somehow been confused with the concept of the no-maintenance garden, became sadly disillusioned with these plants. Native gardens became synonymous with dry, dusty and generally unrewarding horticulture.

Contemporary Australian garden design

The latter years of the twentieth century saw extraordinary changes in attitudes to gardens on a world-wide scale. In many parts of the world, the role of a garden designer was as vital to the creation of a house as the employment of an architect or builder. Where it had once been an exception to have a home garden designed, it now became an exception to not have some professional help with the garden. On new housing estates, gardens were designed by landscape architects as part of an overall package.

Individual homes were provided with designed gardens by an increasing number of garden designers, most of whom had qualifications from an increasing number of garden design courses throughout the country. Australian garden design was becoming internationalised and Australian garden writers became recognised around the world and travelled widely to extend their influence (and further sales of their books). International publishing brought more pictorial information about gardens to designers and garden owners alike than had ever occurred previously.

Influential as this was, it was perhaps television that had the greatest influence on the popular appetite for garden design. Not only did local television presenters bring images of gardens to every home, the public were shown how easily and at what low cost a beautiful garden could be created. International series showed not only the history of gardens, but also the achievements of many contemporary designers.

In the words of Melbourne designer Andrew Secull: 'Gardens have never been so popular, but so few actually garden.' Increased wealth and a paucity of free time, a reduction in the need for home-grown fruit and vegetables and a rise in the perception that a designed garden was a prestigious item, brought a flock of clients to garden designers.

There was a sense too that a whole generation had lost contact with the earth. A time-honoured tradition of learning about growing food in one's own garden, handed down from parents to children, had been lost. Gardens had become a challenge and not just because of the complexity of plants but also because of the vast range of garden accessories that were now available, including outdoor lighting, irrigation, paving materials, pools, fountains etc.

Such was the capital cost of a garden and such was its potential benefit to a home (real-estate agents suggest a well-designed mature garden increases a home's original value by 10%) that the involvement of a professional designer had distinct benefits.

Today, Australia's garden designers work in every state, providing a broad range of services for every type of garden. Garden styles vary as much as the architecture they address, from inner-city roof gardens and terraces to heritage gardens and contemporary sites, from rural farmscapes to coastal hideaways. The designs reveal international trends and tastes and, increasingly, specifically Australian responses that reflect a strong sense of place: geographically, socially and historically.

While Australia has been a sponge for international design styles, there is now evidence to suggest that its garden designers are beginning to make their own impact internationally. The successes of Australian designers at the Chelsea Flower Show reflect their increasing confidence at showing their talents on a broader stage. Jim Fogarty, Jack Merlo, Dean Herald, Mark Browning and most recently Jamie Durie have each exhibited with great success and have shown that Australian designers sit at the forefront of design trends. Harris Hobbs has also received international recognition for its work at the International Garden Festival – Emo 2007 in Ireland and an International Garden Design Competition. In part this is a reflection of the fact that an Australian approach to outdoor living is being accepted elsewhere in the world. Where John Brookes and Thomas Church made tentative steps, the Australian climate and its egalitarian community have encouraged designers to take this approach further than elsewhere.

Identifying common strands among our garden designers is difficult, for their work reflects a wide range of styles. Yet there are trends that reflect new sensibilities and a strong sense of place. Increasingly, Australian gardens are responding to their environment. In part this is a reflection of the diverse climate and ecology of the country, from the tropical climates of the north with average daily temperatures in the summer months well in excess of 30 degrees Celsius and in winter of 18 degrees Celsius, to the cooler climate of the south-east where temperatures are generally in the 20s but where summer temperatures may reach into the low 40s on occasion and winter may fall below 0 degrees Celsius. Variations can occur within short distances, however the broad view of Australia as an environment for an active outdoor lifestyle holds true.

While temperatures and the presence of the warm summer sun may dictate which items are commonly included in the Australian garden, it is rainfall that is causing the greatest change in the realisation of our gardens. While rainfall has always been seen as a constraint in gardening, and, drought has always (intermittently) affected the eastern seaboard where the greater part of the population lives, these patterns seem to be changing. Rainfall appears to be increasing in some areas, for example to the north-west, while it is decreasing for the greater part of the eastern seaboard.

Traditionally, the south-east has experienced up to 1200mm of rainfall a year with many areas in the 600-800mm range. Higher rainfalls may be experienced in tropical areas to the north of the country, for example 1600mm in Cairns and 2000mm in Townsville and in areas to the north-west. Rainfall patterns are changing too, switching from reliable late winter–spring rains in the south-east to occasional heavy summer deluges.

As a result, garden designers are preparing designs that recognise these changing conditions. Indigenous vegetation and the use of new technologies such as drip irrigation systems are becoming an inevitable part of contemporary garden design.

Fiona Brockhoff and John Sullivan in different extremes of the country are evidence of this. Fiona uses a palette dominated by indigenous plants in her coastal gardens, imbuing her gardens with a remarkable sense of place by recycling local materials like pier timbers and coastal detritus and selecting local stone and placing these elements in a planting scheme of local plants. Her approach is exemplified by the Mornington Peninsula garden in this book. Her passion for native plants extends to investigating their tolerances as she manipulates them for horticultural purposes.

At the other extreme, John Sullivan is exploring the potential of the, as yet, under-utilised flora of Far North Queensland, looking not only to harness them for decorative use but to explore their value as productive plants. In conjunction with architects, John is looking to harness local rainfall by creating rain-gardens: encouraging re-charging of water tables by capturing water on the site and allowing it to slowly soak into the garden rather than being drained away.

These are just two approaches to design that suggest an increased awareness of sustainability. Yet there is also a greater sense too that designers belong to the landscape and feel more comfortable there. Kate Cullity and Kevin Taylor have long been champions of this more sensitive approach to design, incorporating brilliantly subtle interpretations of the landscape of Australia into their designs. While much of this has been expressed in larger scale projects, for example at the Cranbourne Botanic Gardens near Melbourne, their own private garden reveals a similar sensitivity, viewing and interpreting the landscape as visual poets and incorporating sculptural elements by local artists that enhance the story they tell.

Interestingly Catherine Shields takes a similar approach, treading lightly on a landscape that she sees as the property of others—long-term residents who were more at one with our country than more recent settlers. Her work makes use of mouth-wateringly beautiful settings on the edge of Tasmania's coastline and treats it gently to allow a sense of place to shine through.

Incorporating the work of artists, as Kate Cullity and Catherine Shields do, is a growing trend in garden design. Neil Hobbs and Karina Harris see their garden as a gallery, a setting for a diverse palette of work incorporating humour, social comment and contemporary art: an extreme example of an approach that is increasingly present in our gardens. Michael McCoy who is a noted plantsman but still sees the value of incorporating sculptural elements in his garden, demonstrating the breadth of his design approach, and Jeremy Ferrier, whose garden is as much environmental sculpture as it is garden, both reveal the value of sculpture to garden design. The sense of garden as sculpture is borne out by Mira Martinazzo whose spare design resolution for a garden surrounding a home

by Harry Seidler sees the house as a sculptural piece in a landscape. Her delicate resolution of the site sees the qualities of the house echoed in the landscape and at the same time defers appropriately to a breathtaking setting on Sydney's middle harbour: a view of Sydney with one of its inlets shrouded in woodland below that overseas visitors would consider typical.

Georgina Martyn, too, recognises the inter-relationship of planting and sculptural form in her superbly crafted garden. In a small space Georgina has developed a scheme that is innovative and exciting, revealing a sense of adventure and a willingness to explore new avenues that reveal the garden as a place of celebration and excitement.

Yet throughout the book, what speaks out loud and clear is the Australian love of an outdoor lifestyle. Several of the designers within the book explore the lifestyle opportunities offered by Australia's climate. For Marisa Fontes and Suzan Quigg, gardening in the far north of the country, the swimming pool is a focus to outdoor lives. Such was its importance in one Darwin garden that it compromised access to the home, and Marisa had to resolve the conflict between the pool and the house's front entry. Suzan faced no such problem, the pool being the major celebration of her garden near Cairns. It provides the focus for both the garden space and the home and illustrates how barriers between indoor and outdoor spaces are being progressively broken down.

Dean Herald takes this to an extreme. His New South Wales garden is an exercise in providing for life outdoors, extending not only to a pool and spa but also tennis court, kitchen and even a few holes of golf. His garden, viewed as a 'resort at home', is about enjoying the pleasures that the Australian climate allows.

Matt Huxtable and Ryan Healy reflect this too on the other side of the continent, revealing not only a garden designed for play and recreation but one where water is used as a design feature to bring refreshment to a dry environment.

As Australia becomes an increasingly urban country, garden sizes decrease and designers find themselves responding to a demand for high quality gardens in smaller spaces. Creating the appearance of space in a setting closely bound by neighbouring walls and houses is never easy but is a frequent challenge for designers and it is tackled in many different ways. Paul Bangay has completely changed the expectations of home owners (around Melbourne in particular), with gardens that not only achieve extraordinary character in small areas but do so instantaneously. His work transforms a new home from a naked block to a mature landscape environment overnight. In this he illustrates another aspect of the present trend in Australian garden design, the need for an immediate result. No longer do gardens grow and mature, rather they are put into place as a mature landscape for the pleasure of their owners.

Janine Mendel faces small garden sites consistently, tackling them with a flair that is based strongly on an architectural response and the use of bold colour and form softened by appropriate planting. While Jamie Durie may have expanded his practice to address larger projects, he too faces the challenges of smaller gardens in inner-city Sydney. While the common perception of Sydney is of homes with glorious harbour views, the majority of home owners face a more restricted landscape. Durie addresses this by creating an inward-looking design response. Durie has played a major role in popularising the home garden. Through his work on Australian television especially, he has revealed how effective design can be achieved in a relatively easy way.

While designers respond to specific challenges in Australia's gardens there is little doubt that plants continue to be the focus of Australian gardeners and their design ambitions. Designers happily respond when garden owners express a desire to see a diversity of plants in their garden. Given the wealth of native plants that still need to be explored so they may reach their full garden potential, it is surprising that this does not feature more widely as an aspect of designed gardens in Australia. John Sullivan, especially, is attempting to address this by reviewing plants from Far North Queensland and introducing them into his gardens. Suzan Quigg in the

same geographic area is, by contrast, combing the world for material suited to the climate so that she can bring it into her gardens.

In this, there are echoes of Roberto Burle Marx and his career spent introducing plants from Brazil's jungles into cultivation. Arno King uses some of this plant palette and displays this in a Brisbane garden where the densely planted masses so popular with tropical gardeners world-wide display strong bold foliage. These look especially good combined with water features. Arno's garden conjures up a world of moisture and lushness even if, by contrast, Brisbane's recent climate has been anything but wet and lush. Yet, even in this context there are garden owners who seek immediate impact and traditional gardens.

As the pressure to save water increases, Peter Fudge in Sydney reveals a garden where water-sensitive approaches provide a garden no less exciting than traditional gardens. By appropriate water use, careful and considered plant selection and reducing grassed areas, gardeners can respond responsibly to water restrictions.

Rick Eckersley has championed a fascinating range of plants and also extended the range of materials and decorations available to designers, to the general benefit of the garden scene.

This book attempts to review some of the trends present in contemporary Australian garden design by interviewing designers about their work and most specifically about a single design. The size and style of these projects varies enormously from simple entry areas to large country gardens. What they illustrate is the multiplicity of influences in play in design in Australia today and the way that garden designers are responding to them.

It will be interesting to review garden design in a further 10 years when the effects of climate change are more clearly felt. It could be that this book shows gardens in Australia on the cusp of an important change!

John Patrick

Spray Farm Garden
Bellarine Peninsula, Victoria

'When I design a garden, I want it to be timeless, and that's what I try and give people, something they can keep forever that just gets better with age. Apart from a place of beauty that people want to go out in and experience, I'd like a garden to be somewhere people go to actually "garden"—they're the ultimate gardens for me. There is nothing better than toiling through the seasons on a beautiful perennial border, cutting back, mulching and then waiting as it bursts into spring life, finally exuding all its charm and excitement in the peak of summer.' paul bangay

Biography

In the tradition of French masters of eighteenth-century landscapes, Paul Bangay now sets the benchmark for formal garden design. With their distinctive sense of scale and balance, his gardens epitomise simplicity and elegance, typically relying on a structural framework of hedging and pleaching to define a series of separate yet linked spaces. With refined ornamentation, the romance of water, architectural lines and axes leading to breathtaking vistas or focal points, his gardens transport one to another world, where harmony and emotional responses provide pleasure beyond visual appeal.

While many attempt to emulate the Paul Bangay style, rarely do others succeed in achieving such perfect balance and proportion. Paul considers his natural ability to apply the principles of scale in his work a fortuitous gift, commenting, 'I don't think that's something you can teach'. Groomed for professional landscape design by his gardening mother, an active member of the native plant movement in the 70s and his father, an academic who insisted he attain tertiary qualifications for his craft, Paul believes he was destined to design gardens. Beginning as a child with prize-winning ferns grown in the backyard hot house, Paul was continually encouraged by his parents with sumptuous gardening books that introduced him to Gertrude Jekyll and ignited his passion for exuberant perennials. In something of a rebellion against his parent's native plants, Paul recalls an early obsession with the landscapes of the English Arts and Crafts movement, and admits to gradually converting the family garden to a traditional English affair.

First taken to Burnley Horticultural College by his father at age eleven to focus him on his future, Paul finally graduated in 1985. He immediately established a retail nursery outlet in the Melbourne suburb of Toorak. His Italianate courtyard design at the shop's rear became a window to his exceptional talents and this, combined with a friendship through student work experience with renowned florist Kevin O'Neill, saw Paul's reputation grow rapidly. His five-year association with the Melbourne International Festival of the Arts through the

1 Perfect balance and proportion are a feature of Paul Bangay's formal gardens.

2 Paul's formal garden design was the perfect adjunct for the traditional Victorian building that dominated the site.

'Botanica' landscape design exhibitions earned him a John Truscott travelling scholarship to study with prominent European and American designers in 1994. In his studies with David Hicks in England Paul unearthed a kindred spirit and a source of great inspiration.

Averse to fashion-oriented design, Paul strives to produce timeless gardens that relate to their surrounding architecture. Following an established formula where structural layout remains constant, his plant palette for generous beds and parterres is constantly evolving. He takes great care—and learns from successes in similar Mediterranean climates—to choose improved cultivars and drought-tolerant options for both hedges and ornamental plantings. Rather than eradicating his characteristic lawns, he believes selecting waterwise turf species and an acceptance of seasonal browning-off is the answer, just as gardeners accept dormancy in perennials.

Paul's impact on Australian and international design is acknowledged through countless awards (including a Centenary Medal in 2001), and wide-ranging committee and representative appointments in both the arts and horticulture. Through newspaper columns, ongoing national and international magazine articles and now his fifth gardening book due for release in 2008, he shares his knowledge of design elements with a worldwide audience. Paul also generously supports charity ventures, from various open garden events, design forums and AIDS fundraising initiatives, to collaborating with celebrity chef Stephanie Alexander on community kitchen garden projects.

Design brief

In a sense Paul Bangay has such a distinct style with his well-defined, beautifully proportioned spaces, enclosing trees, gravel paths, clipped box and colourful perennial mass plantings that giving him a brief is almost superfluous, he seems to know instinctively what will be right!

Yet in the case of Spray Farm there were functional issues to be addressed, for while this property had every appearance of a large formal Victorian home with associated outbuildings, in fact it sat at the centre of a winery that was also to be a place for events—concerts for example—but more notably weddings. On that basis Paul's brief was to create a productive garden that would produce vegetables and herbs for the property to be used by the caterers, as well as a place for wedding photographs.

This brief brought with it the necessity of a garden with year-round qualities and one where different spaces had to be available, after all not every bride would want to be photographed in front of maturing brussel sprouts or recently dug potatoes!

Site analysis

While no house can be said to be 'typical' of the sites Paul works upon, his signature style does relate best to more formal homes. Paul believes his designs work best when they build upon architectural form and in this case, the formal Victorian buildings suited a formal design response.

Built around a courtyard, the façade of the house faced northwest across Corio Bay and out to the You Yangs, a landmark range of hills between Melbourne and Geelong. Proximity to the sea is normally an indication of salt-laden coastal winds with all the implications this brings for physical damage to plants from the wind itself and the effects of salt scorch. Yet, in this case, the effects of the sea were mitigated because the house and garden were located on the sheltered side of the promontory, proof that proximity to the sea need not always be a major constraint to effective plant growth.

Evidence of this was present on-site in the form of large, mature trees that surrounded the house—Moreton Bay figs (*Ficus macrophylla*) and Norfolk Island pine (*Araucaria heterophylla*), both with good coastal tolerance, and peppercorn (*Schinus molle* var. *areira*), which usually has less—were all prospering and established a good sense of scale for the house.

Fortunately, to the southwest there was a large area free of trees that received good light and offered an extension

3 Extensive views over Corio Bay provide a magnificent setting for the garden. The land slopes from a highpoint above the property to the south-east of the property from where a long access road makes its way to the house.

to the house where a garden could be created. To the northeast on the opposite side of the house was space for arriving, for car parking and creating links to the surrounding vineyard.

Design response

Paul's design response is interesting and well worth noting by home gardeners. Paul recognised that the site needed areas of garden for display, and to be effective these needed to be quite intensively landscaped. He also understood the need for practical areas where a marquee could be erected and this, by contrast, would be much less intensively worked.

Paul's approach is to provide his clients with a single design that he believes is the best solution for the site. If clients wish to make changes, they do so to this concept, but Paul is at least sure that any design changes made are appropriate. His cues derive from the architecture, and in this case, the location of doors, articulation of walls and alignment of windows told him where hedge, path and step alignments might occur.

The principal solution for this site sees a design of two elongated parallel gardens, the length of which correspond to the built form of the house in a newly created level area to the south of the house. Divided by an intersecting axial path that aligns with a doorway to the house, the result is four distinct garden areas, each contained by enclosing hedges to two metres.

The two areas comprising the first of the parallel gardens, bordered by the house on one side, consist of a decorative parterre at one end and a perennial garden at the other. A central east-west axis in the form of a gravel path links these gardens, with a formal column and pond, made from bricks that match the house, repeated as the centrepiece in both areas. Beyond the perennials and beneath a mature peppercorn that establishes a scale for the space, the garden descends via an impressive flight of stone steps to an open lawn between the house and the sea: the perfect site for a marquee.

In the remaining two defined areas of the second parallel garden, Paul created long vistas and an allée of trees that provide the perfect frame for wedding photographs. Again, a simple gravel path forms the central axis between the two separate areas, providing overall continuity between the garden's discrete spaces.

While the garden is quite simple in form, this is where its appeal lies. The garden could be maintained by any enthusiastic home gardener who would be assured of success.

What makes this design so effective, however, is Paul's sense of balance and proportion, the fact that he provides well-scaled enclosures, path widths and spaces, which, when put together as a whole, create a garden that is comfortable, appropriate and of a human scale.

4 A retaining wall made from local stone extends across the front of the house and retains the two parallel gardens.

5 The central axis of gravel path links the perennial garden to the parterre. Both occupy a newly created level area to the south of the house and offer stunning sea views from their elevated postion.

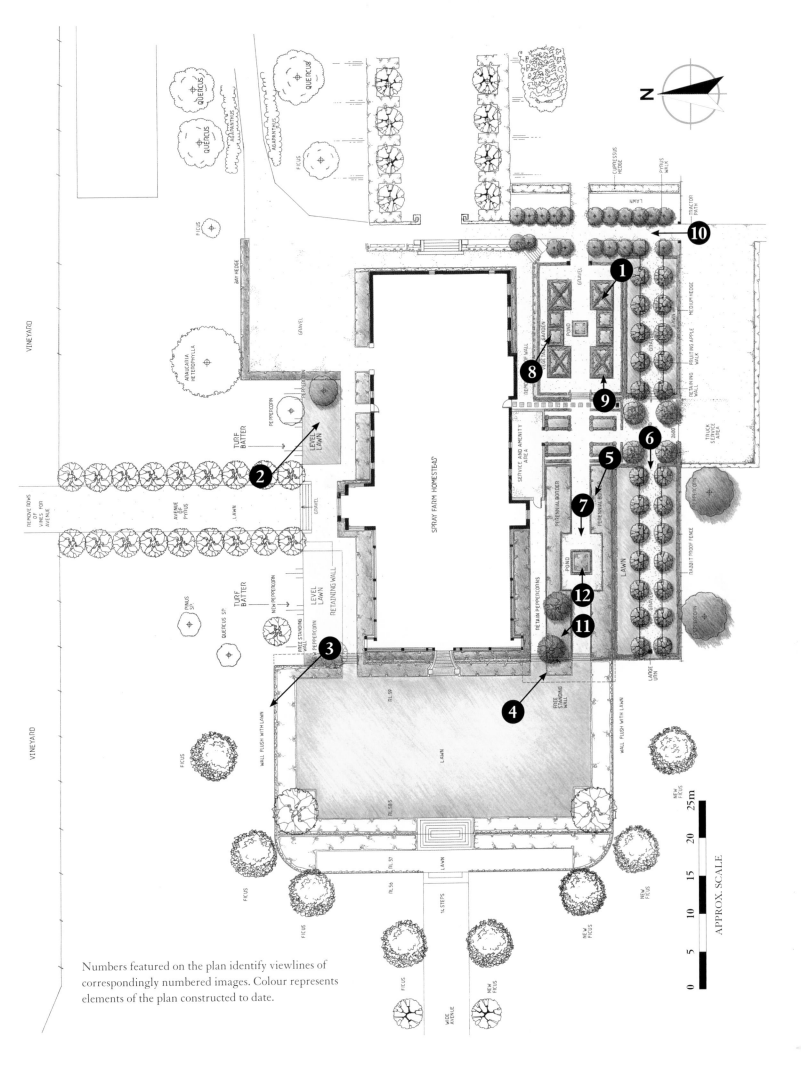

Numbers featured on the plan identify viewlines of correspondingly numbered images. Colour represents elements of the plan constructed to date.

6 Allees of trees provide the perfect setting for wedding photographs and a cool shaded retreat in summer.

7 Formal ponds provide continuity between the upper and lower garden spaces. The introduction of water to the garden brings refreshment through sound, touch and sight.

Planting design

Originally this was to be a productive garden, but with increased use of the facility, and a resultant greater demand for vegetables and herbs, it soon became apparent that production from this area was not practical. Paul designed a decorative potager for enjoyment, rather than a productive one.

Firstly, hedges were established of common privet (*Ligustrum vulgare*) clipped regularly to ensure a dense structure. This hedge has advantages, notably that it is very drought-tolerant and can be cut back to the ground to re-grow if required. However, it produces large numbers of creamy flowers, pollen from which can cause allergies. These can look unsightly when the purpose of the hedge is to offer a slick green backdrop, but regular clipping addresses this problem.

Within the box hedging, Paul uses low-water plants that offer good pattern and contrast with the lush green box. Cotton lavender (*Santolina chamaecyparissus* 'Nana') is one of these, and provided it is clipped frequently it retains dense foliage cover without becoming leggy. Regular clipping has the added advantage of removing the small yellow button flowers that detract from the simple pattern contrast.

In the next space is the green-foliaged *Santolina rosmarinifolia*, offering a gentle but enjoyable contrast. For this garden to appear at its best, regular ongoing clipping is essential as it depends upon a sharp appearance.

Ornamental pears and apples are a feature of the design, establishing attractive avenues that are perfect for spring wedding photographs. The crab apple *Malus* 'Gorgeous' is a major feature, and the grass is shaped between the trees into attractive bays. This crab apple, bred in New Zealand, is not only attractive in flower but also in late summer when its 2cm glossy red fruit are a particular feature. What a contrast is the other crab apple in the garden, *Malus spectablis*, simply stunning in its spring flower but with disappointing fruits.

SPRAY FARM GARDEN – PAUL BANGAY

8 Regular clipping of privet removes the flowers that detract from its green foliage and also removes the potential for production of weedy seeds that can be an issue with this species. Paul recognised that its very fibrous root system can invade planted areas causing competition so he located it within wide gravel paths.

9 Cotton lavenders *Santolina chamaecyparissus* 'Nana' (silverform) and *Santolina rosmarinifolia* (syn. *s.virens* {green form}) provide foliage contrast to each other and to the enclosing hedge of English box to add interest in the decorative parterre.

10 Ornamental pears planted within gravel extend the garden's formal character and provide enclosure to the southern boundary of the site.

Upright ornamental pears, noted for their flowers and more significantly their exquisite autumn foliage, grow from within gravel between hedges to break the line of the hedge and offer a magnificent extension in seasonal interest.

Large peppercorns are consistent elements of Victoria's rural landscape especially around properties and Paul retained them here where they shade the house from western sun. Planting beneath them is never easy; their well-established root systems rob the ground of moisture so that new plantings can battle.

Paul enjoys using perennial plants in country gardens; they allow seasonal change with their slow development from the spring to a late summer crescendo. Choosing perennials that offer long-term impact is important—a week of splendour is insufficient on a site this large.

Sedum 'Autumn Joy' was a great choice for its vast heads of pink flowers—attractive to butterflies in first flush—

which die off to bronze and then, well into autumn, to straw-coloured skeletons of refinement and a delicate beauty. Sages, too, including the South American bog sage (*Salvia uliginosa*) found favour. Reliable in flower, drought-tolerant and visually dramatic, their blue flowers offer a perfect contrast to the large, sub-shrub *Euphorbia wulfenii*. Its grey linear foliage is a perfect foil for large sulphur-yellow flower heads which in the very best forms are immensely dramatic. Its flowers nearly match those of the ladies mantle (*Alchemilla mollis*) also used. This is one of Paul's favourite groundcovers together with snow in summer (*Cerastium tomentosum*), the silver lamb's ears (*Stachys lanata*) and the blue of *Campanula portenschlagiana*, which are all featured here.

Finally, mention should be made of the use of masses of white hydrangea (*Hydrangea arborescens* 'Grandiflora'), its heads of pure white florets are an appropriate replacement for the typical hydrangeas for those wanting a taller growing and truly showy plant.

Ladies Mantle (*Alchemilla mollis*) is an attractive groundcover, especially after dew or rain when its hairy foliage holds water beads like diamonds.

11 *Hydrangea arborescens* 'Grandiflora' is a tall-growing showy hydrangea. Its only problem is that its flower heads may become so large that the stems bend under their weight.

'Paul was the obvious choice to design
our garden, to achieve the understated
elegance, formality and a timeless
quality we sought. Paul worked with
established trees and opportunities
for views to create a garden of great
beauty and stunning vistas that marries
perfectly with the traditional Victorian era
buildings and broader landscape.'

Garden owners

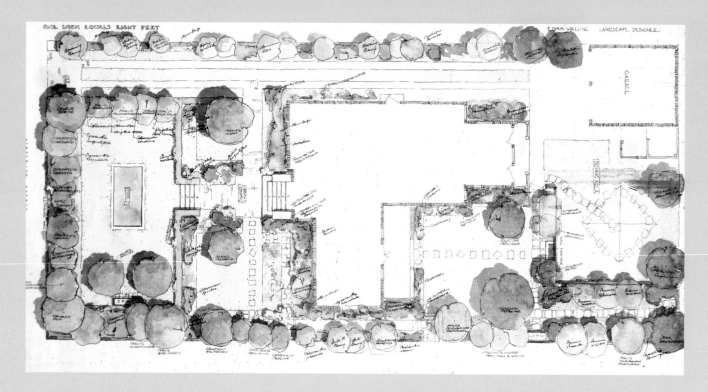

Edna Walling utilised a structured approach to her design using axes and viewlines. Her use of paths, and foci created a strong formal structure onto which she established her diverse planting scheme. Much of the secret of her success lies in the care she took in developing a strong design framework for her gardens.

Balance, scale and proportion

Paul Bangay's gardens reflect a clear and effective grasp of scale, space and proportion and it is this—along with his ability to discipline himself to a smaller plant palette where each selected plant fills an appropriate role—that ensures success in his work. The home gardener generally attempts to include a larger range of plants within a design, greater diversity in furnishings and often a range of materials.

What then are the secrets to the success of Paul's gardens? Paul bases his designs around strong axes created by the geometry of the house itself; it may be views from the windows, or the alignment of a door or walls. This can be seen in his work at Spray Farm where the axes ensure an obvious relationship between the delineation of garden spaces and the built form.

Extensions of wall alignments can provide a basis for enclosing garden walls of hedges or pleached trees, while lines from doors or windows might be emphasised by the placement of sculpture, water or other features in the landscape. The type of response will depend upon the scale of the site. A view from a window or to a narrow side boundary may focus on an urn or small fountain; a view of the length of a larger garden may utilise a rill and terminal fountain or a summer house.

Clear recognition of the scale of the site and an appropriate response to it requires practice. Scale is the relationship between landscape elements of a composition and is apparent in all things, the area of plant groupings, the width of paths, the height of trees compared with a house, or the size of statues or sculptures.

These broad steps typify Paul's approach to scale in a garden. Though initially appearing overly generous, when viewed in context of the garden they are appropriate for their setting.

Paul describes his approach as 'generous', indeed it contrasts with many garden solutions where small-scale landscape treatments are implemented that have a poor sense of fit. In any garden design, it is preferable to make landscape elements too large rather than too small.

The second aspect of Paul's work that has application for the home gardener is keeping the layout simple. Rather than creating a large number of small spaces (that issue of scale again), create a few and make them more generous. These suit the scale of outdoors, of the sky and the landscape, and generally they relate well to a house too.

Clarity of concept continues throughout Paul's design approach. Materials are low in diversity and relate back to the house itself so that a colour or material from the house is reinvested in the garden to achieve an appropriate unity.

Paul is firmly of the view that if a designer gets the proportions and scale of a garden correct then other features simply follow on. For the home gardener, this degree of discipline can be difficult; even more so for those who like plants and wish to grow a significant diversity. Yet Paul's characteristic technique of crisply delineating garden beds with English box or other clipped hedging varieties allows a mixed planting that can still be enjoyed within the garden bed without compromising style and order. It is the strong geometries of the hedges and repetition of shapes and form that create harmony and balance in Paul's work.

Critical to success is training the eye. Pacing out dimensions and looking at spacing of trees, the width of paths or the size of a plant massing are all important to successful design. While books and magazines are a great aid in design analysis, visiting gardens allows for this in a direct physical sense—Paul recognises that his innate skills have been honed by travel and visits to other gardens.

Paul used traditional principles of garden design to achieve his signature elegance and simplicity. The principles of proportion, scale, focal point and repetition are used equally successfully in a grand French garden, Eryignac (*left*), and around a small town house in this Paul Bangay-designed Elwood garden (*right*).

Flinders Garden
Mornington Peninsula, Victoria

'The design of rural or coastal gardens is about acknowledging the broader landscape setting, often preserving views and designing an "outward-looking" space. Plants with foliage texture and form that echo natural vegetation are more important than flowers, which are more likely to compete with external views and struggle in challenging conditions. Conversely, inner-city design is usually about "inward-looking" gardens, where striking courtyards, colour and sometimes flowers play an important role in providing a focus to internal living areas.' fiona brockhoff

Biography

Fiona Brockhoff has a reputation for a uniquely Australian approach to landscape design. Her own predominantly native coastal garden designed in 1995, 'Karkalla', established a prototype for sustainable design that is also sympathetic to its setting of sand dunes and sea. Difficult and hostile sites form a common thread through her work yet, in Fiona's view, the challenges of harsh environments often simplify her job. Solutions are clear cut due to the restrictions imposed by natural conditions, with designs driven by these constraints and inspired by the broader landscape. By using a restricted palette of proven plants, materials and design elements, she achieves simplicity and strength in design.

Known for her sculptural use of Australian native plants, Fiona often prunes, shapes or 'tortures' plants to produce living art forms in her gardens. Acknowledging that careful selection of species is necessary for success, she experiments at home with a range of plants to assess their

appropriateness before 'inflicting them upon clients!' Fiona's philosophy is to both use and encourage more natives in gardens, and believes opening her own garden to showcase their potential inspires confidence in others.

Fiona spent a year between studies travelling and visiting gardens overseas. An opportunity to study with John Brookes at his renowned gravel garden in England was tremendously inspiring. Now heavily reliant on gravel in design, Fiona recalls that Brookes' advocacy of gravel made a lot of sense to her—no need to dig, mow or mulch, and plants, if chosen correctly, performed brilliantly. She continues to encourage the use of gravel over lawn, particularly in coastal gardens, where its organic nature and colour melds with the environment and provides waterwise, low maintenance and affordable surfaces. Fiona noted with amusement that her 'lawn rebellion' contrasts sharply with her father's obsession with it, and his devotion to their family 'bowling green' backyard.

Edna Walling was also hugely influential, particularly her use of architectural elements, such as pergolas and stone walls, to link garden areas and provide relationships

1 Gravelled terraces provide an appropriately scaled response to John Wardle's elegant contemporary architecture. Fiona's landscape response integrates the built form within the setting of its landscape.

between buildings and landscape. Her later roadside restoration work and use of natives continues to inspire Fiona in her revegetation projects.

Encouraging edible content in a garden is also a passion for Fiona. Chooks, herbs, vegetables and orchards are enthusiastically incorporated into her designs without sacrificing style. Trained in permaculture, she actively promotes sustainable gardening. She also believes even designed gardens should be allowed to evolve naturally, claiming too much control stops a garden 'making its own pictures'.

With 'low energy input' a priority in garden construction, she utilises recycled elements and local products or materials. Using indigenous plants and local stone, timber, gravel or shell grit to connect a garden to its setting adds credibility. It also reduces reliance on overseas imports and supports local communities.

Fiona's practice is supported by her partner, David Swann, a landscape contractor who constructs most of her designs and ensures quality control. Their work is predominantly residential in rural or coastal areas, though after relocating to Melbourne in 2007, it now extends to suburbia.

Design brief

Fiona's clients, retired nursery owners, were well-versed in plants and recognised that their earlier garden with box hedging and camellias was not appropriate for their new home designed by Melbourne architect John Wardle, or for its coastal setting. Their understanding of plants and the broader landscape led them to seek out a professional designer with a specific knowledge of, and appreciation for, the native flora of the area surrounding Flinders on the Mornington Peninsula. Fiona was an inevitable choice.

Having selected Fiona as designer, their brief was then clear and concise. The garden was to be low maintenance and able to survive their trips away for travel and golf, and provide ample space for their grandchildren to play. In addition, an area to the rear of the house was to be paved to provide outdoor eating opportunities. Fiona, knowing the Flinders environment well, doubted whether this shaded space away from coastal views was appropriate for outdoor eating.

In an attempt to flesh out this limited brief, she approached the architect to understand his view of the house and its potential garden. Fiona saw the garden supporting the house and responding to it; however, on approaching Wardle he observed, 'I'm sure you'll do a good job', a confidence-building response but not one that further clarified her design approach.

Site analysis

Wardle had designed a house for the site that maximised views over its broad landscape setting by placing the house to the rear of the half-acre block on the highest part of the site. There were advantages in this beyond the benefit of views, in that the greater part of the garden was retained as open space and the house was accommodated beneath a magnificent row of mature Monterey cypress (*Cupressus macrocarpa*), so often a sculptural icon of the Mornington Peninsula where they form effective windbreaks. The trees offer protection from south-westerly winds and, since they are to the rear, do not impinge on views. Yet their roots and the shade they create place considerable restrictions on the cultivation of plants close to them.

The substantial house extends the greater part of the width of the site. A dramatic wall of glass at first floor level permits views of the local golf course and the picturesque coastline.

A balcony area to the north end of the house allows for outdoor eating so that the broad views can be enjoyed, while the cypress provide containment above. In the foreground a gazebo in the neighbouring garden adjacent to the boundary required screening. Fortunately, the fall of the land permitted screen planting without intruding upon the view.

2 The mature cypress row to the rear of the property not only contributes to site character, it forms a dramatic backdrop and provides an appropriately scaled setting for the house.

3 Granitic sand offers mulch and a surface for the path that winds through the planting (footpaths don't exist in this locality), with only the absence of plants indicating the pedestrian's route.

The house sat above the site so that it needed to have a platform established to give a sense of solidity and structure and a link between the house and the garden. Main living areas would always sit above the site but the bulk of the house needed to be anchored in the landscape by establishing terraces of an appropriate width.

Access for cars was by way of a gate in Wardle's dramatic 'piano' fence—the vertical timbers appear like piano keys—and this was set back behind an exceptionally wide nature strip. Fiona saw opportunities in this for new landscape areas that would assist in integrating the garden.

Fiona's analysis returned again and again to the house and she was astonished by how little contact it made with the ground. There are entry points, one at the front door, one from the laundry, but in general the house floated above the garden, paths through it generally being passageways and links that allowed for movement.

Design response

Fiona's design response brilliantly captures a real sense of place and locates the large house within the landscape setting in a way that is sensitive and sympathetic. She does this while also respecting and protecting existing site views.

Central to the success of her design is the establishment of generous spaces: a broad sweeping driveway, an extensive informal lawn for grandchildren's play, and two gravel terraces contained behind retaining walls built of vertical timbers. These augmented Fiona's belief that the garden required organic shapes that moved away from the squareness of the house and incorporated the land's natural contours. The addition of carefully placed swathes of planting created intimate spaces for eating and relaxing within the gravel terraces. Moving away from the house, the space opens up with planting simpler and stronger to relate more to the landscape beyond.

Fiona often uses old pier or recycled timbers (smoothed over time) to create fences and retaining walls. Here, she used red gum posts driven vertically into the ground. Fiona's aim was to create a landscape that was gentle and allowed the character of the house to be revealed without competing with it. None of the garden's features are especially strong or bold; the retaining wall, for example, forms attractive curves with the timber cut to different heights to allow flow both vertically and horizontally.

Landscaping the nature strip has not only given the house privacy from passing traffic, but also blended and extended the property into its setting. It provides a refuge for wildlife and forms a strong visual component of the streetscape. Its clever design accommodates practical elements of footpath and visitor parking as well as seamlessly extending the garden. Not surprisingly, the nature strip is the focus of much attention from local residents and visitors who are charmed by its insouciance.

An area between the house and cypress row was paved, using a tombstone builder's granite offcuts, to accommodate a table and chairs for outdoor eating.

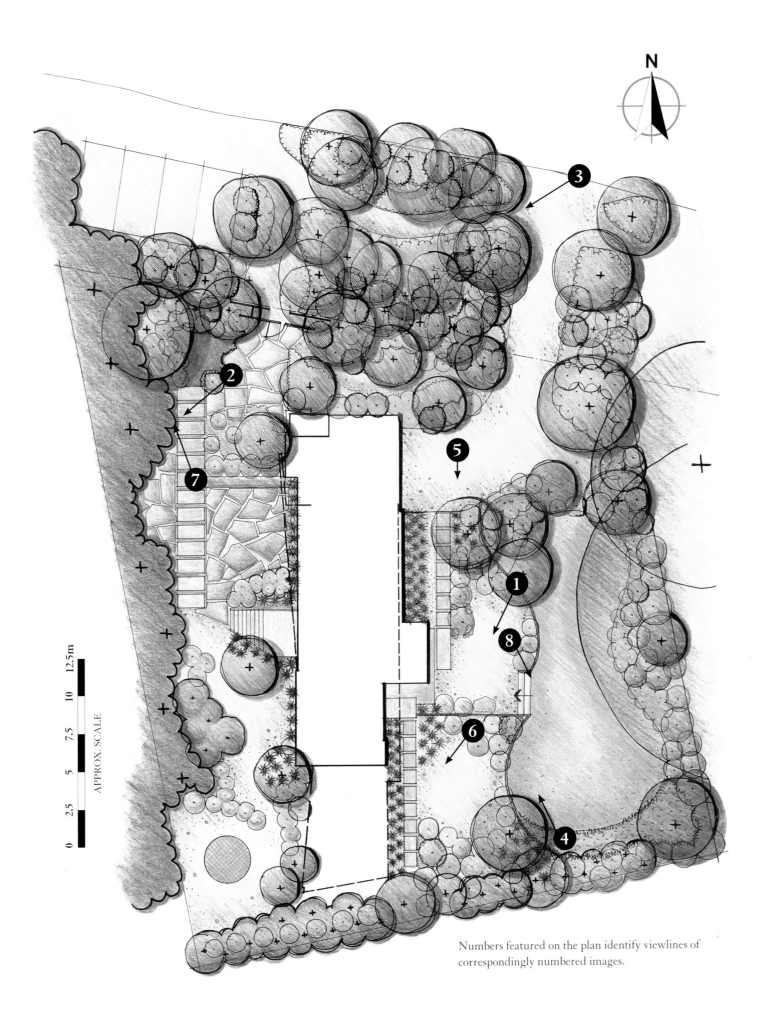

N

APPROX. SCALE

0   2.5   5   7.5   10   12.5m

Numbers featured on the plan identify viewlines of
correspondingly numbered images.

4 Use of vertical timbers allows Fiona to create curving retaining walls and provide a contrast to the geometry of the house.

5 This is a garden of subtleties, changing light and shadow patterns. Seasonal changes in foliage and the reflections created in the generous windows all contribute to its beauty.

Though a visually attractive space, as Fiona foresaw, this south-facing area beneath the cypress canopy has proven cold and uninviting, the northeast-facing house balcony providing a preferable outdoor area.

Fortunately, the owner of the garden was involved in its development. He built the fence and retaining wall himself, giving Fiona a valuable opportunity to work on-site, locating the retaining wall and assessing its impact so that she could judge in situ that its width appropriately accommodated the house. There is much to be said in favour of a designer being on-site during construction since it permits on-the-spot decisions that might alter the impact of a design.

The landscape provides complementary texture and colour to the site, particularly referencing colours present in the house, including its grey timbers and colorbond. Fiona's use of gravel as the predominant paving material and mulch is entirely appropriate for the relaxed coastal setting, particularly as her choice of Dromana topping, a locally sourced granitic sand, provides further tonal consistency with the house and nearby sandy beaches, but also uses a local material which reinforces a sense of belonging and fit with the broader landscape. Fiona's sympathy and sensitivity towards local character is apparent throughout her design. This garden is one of a series she has created that establishes new directions and style for the contemporary Australian garden.

Planting design

A love of plants and a thorough appreciation of their qualities and needs is fundamental to Fiona's planting design. Here, her selection was based on ability to grow quickly, provide a habitat for local wildlife, and create rich pictures through foliage colour, texture and form.

Fiona's replacement of the grassed nature strip with indigenous planting sets the scene and captures her approach to planting design as well as any part of the garden. Familiar with how plants grow, she appreciates the spaces between plants as much as the plants

6 Fiona's planting design shows her preference for foliage impact over flowers, which can inappropriately compete with the more important broader setting. Here she uses (*left to right*) speer grass, bronze New Zealand flax, blue chalksticks, correa and dionella for foliage diversity.

themselves. She explains, 'The way I placed them was to look at the space that I wanted left open and then think about how these elements worked, the pattern and the relationship to each other, which one would I like to have predominant, the grey over the green one, the strappy over the tall one, how growth of trees would affect them, what the background is like, how will shapes relate to that.'

Coastal rosemary (*Westringia fruticosa*) is clipped into mounds to contrast with the loose forms of white iron bark (*Eucalyptus leucoxylon* 'Rosea') and drooping she-oak (*Allocasuarina verticillata*). Coastal banksia (*Banksia integrifolia*) offers a stiff, upright contrast. Other shrubs, including sticky daisy bush (*Olearia glutinosa*), contribute

but it is the grasses dominating towards the road edge (deliberately lower growing for the sake of visibility) that steal the show.

There have been minor conflicts between Fiona and her client for the original scheme involved use of *Poa labillardierei* in extensive drifts designed to sway and dance in response to coastal winds. Sadly, their need for pruning left tufty mounds once a year that Fiona's client disliked so they were replaced with the stiffer, indeed very spiky, spear grass (*Austrostipa stipoides*), familiar to Fiona from her own garden where after fourteen years they remain beautiful, symmetrical mounds.

The nature strip palette dictates much of the internal planting, though there are changes. Selected introduced

Coast Banksia (*Banksia integrifolia*)

plants, for example the purple flax (*Phormium* 'Anna Red') planted above the retaining wall, and low mounds of chalky sticks (*Kleinia mandraliscae*) provide a delightful link between emergent planting and the Dromana gravel paving. The latter's bright blue foliage shines out against the duns and fawns of surrounding planting. Fiona's signature use of natives such as white correa (*Correa alba*) and sea box (*Alyxia buxifolia*) as clipped spheres adds a sculptural contrast to informal plant drifts. This is a garden without hard edges so that planting subtly establishes boundaries to gravelled open areas. Massed Tasman flax lily (*Dianella tasmanica*) forms an apron to the base of the house, growing willingly in quite deep shade. This is one of the few plants that should have a boundary because it grows adjacent to steppers that offer the line to the front path, but it ignores this intention and its quite vigorous growth sees it shooting into spaces between pavers. Fiona quite likes this, however, and her gardens often call for a relaxed maintenance regime, with looseness in planting and an acceptance that plants have a will of their own.

Fiona used her experience of growing plants in the challenging local conditions wisely, introducing seaberry saltbush (*Rhagodia candolleana*) into the garden after seeing it grow naturally in the shaded and dry microclimate beneath cypresses just beyond the site boundary. Other successful plants inlcude wirilda (*Acacia retinoides*), coastal tea tree (*Leptospermum laevigatum*) and large groupings of spreading flax lily (*Dianella revoluta* var. *revoluta*).

Establishing the required screening of the adjoining property to the east, Fiona used native *Callistemon pinifolius* 'Green' for its medium 3–4m height, ensuring sea views were maintained. A sensible choice for this informal, coastal setting, it also offered Fiona 'something that wasn't going to be an obvious screen, that was just a sort of dirty green with reasonably fine foliage so you could hedge it if you needed to'.

7 Seaberry saltbush (*Rhagodia candolleana*), discovered growing successfully outside the garden, prospers as a self-sufficient groundcover, its bright green succulent foliage bringing light to a dry shaded area.

'Fiona's local knowledge and experience
gave us confidence that she could create a
garden that complemented our house and
the surrounding landscape. We're thrilled
with our striking, low-maintenance garden,
and with its clever extension into the nature
strip, we're also delighted we can share it
with our neighbourhood.'

Garden owners

8

DESIGN TIP

Clipped She-oak (*Allocasuarina verticillata*) underplanted with the fountain-like foliage of Spear grass (*Austrostipa stipoides*) add a stunning architectural edge to this relaxed native setting at 'Karkalla', Fiona Brockhoff's renowned coastal garden in Sorrento.

Native plant manipulation

Fiona has always been interested in experimenting with Australian native plants to assess their tolerances from a horticultural viewpoint. She uses manipulated plants to offer attractive contrasts to the free form of more traditional native plantings, believing also that rounded or sculpted plants anchor the garden and provide necessary mass or solidity.

Manipulation of plants, that is clipping or pruning plants to create desired outcomes, is an ancient art. With Ancient Greek origins, the word *topiarius* was the Roman name for the gardener who clipped plants to shape. We use the word 'topiary' in this context, but it is not the only word that describes manipulation of plants. 'Hedges' consist of plants clipped to provide a barrier to vision or movement; 'pleaching' is when a hedge is formed at the top of a clear trunk; and 'coppiced' is when plants are cut back to ground level to create new stems and foliage. Simple pruning, too,

is plant manipulation, designed to achieve increased flower, new foliage or maintain structure. Each is a legitimate gardening practice; each can be applied to native plants. Use of native plants for hedges has taken place for many years. In deciding what plant to use, consider the ultimate size and character you want your hedge to achieve. Lillypillies have been regularly used and offer an excellent evergreen screen. Many new cultivars that grow to different heights are being introduced; *Syzygium* 'Aussie Southern' is excellent to about 6m, whereas the aptly named 'Tiny Trev' suits dwarf hedges to about 1m.

For low hedges, the white correa (*Correa alba*) is excellent and coastal rosemary (*Westringia fruticosa*) is ideal up to 1.5m. Given their greyish colour they are appropriate backdrops for rose gardens and perennial plantings. These are hedges for sun but in shade the native laurel (*Eupomatia laurina*) is an excellent choice.

Di Johnson's renowned Mornington Peninsula garden in Victoria, The Garden Vineyard, uses clipped natives, spheres of Coastal Rosemary (*Westringia fruticosa*) beneath Lemon Scented Gums (*Corymbia citriodora*) and pleached Syzygium varieties, glimpsed in the space beyond, to provide structural contrast for loose perennial plantings elsewhere.

In theory, any plant that responds by producing new shoots following pruning is suitable for hedging or topiary with regular clipping promoting strong, dense growth. The best appearance will derive from those with tight small leaves, rather than large foliage which will become ragged and incomplete when clipped (the reason box is used so commonly). Among native options, tea trees (*Leptospermum* spp.) and *Melaleuca* spp. have much to commend them.

Pleaching is a special form of hedging. By growing trees on straight, tall trunks and then clipping their upper growth into a hedge form, splendid formal effects can be achieved, useful both for screening above a fence where passage is required below or for creating definitions to paths. The native tree weeping lilly pilly (*Waterhousia floribunda*) provides outstanding pleached specimens but other natives are less successful. Many eucalypts are too free-spirited; it is vital to success to have foliage that clips well to shape and has good straight stems to form the framework before being cleared to remove lateral branches.

Finally, coppicing, or cutting plants to ground level to encourage new growth, produces appealing results. Coppiced Snowy River Wattle (*Acacia boormannii*)

produces new dense and attractive silvery growth. Pruning eucalyptus to the ground encourages juvenile foliage sprouts, often seen when red box (*Eucalyptus polyanthemos*) is mown over. The resulting exquisite round, silver leaves are fabulous for cut flower arrangements. Annual cut-backs provide shrubby growth; leave it longer and you obtain small trees as happens with suggan buggan mallee (*E. saxatilis*). The multiple stems, each covered with white wax, are delightful and offer a superb feature in a garden.

Fiona's palette of manipulated plants includes coastal rosemary, all the correas, *Pimelia* spp., *Alyxia buxifolia* spp., *Alyogyne huegelii*, *Olearia glutinosa*, *Pomaderis paniculosa peralia* and *Allocasuarina verticillata*, though after twelve years she finds specimens of this she-oak have begun to fall apart. This reflects one of the most interesting aspects of manipulating Australian native plants—you become a pioneer when experimenting with them and will no doubt experience successes and failures along the way. The plants mentioned offer a starting point for use in the home garden, but research of plants in your local area will no doubt reveal many suitable species. However, Fiona cautions that for successful manipulated specimens, choose healthy plants culturally suited to the particular position in the garden where you intend to feature them.

Russell Page's garden at Haras de Varraville shows highly sophisticated plant manipulation. The crisply clipped box (*Buxus sempervirens*) and hornbeam (*Carpinus betulus*) provide a strong geometry that have great effect, obviating the need for additional colour planting.

Cammeray Garden
Sydney

'My design style is simply to design with soul. You have to make your gardens human, they should be liveable and interactive, not purely visual. I won't build art for art's sake and I don't let ego be the driver. It's very easy to fall into that trap as a designer, but you've got to be a good listener with a keen sense of observation, so you can create a garden that responds to the owner's brief and the landscape around it.'   jamie durie

Biography

Jamie Durie needs no introduction in the horticultural arena; he is known for his infectious, high-energy, public involvement in landscape design. A natural, yet down-to-earth showman, he has emerged from a humble Western Australian mining town childhood and subsequent Las Vegas teenage rebellion to create a gardening empire.

Turning his back on the trappings of fame, in 1997 Jamie exchanged his lavish lifestyle for a carefree 'tree-change' experience. Willing to get his hands dirty, he returned to Sydney to rub shoulders with nature-loving students and acquire his landscape design qualifications. He then established his now multi award-winning design business, PATIO Landscape Architecture and Design, with a modest garden design shop on Sydney's North Shore. A discovery by *Burke's Backyard* guru, Don Burke, saw his life in the spotlight resurrected and he now spreads the gardening message through his landscape design, media, publishing and business enterprises to huge national and international audiences.

Despite his celebrity status, Jamie insists that foremost he is a landscape designer. Genuinely passionate about nature and gardens, he attributes his Sri Lankan garden-obsessed mother with 'planting a seed that wouldn't germinate until many years later'. Particularly inspired by the works of Sri Lankan architect, Geoffrey Bawa, Jamie has a special love for designing lush tropical spaces that entice and invite exploration. He sees his gardens as an extension of the home, designed to increase internal living areas through the addition of a perfectly integrated 'outdoor room'.

Jamie's gardens are known for their contemporary, relaxed style with an interplay of sophisticated and innovative elements that offer function and fun in the garden. Proud to be Australian and part of an open-minded, ambitious young nation, he believes it's time to shake off the European gardening style of our forefathers and carve out our own groove. He hopes to encourage a love of a more weathered, Australian look through natural materials and native plants that, in his view, should be regarded as 'more of a sexy palette' for landscape design.

1 With its elevated theatrical deck, Jamie's design harks back to his previous stage career and years of experience in set design.

A silk screen of irises acquired by Jamie's clients on travels to Kyoto provided the theme for the design of the garden.

2 The upper deck sits like a stage atop three curvaceous masonry steps. *Cyperus papyrus* and *S. involucratus* emerge from the water course, while *phyllostachysnigra* adds vertical interest.

Though Jamie considers himself a relatively new kid on the block, he acknowledges his evolution as a designer. Now an avid supporter of Planet Ark and environmental initiatives, his approach to design reflects this. Sustainability is paramount, reflected in both plant choices and eco-friendly construction materials.

Despite his impressive achievements and unparalleled success, Jamie continues to abound with enthusiasm for his industry. With opportunities through American television, he encourages gardening and environmental responsibility globally, promoting Australian plants and places in the process. Honoured with a gold medal at the 2008 Chelsea Flower Show, Jamie's Australian Landscape exhibit featuring homegrown products, textures and colours continues his showcasing of our horticultural heritage to the world. Having discovered his own path to contentment through nature, Jamie hopes he might 'teach some kids as well, get them off computer and TV games back out into the garden'. Concerned for the earth's future, he intends using his profile to help in its preservation—hopefully engaging the public in their humble backyard, their nation and, ultimately, their planet.

Design brief

In this small backyard the brief was clear and concise, in fact it no doubt reflects the aspirations of many typical Australian home owners. 'We want the garden to be low maintenance, to come home and relax and enjoy it from inside and out, and to entertain in it over summer.' His clients sought an outdoor living space, without lawn, for entertaining six to eight friends, that flowed from and extended their indoor living area. They also admired the simplicity and Zen-like qualities of Japanese landscapes and were keen to capture those elements in their garden.

The simple brief allowed Jamie to have a clear direction for his work. Sensibly, Jamie's clients extended their brief by providing colour boards and samples of materials they liked, together with photographs in books and magazines to help Jamie develop a picture of their taste and style.

Site analysis

This small, rectangular, slightly sloping block is representative of many suburban blocks, yet every site has distinct characteristics and qualities. The designer's skill lies in identifying and unravelling the specific qualities that contribute to a garden's design. Jamie's analysis started inside the house, even before venturing outdoors. His clients had a neat, well-ordered home, with abundant artwork, including an exquisite painting of Japanese irises brought home from Kyoto. The house interior had a distinctly restful Japanese theme, inspiring Jamie's ultimate design.

The whole house block measured about 700sqm, with the rear garden approximately 9m wide by 16m deep sloping upward to the rear. 'Nothing turns me on about a flat landscape,' says Jamie. 'The challenge here was to work with the slope to introduce distinct level changes and make the most intimate areas of the garden feel like they're sunken and protected.'

Two trees on adjacent blocks were, in Jamie's terms, 'money in the bank', providing him with borrowed landscape elements to include in the garden, yet avoiding the need for large trees within it that might have overwhelmed the small space. Fortunately, these trees were beautiful evergreen Sydney natives, smooth-barked apple myrtle (*Angophora costata*), that provided effective screening and dappled shade.

Design response

Jamie's response to the brief was to simply sketch a plan, with broad sweeping lines, on site in front of his clients. He was then able to secure an approved general design response quickly and effectively.

Jamie had a vision for the garden, one that responded to his clients' needs and their elegant home. He says, 'I wanted to make the garden really fluid. I wanted to avoid feelings of square corners and sharp lines. This was meant to feel more like a puddle of wood than anything else, an oasis of timber.'

3 The use of graded pebbles and bamboo is reminiscent of serene Japanese gardens and perfectly addresses the clients' brief.

4 The natural timber colour of the deck melds with the nature reed cleverly used to disguise paling fences, giving the site a consistent sense of colour and form against which the planting is set.

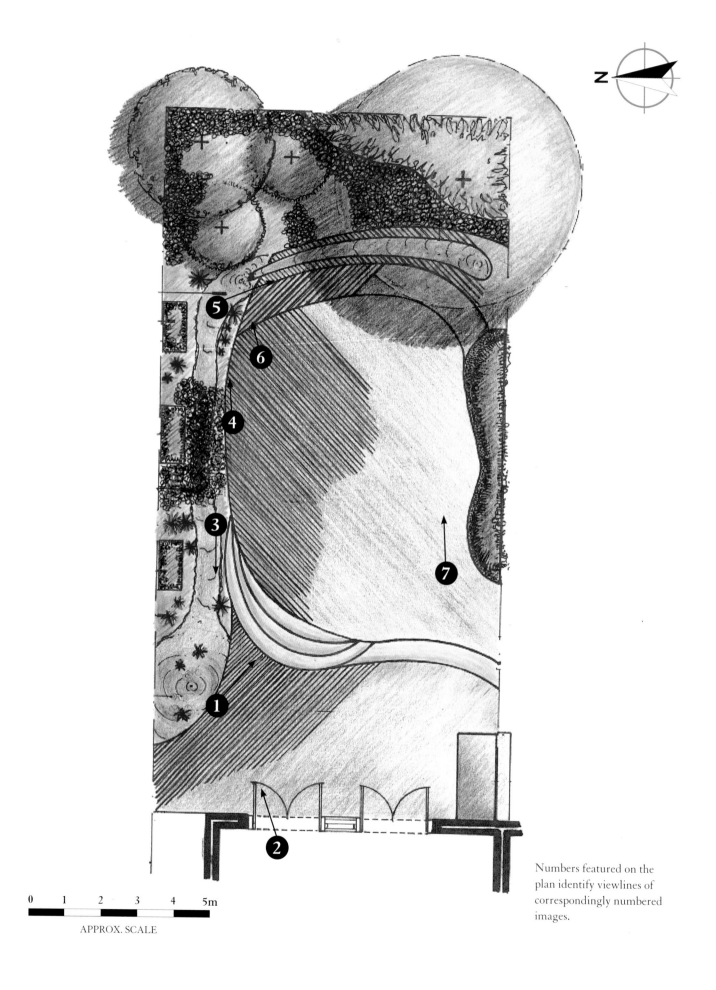

N

0 1 2 3 4 5m

APPROX. SCALE

Numbers featured on the
plan identify viewlines of
correspondingly numbered
images.

5 A planted water channel at the rear of the bench seat provides for refreshment and distracted finger play.

His approach was simple. The garden was built as a series of stages, rising from the level of the house, so that viewed from inside, each layer could be thoroughly appreciated. 'I think change of level is one of the most useful devices in design today,' Jamie says, 'because you can turn anything into something much more seductive, interesting and evocative.' The foreground comprises a deck extending from the house with a corresponding seat hung from the face of a low retaining wall. This is the perfect adjunct to a barbecue and ensures the cook can interact with guests.

Three gracious curved masonry steps at one end of the lower deck lead up to a free-form spacious upper deck, with the middle step extending into the lower level seat. This upper level is the main outdoor eating space where a table and chairs are accommodated. Changes in levels are not so great that safety rails are required so there is no intrusion to the view from inside the house.

A second rendered wall wraps around the upper terrace, forming a planter box to the side and a curved sitting wall to the rear. Cleverly, the rear wall also houses a water feature, a rill that flows around the terrace and splashes over a small cascade at one end. The rill adds the delightful sound of water and creates a sense of coolness, before following the line of a pebble-filled brook to the lower pond, with water logically flowing around the site according to original land contours. Water is then pumped back to the first pond and recycled. The pebbles in the brook are decorative in their own right and carefully graded in colour and size—larger and white to the outside, smaller and black to the middle—to give a sense of deeper water in the centre.

Jamie sees the garden offering two levels of 'cradling' to its owners. At one level the curving form of the upper terrace feels like the garden has cradled its occupants, sheltering them and giving a sense that they are enveloped and protected in their outdoor world. Yet at a more practical level, the curving rear wall that carries the water offers lumbar support, allowing the garden's users to lean back and relax. With the water so close, they can play their hands through it and be cooled, bringing a sense of refreshment and touch to the garden. The seats, hard given their masonry surface, are softened by specially made cushions which also add a splash of colour and comfort.

The garden's dominant character comes from timber, in this case decks of 65mm x 19mm oiled ironbark that has silvered over time. The two decks have timber laid at different angles for visual interest. Their edges are curved, a feature easily achieved with timber and surfaces like gravel and concrete, but more difficult with unit pavers.

Finally, the garden is extensively lit by halogen lights in the steps and retaining walls to give it a night-time life and the sense of an illuminated stage for an evening's entertainment. They fulfil Jamie's mission to satisfy his brief and produce a garden that is as appealing to be in or look out onto during the day or night.

Planting design

Jamie's experience tells him that well-designed small gardens do not require diverse planting. Simple planting solutions not only help contribute to low maintenance, they also look visually stronger. Jamie's plant palette here is small, but chosen with great care.

6 A black pine (*rear*), so loved in Japanese landscapes where it is clipped to give illusions of clouds, is appropriate for the subtle Asian-inspired setting.

Iris was an inevitable choice building upon the beautiful irises in the painting indoors. Their use in the upper terrace gives both flower colour and strappy foliage, a theme that is continued in the use of Japanese sweet flag (*Acorus gramineus* 'Ogon') in the upper water trough, introducing a softness to the otherwise hard masonry backdrop.

Left: Black Bamboo (*Phyllostachys nigra*) produces green stems in its juvenile stage, the lustrous black stems that follow are well worth the wait. **Centre:** The presence of iris in the garden refers to the iris silk screen that established the theme for the garden. **Right:** Attractive aquatic species, Japanese sweet flag (*Acorus gramineus* 'Ogon'), softens the masonry sitting area.

Bamboo, in this case the black bamboo (*Phyllostachys nigra*), is extremely versatile in smaller gardens. Here the layers of stems, one above the next, create shadows within their form and against the fence behind, bringing depth to the garden. Its vertical form provides shade, enclosure, and the perception of space and depth.

Two sedges help to decorate the lower brook feature. Umbrella sedge (*Cyperus involucratus*) and papyrus (*C. papyrus*) break through the water surface to provide reflections and scale, adding a further dimension to the use of water in a garden. They must be contained or cut back regularly to keep them from spreading, but this routine task is worthwhile as they offer great value in the water garden.

Finally, Jamie added a black pine (*Pinus thunbergii*), providing a fitting oriental touch in a delightful garden that is simple in concept, yet rewarding in use.

'Jamie and our fabulous contractor, Nick McCarthy of Urban Escape, were a delight to work with, producing a wonderful, peaceful space that incorporates simple Zen elements whilst acknowledging Australian lifestyle needs. We especially love the way the design flows and that all the water within it re-circulates and renews— much like nature itself.'

7

Garden owners

Thomas Church in his classic garden El Novillero in California introduced deck to extend a concrete paved area where land sloped away steeply. The point of junction between the two surfaces must be carefully calculated to ensure a trip-line does not ensue.

Timber decks

Timber decks provide a useful garden treatment and if they are appropriately designed and constructed, offer a great alternative to paving. When designing a deck, it is important to consider how it will appear in the context of a garden and how it will fit with the garden's style and character. The organic nature of timber makes the use of decks particularly appropriate in informal or relaxed gardens, though with careful thought they can be designed to suit any style of property. In Jamie's design, it is the deck itself that creates the style.

On a purely functional level, particularly on sloping land, it can be much easier to create a deck to achieve a level platform than it is to use paving where retaining walls and fill are required to establish a secure paving base. Freestanding decks, linked to each other by steps, can be submerged within planting to great effect and varied in size to provide communal spaces or solitary enjoyment. Decks connected to a dwelling need to respond to the style of the house and offer good opportunities to link

indoors and outdoors, as well as extending internal floor space. Supplementary hand rails are a legal necessity where the deck is 1m or more above the ground. Rails can be extended to include a pergola and screening lattice if desired.

Decks also have a practical value when existing mature trees need to be retained and paving may cause damage to roots through excavation or changed drainage and aeration patterns. With care, vertical posts for deck structures can be located within the ground to avoid roots. This may need some exploratory digging to locate, or rather avoid, existing roots, work best undertaken by an arborist. Bearers can then be laid above the ground, securing entry of water and air into tree root zones. While this does involve cutting openings in the deck to accommodate the trees and enlarging these as the trees grow, the result is worthwhile as the trees bring immediate shade and drama to outdoor areas and are dramatic features.

This timber boardwalk in Phil Johnson's Olinda garden in Victoria's Dandenong Ranges demonstrates the ability to create curves using timber decking materials.

Decks also allow for variations in level to be established easily. Indeed a step within a deck can form a separate conversation pit within the overall deck structure, thereby accommodating various uses including both a relaxed informal gathering area on the lower step and a larger area on the main level for more formal outdoor entertaining. Cushions on steps can provide character and an opportunity to create different moods and styles.

Roof and terrace gardens are other areas where decking provides a valuable surface. Timber, being relatively lightweight, is more easily carried to less accessible areas compared to heavy paving materials. Decking can also link to raised or portable timber planters, often used in these situations, to provide continuity.

There are practical considerations to be addressed when creating a deck. Timber can be slippery so consider using a milled surface to give extra texture, a small gap between timbers for drainage, and hand rails, especially for older garden occupants. Timber can also be laid to carry the eye along a particular plane. In this case, Jamie laid the timber at an angle, leading the eye across the deck, creating the illusion of depth.

It is important to consider the source of timber used for decks. It should be sustainable and while timber from managed plantations may appear renewable, original forest cover has often been felled for these planting areas.

Different maintenance options provide choices in appearance. Oiling a deck 2–3 times a year will guarantee a rich finish and a degree of protection for the timber, while leaving it to weather naturally produces delightful silvery-grey hues that fit well into a garden context.

Tubs and pots can be placed on decks to soften and decorate, provided they are slightly raised to ensure water doesn't pool beneath and cause damage. Plants can also be trained across deck surfaces, with climbers meandering from the ground below giving a softening effect. Incorporating a pergola with a deck promotes integration and provides a framework for dramatic overhead climbers such as wisterias and roses which combine with the deck to create an intimate garden room.

Construction of a timber deck around existing mature trees in El Novillero minimises root disturbance and ensures healthy trees for instant shade to outdoor areas.

This charming timber deck left to age gracefully in its natural state provides a restful poolside setting for this John Patrick-designed Mornington Peninsula garden.

Toorak Garden
Melbourne

'I believe the essence of a garden is how you feel in it, it doesn't really matter how it looks, it's how it makes you feel. A garden that really works is one where the longer you stay in it, the more sensory reactions you encounter. Through fragrance, billowing plant massing or subtle contrasts in colours or textures, mood can be cultivated in a garden so that people actually feel good within it. I also try to reveal clients' personalities in my designs so they can respond positively and take ownership of the gardens I give them.' rick eckersley

Biography

An uncompromising attitude and pioneering approach for more than 30 years in the horticulture industry has earned Rick Eckersley the highest respect as a visionary landscape designer. His practice, Eckersley Stafford Design, with origins from 1975, is synonymous with sophistication and style, be it for garden renovations or the creation of a diverse range of new residential and commercial landscapes. Having built a reputation for quality, innovative design with his now retired partner, Lisa Stafford, Rick continues the business with four talented staff from his Richmond office, though increasingly works from his Flinders base on Melbourne's Mornington Peninsula.

A grazier's son, Rick took an agricultural route to horticulture. Never shying from new challenges, at 22 he exchanged the rural landscapes of Victoria's Western District for the Kalahari Desert, working as a foreign aid agricultural volunteer. A transfer to Vanuatu saw him begin to garden, establishing productive market gardens to feed local children. Inspired to further his land management knowledge, Rick sought entry to Burnley Horticultural College, unaware that a career in landscape design lay waiting. Offered a newly created mature age student position, he returned to Australia in 1972, graduating in 1975 when residential landscape design was a new phenomenon.

Like most in his era, his career began 'on the tools', where opportunities for paid work were essentially in garden construction. A commission to quantify the financial loss from the Ash Wednesday bushfires in Macedon gardens finally enabled him to expand and move into dedicated design. His characteristic forward thinking continually led him to numerous integrated horticultural pursuits, from small retail nursery outlets, an upmarket florist and decor shop to a boutique wholesale nursery business. His constant search for individual expression gave rise in 2001 to his retail enterprise supplying a range of lifestyle products and landscaping materials.

---

1 The use of 'eggshell' cobbles is reminiscent of an English stable yard and offers delightful contrast to the smooth plane of sandstone, particularly as moss has gathered between the pebbles.

Informing and entertaining gardeners through books (*Outside* in 2006 and *Living in the Garden—Australian Style* in 1993), award-winning exhibition gardens, magazine articles and editorials, charity open garden events and via fifteen years on gardening talk back radio, Rick modestly plays down his influence on trends and directions in Australian landscape design. Often misinterpreted as arrogance, his frustration with conservative, formulaic gardening has seen him continually pioneering new products, plants, and perceptions of good garden design. He has often paved the way for others, popularising patterned pebbling, natural stone, textured paint, sculpture, lighting, simple plant massings and gardens without lawns. Acknowledging influences from Asian rather than European design, Rick often incorporates swirls and textures to provide interest at ground level, adding luxurious, softening plant drifts to stimulate the senses.

Redirecting reflections on his notable achievements, Rick says, 'It *would* be a great achievement if you could get people to change their approach.' He hopes climate change is the catalyst for an overdue appreciation of our own subtle hues and organic coloured landscapes, where, in his view, browns and greys are more beautiful than greens. Despite a preponderance of greenery in clients' gardens, he personally prefers a predominantly native plant palette, convinced that, in cultivation, natives can be as successfully manipulated and reliable as exotics.

Those who have experienced a Rick Eckersley garden will understand the intangible pleasures his gardens evoke. Where many 'designed' gardens lack personality, Rick warmly imbues his beautifully proportioned, functional spaces with soul and the charm and elegance of a lovingly created, traditional country garden.

Design brief

Development of large homes in urban areas that meet current lifestyle expectations often results in garden spaces being fragmented. The building footprint and boundary set-backs contribute to this. Most garden owners still require effective outdoor spaces to support their lifestyle.

This garden was no different with the client wishing to have spaces that not only allowed outdoor entertaining and relaxation but also provided strong visual links to the house.

In part, links to the house were achieved by the owner's own collection of sculpture, significant pieces that were to be located through the garden. These would provide significant focuses within the design and Rick's experience ensured that they would be appropriately highlighted by lighting and planting that permitted their qualities to be appreciated.

Landscape design responses had to recognise the scale of the house and ensure that it would be appropriately settled within the landscape. Massing of plants was required to ensure the overall effect matched the scale and character of the home.

On a more prosaic level Rick's clients wanted a pool as a focus to an outdoor living area.

Site analysis

This large site occupied a corner position in a street of large homes. The architect had wisely chosen to position the house towards the site's eastern boundary and in doing so ensured that realistic spaces were available to accommodate outdoor lifestyle. Thus to the north was a relatively narrow space to the front of the house accommodating entry to the basement garage, while to the east the sloping ground had been terraced to create a narrow strip to what was practically the rear of the house. Few windows opened onto this area.

The largest garden areas were to the south and west. Because the site was wedge-shaped, these spaces were both compromised. To the south the slope was cut away so that changes in levels at the boundary of the site would require a significant retaining wall. The space was triangular, generous to its eastern edge but more confined to the west. Here it linked to the largest open space, an extensive triangle that was open to good light access and was level, albeit adjacent to the street junction. Traffic flows were so light that noise was not an issue.

From the street, little can be seen of the house and it is only appreciated from within the site where its strong form and clean lines with exquisite detailing can be seen. It provides a strong mass, demanding a design response in which landscape can match its powerful impact.

Existing vegetation was of little consequence. There was some cover on the neighbouring property to the south but its elevated position meant that it had little effect on Rick's site. The view of the property from the street was of enclosing walls that secured privacy but more practically provided a retaining wall to ensure a site for the garden that was more or less level.

Design response

Rick's design response recognised the constraints established by the site by clearly delineating specific purposes to the garden's precincts; to the east was a service area, the north provided for site entry while the south provided for more passive outdoor living and,

significantly, as a backdrop for views from the major living areas in the house. By contrast, the largest open space in the site, to the west, was earmarked for outdoor recreation and entertainment.

The architectural interest and style of the house demanded an appropriate entry scale. Rick provided this in a broad set of steps within masonry walls. To their east a driveway led to the basement carpark.

While the treatment of the garden's east side is essentially a service area, it is in fact a service area with some style, with an axis of paving extending the length of the site. Formed from 'Almond' Tasmanian sandstone in squares, this paved area widens and narrows as required.

Walls form the garden boundaries throughout the site, acting as retaining walls as well as offering enclosure. All are treated consistently with Murowash 'Kohl' to which 30 per cent sand is added to provide a more textured surface than the paint alone would offer. This extent of

2 Links were established between adjacent areas of the site to increase the sense of spaciousness as well as provide greater opportunity for family recreation.

3 Service features such as clothesline and airconditioning equipment are accommodated on the east side of the house. Rick changes paving widths to locate these within a mass of lush and luxuriant planting so that any sense of this as a service area is diminished.

paving and walling suggests a hard landscape outcome but with Rick's intense planting treatment, this is far from the truth.

To the south and west of the house, metre squares of the Tasmanian sandstone set at right angles to the house are divided into rectangles by the use of pebbles in bands. This combination of treatments ensures that the paved surfaces not only contribute positively to the site's design but also maintain visual interest on the ground plane. This is most notable where the eastern axis is separated from the southern courtyard, where loose 'Eggshell' cobbles of 10–15cm diameter were placed around trees following their planting.

Retaining walls to the angled south boundary run parallel to the house, reinforcing lines established by the paving. A series of zigzagging garden beds retain the acute-angled line of the boundary fence at their rear, giving the illusion that the beds are parallel to the house. This clever design trick creates depth for planting and simultaneously ensures the shape of the beds corresponds to built form.

4 Rick is a great believer in using large paving modules. Here 1m by 1m Tasmanian sandstone slabs reflect the space and scale of the garden. Retaining the same paver as the pool edging ensures the pool can be seen as an intergrated element.

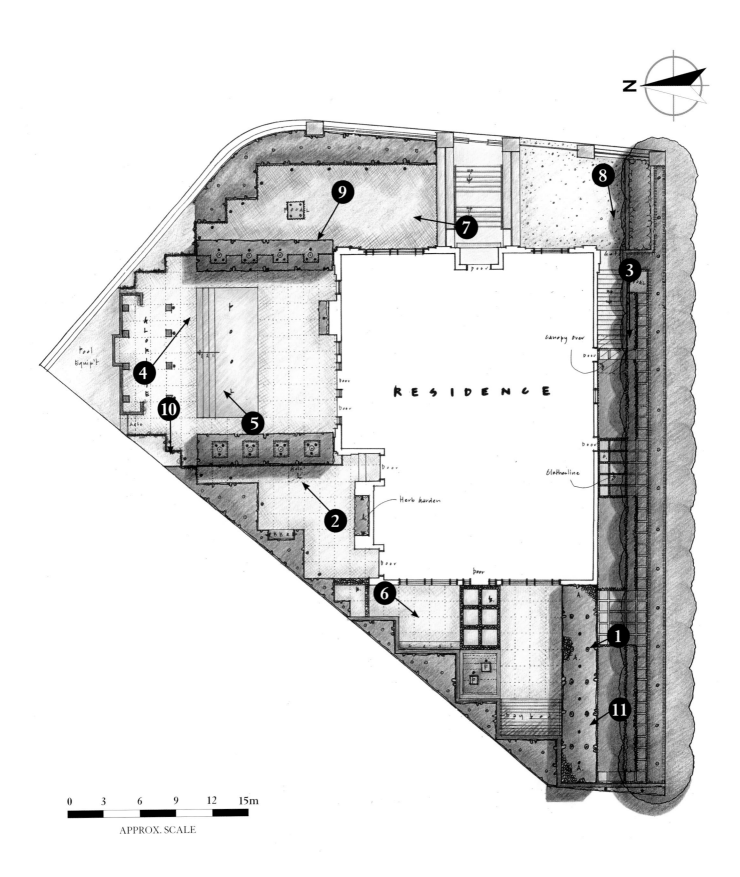

Numbers featured on the plan identify viewlines
of correspondingly numbered images.

5 The cabana is put to good use. Not only does it provide a shaded outdoor area and privacy, it also isolates and screens a second service area that includes the pool equipment behind its western end.

6 The dimensions of the paving feature to the rear of the house match those of a reflective pond and continue the lines of the pond through the paving. The pond accommodates Jane Valentine's sculpture, carrara marble pieces offering reflection in the water's surface, and appearing translucent when uplit at night.

7 To the north of the site, an extensive area of mondo grass provides the setting for an Anthony Prior sculpture positioned to offer a focus to both the pool area and the entry.

Immediately adjacent to the back door of the house, 'Eggshell' cobbles of 5–7.5cm diameter are repeated, in this case the surrounds to sandstone paving slabs. Relaxation and passive recreation dominate this southern garden as is identified by the presence of an outdoor lounge.

To the west a swimming pool drops seamlessly into the 1m x 1m pavers. Behind it a fully serviced cabana, complete with retractable shade awning, holds an Andrew Rogers sculpture. Tree planting within the paving ensures foliage canopies above the paved area, assisting in achieving separation and spatial definition from gardens to the south and north.

One of the most impressive characteristics of this design is the way attractive spaces are achieved in a site that is not large; and while these are separated, there is a flow between them that gives the garden an attractive sense of unity.

Planting design

Rick is at the forefront of using foliage plants in garden designs to achieve year-round lushness that ensures his gardens are always at their best. While there is seasonal change, for example from the autumn colour of selected plants and the flowering of different plants in season, his design's overall impact is of delightful greenery enveloping walls and fences.

Plant selections are not always predictable. To the site's eastern boundary, screening is provided by Chinese tupelo (*Nyssa sinensis*), notable for its dramatic autumn colouring. In the shade at its base, jaburan (*Ophiopogon jaburan*) prospers.

There is a special feature to the northeast where retaining walls hold the slope on a steep site at the edge of the driveway to the basement carpark. A wonderful planting effect is achieved through the use of the fashionable oak-leafed hydrangeas (*Hydrangea quercifolia*) and the unfashionable *Cotoneaster dammeri*.

At ground level to the east, the use of scented plants includes *Philadelphus* 'Virginal' and white daphne (*Daphne odora* 'Alba') underplanted with the dwarf mondo grass (*Ophiopogon japonicus* 'Nana'). The result is lush and green. Japanese sacred bamboo (*Nandina domestica*) and the small-leaved form of Boston Ivy (*Parthenocissus tricuspidata* 'Veitchii') complete planting

8 The combination of oak-leaf hydrangea (*Hydrangea quercifolia*), appreciated for its autumn colour and cream flower heads, and the groundcovering *Cotoneaster damneri* serve well to soften the steep walls above the driveway and offer fascinating contrast in leaf form and texture.

9 *Magnolia* 'Heaven Scent' produces delicate upright pink flowers on naked branches and bring splashes of colour that herald the arrival of spring.

10 Star jasmine is grown over a metal mesh frame, offering an effective screen without consuming valuable garden space. Once mature, it provides a green wall that completely obscures the framework and when in flower brings a wonderful scent to the garden.

to the eastern garden by covering the large wall at the southern end. Their combination of textures and foliage colour bring drama especially in autumn.

In contrast to the eastern boundary, the site is enclosed to the south and north by the fastigiate form of the western red cedar (*Thuja plicata* 'Fastigiata') clipped as an enclosing hedge.

As a complete contrast in form, foliage and seasonal character, cultivars of magnolias have been used as feature trees that emerge from paving. To the south, *Magnolia* 'Heaven Scent' emerges from the cobbled paving where it is pleached to form effective, light, spatial definition. It is the flower's scent that is perhaps most arresting, filling the garden with an exquisite sweet perfume. *M.* 'Royal Crown' offers deep violet-red flowers before foliage develops at the edge of the pool courtyard west of the house. They reinforce the line established by the glass pool fence that secures this area.

Given that space here is restricted, vertical enclosure is provided by star jasmine (*Trachelospermum jasminoides*). It is a valuable contrast to the fastigiate western red cedars that demand far more space, in spite of their vertical form.

Finally, it is interesting to consider the 'lawn' area at the northwest corner of the site. Recognising the constraints that drought places on the cultivation of traditional turf, Rick has replaced its use with a dense planting of dwarf mondo grass (*Ophiopogon japonicus* 'Nana') at 20cm-centres. This is cut back annually and responds with vigorous growth that maintains a splendid, consistent green cover and, because of its density of planting, precludes weed entry. The whole area is irrigated with sub-surface irrigation. This treatment has proven so successful that only occasional plants have needed to be replaced.

Created in 2002, this garden has matured quickly to provide a haven from the streets beyond the enclosing walls. In part, its success lies in good plant selection combined with a density of planting that secures good cover and plant growth to offer an almost immediate lushness.

'The simple elegance of Rick's design not only perfectly complements the rectilinear architecture of our home, but it has enhanced our lifestyle immeasurably. The garden is both a restful retreat and a stimulating, artistic endeavour that, depending on how the mood takes us, offers a variety of separate yet integrated spaces to enjoy.'

Garden owners

11

DESIGN TIP

Rick's innovative use of pebbled paving has great impact, yet he cautions the pleasing visual effects of an uneven pebbled surface should be weighed against the functional limitations of placement of outdoor furniture or frequency and the age of pedestrian traffic as such paved areas, particulary those with loose stones, are less stable than other forms of paving.

Paved surfaces

Rick recognises that paving can contribute to the decorative success of a garden just as much as planting. On a purely functional level though, paving should be appropriate for its purpose. It should carry the load placed upon it, be non-slip, drain effectively (to garden beds where possible) and be appropriately dimensioned to support the activity for which it is intended, for example as a sitting area or path. Careful design, however can take paving to another level.

Firstly, appropriate selection of material can link the house to the garden design by extending an internal paving material or relating the colour of the house to the selected paving. When designing your garden obtain paving samples and place then in context against the house, reviewing their effect in sun and shade and both wet and dry.

Natural stone represents one of Rick's favoured paving materials but he notes the hesitancy of some clients to use it because of a lack of consistency in its form and colour. However, as the paving is the charm and beauty of natural stone is that it reveals variations in colour and texture, and ultimately in wear, that are not apparent in the consistently charactered manufactured materials. Currently, with sources now opened up in China and India, natural stones are very competitively price when compared with manufactured products.

Extended areas of a single paving material can be monotonous so Rick takes the opportunity to divide areas by introducing a second paver. He takes great care in how he undertakes introduction of pattern into paving because in doing so paving scale can be modified and elements of

In this garden, Rick changes the pool edge material to frame the pool. His use of large-particled exposed aggregate complements the style of the featured art work and is an alternative to commonly used small particle exposed aggregate finishes.

the garden may be highlighted. For example, the use of a contrasting paving trim for a swimming pool highlights the pool within the design.

Similarly, a small ornamental pond within a paved area may benefit from being highlighted to make greater visual impact as a result of the paving change. It is vital to consider the overall design context of different finishes. In the Toorak garden Rick has created change in paving by introducing beds of cobblestones, reinforcing pattern in the design and, as paving is loose laid, it also allows for growth of tree trunks and water soakage.

Not only do pebbles provide a striking visual impact, they also can act as a barrier to movement because they are less comfortable to walk on. Just as with other aspects of design, alternative approaches to the use of pebbles within paving can achieve different effects. Pavers laid in a regular pattern within gravel highlights direction and creates an interesting visual impact. Alternatively pebbles might be laid between pavers to create banding patterns.

The use of pebbles to create mosaic-style paving patterns using contrasting coloured pebbles is increasingly popular, reminiscent of Renaissance gardens in Italy where geometric patterns were created to give interest to the garden's horizontal plane.

Interesting as this is, it is not especially subtle and does not always meet Rick's objectives of creating a more natural garden appearance. By contrast, exposed aggregate paving in which gravels are used within concrete slurry and the fines washed off to give an appropriate finish, has an attractive natural look without the risk of the gravel moving or being tracked indoors on footwear.

Paving offers a diverse range of finishes for a garden but most significant in the process of designing paving is appropriateness for the site, style of garden and for purpose and this becomes apparent only when you observe paving in different settings and ask questions about suitability and preference.

In contrast to planting, paving once down is expensive to change. It is therefore important for the home gardener to visit a range of gardens and review different paved surfaces, to collect samples and compare different finishes. No doubt cost is another consideration but overly compromising on this area of design is false economy as paved surfaces need to be long-lasting.

Setting pebbles within mortar avoids maintenance issues of replacing them after inevitable dislodgement and the difficulties of removing debris such as soil, weed seeds or leaves. A simple sweep of this striking path, designed by Phil Stray of Crafted Landscapes, is all that is needed to maintain its impact.

Kenmore Garden
Brisbane

'The great thing about designing for me is the opportunity to take clients a little bit further than they ever anticipated. If you don't, then it's sad and fundamentally you've probably failed as a designer. People should say, "I never expected that." If they remark, "That's exactly what I expected", then I think essentially you've failed. I can't imagine you could have done your job successfully if you have designed something they could have envisaged themselves.' jeremy ferrier

Biography

Jeremy Ferrier brings to gardens his love of both fine art and the discipline of design as an art form. This parallel attraction to both art and design, and an appreciation of the 'living pictures' created in landscapes, eventually led him to the field of landscape architecture. After brief forays into studies of history, english and law, he was introduced by a friend to the idea of landscape architecture as a career. Inspired by early memories of an Edna Walling book of garden plans owned by his parents, he was soon captivated by a profession where he could potentially earn a living from what he saw as the indulgence of 'drawing beautiful plans of gardens and the landscape'.

After completing his studies in landscape architecture, Jeremy began his career independently in 1984, designing for local contractors from his office in the inner Brisbane suburb of Paddington. He now operates his practice of five staff from Brisbane's West End, primarily designing residential gardens, land subdivisions, townhouse developments and educational facilities. Recently, these have included private school grounds where, through his innovative approach, he has created unique and stimulating play environments that have challenged the traditional approach to schoolyard design.

A highly respected landscape architect in Queensland, Jeremy has won numerous awards for his varied landscapes. His work is regularly featured in lifestyle magazines and industry journals, and also used as reference material for landscape design students.

Although much of Jeremy's designing is structured in style, he neither aspires to nor believes there exists a recognisable pattern to his work. Indeed, he is fascinated by the ability of others to create gardens that portray a predictability of style, easily identifiable to a particular designer. He maintains that in his work no two sites or briefs are alike and every garden deserves an individual approach that cannot be replicated elsewhere.

---

1 Viewed from above, the entire garden captures the imagination with sculpture, movement and pattern. The butterflies sway in the breeze bringing a dynamic quality – reflecting light and introducing a sense of wonder.

Motivation and influences on Jeremy's work are absorbed directly from the world around him. Rather than images in books or gardens he has visited, he credits the daily observations of everyday objects, architecture, art and nature with the inspiration for his creativity. Each design is a natural response for him, not laboured over or researched extensively. Never happier than with pencil in hand, a quarter of a century on, it is the intrinsic process of design that still captivates him completely. Genuinely excited by design opportunities, he attempts to push boundaries wherever possible; to encourage a sense of adventure in clients and maintain enthusiasm in every new project.

A garden to Jeremy is a place for artistic expression; a medium for the communication of artistic feelings and ideas through the beauty of nature. He greatly admires Roberto Burle Marx for his expression through landscape and, like Marx, views design as an opportunity for discovery—to extend ourselves, even in some small way, in a direction that we might never before have contemplated.

Design brief

'Barb, I think we better design a garden for you.' So began Jeremy Ferrier's brief for his mother-in-law's garden. It was actually a response to the removal of a large Chinese elm (*Ulmus parvifolia*) to permit light entry into a recently extended deck and renovated kitchen. The thought of removing the tree had horrified Jeremy initially, it was so beautiful, not only in its bark and foliage but also in the shadow pattern it provided. Its removal, however, did open the garden to new opportunities, providing Jeremy with a blank canvas and the simple brief, 'The tree has gone, what are we going to do?'

As an artist, Jeremy's client Barbara gave him the opportunity to explore ideas outside his normal zone, to create a design that was artistic, without any specific functional purpose. The semi-retired professional couple no longer had children at home, so the need for practical elements in the garden was removed. This was extremely liberating for Jeremy in terms of his approach to the design. Also, the garden area lay about 10m below the living areas of the house, thereby limiting physical access to the garden, yet providing a perfect opportunity to design a space purely for visual delight and introduce a pattern to be viewed from above.

Barbara's love of abstract art is apparent as contemporary style paintings, including many of her own works, decorate her walls. The challenge to Jeremy was to extend

The removal of a large Chinese elm (*Ulmus parvifolia*) revealed an enormous hole in the existing landscape canopy.

this inspiration out into the landscape. The garden also had to achieve its objectives while requiring minimal maintenance.

Site analysis

Removal of any established tree leaves a gap—without the enormous Chinese elm this garden was completely bereft of character and form. The tree canopy had spread into the terrace of the house but, more than this, it extended to the property boundary, a creek some distance beyond the house. The result of its removal was a huge void extending out over the now open ground as it sloped away towards the creek bed. The extent of the Chinese elm's canopy meant there was little screening left on the site as it hadn't allowed any other trees to grow beneath it. Views were now exposed of the adjacent suburban street, with houses built on the slope beyond appearing to head directly for the garden.

Fortunately a large clump of bamboo, reaching 6m in height, contributed a restricted screen to lower parts of the garden. Repairing the scars created by the removal of the tree was a vital first step in the design, yet it was also apparent to Jeremy that there were benefits accruing from the tree's removal. There was now an abundance of sunlight and open space, bringing warmth to the garden and enlarging the area visually. The reintroduction of the impact of sky, with its ever-changing moods and colours, also brought a new dimension to the garden.

Analysis of the area showed that some of the local trees performed especially well in the garden, notably the weeping lillypilly (*Waterhousia floribunda*) and there were some good young specimens growing along the creek. Their extended use might allow the openings in the garden's boundary vegetation to be closed quite quickly, while also offering continuity in the design.

Yet the single most important aspect of the site was the distance between the viewing point on the terrace above the garden and the garden itself.

The garden was a focus for a view rather than an extension to the house, and any design had to recognise this.

2 With the vertical distance between the house and garden, it was impossible to design a direct physical link between them; any link had to be visual.

Design response

Jeremy's design resulted from his quick appraisal of the site's constraints and opportunities. On the negative side, as a result of the removal of the Chinese elm, there was the newly exposed view of neighbouring suburban roads and houses. However, the positive elements far exceeded the negatives for not only did he have a large open space to work with, there was also a big clump of bamboo that gave the garden both a maturity and a strong background for any new design.

The bamboo set a theme, that of a jungle character. Jeremy began to develop lines on his drawing paper over a base plan of the site, as he does in all his work. He explains, 'Like most of my designs, I didn't think deeply about it. The design came from pencil lines on a piece of paper—two to three lines and you start to get an idea about the possibilities of the site.' As the plan evolved, Jeremy explored the concept of the garden as a clearing in the jungle. He envisaged a snake coiled up, basking in the sun, then its movement, perhaps disturbed by a

3 Rippled grey concrete pavers simulate the flow of water beneath the sandstone blocks that take on the appearance of stepping stones over a running watercourse.

4 Existing bamboo contributed an immediate sense of maturity and a framework for the new design.

viewer on the terrace, set a flock of butterflies into flight. He says, 'The spiral of the design came first, the rest of the design flowed from that.'

Development of the plan resulted in large sandstone blocks, which were carried into the site individually because there was no bobcat access, coiling like a snake through the design to provide a focus to the garden. These blocks are placed against a mass of pebbles of a similar colour, as if the sandstone blocks themselves had eroded. They also pass through a broad channel, or 'water rill', that runs from below the house in the direction of the creek.

Budget constraints prevented this rill from being a working watercourse, but because of the viewing distance from the terrace above, water was easily simulated through construction materials. The result is a stylised creek bed developed from textured paving stones so that even when conditions are dry, it appears to run to the creek line below. When it does rain, and in normal circumstances heavy rainfall in Brisbane is not uncommon, it channels water to the creek.

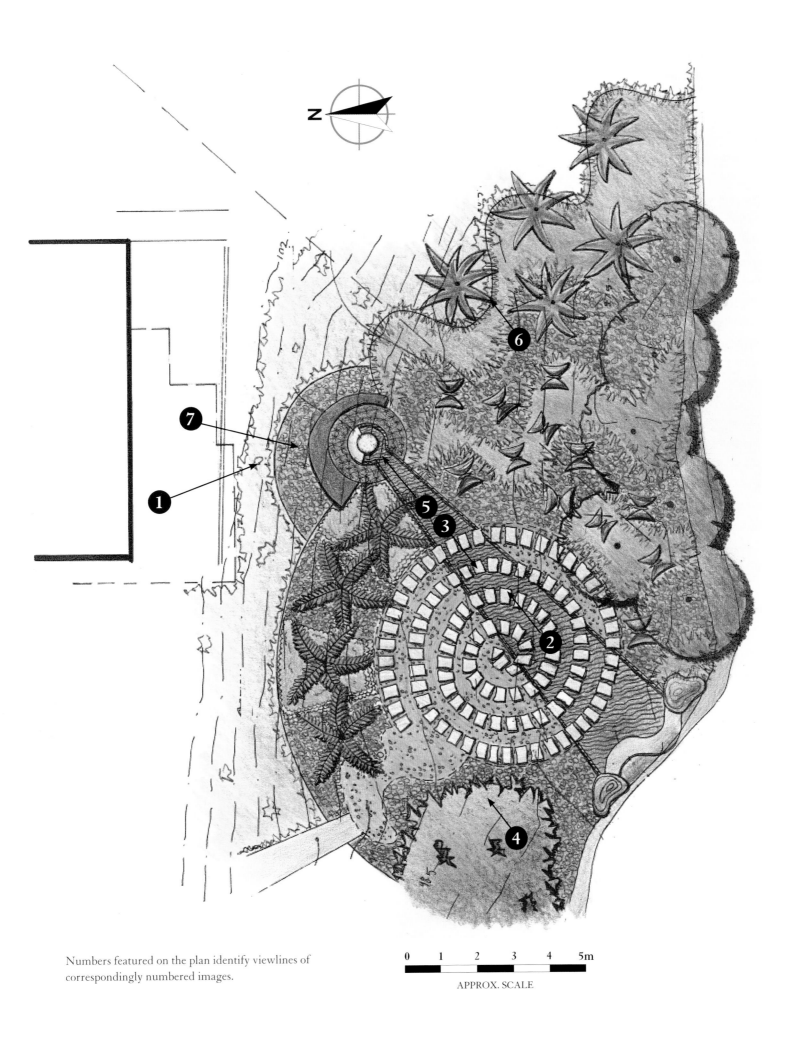

Numbers featured on the plan identify viewlines of
correspondingly numbered images.

APPROX. SCALE

5 A large orb within this sculptural piece appears precariously placed bringing tension to the design. White-flowered impatiens contrast with black mondo grass.

Where water features are normally a valuable part of any garden design for the sound they offer and the way they refract light, in this case distances between the garden and the viewing terrace were too great for either of these benefits to be enjoyed. Yet the rill across the site required a source. In response, Jeremy designed a fascinating sculptured piece that offers tension within the design, the large orb appearing to be precariously held on its substantial solid base. It brings a finality to the alignment of the rill and a strong focus to this portion of the garden.

Extending the concept of the garden as a clearing in a jungle, a sculptural feature was introduced in the form of a flight of butterflies. The butterflies also provide the essential quality of movement—this is often created by water which was not appropriate in this garden. Mounted on metal poles of differing heights sunk

into sleeves in the ground, the concept of butterflies in motion, recently disturbed by movement of the snake, is reinforced. Further, they carry the viewer's eye across the garden, deeper into the shadows of the more densely planted far corner. The slender metal poles used ensure the butterflies sway in the breeze, reflecting light and bringing imagination to the garden. (All this without any damage to vegetation from the activities of their caterpillars!)

It is difficult for many gardeners to understand how an actual garden will look and feel from a two-dimensional plan. In this case, because the garden is experienced predominately from above in what is essentially a plan view, Jeremy's plan gives a very strong sense of the finished garden. While it is usually the vertical elements that give a garden character as a visitor walks through, here it is the patterned swirls and shapes that provide personality.

Importantly the garden has an elegant simplicity, reflected in both hard and soft landscaping elements, so that the patterns created in the design are readily apparent when viewed from above.

The design approach focused on the central part of the garden, after all, this is the feature space to be viewed and admired, yet its boundary had an equally important role to fill, for this offered a setting for the pattern. To be effective, the boundary planting needed to be low key as well as sealing out external distractions. Jeremy chose to enhance existing vegetation, planting weeping lillypilly and Alexandra palm (*Archontophoenix alexandrae*)—indigenous to the creek banks—to secure enclosure for the site.

Planting design

Traditionally, pattern in gardens has been achieved by developing geometric shapes using a dwarf hedge—box, for example, and combining this with gravel or colourful planting. Jeremy's response is a more contemporary approach, drawing its inspiration from cubist art and the work of garden designers of the mid-twentieth century, such as Roberto Burle Marx.

In Jeremy's design, the pattern created by planting is secondary to that of the paving and stone blocks, which are the real focus of the garden. Here is an outstanding example of what can be achieved when plants are selected for form and shape over flowers; the presence of colourful flowers could detract from the appeal of the design. Critically, the planting is closely established so that a dense cover of foliage is provided. Not only does this reduce maintenance, it also ensures the planting creates strong visual impact.

Jeremy recognises the importance of plant selections: 'I wanted nice bands, bands of different colour and different texture. So as a designer I asked "What would achieve this for me?" In this case it was philodendrons and variegated mondo grass. I didn't want a lot of colour, I wanted something very subtle.'

There is no doubting that Jeremy achieved his objective. There are flowers from the white impatiens that light

6 Planting simply merges with the forest edge, consumed by the shadows as if the garden genuinely was a clearing in the jungle. (Rear to foreground): *Archontophoenix alexandrae*; *Philodendron* 'Xanadu' (repeated in foreground) and *Ophiopogon planiscapus* 'Variegata'.

China Gold (*Bambusa eutuldoides* var. *viridiuittata*)

up some of the shaded areas of the garden, as do the variegations of the mondo, but in general the garden foliage is neutral, deep green and green-black.

Many home gardeners are often tempted to increase their plant diversity. Jeremy disciplined himself to a limited palette, using three different forms of one plant in his very restricted range. The traditional mondo (*Ophiopogon japonicus*) is joined by the dark foliage of *O. planiscapus* 'Nigrescens' and the variegated *O.* 'Variegata'. Even this small palette creates contrast of

texture and colour. To this Jeremy added the similarly textured giant turf lily (*Liriope* 'Evergreen Giant') and in complete contrast *Philodendron* 'Xanadu', a low-growing, maximum 1m, evergreen shrub with lobed foliage.

By carefully restricting his plant palette, Jeremy has ensured that his plant-massing effectively responded to his hard surface selections in the garden and balanced their impact. His planting does not compete with the overall effect of the sculptural design.

Contrasting the static and solid elements of the design, the butterflies bring a delicacy and exquisite sense of life to the garden.

'Our garden is a living, breathing work of art that I never tire of. Even our grandchildren are enchanted, endlessly hopping between and counting the stones—but never agreeing on the number! In contrast to the seasonal change, I love the permanent beauty of this garden and the more subtle changes of light and shadow.'

Garden owners

Modelled on nature's own landscape designs, vibrant red sand, cresent-shaped dunes and contrasts of grey-green foliage provide pattern in the Red Sand Garden at the Royal Botanic Gardens, Cranbourne, Victoria. Mark Stoner's 'Ephemeral Lake' sculpture uses white ceramic to recreate the patterns of the salt-encrusted surfaces that remain after water has evaporated.

Pattern in the landscape

Pattern in the landscape can meet functional needs, such as directing movement or defining special-use areas, or be purely decorative. Critical to the success of Jeremy's design for the Kenmore garden is the creation of pattern on the ground plane that allowed full appreciation of the garden from above. Not every garden is suitable for this approach, but gardens viewed from above offer a unique opportunity to re-create the two-dimensional view presented in a plan.

Throughout history, pattern gardens have been popular. Roman gardeners created pattern using box (*Buxus sempervirens*), gravel and planting and this approach continued for centuries. Traditionally, patterns have tended to be formal, often they were focused on the centrepiece of a fountain or pond. Today, more

flexible, informal patterns are developed, as witnessed here. Modern approaches are often sophisticated and interesting, utilising a range of materials as well as plants.

In most gardens, the height from which a pattern may be observed is not great. Jeremy was fortunate in that the viewing verandah was 10m above the ground but, in many cases, the distance of view is 2–3m from a balcony or upper storey.

There are a number of aspects to be considered when preparing a patterned garden. Remember that a pattern garden requires a strong delineation of design. Use subtle differences in texture and form, and contrasts will be lost. For pattern to be clearly appreciated, you need to prepare

Annie Coney's garden in Auckland uses box hedges clipped to achieve pattern, highlighted by a groundcover of scallop shells.

a design where there are reasonable areas of different planting and contrasting colour and texture to achieve good visual impact.

Colour is an easy way to delineate pattern. Many French gardens do so by using colourful annuals within box hedging, but remember that flowers of this type are fleeting and seasonal—glorious at their peak, dull in their off-season.

The use of evergreen plants does offer permanent impact. You could create a frame of box and interplant with different foliage colours, perhaps the gold of golden oregano (*Origanum vulgare* 'Aureum') and the silver of cotton lavender (*Santolina chamaecyparissus*). The traditional potager, where herbs and vegetables are grown within a frame of planting—normally box but consider using rosemary (*Rosmarinus officinalis*) or cotton lavender—utilises pattern and can offer remarkable effects. The great French garden of Villandry is testament to this.

Jeremy has used foliage for contrast, looking firstly to colour, by using the variegated form of giant mondo with other green foliage plants, and then to leaf shape to create variation. This approach can also build upon layers of foliage, drawing from changes in plant height; and with the use of free-form plants, not dependent on clipping, this allows for a bolder effect of sweeping bands and curves.

In addition, Jeremy has looked to hard surfaces to offer pattern. In some respects this is an easier option than that of planting because the materials and colours are permanent. Traditionally, black and white checkerboard pavers have offered pattern but today more subtle, more complex or less obvious patterns can be created using a range of materials. Choices in hard surfaces allow an extraordinarily broad variety of pattern to be pursued. From gravels to slabs of stone, sea shells to mulches, the range of patterning materials is endless.

Pattern design is available to all gardeners and, in some respects, design is made easier, for what you place in your plan is what you will see in the ground—and patterns are relatively simple to develop. For a formal approach, there are examples in many books showing gardens throughout the world. For informal, flowing pattern, fabric designs and samplers offer inspiration. Trace these onto or re-draw them in your plan. Nature itself can also provide sources of pattern; aerial views of land contours, sinuous curves of rivers or mountain ranges, and swathes of natural vegetation can all be translated to pattern on a smaller scale. Developing a picture in your garden using pattern is a great way to express your own creativity or personality. If you have an opportunity to view a garden from above, be encouraged to introduce pattern for great reward.

Even the simplest of patterns can be effective as Kate Cullity demonstrates in her imaginative take on the routine task of lawn mowing in this suburban backyard.

Darwin Garden
Northern Territory

'Living in Darwin occurs mostly outdoors, with the climate and relaxed lifestyle such that people are almost permanently outside. Gardens are for living in, literally, and textural and material changes are not just something to look at, but to be experienced with bare feet and lightly clad bodies. People are not hidden behind layers of clothing—personalities and emotions are exposed so that their needs in a garden are more obvious. This openness and connection with people makes designing in Darwin a unique and sustaining experience.' marisa fontes

Biography

A childhood spent roaming on an expansive villa-style property in her birth country, Uruguay, seems far removed from principal of Outsidesign, the landscape architectural practice Marisa Fontes now operates in Darwin, Northern Territory. Yet there, on her grandparents' estate, Marisa's passion for landscape design began. With an imagination fuelled by her exotic surroundings, including the roar of lions from a neighbouring zoo, Marisa recalls countless hours digging in the dirt, designing and constructing detailed landscapes from sticks and mud, before her family moved to Sydney when she was seven.

Stumbling across her current profession, which promised to appease her appetite for design and the environment, Marisa studied landscape architecture in Sydney. Part-time work required for her study provided experience in urban landscape design—as well as hands-on physical work that confirmed her preference for working from a drawing board!

Marisa graduated with Honours in 1989 and subsequently combined a journey of self-discovery to South America with a trip visiting gardens in Europe. Brief employment in a working-class suburb of London proved challenging, with any notion of creative design stifled by practical needs for indestructible, 'vandal proof' public landscapes. She returned to Sydney to previous employment with a small landscape architectural firm, quickly becoming disillusioned with designing 'leftover' spaces in inner city developments. Fresh from exposure to cultures and lifestyles overseas, she sought an alternative avenue for expression and moved to Darwin on a 6-month assignment with Clouston Associates, an established Sydney-based Landscape Architecture firm, in its new Northern Territory office.

Reinvigorated by the relaxed lifestyle in Darwin, and unusually for her, especially in such a transient city, Marisa stayed permanently. Embracing the challenges of a new culture, climate and plant palette, she now recalls appreciatively her twelve years of learning with Clouston Associates. She feels privileged to have explored the

1 A welcoming 'sense of entry' for this Darwin family garden was achieved through innovative textural and colour changes in both hard and soft landscaping elements.

2 The presence of majestic Royal Palms (*Roystonea regia*) certainly gave the site its character and indeed the house itself was established among them, some growing within a few metres of its walls. Fortunately, with their fibrous localised roots they posed no problem to the house, though they were causing some damage to paths and paving because of their bulk.

breadth and soul of the region through her work from Uluru, Pitjandjara lands in the Great Western Desert, Kakadu and Katherine, to Darwin itself.

Balancing family and professional life, Marisa now enjoys the freedom to operate independently and create on a more personal level in her own practice. Marisa uses her travel experiences and local knowledge of plants, climate and soil to create gardens that incorporate the excitement of foreign influences and the character of Northern Territory life, aiming for a truly unique Australian 'Top End' perspective. She sees garden design as an interactive process involving extensive liaison with clients and allied professionals who will contribute to the creation of a garden. She believes a landscape architect's early intervention in a project will produce a unification between house and garden, guaranteeing 'a final product that is complementary to its surroundings, effective for its users, efficiently procured and environmentally sustainable'.

Collaborating with local Territory architects, her projects have produced award-winning landscapes and her residential designs have had regular magazine and television exposure for their uniquely Australian 'Top End' perspective. She has contributed to environmental publications and been actively involved in membership of the Australian Institute of Landscape Architects (AILA) since 1994.

Design brief

Owners of large gardens often face the dilemma of whether to landscape their whole garden or concentrate on a portion of it to achieve a high standard in a smaller, key location. In the case of this Darwin garden, the owners chose to focus on a small area adjacent to the house, as the most visible and interactive section in greatest need of attention.

Accordingly, the brief reflected the owners' need for an intimate area for entertaining where three young sons could play safely, especially in the context of the existing swimming pool. Whatever the solution, it had to be robust, for the boys already placed considerable pressure on the garden. The clients also realised their house—comprising two separate buildings, main house and guest wing with a breezeway between—needed a focus that brought style and character and, importantly, linked the two buildings. The intrusive pool fence did little to benefit the area. A resolution of the role of the breezeway space was required, as it was the main access to the home, pool and the boys' play area.

Providing a more formal sense of welcome and arrival for visitors was a vital part of the brief. So low-key was the existing entry that visitors tended to park 'out the back' and enter the house from the rear. The clients hoped to address this by introducing a water feature at the front entrance.

Darwin's outdoor lifestyle and the home's position within a broader landscape meant the creation of an intimate outdoor eating and relaxation space for the whole family was essential. Works had already commenced on a rear deck, developing the garden as an oasis in the centre of the larger site. Marisa's brief was to take a site overview, bring the initial work into a bigger picture and achieve a satisfactory design whole.

Site analysis

The 2-hectare site is dominated by mature palms, as it was originally a nursery where mature plants were cultivated. Those that remained gave maturity to the garden and, as they were grown in a nursery grid pattern, provided an attractive formality. On this basis, that part of the garden was retained, with the new design focusing on the area around the house.

While palms characterised much of the property, behind the house were extensive areas of open lawn extending to natural wetlands, filled with native water plants, birds and wildlife. It provided a source of fascination for viewers from the house.

Both buildings that made up the home had gently pitched roofs and sat comfortably within their landscape setting.

The house had recently been refurbished by Darwin architects, Troppo, who introduced open-air bathrooms, well-suited to Darwin's climate. New windows gave views to outdoor areas, providing an opportunity for the creation of a garden focus that could be enjoyed from indoors.

The form of the buildings, U-shaped with limbs extending towards the west, resulted in the driveway bringing cars to the end of the house, bypassing the front door at the centre of the 'U'. A pool existed within the 'U' shape and a pool fence jutted out into the approach path to the front door.

The simple architecture of the house was attractive, yet it lacked personality and character. The dull, straw-coloured, brick paving lacked vigour and, extending the unremarkable colour of house walls, created an overall character that was low-key in the extreme. Fortunately, Troppo architects had injected life to the site by selecting bold colours to enliven internal and external feature walls. This gave Marisa a cue for her design response.

3 The breezeway between the buildings was cramped and uninviting, particularly as construction work had been poor. It had become a place to deposit bikes, prams, shoes, balls and other detritus of family life. A need for storage space was apparent.

The location and colour of the pool fence adjacent to the entry path made it an undesirable, visually intrusive focus for visitors to the home.

The massing of the palm roots had caused lifting of existing paving, with protruding bricks rendering the front path dangerous for visitors and unusable for the boys on their bikes. A step between paving levels in the breezeway area restricted their ability to ride between the spaces. Awkward changes in level extended to the pool where a narrow paved rim was raised 10cm above the pool surrounds. It achieved little beyond providing an inconvenient trip line that caused problems for unsuspecting visitors.

An immature weeping rosewood (*Pterocarpus indicus* 'Pendula') existed to the east of the house, just beyond the breezeway. From Marisa's knowledge of tropical plants, she knew this fast-growing tree would soon bring changes to light and shade in the garden. In three years, as anticipated, it has reached 12m, significantly altering available views and the original microclimate, providing shade and containment to the breezeway area.

Design response

Marisa began this project by getting to know her client thoroughly, in this case, the whole family, so that she appreciated their vision and their expectations from the design. She is careful not to impose her own ideas onto her clients, but to work with them to explore their needs, though her professional expertise comes into play as the project develops.

Marisa's aim was to create interest at ground level that took the eye away from the buildings and provided significant impact to give the garden character. By creating an attractive and interesting ground pattern, Marisa hoped to link the two buildings, bring the site to life and provide visual interest that needed little supplementary planting for effect. This was important for, as well as having little room for planting, there was a need to limit plant maintenance in light of upkeep elsewhere on the property.

The design that was implemented represented Marisa's initial design response. Contrasting with the lines and compartmentalisation of the rows of palms (into which the house appeared to have been 'plonked'), the new randomly angled design using geometric shapes in various concrete surfaces, decks and pebbles, broke out of the palm tree grid and created a more interesting ground plane. Marisa describes the result as somewhat 'whacky'— a plan of complex lines and angles—yet it was adored by the owners for its originality and innovation. It also responded to the excitement of architectural additions, and provided a delightful contrast to the predictability of the broader setting.

Marisa derived the complex pattern of geometries from the site analysis itself: by linking doors and drawing connections between spaces, the pattern evolved naturally. Marisa's initial intuitive design, however, proved a little too complex to construct and some modifications were made, yet Marisa's original vision provided the overall theme.

Corresponding to a similar concept at the rear of the house, the suggestion of a creek bed was included in the front entrance path, with its curvaceous form and scattered pebbles offering an informal contrast to the geometries of the paving. A water feature in the form of a raised red pond and wall, echoed further along the path in a red masonry square planter which was constructed around an existing palm, is the focus to views from the house.

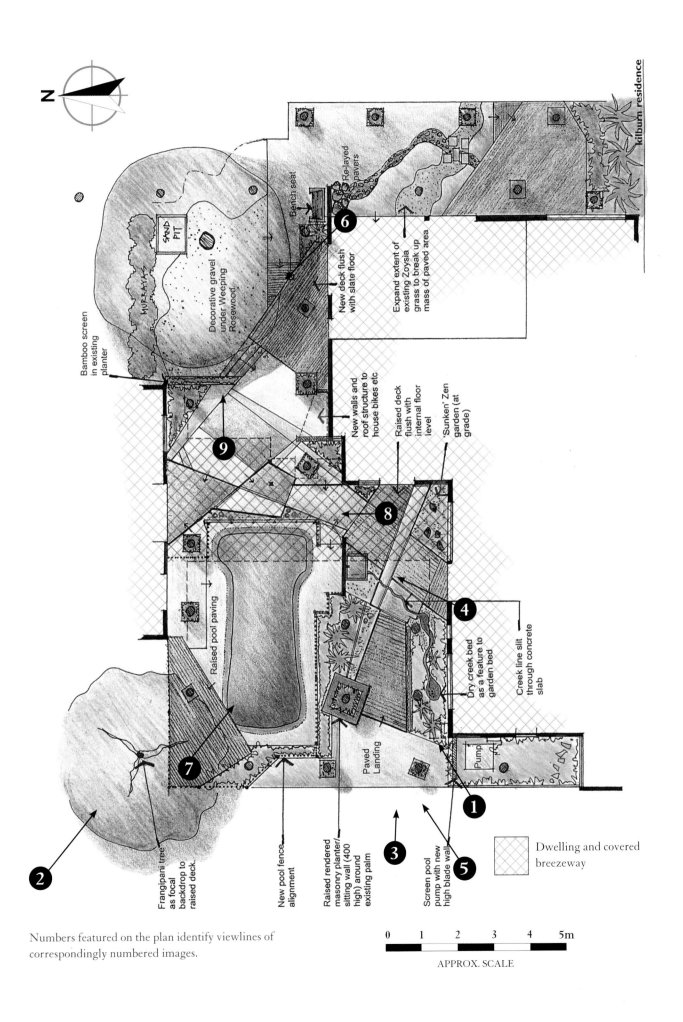

kilburn residence

N

Re-layed pavers

Bench seat

6

New deck flush with slate floor

Expand extent of existing Zoysia grass to break up mass of paved area

SAND PIT

MURRAYAS

Decorative gravel under Weeping Rosewood.

Bamboo screen in existing planter

New walls and roof structure to house bikes etc

Raised deck flush with internal floor level

'Sunken' Zen garden (at grade)

9

8

4

Dry creek bed as a feature to garden bed

Creek line slit through concrete slab

Raised pool paving

Pump

1

Frangipani tree as focal backdrop to raised deck.

7

New pool fence alignment

Raised rendered masonry planter/ sitting wall (400 high) around existing palm

Paved Landing

3

Screen pool pump with new high blade wall

5

2

Dwelling and covered breezeway

Numbers featured on the plan identify viewlines of correspondingly numbered images.

0   1   2   3   4   5m

APPROX. SCALE

4 The creek originates at a formal water feature located as a focus to views from the house. The pond overflow falls onto a black pebble bed that flows through the path to a simulated dry creek bed adjacent to the house.

Small changes in gradient on the site have been addressed by using a variety of paving materials—wooden decks and concrete of different colours and surface treatments—all at a single level. The varied surfaces not only provide visual interest, they offer children a level playground and their distinct shapes and textures stimulate imaginative play. Although a realignment of the pool fence meant the size of the pool area was reduced, the play area available to the children was actually increased by raising its paved surrounds 10cm, creating one uniform paving level and removing the existing raised pool edging. The construction of an angled merbu deck over existing garden beds to the northwest of the pool repeated the use of timber and angles elsewhere and greatly increased useable space, doubling as an exciting diving board for children and a relaxing poolside lounge area for the parents. The pool was originally surrounded by a fence of glass framed in white metal that closely followed the entry path, making it a prominent feature of the entrance. Cleverly, its realignment closer to the pool, also significantly enlarged the entrance area, contributing to a greater 'sense of arrival' pursuant to the brief. The glass

5 Re-coating the original pool fence to a dark charcoal achieved a successful balance between costs, aesthetics and function; restricting pool access, the darker frame colour helping it to recede and the glass panels providing parents with visibility into the pool. Its realignment beyond the palms also created a more generous entry.

6. Apart from pool access this outdoor living area now provides a restful shaded place to view the wildlife in the distant wetland or to enjoy the rich pattern of shadows that the palm foliage casts dramatically upon the paving and walls at certain times of the day .

fence joins the 1.2m-high red masonry wall that doubles as pool enclosure and backdrop to the entrance fountain, before turning 90 degrees along the breezeway that became an outdoor entertaining space. The fountain's masonry back wall had the added benefit of diffusing the sound of the water feature so that from the entertaining area the provocative movement of water is a soothing backdrop rather than an impediment to comfortable conversation.

From a purely practical viewpoint, Marisa created new 1m-high masonry wing walls to the northern end of the main house to hide bikes and play items. She also enlarged the outdoor living area by extending the paving and pushing out the steps to the lower level towards the rear of the house.

This is an effective design solution for a small space within an expansive setting. With innovative angles and diverse surface treatments, the intimate garden area around the home now has a vigour and life that transforms a dull, low-key outdoor environment into one that is

dramatic and lively, with just a touch of formality—as is appropriate for Darwin!

Planting design

There are times when planting inevitably takes a secondary role to the effect of hard elements such as paving, water features and other constructions. Fortunately, existing vegetation such as the palms fitted into the scheme and imbued it with an initial maturity that Marisa was able to build upon. The fast-growing weeping rosewood (*Pterocarpus indicus* 'Pendula') located to the northeast of the garden also provided immediate maturity. Originating from southeast Asia where it is grown for its timber, here it is especially appealing for its elegant, slightly pendulous foliage that provides protection from unrelenting sun.

Royal palms also played an important role. Providing both a tropical feel and vertical interest, they formed a grid throughout the garden that the house had been fitted into. But, for Marisa, the purpose of smaller plants

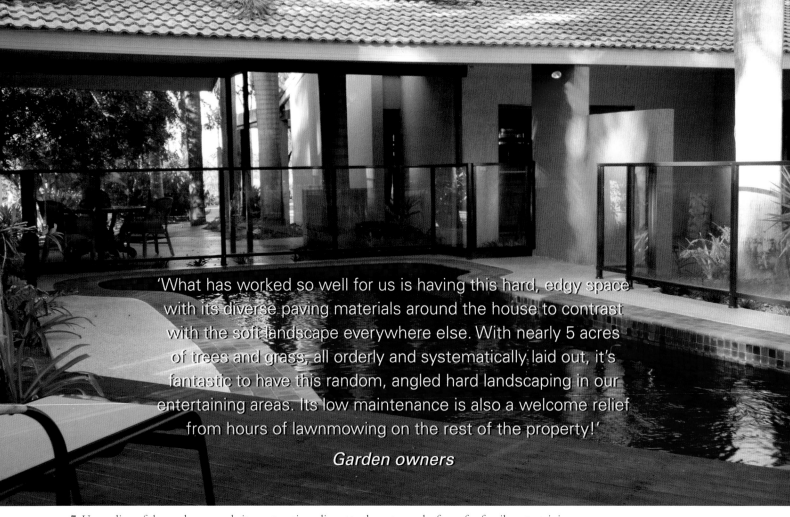

'What has worked so well for us is having this hard, edgy space with its diverse paving materials around the house to contrast with the soft landscape everywhere else. With nearly 5 acres of trees and grass, all orderly and systematically laid out, it's fantastic to have this random, angled hard landscaping in our entertaining areas. Its low maintenance is also a welcome relief from hours of lawnmowing on the rest of the property!'

Garden owners

7 Upgrading of the pool area made it an attractive adjunct to the entry and a focus for family entertaining.

8 The varied surfaces in the breezeway not only provide visual interest, but also offer children a playground where they can use their imagination on the distinct shapes and textures.

Changes in material and shape were fundamental to Marisa's design solution for the site.

was to create interest at the ground plane where plants could provide visual focus to the design. In the Darwin climate, she has the advantage of plantings that offer year-round interest, important since Darwin's gardens also provide for a year-round lifestyle. Interestingly, in her plant palette, foliage textures play a more significant role than flowers. Dragon tree (*Dracaena draco*), *Dracaena marginata*, the variegated form of furcraea (*Furcraea foetida* 'Albo Marginata'), and the large-growing *Yucca elephantipes* all fill this role. However, there are plantings that contribute only flowers, though most offer both flower and foliage quality.

Also included are bromeliads, such as the South American native *Guzmania lingulata* with copper foliage and a strong architectural form; crinums, particularly the gold crinum (*Crinum xanthophyllum*), native to Melanesia and boasting not only fascinating yellow foliage but the most exquisite delicate white flowers; spider lily (*Hymenocallis speciosa*); and both hanging and terrestrial orchids. In the context of this site, planting is used to support the richly patterned paving. It provides texture, foliage colour and flower, though as a secondary element to the

White frangipani (*Plumeria obtusa*) is used to the north of the pool as a feature tree. It provides a fine focus to views across the site and summer fragrance.

decorative paving. In this respect the planting palette in this garden contrasts markedly with planting design in many other gardens, revealing the way that plants can take a secondary and supporting role in the context of a landscape design.

9 Between the paved area and the lawn to the north-east is an informal, pebble mulched children's play area. Here, a Weeping Rosewood is the dominant feature, its shade providing perfect protection for a sandpit and swing.

DESIGN TIP

A generous pathway always provides an effective sense of arrival. In this Melbourne garden designed by Eckersley Stafford Design the entry path becomes a feature in its own right, wide enough to accommodate an attractive fountain.

Garden entry

The experience a visitor has when arriving at a garden is important, for it defines their attitude to a home. A clear, well-defined transition from a street to the front door helps to make a home welcoming and friendly, as well as clearly identifying the point of entry for first-time visitors.

It is worth recognising that for all the spaces we create in a garden, there are functional requirements that need to be fulfilled. For example, a dining terrace needs a level area with a comfortable surface treatment, close to the house and of an adequate size to accommodate tables, chairs and possibly a barbecue. It requires sun and shade at different times, perhaps on the same day. Home garden designers should identify the characteristics required for each functional component of their garden to ensure an appropriate and logical apportionment of space in their plans.

The entry to a home is no different; it has its own specific character and requirements. While there are no specific climatic needs and in fact the climate will be pre-determined by its orientation—sunny if north-facing or shaded if oriented to the south and either sheltered or exposed—clearly there are design approaches we can take to improve its function. Importantly, the character of an entry garden tells a great deal of the values and personality of its owner.

An entry needs to accommodate movement. A path provided as the main access for pedestrian entry should be sufficiently wide to accommodate two people abreast, preferably at least 1.5m. Surfaces should also be comfortable and level. Remember, visitors may be using an entry path for the first time, and, if arriving at night, may not be able to see the path clearly.

A 'sense of arrival' at a garden is important and should include a clear entrance element, perhaps a decorative gate or pergola. The entrance may also be associated with a driveway as a paved plinth extending from parking areas. Selection of a contrasting paving material for pedestrian paths helps to differentiate vehicle and pedestrian access and points visitors in the right direction.

In most cases, the entry route to a house should be logical with a degree of predictability. If not, frequent visitors will inevitably define their own impromptu access path according to 'desire lines'—the most convenient and often shortest possible route of access to the front door. We have all seen these informal paths develop where corners are cut or paths are avoided if they form a circuitous route to the desired destination. However, if properly designed, indirect paths can be successful and bring a sense of intrigue or mystery to a garden.

The use of an apron at the end of a path, where it widens out to offer the sense of a welcome mat, is an attractive and practical option. It also presents an opportunity to link the character of the path and the house, possibly by using similar or contrasting materials for effect. Similarly, a weatherproof porch is a sensible addition at the house entry point, offering a comfortable and sheltered area where conversation can occur—or to leave wet coats and shoes.

A front entrance path can be a place to express personality in choice of finishes and materials as in this Sinatra Murphy design in Kyneton, Victoria.

In Marisa's Darwin garden design, the front door was hidden from visitors' direct view and was located in a shaded area with little visual impact. Marisa's innovative design resolution using bright painted walls, a water feature and contrasting paving materials injected vitality into a previously dull area. By recognising the importance of the arrival experience, the garden entry was transformed and visitors had a strong sense of the direction they should take. Simple design planning can achieve a similar solution for any garden.

Lighting is a sensible inclusion to entry paths to direct the way where the front door is not visible from an entry gate and ensure safety, particularly where steps are involved and negotiation could be tricky after dark. Marisa's use of lighting makes the entry area more appealing and offers clarification of access at night.

Killara Garden

Sydney

'For me, one of the most wonderful aspects of the whole design process is the psychological component, where I need to get inside people's heads to come up with something that I'd be really happy to look at aesthetically that also fits their practical and visual requirements. Balance and restraint are all important, and often it's knowing when to stop that is the critical ingredient to a garden's success.' peter fudge

Biography

Peter Fudge is a household name in Australian garden design. With more than twenty years experience, he is widely regarded as one of Australia's most influential garden designers. His gardens exude a remarkable sense of style, combining an understated elegance with contemporary appeal. Best known for his French-inspired classical approach using hedging and garden rooms, today Peter confesses to a more asymmetrical approach, yet maintains that balance and proportion are critical elements of any design. He attributes this shift in focus to the inspirational Australian architecture emerging around him, believing the use of organic materials in housing today calls for a corresponding organic approach to gardens, where informal layouts and less structured planting both complement and relate to their construction materials.

Peter had the good fortune of spending countless days as a child and young teenager exploring the local wilderness of Ku-ring-ai National Park, north of Sydney, 100m from his family home. He fondly recalls swimming in rock pools, exploring caves and a strong sense of a oneness with nature that has undoubtedly contributed to his love of gardens today.

Faced with the decision of selecting a career, Peter broke with the conventional options open to his classmates, choosing horticulture over medicine and law. This proved an inspired decision, Peter undertook part-time study to gain practical work experience from the outset. He credits working as project manager for Parterre Garden during his study as the foundation of many of his established design principles. To Peter, simple, clean, uncluttered spaces are the essence of sound garden design, ideals instilled early on from both his mentor Annie Wilks at Parterre Garden and his visits to European gardens.

In 1988, Peter returned from inspirational visits to gardens such as Versailles, the Alhambra in Spain and Sissinghurst with a clear vision and passion for his craft. He opened up his own boutique nursery in Wahroonga, on Sydney's North Shore, and used the retail outlet as a platform to

1. The pond on the central terrace is the key feature of the garden and can be appreciated from the upper and lower terraces. Its disappearance around the corner encourages exploration of the garden.

develop his design and construction business. He now concentrates fully on his design. His design staff of six and a construction company of ten form a thriving enterprise where all manner of gardens from the traditional to the modern are created from the drawing board up.

Refreshingly down to earth, Peter is still motivated by the simple pleasures of his work. He loves the challenges of working with new people and turning up at sites that take him out of his comfort zone, forcing him to be flexible and creative in his design resolutions. Plants themselves also captivate Peter, who admits to getting a 'buzz out of choosing really punchy and eyecatching planting combinations'.

Peter's considerable talents, award-winning designs and natural flair have made him a highly marketable commodity. He enjoys a high profile in the industry. His first book *Peter Fudge Gardens* was published in 2006, with a sequel in the pipeline.

Design brief

Being well-known to a client has considerable advantages—they are familiar with your style and approach and have confidence in the outcome, making them relaxed and comfortable in the design process. In this case, Peter was engaged by the son of an ex-colleague, hence his client was very clear about what would result from Peter's appointment.

But Peter was doubly lucky, for his client loved plants and his garden and had a good idea about garden maintenance. It allowed him to work on a design that he felt confident would be well-maintained. Being familiar with his client meant he also knew the family's lifestyle; consequently much of the brief was implied rather than stated.

Sydney lifestyle was important, outdoor space to relax and entertain quite large groups of people, such as friends with their children, and both formal and informal spaces were required.

Screening, too, was crucial and part of this process was the retention of a large peppercorn (*Schinus molle* var. *areira*) in the garden's northeast corner. While a northern

aspect is, of course, the main source of sunlight, and retaining solar access is important, protection from the fierce summer sun in any outdoor eating area is always a priority.

The owners were keen gardeners willing to do much of the implementation of the garden themselves, but they lacked the skills and time to complete the hard landscape elements. The site was steeply sloping and the designer needed to establish effective levels, including terraces, steps and retaining walls. To reduce overall costs, the owners were happy to fill these areas with imported soil themselves. This was potentially an enormous amount of work, but it ensured a thorough and direct influence on the garden by its owners.

Storage and service areas were also important; the owners needed a place for compost bins and clothesline and, if possible, a place where dogs wouldn't destroy the garden but could live comfortably as part of the family. In fact, this garden had a fairly typical brief for a family garden.

Site analysis

The site was north-facing, giving Peter every chance to have the garden benefit from the Sydney climate with its summer warmth and year-round sun. The main constraint, however, was the site's slope: from a high point at the rear northern boundary to the level of the front street, there was a total fall of approximately 4m, and of that nearly 2m from the rear fence to the house alone. This needed resolving, and Peter created terraces to break up the site into a series of manageable spaces, and to offer visual interest in an effective and logical way.

While there was a fall from the back to the front of the site, there was also a cross slope so that the neighbouring garden to the east was considerably lower. Some screening here helped to overcome a sense of overlooking and, reduced the feeling of the garden slipping down the hill. At the same time, this direction offered good views, allowing the garden access to open sky and distant greenery.

By contrast, a tall brick apartment building sat close to the northern boundary, though the garden's length made this

2 The ground floor rear portion of the house was specifically designed to link with the garden, visually by windows and physically with sliding doors that offered a seamless transition between spaces. Indoors and outdoors could effectively be a single space.

quite remote from the house. To the west, a brick house sat on a site likely to be subjected to redevelopment. It is always a good idea to consider the future of adjacent sites when designing a garden so that appropriate screening can be implemented in advance.

The new garden was being constructed at the same time as an extension to the family home. Upon completion of the renovation, access to the rear garden would become limited as there would be no rear site entry point. However, through the early stages of construction, there was access to the rear garden by way of the ground floor garage. Timing issues are not always a site analysis issue, but they were on this project; all retaining walls and terraces had to be established early to permit movement of the many cubic metres of soil that were critical to the success of the design. Miss this window of opportunity and the effort involved in transporting the soil would have become much greater.

Design response

Peter's approach to this design shows some influences from his travels spent visiting foreign gardens. French gardens, with their clean lines, appealed to him above all and examples of French elements often infiltrate his work. This design marries clean lines and great spaces with lush, decorative planting.

To start with, Peter needed to establish levels and determine exactly where to create retaining walls and steps so that a series of terraces was available for the garden's users. Balancing cut and fill goes a long way to minimising quantities of soils that have to be imported (or exported), an important issue in keeping clients happy when they are doing the work!

Sensibly, Peter worked with the topography of the site, retaining the northwest corner as an upper garden terrace, creating an extensive middle section on a lower

3 By creating terraces Peter established a garden consisting of two contrasting outdoor living areas with a decorative garden as a linking element between. The more remote upper north west garden was designed to provide a relaxed, simple shade space where teenagers could hang out, while the lower terrace adjoining the house was the formal area. The Peppercorn that was a feature of Peter's site analysis can be observed to the rear centre right of picture.

level forming the mid part of the garden (by far the largest section) then establishing a third level at floor height of the house to provide for outdoor living space.

This was a practical and attractive solution to the site design; the plan contained hidden corners where one could walk, explore and gain a distinctly different experience of the garden, and there was an area that would be the focus of planting, where the planting design itself created interest. For a family who enjoy their garden and social life, this was a perfect solution.

Access through the site was also carefully orchestrated and modulated. Generous steps lead from the formal lower terrace, inviting visitors into the flower garden. By contrast, a narrower flight of steps links this middle area to the more private upper space. Realistically, there are few options for those using the upper steps—they only lead to an elevated lawn—whereas the lower steps enable

access to the water feature, the service area, and upper steps and thus are logically of a greater scale.

The upper northwestern garden is not yet complete. It illustrates the way a garden can be developed over time, if an effective master plan is prepared. In the short-term the upper terrace comprises lawn under an informal mass of birches, perfect for casual activity for young teenagers (or for weary parents to retreat to!). The long-term plan is to include two decking areas, a small one at the top of the steps and a second larger one at a slightly higher level. This will be dressed by colourful outdoor cushions to provide an attractive shaded gathering space.

On the central terrace the garden divides comfortably into two halves: to the west, massed planting, a stepping stone path and a formal L-shaped pond create a visually rich focus. Viewed from the family room or outside table, both pond and stepping stones disappear around a corner,

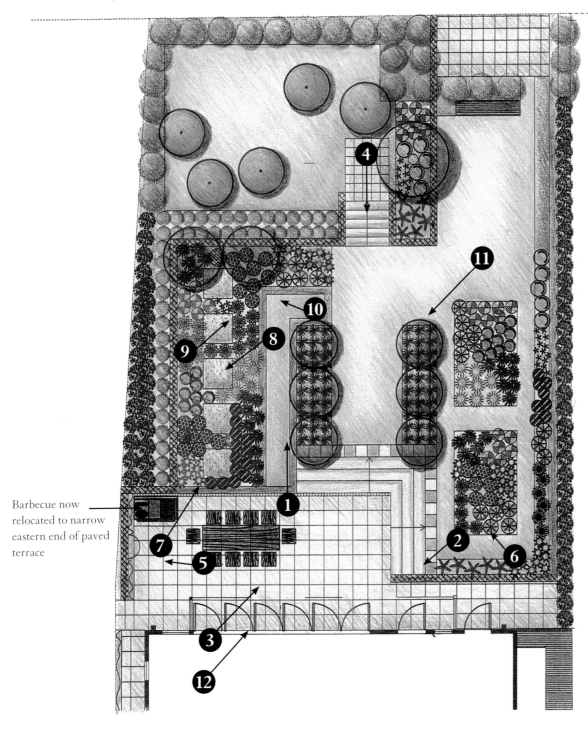

Barbecue now
relocated to narrow
eastern end of paved
terrace

Numbers featured on the plan identify viewlines of
correspondingly numbered images.

0   3   6   9m

APPROX. SCALE

4 The central axis through the garden is framed by the retaining walls containing the steps, but more importantly by the six pleached cumquats (*Citrus x microcarpa*) that reflect Peter's love of French garden design and are essential elements to the structure of the garden.

5 'Kohl' retaining walls are complemented by tonal *Phormium* 'Chief', used to frame a formal wall ornament. Boston ivy, (*Parthenocissus tricuspidata*) adheres to the wall.

intentionally enticing the viewer into the garden to see where they lead. This concentrated area contrasts to the eastern half of the terrace where lawn is more dominant. Beyond to the north west is a small rectangular lawn going into the paved service area, complete with compost bins and clothesline. Evergreen planting that extends directly along the northern boundary wraps around the service area to provide enclosure and screening.

Most importantly an axis extends through the garden effectively creating a spine, binding the design and linking the house to the narrow steps to the upper garden.

Where the upper steps are subtle and narrow, the lower steps are features in their own rights. L-shaped, they echo the shape of the formal pond in the middle level.

Their form reinforces Peter's fondness for 'uncluttered, very simple architectural lines'. However, these steps won't always be 'uncluttered'—Peter's clients see them as a place to put cushions, an ideal location for young people to gather.

The steps also assist in modifying the form of the paved terrace. Instead of crossing the site as a single broad series of steps, the return of the steps narrows the terrace so that to its east end it provides access to the side of the house, as well as a discreet location for a barbecue; whereas to the western half of the terrace the steps added to the retaining wall give the effect of a conversation pit. Too often the presence of a table and chairs clog a terrace and can prevent movement, but not in this case. At 4.5m by 9.5m, the area is sufficient size to accommodate both outdoor eating and movement. This is a large mingling space, perfect for parties and, being at the same level as the family room, passage between them is comfortable and convenient.

By having larger retaining walls and steps close to the house, Peter could reduce the height of the walls to the rear. In some ways, he would have preferred fewer steps and lower walls but, as previously explained, the establishment of levels is an issue of balance and a deeper cut in one area results in higher retaining walls.

6 Island beds dot the lawn on the central terrace. These are formal geometric beds, clean crisp and full of colourful planting.

Interestingly, the retaining walls are not capped by a paving stone but instead are clean and neat, leaving the use of bull-nose stone to the steps matching the terrace paving. 'Kohl', the colour chosen for the retaining walls and step risers, is used throughout the garden. Peter sees its value in its capacity to contrast with all other colours, so that it is perfect against foliage, ensuring appreciation of colour and form when used as a backdrop.

Planting design

Plants have always been one of Peter's great loves. New plant releases excite him with the opportunities they provide for experimentation with colour and textural contrast. Despite his client's plant maintenance knowledge, Peter still attempted to use plants here that offered really good effect with the lowest possible maintenance input. The driving philosophy behind the planting was to soften the formal lines of the garden and, by so doing, assist in creating a garden with a strong visual quality and character.

On a purely functional level, native evergreen plants were selected to provide boundary enclosure; lillypillies (*Syzygium* sp.) to the side boundaries and the beautiful Eumundi quandong (*Elaeocarpus eumundii*) to the rear. This rainforest species enjoys a wide distribution from Cape York Peninsula to northeastern New South Wales, but is rarely used in gardens perhaps because ultimately it can be a very large tree. Yet with its handsome, cream, delightfully scented flowers, borne in November and December, the dark blue fruit that follow in early winter and its slow growth rate, it makes an excellent garden subject that is never likely to become too large, particularly if hedged where competition restricts growth.

Whether plants are native or exotic is unimportant to Peter. He is happy to mix plants from different origins, here confidently using the quandong to provide a setting for a group of five river birch (*Betula nigra*). This birch,

native of eastern USA, has proven to be more tolerant of drought and heat than so many other forms, and is now widely called 'tropical birch'.

The noticeable feature of the perennial plantings that dominate the main terrace of the garden is that the planting blocks are large so that each plant chosen for the design makes considerable impact.

Silver-grey foliage in the borders offers a foil to the lush green that is otherwise dominant. Here, society garlic (*Tulbaghia violacea*), the American *Artemisia ludoviciana*, available in a number of cultivars with different leaf forms, and catmint (*Nepeta* x. *faassenii*) contribute good silver effect—and show good drought tolerance. The grey foliage hues are extended by the use of renga renga lily (*Arthropodium cirratum*), spurge (*Euphorbia characias*), pride of Madeira (*Echium fastuosum*) and Adam's needle (*Yucca filamentosa*), the latter offering a striking visual highlight especially when flowering with its pendulous, waxy cream bells reaching 3m skyward.

7 As they mature, a copse of five river birch will provide an outstanding focus at the rear of the garden as well as welcoming shade to the lawn beneath them. Besides the delightful light green foliage, always so lush in appearance, this species produces superb yellow autumn leaves and bark that ages bronze, before peeling off in narrow strips around the trunk to reveal fresh silver birch colours.

8 Peter rarely plants in groups that contain less than five plants and in large gardens uses correspondingly larger group plantings. **From left to right:** Autumn Joy sedum, lambs ears, lime-coloured Mexican sedum, society garlic, *Helichrysum* 'Limelight' and pride of Maderia.

9 Peter terms his planting design here an "Australian herbaceous border", though recognises this is not strictly correct. There is a wealth of woody and evergreen material as well. **Foreground:** bronze *Loropetaium chinese* var. *cubrum,* Lambs Ears (*Stachys lanata* 'Big Ears') and Spurge (*Euphorbia wulfenis*).

10 Peter is often surprised by the unpredictability of plant performance. Pride of Madeira (*rear left*) has a reputation for struggling and being short lived in clay soils. Yet here it prospers in clay, while at Peter's own home, in what ought to be a perfect open soil, it struggles, reinforcing his view that only by growing plants can the gardener become informed and confident about their suitability.

11 *Helichrysum* 'Limelight' has proven to be an outstanding plant, less likely to scorch than the silver foliaged species, *Helichrysum petiolare,* of which it is a cultivar. Occasional tip pruning keeps it in shape and its lime foliage is a real highlight.

Despite these grey highlights, the greater part of the garden's planting consists of lush greens. This starts with the lawn, when at its best it is a delightful green foil to other planting. In fact, Peter contends that much of the lawn could have been replaced with gravel as the lawn defines spaces too sharply. By contrast, gravel allows plants to spill over the edge of garden beds, to create softness and a sense of space and character so rewarding in gardens. As water becomes a scarcer resource, it is likely that the use of gravel will become more common. However, there is no doubt that in this garden at least, the lawn does offer a lush coolness that provides an effective contrast to the areas of paving.

So many plants bring green lushness to this garden—Oak-leaf hydrangeas (*Hydrangea quercifolia*), groundcovering bugle (*Ajuga reptans* 'Jungle Beauty'), different dwarf escallonias (*Escallonia* spp.), and perhaps most visually striking, *Helichrysum* 'Limelight'.

For contrast, Peter includes strongly textured plants. As well as the previously mentioned yucca and society garlic, the grassy-leafed *Acorus gramineus* 'Ogon', the bronze sedge *Carex buchananii*, the New Zealand flax (*Phormium* 'Chief'), and the giant turf lily (*Liriope* 'Samantha') all make valuable contributions.

Viewing this garden, it is hard to believe that Peter usually designs gardens that show restraint in planting, yet the key here is to remember that this garden has been designed to suit its owners, people who enjoy gardening. This has permitted him to use a broader palette of plants than usual, though that said, his focus has been on plants with low maintenance demands. The result is a garden of great beauty, one that satisfies the criterion of a 'gardener's garden', but not one where its owners feel enslaved.

'We love both entertaining and gardening, and are thrilled that Peter's design accommodates these passions. Our confidence in Peter allowed us to give him enough scope and to trust in his design expertise; this has reaped its rewards, giving us a much-admired garden perfectly combining water, plant foliage, colour and texture, structure and style.'

Garden owners

12

David Kirkpatrick of Outdoor Creations used this sloping site to great advantage, creating an upper terrace and waterfall cascading into a pool on a lower terrace.

Level changes

Changes of level can bring interest to a site and allow for creation of different spaces within it to support various activities. Peter recognised this when he prepared his design, providing an outdoor eating terrace at the level of the house, a middle terrace for lawns, planting and services, and an upper level as a more remote retreat.

What issues need to be addressed when considering a sloping site? Start by calculating the fall. The most reliable method is by undertaking a site survey. This may be costly, so you could estimate falls yourself by using a small spirit level suspended from a taut string line, extending from the highest point of the slope to the lowest and measuring vertical distances to the ground at intervals in between. You can also measure changes by following level courses in brickwork in existing walls or fences. Changes to number of courses indicate level differences and a simple calculation of their height will give an estimation of fall.

Changes in level usually require retaining walls if you are going to create useful terraces and steps to link the levels. Retaining walls are expensive, whether in the simple form of sleepers or as more costly masonry construction. Yet these are better options than inexpensive rock banks in terms of the little comparative space they consume. Retaining walls about 45cm high and at least 25cm wide make great sitting walls, too. Add a coping to the top to make it more comfortable. Do try to make the 'cut' (the soil removed to create a level terrace) equal to the 'fill' you need (the soil needed to fill behind the wall). It saves work and cost. Retaining walls taller than 1m need to be designed by an engineer and may involve obtaining a building permit.

Keep retaining walls to a minimum by creating large areas at each level. In Peter's case he formed a broad lower terrace, though he added interest by varying that width, narrow to one side, expansive at the other. He also balanced the areas at each level to provide an interesting garden form.

Linking levels by use of steps is appropriate. As evidenced here, these can be narrow so they link levels discreetly or broad and generous. Broad steps invite passage from all parts of the terrace and lead to all parts of the garden, while narrow steps are more focused. Peter's wide steps also act as informal seats.

By using the colour of the retaining wall for the riser or vertical part of the step, continuity through the design is established and steps and wall are integrated. The treads, the flat part of the steps, stand out because of their contrasting colour.

Regardless of the type of steps you implement, wide or narrow, curved or flat, there are golden rules to follow. Make tread depth and riser height consistent in any flight

In this informal Victorian garden designed by Emma Plowright, a sympathetic stairway of timber and natural retaining boulders effects change in level without traditional retaining walls. Plants are left to clamber down the slopes maintained on both sides of the steps.

A change in level becomes a feature in its own right in this Tasmanian garden designed by Susan Small with the use of local stone to create a generous flight of steps beneath a stunning Japanese maple (*Acer palmatum*).

and design them to shed water to the side. Outdoor steps should be comfortable and relaxed. They work best if following the relationship that twice the height of the riser plus the tread depth are equal to 65–67.5cm. If the riser is short, say 10cm, then the tread becomes deeper; if risers are taller, say 18cm, the tread becomes narrower. This helps to modify the experience of climbing steps, relaxed and gentle with shallow risers, more demanding with taller risers. However, shallow risers and deep treads take up a lot of space so you need to balance the height of the riser against the vertical level change and the space available. Even where informal rock steps are being formed, this formula provides a useful guide.

Locate steps where they fit into the movement pattern around the garden and carry the eye through the site. You can decorate steps with pots of colourful plants where space allows or use cushions to turn them into resting points.

Peter's design provides an excellent example of how changes in level, steps and retaining walls can be used to give style and personality to a garden. Handled with care, they combine to form the basis of very successful and functional site plans.

Deakin Garden
Canberra

'Art in a garden provides an extra dimension to spaces that would otherwise be solely dependent on plants. Using plants and art to complement each other results in multi-layered spaces that provide stimulation and engagement on many levels. It also provides an opportunity for expression on a particularly personal plane, where pieces of art, sculpture or text are chosen to reflect the individual tastes, style and personality of the garden's inhabitants.' karina harris & neil hobbs

Biography

Karina Harris and Neil Hobbs are talented landscape architects who have married their philosophies towards landscape design, as well as each other. Since 1991 they have worked together in their dynamic Canberra-based practice, Harris Hobbs Landscapes. Renowned for its distinctive and experimental qualities, Karina and Neil's innovative landscape design often incorporates art in one form or another, introducing an intellectual and interpretive element to a garden.

Karina initially began arts/law studies (though half-heartedly) and thought nothing of pursuing a landscape architecture career until it pursued her! Sent an application from her parents to enrol in a landscape architecture course while on study break in Europe, she reconsidered her future and returned home to undertake a landscape architectural degree at Canberra University. With her innate passion for art, gardens and design, it proved an inspired decision, albeit the inspiration was not not originally her own.

Neil was equally nonchalant, originally intending to study architecture. Through a series of friendships and experiences, most notably with his McMahon's Point neighbour and renowned landscape architect Harry Howard, he too undertook a landscape architectural degree at Canberra University. Neil enjoyed working for Harry as a Sydney school boy, propagating native plants and tinkering with small construction projects. So, with his interest in plants, building and architecture, he too ventured down the path to landscape architecture.

During a year off study, Neil worked in Sydney in design and construction, gathering invaluable experience in the installation of gardens (punctuated by extended breaks to watch the cricket over summer!). Eventually compelled to complete his degree, he returned to Canberra, met Karina and upon graduating in 1984 they returned together to Sydney.

Ensuing jobs included positions with landscape architectural firms and later, intent on acquiring more practical knowledge, self-employment constructing gardens throughout Sydney and the Blue Mountains.

1 Critical to the garden's success as an outdoor gallery and display area for hard and soft landscaping material is spatial separation, achieved here through hedging, potted plants and a patterned ground plan.

With the onset of age, parenthood and frustration at Sydney's traffic, they downed tools, moved to the more relaxed environment of Canberra and concentrated purely on design. 'Trained as shiny bums,' as Karina says with amusement, they felt comfortable at their drawing boards, once satisfied that their construction experience had equipped them with a practical base to inform their designs. They also felt the need to separate themselves from the implementation phase of their work, aware of a potential conflict for clients in the packaging of design and construction together.

Now, their much awarded and regularly published work displays their confidence with construction materials and is renowned for its progressive treatment of surfaces and spaces to introduce elements of movement and rhythm in the landscape. As passionate art enthusiasts, they often incorporate sculpture or art pieces in their designs, believing that, particularly in Canberra with its bleak winters, the permanent beauty and provocative influence of an art piece can carry a garden through the seasons. The displaying of text as art—be it for what it says, its

Karina and Neil attempt to create spaces for sculpture or art but in a general way so that an area of stone, for example, can be used not only as a setting for sculpture but also for varied displays, such as pots or a bowl of water with a camellia flower floating upon it.

interesting typography, relevance to clients, humour or ability to provoke discussion and opinion—is a signature element of Harris Hobbs landscapes. As they often use art to fill spaces that would otherwise be planted, Karina and Neil believe art in a garden is also a waterwise option.

Their practice has a broad client base, bridging residential, public sector and commercial spheres and, though big on awards and achievements, is deliberately small on staff. Karina and Neil operate their 'hands on' practice independently, apart from one casual employee, ensuring control and integrity of design is maintained. Outside their design practice both contribute their considerable expertise elsewhere: Neil through involvement in Australia's Open Garden Scheme and the Australian Institute of Landscape Architects culminating in his 2007 appointment as President, and Karina as a lecturer in Design Research and History at the Canberra Institute of Technology.

Design brief

As landscape architects, Karina and Neil's brief for their own garden was much more more relaxed than their usual client briefs, yet no doubt reflected a fairly typical approach to a home garden design. Initially their garden needed to meet family needs— a place where children could ride bikes and enjoy other playful activities.

As their home-operated practice grew, they also wanted a garden where they could stroll from the studio office, to drink coffee, seek inspiration or enjoy a relaxing few minutes with their pets before returning to work. In this way, their garden was to become an invaluable adjunct to their work space.

Their fascination with art, particularly text, drove much of the form of the garden, as it does their work. The opportunity to create a garden as a beautiful work of art was a driving element and for this a sense of enclosure was valuable so that the garden became a place 'where you could really just shut a door and be alone surrounded by beautiful things. We love text. We love art; we buy a lot of it.' Consequently, their garden was to accommodate an extraordinary art collection.

2 At one level, spaces are developed to meet functional purposes, such as access to the house and places to sit, but spaces are also provided for the extraordinary range of art pieces on display.

Yet, on top of this highly personal and private space was a need for their garden to act as a sampler for clients, ultimately so it became an amalgamation of personal and professional needs. Where their ideal design might reflect 'minimalism', they realised there was much to be said for providing demonstration areas of different materials and plants to inform clients, and this had to be achieved within an overall design unity.

The design has grown organically to a brief that evolved as family needs changed. It reflected the changing nature of many home gardens and underlined their dynamic character. They are rarely static and any brief should provide an opportunity for change within a well-structured design.

Site analysis

Just as the brief for this garden has evolved, so too has the site analysis. Elements of the design that Karina and Neil added to their garden in one iteration became parts of the site analysis in the next.

Their garden grew out of a typical late 1950s Canberra block of about a quarter of an acre or 1120sqm. Their home is central on the block, meaning they have a surprisingly large front garden, quite atypical in Canberra suburbs, and the garden wraps around the house offering a sense of a home enclosed by landscape. As windows extend to ground level, the old maple and apple trees in the front garden have survived the garden's numerous incarnations as they have always been always much appreciated site fixtures.

When they first arrived the garden was low key. Scrubby grass, concrete, black plastic and white pebbles covered much of the site and the addition of new plants shoved into holes cut in the plastic was far from appealing! Fence lines were open-wire mesh giving little sense of enclosure. These were filled with seedling cotoneaster and firethorn (*Pyracantha* sp.) whose masses of ornamental berries each autumn were sources of weed infestation for local bushland. A new brick boundary wall from a neighbour's proposed garage was welcomed enthusiastically as it gave enclosure to one area of garden and a theme to build upon in creating enclosure elsewhere.

Enclosure at ground level would offer privacy, but from the upper storey there were superb views of Black

Construction of a wall by a neighbour was welcomed since it provided enclosure and spatial definition. It was turned into a great feature by imaginative planting and its use as a site for art display.

3 At the front door, the garden's cubic forms are present in a series of low hedges that define a diagonal line guiding the visitor to the entry.

Mountain Tower, a night-time feature in Canberra, and views to the surrounding mountains. One objective that drove the design of the garden was their instruction to the house architect: 'We want to feel like birds in a nest and to look down onto the garden in plan.' Karina points out that 'from upstairs, now that the canopy has grown up, we don't actually see a house, just trees.'

Mundane issues do come onto the scene: a driveway to the south of the site leads to an elegant carport specifically designed to have its own character yet allow the character of the house to stand free from it.

Design response

Neil and Karina's garden is proof that a design can gradually evolve and yet achieve a very high final standard. Perhaps it is their realisation that gardens are dynamic and experience change that has allowed Karina and Neil to develop their own garden in a progressive way. Even now, with a garden that has won international recognition, they see it continuing to change and evolve so that when open for the Open Garden Scheme, as it regularly is, it is different on each occasion.

Yet there are permanent elements within the design that, in spite of the garden's evolving nature, offer the site consistency and unity. The use of the garden as both gallery and showroom has given rise to a number of separate 'display' spaces within the design. While the very nature of these experimental spaces calls for diversity, an overall cohesion has been maintained through repetition of shapes and themes. As with any garden, implementing consistent themes creates unity into which variety from art pieces and planting can be injected. The use of cubic forms here, for example, is a repetitive element, taking the form of clipped hedges of various heights, varied forms of masonry blocks used as stands for pots, and places for art installations such as the wraparound graffiti block in the rear garden which are also used as sculptures in their own right.

Clipped hedges are used to create the spatial definition so vital to the garden's success, but are not the only method employed. The checkerbox pattern of foliage and concrete in the front garden forms an individual space at ground level, while its grid pattern continues the geometric theme used elsewhere. A similar use of contrasting paving in the rear garden further unifies site design. These geometric shapes are also clearly read when viewed from upstairs,

Squares of planting, mod-grass and textured paving are laid intermittently between smooth paving, offering subtle delineation of space, repetition of geometric shapes, and an experimental showcase for clients.

satisfying Karina and Neil's wish to look down on a garden in plan. Inclusion of other cubic forms of modified height and depth, including concrete blocks, stone walls and two innovative cubes covered with artificial turf, further help to differentiate spaces, continue themes and provide year round structure.

4 Varying sizes of terracotta pots feature throughout the garden. Plants are rotated: evergreen topiary specimens, succulents, patio roses, grafted maples and colourful annuals all feature, but the consistency of pot form is the secret to a cohesive result.

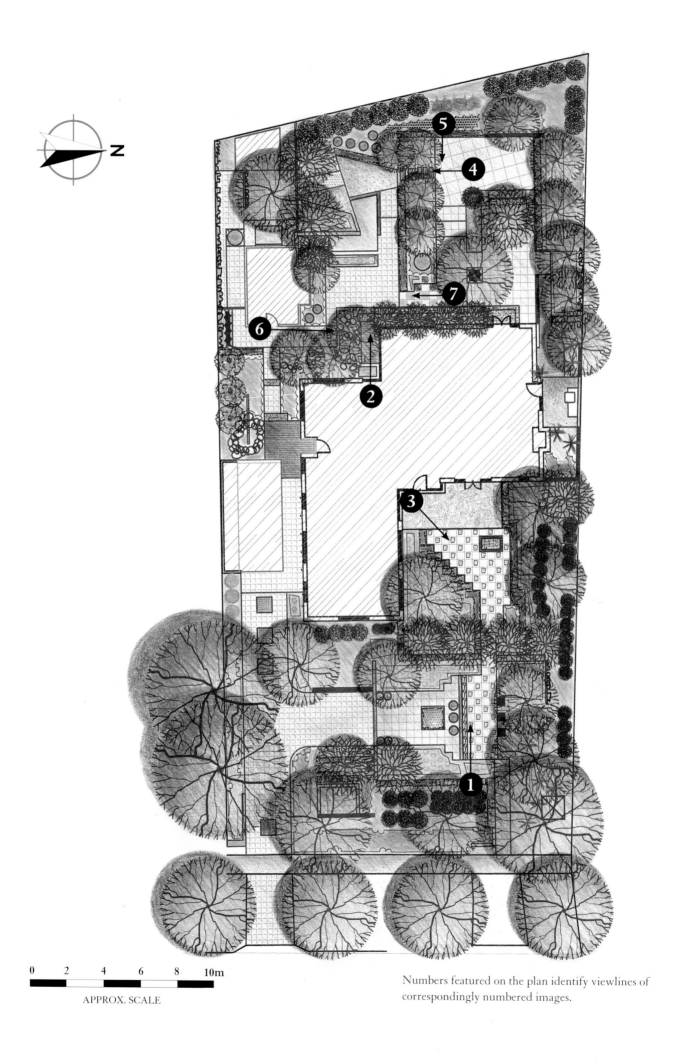

APPROX. SCALE

0 2 4 6 8 10m

Numbers featured on the plan identify viewlines of
correspondingly numbered images.

Another unifying element in the design is the extensive use of terracotta pots. Though variable in size, they are of one colour and form to provide links throughout the garden's individual areas.

Karina and Neil's love of text as a garden feature inevitably sees text used in this garden. One example at the front gate, a red and yellow art installation of '16s' not only delineates the site boundary but provides an amusing identification of the house number. On the horizontal plane are the letters 'Sweet', an example of how art can be read at many levels. On one hand it reflects an Australian use of the word, indicating things are good, on the other it celebrates their daughter's sixteenth birthday – Sweet 16. Whether visitors fully grasp the levels of interpretation at play in the garden doesn't concern Karina and Neil, but they are pleased when visitors stop and question the purpose and meaning of their sculptural pieces.

Despite repetition of certain design elements there is a diversity of paving and construction materials that appear to fly in the face of accepted design principles. This is

Typography is a continuing theme, reflecting Karina and Neil's particular interest in text.

The use of artificial turf to cover large cubes in the rear garden takes a landscape material away from the mundane to provide an exciting visual effect and a contrast to the norm.

Spaces are vital to the gardens' success. Importantly, each art piece is separated, becoming an individual focus for its own space, in this case by utilising *Buxus sempervirens* as an enclosing hedge.

where the garden fulfils its educational role, providing clients with an opportunity to appreciate the qualities of a range of paving materials. Brick, natural stone, pre-cast and in-situ concrete, pebbles and cobbles each play their part in the design.

There is a strong sense that this is a garden that marries experimentation with confidence. It bridges many aspects of design including an interest and acknowledgement of landscape as poetry and a love of plants that recognises their diverse values.

Planting design

Talk to Karina and Neil and their appreciation of, and love for, plants comes through clearly. Plant diversity in their garden is included not only to provide instruction to clients but to satisfy their own passion for plants.

Importantly, plants are used to provide strong blocks in masses that define and divide space, creating areas for display of sculpture. The boxes (*Buxus sempervirens* and *B. microphylla* var. *japonica*) and the box-leaf honeysuckle (*Lonicera nitida*) are fine examples of plants meeting these roles. The boxes are also used as topiary in containers, as pyramids, cones and balls to offer textural continuity. On a larger scale, these shapes are repeated in the form of clipped bay (*Laurus nobilis*) domes in large planters. Spatial separation though doesn't need to be total, just the presence of plants can suggest separation, achieved here by the trunks of three silver birches.

Vital to the planting balance within the garden has been the use of a combination of deciduous and evergreen plants. On one hand the use of deciduous plants recognises seasonal change; however, if a predominance of deciduous material is used then the garden is left too exposed in winter, too much of its structure is lost. Use of balanced planting ensures that the garden retains form through winter and the joys of autumn colour and spring flower are also available.

Nowhere is the garden's changing nature more evident than in the planting. Because they love plants, Neil and Karina enjoy changing their garden. An area that is

5 A row of the Himalayan Birch (*Betula jacquemontii*) with their superb silver trunks offers subtle spatial separation through the centre of the garden and gently delineate garden areas.

6 The kitchen, hub of family life, has glass walls that permit complete integration with the surrounding garden which, in part, has its experimental character reflected in the combining of Australian native plants, such as Mat Rush (foreground) with exotic species including the silver birch.

Front to rear: *Dianella* 'Little Rev', *Dianella* 'Little Jess', *Olea europaea* 'Verdale', *Melaleuca linarifolia:* part of changing garden planting.

currently filled with the dwarf flax lily (*Dianella* 'Little Rev') was firstly planted with irises, then with euphorbias. The degree to which planting can be changed depends upon growth rates. Trees and many woody plants take time to mature, their placement tends to be permanent. By contrast, perennials mature quickly and, as a result, offer flexibility and change. They also allow different effects to be conjured up. Here, there are architectural and textural plants that offer a foil to sculpture, such as sedges (*Carex appressa* and *C. glauca*), the enormous gymea lily (*Doryanthes excelsa*), flax lilies (*Dianella tasmanica* and *D.*' Little Rev') and mat rushes (*Lomandra* 'Little Pal' and *L. confertifolia*). Balancing these and bringing informality to the garden is a selection of what might be described as 'romantic' planting including flowering trees—*Magnolia* 'Rustica Rubra', M. 'Elizabeth', *Malus ioensis* 'Plena', *Cornus florida, Pyrus Calleryong* 'Red Spire'—that bring colour and impact to the spring garden; and shrubs including camellias, azaleas, daphne, lilacs and roses.

Changing microclimate and increased shade has reduced the rose palette to rewarding cultivars, including the shrub rosas 'The Fairy', 'Buff Beauty' and 'William Shakespeare', and the climbing roses 'Mrs. Herbert Stevens', 'Mermaid', 'Paul's Lemon Pillar', and 'Sombreuil'.

Neil and Karina's love of plants is complemented by the value they place on simply being gardeners. The process of working with plants provides them with familiarity and knowledge, and also extends to a willingness to experiment. A recent visit to Tasmania has seen them introduce Tasmanian plants into a specific garden area where *Richea dracophylla*, *Tasmannia lanceolata* and celery pine (*Phyllocladus trichomanoides*) are now growing, benefiting from the cool Canberra climate.

The home office is a discrete building, beautifully scaled so that it does not dominate, but still accommodated within the garden. Its role as a meeting place for clients dictates many of the garden's themes.

'Our garden is constantly
unlike architecture which
the landscape is always c
around us with a range o
coming into play, not lea
fact that the garden is de
and the micro-climate a
accordingly. In many way
the significant dynamic
of garden design

Garden owners

7

DESIGN TIP

Painted poles installed on an angle bring a modern artistic twist to the garden of John Van de Linde in Victoria's Yarra Valley.

Garden features

Neil and Karina's garden extends their remarkable collection of Australian art outdoors. While most home gardeners would not wish to see their garden as an outdoor gallery, garden features can undoubtedly provide valuable focal points within design, carrying a garden through seasonal downtimes and reinforcing a garden's style.

While the idea of using a piece of original art is attractive, its cost may be restrictive. Yet today there are any number of affordable materials and decorative items to enhance every style of garden. Marrying decorative elements with a garden's style is important. For traditional geometric gardens, a formal, classical urn is appropriate, either beside steps or a gateway or as the centrepiece to a paved area or herb garden. Here, the emphasis is on scale, balance and symmetry.

By contrast, in informal gardens the feature can be more relaxed and located asymmetrically. Such gardens present an opportunity to use features that reflect a sense of place. On a rural property, rolled barbed wire or weathered timbers would fit well. At Karkalla, Fiona Brockhoff's Victorian coastal garden, she uses Tepi Islander's decorative poles as a focus to informal planting, a delightful tribute to Australia's traditional land owners. Elsewhere, she uses sandstone columns and a 'thong' pyramid as sculptural elements. Both symbolise location and site character, the latter also being low cost, colourful and humorous.

Apart from sense of place, garden features may be chosen to reflect personalities and interests of garden owners, providing an appealing personal element or meaning to a space. Much pleasure can be derived from the selection of a garden feature that evokes memories of loved ones, exotic holiday destinations or important moments in time.

There is an enormous range of materials for use as a focus within a design. Water features, sculpture, seats, urns,

This delightful bronze statue by a pond in Normandy, France reinforces the relaxed atmosphere produced by water in a garden. Its lifelike character is gentle and appropriate and part of its charm.

sundials, trees (particularly those of strong form), boulders or elements of modern life can all be suitable. Text, not usually considered by gardeners, is often used by Neil and Karina as a decorative element for its ability to express values or ideas, inject humour and stimulate discussion.

By selecting a decorative element with colour or textural interest, either contrast or harmony can be achieved. Furniture could be painted to complement planting, perhaps in a little deeper colour than the surrounding flowers. The use of a polished metal ball will permit reflection of nearby plants, offering a contrast as rich as within planting schemes themselves. Integration of a feature within planting may provide a more subtle

appeal, especially effective where partial coverage can disguise a poor quality or less individual piece.

Selection of features that are appropriate in scale is important; pieces need to relate to the scale of the broader environment unless a specifically prepared location is used that changes the scale. In general, focal points need to be large enough to be successful and it is better for a piece to be larger rather than smaller. Small features trivialise a garden and it is better to combine a group of these pieces so that their total impact is enhanced. However, there should be some consistency between them—of shape, style and material—to give a sense that they belong together.

Features can be framed, leading the eye to them—in, for example, a pergola or tunnel of hedges where their structure provides enclosure. Equally, the use of a circle of paving may serve this purpose, offering a setting for a feature which should be either centrally located or placed towards the rear.

It is important to separate focal points within a space to avoid duality and conflict where several items may be competing for our attention. Use of uplighting can emphasise or transform the effect of garden features at night.

A sculptural representation of plant cell structure used in a metal gate in the garden of Kate Cullity and Kevin Taylor illustrates how a decorative feature can double as a functional element.

Rusted shoes and handbag provide a perfect potted feature in the garden of Sue and Warwick Forge, being both personal and appropriate to the romantic nature of the garden and historic home.

Peppermint Grove Garden
Perth

'In designing landscapes you have the ability to affect and manipulate the way in which people interact with their surroundings. The reward comes when we see people thoroughly enjoying their existence in a space we've created. By attention to detail, and drawing on everything we've ever read, seen, learnt or experienced, we strive to produce gardens containing functional spaces that obviously, or often subconsciously, enlighten the experience of the inhabitant.' ryan healy & matt huxtable

Biography

Newforms Landscape Architecture, established in 2001, is the result of the joined forces of Perth friends formerly operating independent practices, Ryan Healy and Matt Huxtable, who met when studying for landscape architectural degrees. As the name suggests, their business is founded on the principle of bringing 'new forms' to the realm of landscape design, be it through their adventurous ideas and construction techniques or their innovative use of plants and materials. With a passion for residential design and the opportunities it provides to shape both the look of the land and the outlook of people, Ryan and Matt have established a reputation for contemporary and inspirational gardens.

Ryan and Matt share design responsibilities in their practice, yet Ryan's original studies in commerce underpin his role as managing director. Now grateful he transferred to landscape architecture, he attributes his flair for art and economics, and his part-time student work as a landscape contractor, with enabling him to

successfully run the business as well as design distinctive gardens that showcase the firm's skill in construction. Matt, too, has practical experience in technical aspects of garden-making, building his own designs prior to their partnership. This layering of skills brings a higher level of expertise and a holistic approach to the design process.

Matt developed his interest in gardening and the outdoors by osmosis, having grown up in a large garden enthusiastically cultivated by his artist mother. He believes her creative influences played an important part in fuelling his enthusiasm for design. Both directors now believe their design ideas challenge and complement each other, giving strength and resolve to their creations.

Matt and Ryan place great importance on site architecture in shaping landscape design, with Ryan citing the architectural icons of Frank Lloyd Wright, Richard Neutra and Santiago Calatrava as motivational influences. Believing architecture and landscape design should exist as one, Ryan states, 'They are the same thing as far as I'm concerned. The only difference is one strives to keep water out and the other to keep it in.' This philosophy

---

1 Paving slabs across the water in the front garden allow close inspection of the fish that inhabit the pond.

governs much of Newforms' work and results in gardens that show a strong relationship between building and landscape.

Both Matt and Ryan have a firm commitment to environmental issues, believing successful Australian design results from a creative response to the limitations imposed by our challenging climate and scarcity of water. Recognising that solely using native plants to overcome these constraints is restrictive, they believe that by combining more architectural and structural elements in a garden, as well as using a palette of carefully selected, proven, dry climate species, both a sustainable and visually striking garden will result.

With an ambition to develop their practice on the international stage, they are enthusiastically looking to a future in the residential, commercial and show garden fields. Already achieving both design and construction awards, their highly respected and much sought after gardens indicate their goals are firmly within reach.

Design brief

An existing garden can sell a house but it may then be inappropriate for new owners. That was the case in this Peppermint Grove garden when Ryan and Matt were invited to redesign it. Their initial brief was to remove the large pool extending across the entire rear garden and relocate it to the front garden, enabling a subsequent redesign of the rear as a space to accommodate entertaining on a large scale. Overlooking was a concern on the northwestern boundary and a guesthouse at the rear of the property, currently isolated by the pool, needed to be linked to the main dwelling by improved access.

The front garden was untidy and needed an overhaul. A glass wall separating inside and out meant the area was a major focus from indoors, as well as the arrival point for visitors. The clients sought a modern upgrade, though nothing too abstract or hard-edged, that offered a sense of arrival with WOW factor, capable of providing a multitude of features, including a fish pond, kids play area, a viewing terrace for the tennis court below and

a strong visual focus from inside. The area also had to retain a car turning circle directly associated with the entrance to the house.

Continuity through the site was vital too, though difficult to establish with two very discrete areas. With the swimming pool to the rear of the site and the tennis court to the front, there was a sense that the site simply didn't flow. Narrow boundary spaces prevented a more obvious link but Matt and Ryan were asked to provide a stronger sense of a visual continuity through the site.

Site analysis

This was a steeply sloping and very long block, entered via a 60m driveway from the lowest level at the street and rising over a height of 3m to the level of the contemporary two-storey house. The house and rear garden rise a further 3m to the rear boundary.

There is a strong sense of place on the site derived largely from a limestone retaining wall to the north end of the grass tennis court immediately to the east of the driveway. The house itself is built of concrete blocks painted cream to marry with the limestone that characterises this part of Perth. Grey-framed windows provide a strong contrast to this cream stone but they also give extensive views not only over the garden but across the house's broader landscape setting.

To the eastern boundary, a second limestone retaining wall extends along the length of the upper part of the site, until at the site's northeast corner a small guesthouse occupies the width of the block. This gives privacy from the north and, being only single storey, permits excellent light entry to the large courtyard almost entirely occupied by the swimming pool. There was inadequate space remaining for outdoor entertainment.

In the front garden, mixed vegetation clothed much of the south-facing slope to the tennis court. Worthwhile trees were identified for retention but, given they were located on a sloping site, the level of their roots and the base of their trunks placed some constraints on the works implemented around them.

The site is extremely exposed. The northern aspect makes much of it unacceptably hot, except where the guesthouse and existing trees give shade. Being on a site that is, for Perth, quite elevated, the garden is also exposed to strong winds. Climate modification was important if the garden was going to provide an appropriate family setting.

Design response

On a site where a garden has already been created, a designer has the role of retaining the best of the original while introducing new themes and directions that reveal their own skills and meet the needs of their clients. Here, there were functional components that did work, the tennis court and driveway, for example; others, as explained in the brief, required attention.

The swimming pool clearly needed resolution. After consideration of the northern orientation of the existing pool and access issues which would severely complicate and increase costs of filling it in, the designers presented their clients with an alternative to relocating the pool to the front, south-facing garden. They suggested the pool be reduced in size to accommodate both swimming and entertaining areas, simultaneously providing transition and linkage to the guest wing. This option was accepted.

The next task was to establish a unity for the site to give a sense of continuity and cohesion. Spaces to both the east and west of the house were constricted so passage between the two areas would always be difficult, yet a sense of continuity and flow could be established by design elements. Working with the character of the area, the designers recognised the appropriateness of local limestone, choosing to make it one of their consistent site elements, albeit not always as a natural material. In the rear garden, a limestone-coloured manufactured paver was recycled.

Neither Matt nor Ryan was comfortable with the slope to the front of the house. It failed to provide an appropriate outdoor sitting area, lacked a sense of place and was

In the rear garden, the pool was reduced in length by a quarter. The additional paved area provided a visual link and direct access to the guest house.

2 Matt and Ryan specifically identified tree levels so they could take measures to protect mature specimens which would offer shade and an established air to the new garden.

3 Tree trunks are located in holes through the deck which are easily enlarged as the trees grow. The sweep of the deck, curving around existing trees enhances the feeling of movement.

Replacement of a wire pool fence with a glass one provided a sleeker finish and created a strong sense of continuity through the site.By shortening the pool, an alfresco dining area was established that included a barbecue built into a low retaining wall against the eastern boundary. A limestone coloured paver previously laid on a sand base was recycled saving clients' money and reducing waste. New pavers of the same material were interspersed with the old so that discrepancies between colour of old and new pavers were disguised.

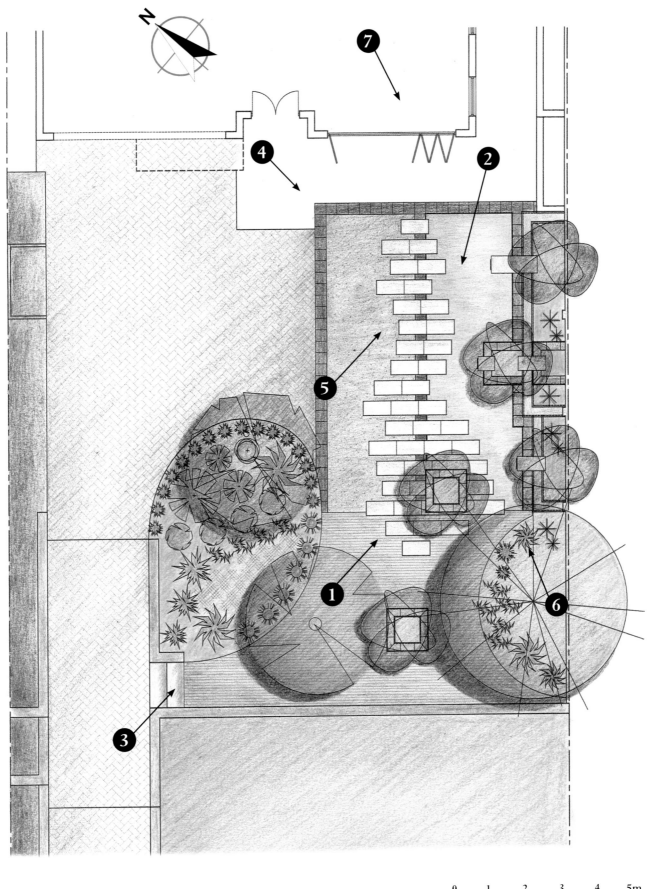

Numbers featured on the plan identify viewlines of
correspondingly numbered images.

4 Clever lighting design ensures the garden's beauty continues into the evening.

5 Three sheer descent waterfalls tumble from Donnybrook sandstone pillars enhanced by fibre optic lighting that creates shadow and drama after dark.

difficult to maintain. To pave the area would have required a filled base, potentially damaging existing trees by compacting and burying their root zones. In addition, it would increase the height of the tennis court wall and place further load on what was already a significant weight-bearing wall. Their decision to build a deck bridged the tree roots, allowing permeability for air and water to maintain tree health.

Matt and Ryan's response to the requirement for a fish pond was exciting and innovative. Recognising that the front garden was visible from a mezzanine office within the house, they saw an opportunity for a design 'to be an art piece in plan'. In a major technical undertaking, a long rectangular pond, covering approximately 32sqm, was built along the eastern boundary using the existing limestone retaining wall as its foundation. Constructed landscape elements were designed to double as housing for the working parts of the water feature.

Rectangular limestone-coloured pavers form a central spine to the design with all other landscape elements converging upon it. The steppers, protruding at various lengths into the pond, appear to float over the water in an attempt to blur the segregation of water and stone. Charcoal-coloured pavers interspersed between the floating steppers link to the capping on the three raised planters within the design. The paving spine extends into an area of Ord River pebbles. Their soft brown colour links with the oiled batu timber deck, providing a sense of visual cohesion. Repetition of charcoal-coloured pavers in a strip border provides separation from the driveway.

The existing driveway curved around a magnolia tree (*Magnolia* x *soulangeana*) towards the entrance to the house. The curve was continued to completely wrap around the tree before making its way to steps leading up to the deck from the driveway.

By framing the pool in a charcoal bull-nosed coping the form of the pool was highlighted. It also unified site design as it repeats the use of charcoal pavers in the front garden.

It's not only the repetition of limestone elements that now links the front and rear garden. By painting the boundary walls a claret shade, specifically created to reflect the claret in the feature clinker bricks of the home, Matt and Ryan provided a link that extended through the length of the garden, but also selected a colour that was a dramatic foil to their planting. Throwing foliage and branches into silhouette, this colour brings warmth through the winter and a sumptuous character and feel to the garden at all times.

The claret paint finish was also used to the pool's western end where there was a need for increased privacy. Creation of a water wall using limestone-coloured schist stone cladding achieves this and with the repetition of the cladding and the claret tones in both the front and rear gardens, this whole courtyard space is reinforced as an element of the larger site.

Establishment of the greater part of the site for recreation is completed by careful placement of all the site's service elements—airconditioning, clothes drying and bins—in a narrow space to the west of the house, ensuring that the original aim of the brief, to maximise the sense that the garden was a single space, is achieved via the passageway to the east.

Planting design

Being an existing garden, integrating established trees was a priority within the planting design. Enveloping them with new beds of complementary planting, as well as incorporating one of the existing two mature honey locusts within the deck structure, achieves a successful blend of the old and the new.

The background claret wall colour featured throughout the garden was a major influence on plant selection. Three crepe myrtles were added in raised planters, specifically chosen so that their summer flowers provide a perfect match to the painted walls. Underplanting of existing trees with spiky, architectural foliage, and then using a similar plant palette along the eastern boundary, maximissd the drama of the background colour as a foil for planting and, at night, it positively glows under the glare of lights.

(*Crinum pedunculatum*), with their stunning white, fragrant flowers and bold green strap-leaf foliage, provide an eye-catching contrast to the claret wall along the shaded eastern passageway.

Other plants with complementary burgundy shades are used throughout, including double-flowering plums (*Prunus blireana*), burgundy cultivars of New Zealand flax (*Phormium tenax*), Moses-in-the-cradle (*Rhoeo discolor*) with its purple leaf undersides, and the purple-foliaged *Alternanthera rubra*.

Silver shades provide contrast, most notably through an olive (*Olea europaea*), bird of paradise (*Strelitzia reginae*), spineless yucca (*Yucca elephantipes*), and cushion bush (*Leucophyta brownii*). The addition of other architectural foliage plants such as turf lily (*Liriope gigantea*), *Draceana marginata* and *Dietes iridoides* reinforces the modern character of the garden, and these are also drought-tolerant.

In the rear garden, filtered light created by a shade sail erected over the entertaining area provides a suitable

Diverse planting forms consistently referencing purple foliage or flower provide screening to the eastern boundary and a softening of the edge to the ornamental pond.

environment for espaliered sasanqua camellias along the south-facing wall of the guesthouse. A Chinese tallow tree (*Sapium sebiferum*), planted to provide a canopy over the built-in barbecue, brings claret shades via stunning autumn foliage to further complement painted boundaries. Espaliered olives decorate the western pool boundary wall, tough enough to tolerate pool splash and children's play.

Evergreen climbers, creeping fig (*Ficus pumila*) and star jasmine (*Trachelospermum jasminoides*) provide coolness and cover throughout the year. The deciduous climber *Wisteria sinensis* adorns the guesthouse and injects spring colour and fragrance with its mauve flowers, as well as yellow autumn foliage tones to the rear garden.

Right: Trained along marine wire, sasanqua camellias bring an elegant restraint to the formal outdoor sitting area. Their underplanting with turf lilly provides an evergreen swathe of foliage at their base.

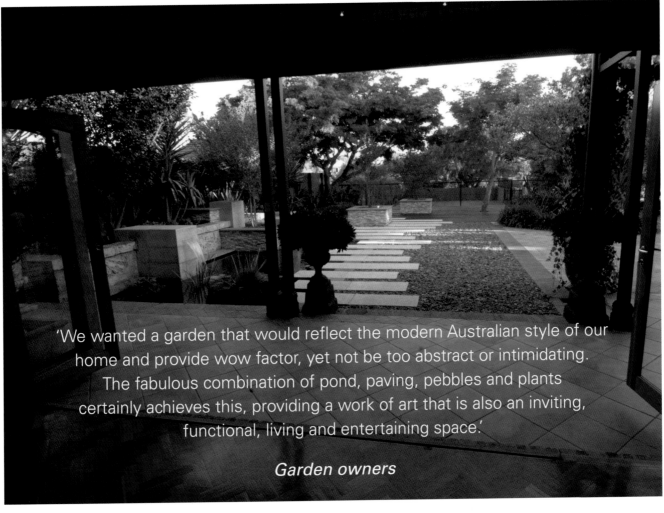

'We wanted a garden that would reflect the modern Australian style of our home and provide wow factor, yet not be too abstract or intimidating. The fabulous combination of pond, paving, pebbles and plants certainly achieves this, providing a work of art that is also an inviting, functional, living and entertaining space.'

Garden owners

DESIGN TIP

Water can reflect architecture, the sky, design features or plant foliages depending upon its setting. In this example, designed by Sinatra Murphy, the latter three are reflected on the surface of the water. Reflection of light itself can invigorate a dark space.

Water features

Without water, gardens as we know them obviously couldn't exist. Apart from the role of water in securing healthy plant growth, water offers the garden designer endless opportunities to bring life and excitement to a garden as evidenced in Ryan and Matt's Peppermint Grove design.

Home owners, too, may consider the potential for water features in their gardens, particularly as modern plumbing technology allows for environmentally responsible use of recycled water for such features. Before doing so, consider what water can provide; reflection, refraction, coolness, habitat, life, movement, humour, play and a wonderful sound—not to mention the life source for our plants.

For reflection, water must be located where light can play upon it. Water in permanent shade can look dull and unexciting, but allow light to play upon it and reflections occur. Establish planting around it and foliage can be reflected, so use bold, exciting foliage for maximum effect.

Light becomes more exciting when it plays through fine water particles, shattering into the colours of a rainbow. Placement of the feature is all important because light will only break into the colours of prism with sun upon water particles.

Water also provides sound. In the case of fine particles, a delicate and refined sound; by contrast, a falling sheet of water provides a loud, splashing sound, suited to overcoming intrusive noises. Home gardeners need to understand the effect of different water jets because they have an enormous effect upon the quality of a space. Adjustable jets are valuable where fountains are concerned; water spillways are less easy to adjust.

A body of water also creates evaporation which can cool the surrounding air, but it does mean you will need to top up the water in hot weather, something that may not be justifiable in dry conditions when refreshment is most needed. Alternatively, a sense of refreshment can be achieved by placing a bowl of water at a vital point in a

Water should conform to the style of the garden and for the traditional, formal garden where water is the focus, a symmetrical pond is appropriate as featured in this Paul Bangay design.

garden. Float flowers such as hellebores or camellias for a special effect.

For children, water is irresistible. Swimming pools offer them focus for outdoor life, yet they can be given an extra dimension by jets playing into the surface from within paving or a wall-mounted fountain. Listening to the screams of delight that accompany water play is a clear indication of its value. Water jets, a sophisticated interpretation of a Spanish style of water use, create not only a delightful sound but also refreshment and life.

These approaches to water use are, to a degree, a formal response. Contemporary design, however, is now approaching water in a different way, using its capture and retention on-site to improve sustainability. In the native garden, a more relaxed character works. There are also opportunities to create an effect where water is never actually present, the line of a creek being suggested by no more than natural-looking stone, pebble and debris creating a simulated watercourse. An occasional rush growing through or a sleeper bridge taking a path across the creek line gives a delightful effect. In heavy rain, water can be held here before soaking into the garden.

Where a permanent informal pond is required, use of large boulders and a heavy duty pond liner will achieve the objective; but, if reflection is required, keep the water surface open to encourage light access. If habitat is your goal, however, then encourage plant life, algae and associated animals and insects.

As a design element, water can also provide opportunities to grow aquatic plants and harbour fish, form bog gardens, and encourage bird life with either simple bird baths or through complex wetland designs. Its uses are indeed endless, but for best effects, ensure your chosen use of water meets the style of your garden.

Phil Johnson of Greenmark Landscapes shows how native gardens can be designed to incorporate water in its many moods. **Left:** In Phil Johnson's Olinda garden in Victoria, there is reflection, movement, dramatic sound and habitat creation while also providing a cooling and charming glade. Right: The natural styled billabong in Phil's Silvan design reinforces an Australian identity.

Dural Garden
Sydney

'The depth of talent in Australian design, now proven on the world stage at Chelsea, is a source of pride for our industry. The opportunities here for groundbreaking design are enormous, with more than enough room for every different style. My own 'resort style' focus often attracts critics who disregard the fact that a market genuinely exists for these gardens, just as one does for smaller gardens at the other end of the spectrum and those in between. As members of one exciting, well-respected industry, why not celebrate our achievements together, appreciating and encouraging diversity in landscape design.' dean herald

Biography

Popularising a new brand of residential design, Dean Herald has introduced the concept of retreating to a luxury, resort-style living space 'in your own backyard'. Forging a niche market for his residential design and construction practice, Rolling Stone Landscapes, Dean creates private oases for clients with a desire to enjoy five-star surroundings from their own home.

Ironically, these environments contrast sharply with the ministry rental properties that Dean, the son of a preacher, grew up in. Without regretting those modest yet loving backyard environs, exposure to luxurious settings through the odd magazine or television program sparked his interest in opulent landscapes. Combined with a genuine love of all things outdoors, a flair for drawing and design (and a self-confessed lack of academic aptitude!), Dean left school at fifteen to undertake a landscape construction

apprenticeship. Though not formally trained in landscape design, he is well suited to design and construct gardens through early dedication to his craft, amassing practical knowledge and experience in his formative years. Now acknowledged as a talented designer, numerous show garden medals and landscape awards provide justification. In 2006, a gold medal at the prestigious Chelsea Flower Show in London, regarded as the pinnacle of success in his field, offered a career highlight.

Establishing Rolling Stone Landscapes at nineteen initially brought challenges: Dean found it difficult to obtain the confidence of clients. Rapidly acquiring respect, however, through hard work and commitment to excellence, his industry reputation resulted in regular appearances as a landscape consultant on the popular television series *The Block*, hosted by Jamie Durie. A resultant offer to participate in Sydney in Bloom in 2003 gave him an opportunity to showcase his considerable talents and introduce his resort-style gardens.

Dean remains true to his philosophies by limiting the size of his practice, thereby ensuring protection of his

---

1 Dean plants not only in water but along its margins, carefully leaving gaps where views onto the water surface are especially important and planting would be intrusive. The site plan reveals the way that belts of planting adjacent to the creek alignment allow him to establish flowing lawn areas that contribute to the natural character.

2 Dean's designs provide his client's with five-star accommodation at home.

personal design style. Content to design fewer gardens, but designing those on a particularly grand scale, he enthuses about the opportunity to immerse himself in the needs of his clients, allocating hours to design resolutions, finely tuned to individual lifestyles and dreams. Though often tossing a variety of options around on the drawing board, Dean usually presents one, meticulously detailed, final plan to his clients. He believes preliminary sketches and alternative options confuse clients, or worse still, encourage them to hybridise concepts, potentially resulting in disunity and a compromised design.

Predominantly working with 2 to 3 hecture properties, Dean says his site surveys are his bible, though he remains flexible in reshaping land contours during construction, recognising that a design often evolves as site works progress. He enjoys collaborating with architects—re-siting buildings or features to enhance views, integrate house and landscape or account for site opportunities or constraints. Dean aims to produce a well-packaged result with wow factor and functionality that brings excitement

and satisfaction to clients. Though enjoying prestigious awards, high-profile media exposure, publication of his first book, *Resort Style Living*, and meeting the Queen at Chelsea, it is still fulfilling and exceeding his clients' expectations that is Dean's motivation and personal measure of success.

Design brief

Dean Herald's reputation for resort-style gardens goes a long way to establishing his design brief. His objective is to provide his clients with the type of five-star accommodation they enjoy on their holidays, in the context of their home garden. With Dean's confidence and vision, his clients are willing to allow him to design a garden for them that evolves as his understanding of his client and their site develops, without the need for a detailed brief.

There are refinements that individual clients seek. In this case it was the need to establish a parkland environment as a sanctuary. Having moved from a small, inner city property to a larger site, the owners now sought space to relax and take a more expansive approach to life.

Sanctuary was also important for the owners' grown family, one of whom only visits the garden at weekends. For them the garden was a place to explore, meaning a range of paths and routes was needed. With the clients having one son in a wheelchair and another with intellectual disability, the garden had to be designed to meet specific requirements. Ramps at correct grades were essential for movement, yet needed to blend in unobtrusively.

Dean quickly realised that to satisfy his clients' brief, the garden should have gum trees and a rural character. He could also increase the garden's interest by integrating golf holes and waterways within his design. This was a shared realisation with his clients as they wanted a garden to be used and enjoyed and the golf course encouraged this. A creek was important, too, recalling memories of a swimming hole his clients had loved as children. There was a strong overriding sense that this should be a

'natural' garden albeit with a combination of formal and informal areas.

Recognition of increasing water shortages across Sydney led to the garden being designed as water efficient. Capturing water from the roof and driveways was important while provision of a bore was desirable to allow topping up of dams when required.

Site analysis

This long and narrow rectangular site had a quiet road to its eastern boundary. The land fell 15m from east to west, permitting a view across the site from the road. The slope allowed good views to the west, across to the Blue Mountains in the distance, the childhood home of the garden's owners.

Retention of the view to the Blue Mountains was important. So too was screening of the western sun, especially during the late summer when it can be exceedingly bright and uncomfortable. At the time of the

3 The strong formal character of the house provided guidelines for Dean's design response, formal adjacent to the building, less formal further away.

4 Dean and his team created this waterfall as the starting point for the creek, when it became apparent during construction that the opportunity was available. Its implementation reflects the flexibility that Dean's practical approach to design permits.

design commission, two new houses had been constructed to the site's north. Initially they had limited impact, the houses were quite remote; however, as the project developed a large garage was constructed. Screening became essential, though fortunately this orientation was secondary to the whole project, the site's main focus extending east–west, not to the north.

To the south, it was difficult to predict future land use. Dean attempted to pre-empt change by implementing screening to this boundary. His response is worth noting, reflecting an awareness of a need to predict change that may influence a site in the future.

Dean's analysis of the site revealed that, despite the appearance of a good covering of trees, most of these were old and sparse offering little long-term amenity. Assessing trees and their condition is an important part of any project. Trees with a long useful life expectancy should be protected (in this case 5–10 trees were worth retaining). Others needed to be removed and areas replanted.

The site was agricultural land and the one feature that made significant impact on Dean was an old farm dam at the mid-point on the slope. It contained water when much of the landscape was dry, bringing a new dimension to the site and providing the opportunity for development of a decorative creek.

Finally, mention should be made of the proposed house. Though not built when Dean became involved in the project, much of its style and presence was clear. Dean describes it as 'classic, modern country style'.

Design response

Wherever possible, Dean establishes the house's level on the site. He locates the main driveway and house entry, and resolves details of pool and entertainment area, but retains a flexible approach to other elements of the design. The trust of clients and the experience of his construction employees allows him to take this approach. Unlike many other designers, Dean employs his own construction team and, having worked 'on the tools' himself, fully understands the implications of his designs.

Responding to site architecture and setting, the design solution incorporated an informal and natural garden character through the front garden, becoming more

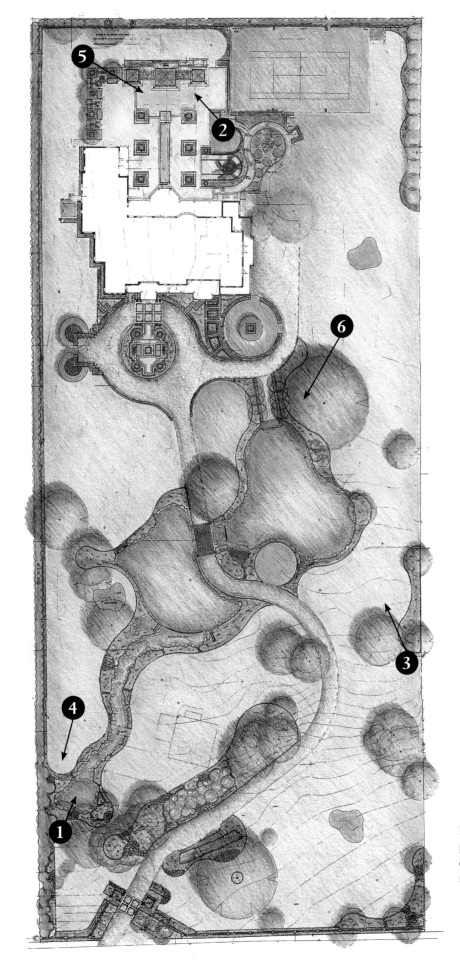

Numbers featured on the plan identify viewlines of correspondingly numbered images.

The main waterfall cascades over a curved eco stone wall, giving a striking and dramatic focus in the landscape above the upper dam. Use of pumps recycles this water to maintain the effect and ensures its sustainability.

formal towards the house. To the rear, the garden showed greatest formality. Here was the sitting area, swimming pool and tennis court. Water gives this garden much of its character and calmness. Dean began by, extending the existing dam so that the water follows a natural flowing contour to form a system of ponds and creeks through the site. Existing sandstone gave an integral character to the site. Dean enhanced this by importing additional sandstone to construct the naturally syled ponds.

The extremely peaceful effect is shattered, however, by three dramatic waterfalls: one of them 15m wide with a 2m-fall that sees approximately 120L of water per minute cascade over, and brings a tremendous energy and excitement to the garden. One of the falls is located near the driveway bridge so that the visitor has the experience of looking across a pond beneath them.

As mentioned, the natural garden character gives way to a more formal response closer to the house to the western end of the front garden. Here, architecture extends into the landscape with a turning circle on axis from the front door and a formal garden within it—the size

The lower waterfall is located beneath the driveway bridge and acts as a weir to a large pond allowing visitors a glimpse of the water upon entry. By breaking the waterflow into a series of chutes, Dean created greater drama clearly expressed in changing conditions of light.

5 The pool is the focus to outdoor entertainment areas, as it is in most of Dean's gardens, and is combined with an outdoor kitchen and a formal water-wall to provide a vibrant focus for family life and entertaining.

of most urban backyards—with the drive extending to the north to access garaging beneath the house. Though this landscape is formal in character, it is not a formality of geometric lines but of curves. One of the aspects that especially pleases Dean's clients is his successful melding of informal and formal areas.

Dean's success in achieving a natural effect to the front garden is evident from the diversity of wildlife that occupy the area. Not only do plovers, ducks and geese graze the lawns, but lorikeets and kookaburras have taken residence, with fish in most of the ponds. For children with disabilities, the garden is not only relaxing, but also a place where they can enjoy a diversity of Australian wildlife, giving it particular appeal.

With the house to the rear of the block, the formal area of tennis court, pool, pavilions and associated paving is more restricted in size, but its relative compactness importantly provides a well-resolved focus to the site. The tennis court in the northwest corner is designed not only for tennis, but also for cricket and basketball. Ramps provide access

for the whole family to all parts of the garden including the swimming pool. This garden has not only become the focus for fundraising charity events, but also allowed the family to sell their Gold Coast weekender. Surely there could be no better testament to the value of a garden, nor to Dean's ability to capture his clients' vision and to realise it on their behalf.

Planting design

Dean explains that he resolves structural design aspects first, with planting design completed as a secondary element. His purpose in this is to allow his clients to appreciate something of the garden character so that planting can reinforce overall style.

Considering his planting design here, it is clear that Dean enjoys using a well-tried palette of plants that will meet his expectations in terms of performance and design objectives, whether it be conjuring up an informal character, offering privacy and screening, formality, or a dramatic mass-planting for visual effect around a formal entertaining area.

6 In the front garden, Dean's design intent with plants was to help integrate his dramatic water features into the overall landscape. This image shows swathes of native grasses beneath a newly planted honey locust (*Gleditsia triacanthos*).

New tree planting was essential in the front garden and included peppercorn (*Schinus areira* var. *molle*) and honey locust (*Gleditsia triacanthos*). At the end of the watercourse where a more formal character was required, the callery pear (*Pyrus calleryana*) was chosen for spring flower and autumn foliage colour, an effect supplemented by use of Japanese maples (*Acer palmatum*).

Critical to integration of water bodies is the use of appropriate aquatic and water margin plants that establish appropriate visual character.

Planting along these margins is restricted in diversity but its impact is dramatic. Intermingled are the variegated leaves of flax lily (*Dianella* 'Silver Border'), an evergreen with blue and yellow flowers and turquoise berries and purple fox tail grass (*Pennisetum setaceum* 'Rubra'). Gymea lily (*Doryanthes excelsa*) brings native drama matched by the South African bird of paradise (*Strelitzia reginae*) and, while knobby rush (*Ficinia nodosa*) is more modest in form, by using it in masses at the water's edge, its impact is equally striking. Japanese sweet flag (*Acorus gramineus*) provides attractive emergent foliage from within the water.

Closer to the house Dean's planting selection changes to match the changing mood of the garden. Formality and perfume becomes more important and orange jessamine (*Murraya paniculata*), Florida gardenia (*Gardenia augusta* 'Florida') and masses of star jasmine (*Trachelospermum jasminoides*) fill the air with their heavy perfume in season. The range of lillypilly now available is witnessed here with the dwarf form as an edging hedge to paths, driveway and formal garden beds, and the larger growing *Syzygium australe* 'Select' used as screening along boundaries. In the rear garden lillypilly is clipped into standard trees along the formal line between the house and gazebo. The benefits of using a reliable palette of plants in this context becomes clear. This area will be intimately experienced by visitors so planting needs to stand up to close scrutiny.

Flower of the west wind (*Zephyranthes candida*), New Zealand flax (*Phormium* 'Maori Chief'), turf lily (*Liriope muscari*), variegated mondo (*Ophiopogon jaburan* 'Variegatum'), and Japanese box (*Buxus microphylla* var. *japonica*) all reappear in his design, selected for their reliable performance.

Just as Dean recognises the role of plants in achieving success in his designs, he also recognises the importance of maintenance. For his clients, this signifies his ongoing interest in their projects, for him it is a guarantee of success in his work.

Purple fox tail grass forms impressive drifts, its smoky purple flowers appealing when swept by wind or back-lit by late afternoon sun.

'We get up every morning and think how lucky we are to live in this place. We derive enormous pleasure from the relaxed feelings our garden evokes, for our own family and our many guests. It's no wonder our holiday home was sold and our boat is unused!'

Garden owners

Thomas Church pioneered the free-form design that was to become a classic approach to pools in the garden 'El Novillero' in California.

Swimming pools

Pools, including their size and form, should be considered within the overall context of the garden, rather than designed as a separate item. Without careful design, pools can overwhelm a garden; indeed with the size of an average pool ranging from 7–10m x 3–5m, a garden has to be large to accommodate one. For smaller gardens, lap pools or swim jets do provide practical options.

Free-form pools need to be integrated into a relaxed, informal garden space, not always available in small suburban backyards. A more formal design (usually rectangles, providing for reasonable exercise and water play) responds more appropriately to average lot shapes.

Paved or decked areas provide an opportunity to link the pool to the architectural form of the house and garden so that it becomes an integrated element. When siting a pool

it is important to consider location of services—sewer, electrical, telephone and gas lines may need relocating to accommodate the pool and this will add substantially to costs. Tree roots should also be considered and affected trees may need to be removed if their future stability is threatened by root severance. Roots of new trees planted in pool surrounds shouldn't pose problems if the pool is properly constructed.

Remember that pools bring with them other requirements, areas of paving or deck for sun loungers, housing of pool equipment (giving consideration to operating noise), roof space for solar heating if used, and a coping area to allow access for cleaning. In most instances an associated area of paving for outdoor eating and sitting are important, and a pool fence for children's safety is mandatory.

Spectactular pool lighting by Light on Landscape ensures this pool is a stunning feature of this Paul Bangay-designed garden.

Size of the pool should fit its function. A small plunge pool may be adequate for children to have fun and cool off, a 20m-long lap pool may be needed for exercise. Circular and elliptical pools bring a calming quality to gardens but are not as conducive to swimming. Adding a spa as a pool element may extend its value. Isolatated from the main pool, it can be easily heated to provide year-round options for communal relaxation and entertainment.

Pool finishes require thought. Dark-coloured pools provide the greatest opportunities for reflection, an often overlooked advantage of incorporating a pool into a garden. Dark pools also offer a smart, modern feel, though their lack of transparency is less inviting to swimmers. The reduced visibility through the water also requires greater vigilance where there are infants and children. While blue tiles are most frequently used, they can appear highly intrusive in the garden and, particularly light blue choices, cause significant glare on sunny days. Greys and greens offer more natural-looking alternatives though they can appear less clean than a blue pool. Tiled pools are most popular, but there are alternative finishes including pebbled and painted treatments that provide more natural effects particularly appropriate for informal pools and gardens, though they often lead to increased maintenance.

Dean creates pools for his clients that are the focus of lifestyle. He offers a valuable lesson in that pool size dictates that associated features—paving and sitting areas, outdoor kitchens and spas all respond to the scale of the pool. Remember that as pools become larger, they need increased equipment for heating, pumping and cleaning, and installation and running costs increase dramatically.

Outdoor recreational items such as tables, umbrellas and barbecues should also be selected to reflect the pool style and size, while planting can help to reinforce site character. Traditional pools suit a formal planting treatment, such as tubs of clipped topiary or hedging. By contrast, planting may spill over the edge of an informal pool, though they will need to be chosen to tolerate chlorine or saltwater splash.

Finally, pools provide attractive settings for evening use. As expensive features, it makes sense to extend their impact beyond daylight. Well-designed lighting can transform a pool at night into an elegant water feature and stunning focal point from indoors. Separate switching to spa lights is useful so that an evening spa bath can offer privacy when required.

Phil Johnson's glorious natural swimming hole is the epitome of a pool integrated within its Dandenong Ranges setting.

Brisbane Garden
Queensland

'My inspiration so often comes from how the average person deals with gardens. I love the intuitive gardener where, particularly in regional centres, people have gardened for 150 years in a certain way or style that's simply intuitive, for fun and without being told "this is what you should do". I feel so much of that is being lost today because of current gardening philosophies; there's almost an academic conceptual idea of what we should have. For generations gardeners have worked with and improved upon the beauty of the Australian landscape and in so doing, brought biodiversity and a pleasing aesthetic to their environment. This manipulated landscape is as much a part of the fabric of our existence as the pristine bushland we also need to protect.' arno king

Biography

The path to gardens for Brisbane landscape architect, Arno King, began in the suburban New Zealand garden he grew up in. With a fascination for plants and animals, he wore a track to the untamed bushland at the bottom of the family garden. Years later, a maths/science tertiary qualification left him unfulfilled and he finally followed his heart to horticulture. After tiring of administrative roles in other landscape architectural practices, he now runs his own design business in Toowong, Queensland, where his passion for the 'hands on' process of designing gardens can be pursued.

As a young horticultural graduate, Arno spent many years working in various landscape design practices. A chance meeting with English designer, Anthony Paul, saw him join Paul's thriving practice in England, presenting an amazing opportunity in the 80's to create unlimited budget gardens in a relaxed hybrid Australian/ New Zealand style for high profile English clients.

Influences on Arno's career include his inspirational university lecturer, Lesley Maughan, who in turn introduced him to the ground breaking work of Roberto Burle Marx—a revelation for Arno. After visiting gardens throughout Europe, a meeting with Marx himself in Brazil was a life-changing experience. Believing much of Australian design today is Marx inspired, Arno also incorporates the characteristic Marx style of bold, colourful foliage and focal planting in his work.

A quest to attain a technical, construction-based understanding of his craft saw him return from his travels to study landscape architecture in Brisbane. Impressed with the climate and strategic opportunities provided by the location, Arno established his current practice there in the early 1990's. Primarily designing residential gardens, his much awarded work also includes the public landscapes of Cleveland Shopping Centre, South Bank and the freeway entrance to Brisbane. Arno draws on the success of local historical plantings in his selection

---

1 Arno's use of bold massed foliage plants can be viewed as a tribute to the great designer, Roberto Burle Marx. The yellow-green leaves of *Alpinia zerumbet* 'Variegata' contrast with the burgundy foliage of *Acalypha wilkesiana* 'Raggedy Anne'.

of hardy, appropriate plants for his gardens today. Ultimately, he believes these 'survivors' of the rigours of the Queensland climate should form the palette of designers, not the instant impact plants often promoted in nurseries.

Arno actively supports a greater community appreciation of horticulture – publicly through media opportunities and his role as a selector for the Queensland Open Garden Scheme and privately, enthusiastically engaging his clients in the complete process of creating a garden. He often asks them to compose a postcard to an overseas relative painting a picture of their dream garden. Using this as a basis for his brief and insisting on the clients' strong level of input to the development of the design, he ensures his clients become connected to the garden, and a lifelong commitment to its care.

Gravely concerned at the continuing degradation of our natural resources, Arno creates environments that encourage greater biodiversity of flora and fauna. To him, the current trend of roadside 'monoculture' planting of one or two species contributes little habitat or aesthetic value and offers no reflection of our culture or social identity. Arno strongly believes that through a community developing an interest in horticulture, potential exists for meaningful sustainability and greater worldwide protection of plants.

Brief

The initial brief for this large suburban garden was confined to eradication of ever-expanding pockets of bamboo. Concerned that it was progressively extending beyond the property boundaries into neighbouring gardens, the clients sought Arno's advice as to the likelihood of successfully removing it. Deending on his response they would either sell the property and begin a garden elsewhere, or remain and redesign their existing one.

Arno's positive attitude to the bamboo's removal and the garden's redevelopment convinced his clients to stay. The eventual brief required retention of a large portion of the

existing site vegetation, including many mature gums. As the garden of an artist working from home, the space had to provide a sense of tranquility and opportunities for relaxation and quiet contemplation. No sculpture, garden art or stimulating features, apart from those provided by nature, were to form part of the design. Existing wildlife habitat and 'sense of place' were to be enhanced, while access to a remote studio needed improvement. Once the clients had committed to remaining on the property, issues of mobility and comfort within the garden as they aged were also a concern.

The intention was a to form a seamless integration of indoors and out. Structural elements within the 1960's home, such as concrete surfaces, were identified as potential links between house and landscape. Garden lighting was also an integral requirement and much of the budget was allocated toward it.

Both willing gardeners, the clients sought a variety of interesting plant material that would offer hands-on gardening opportunities.

Site Analysis

Despite the presence of pernicious bamboo throughout this Brisbane western suburbs garden, Arno fell in love with the one-acre site, complete with its 1960's Don Spencer-designed home and remnant native vegetation. He saw potential in the style and construction period of the house, the existing free-form swimming pool and the sub-tropical location and the possibility of incorporating the design influences of Brazilian landscape architect, Roberto Burle Marx.

Once the bamboo had been removed, the garden took on a distinctly new and open feel. Many tall trees that had been growing from within the bamboo now gave rhythm and form to the landscape as their tall, straight trunks stretched to the sky, yet there were still many separate neglected and overgrown areas of the garden, resulting in a lack of cohesion.

While the pool was the garden's focus, Arno felt existing contours and intervening trees detracted from its appeal

2 Existing native vegetation formed an integral part of the site and was retained to ensure privacy and encourage wildlife.

as the major feature, with small terraces and individual garden beds interrupting the view line from the house. Arno was impressed, however, that the low-key arrival from the street meant the discovery of the rear garden was a breathtaking experience, commenting, 'There was this whole world that ... you never ever saw.' Though the route to the front door needed clarification, Arno resolved to maintain the drama of the rear by making 'the front entry very low key'.

The scale of the house with its floor to ceiling windows called for a corresponding spaciousness in the garden, so some paring back was necessary. Terraces and steps needed reconfiguration to improve flow and provide spaces for enjoyment outdoors.

The site was in two parts: the cleared area close to the house and a bushland area further afield. While the latter was in Arno's terms a 'manipulated bushland', not pristine native vegetation, it was to continue as a more natural garden that looked after itself, in contrast to the area that would be gardened around the house. A dry

Bold mass planting is characteristic of Arno's work. It gives a strong visual effect and achieves low-maintenance results.

3 Bamboos remain a favoured plant of the owners, despite their vigour. Now the bamboo is well contained using 1m deep steel root barriers. At the site entry it is used to great effect as passing through a tunnel of towering bamboo to reach the house adds to a sense of drama and mystery.

creek bed deep within the native forest canopy added to its authentic bushland character.

Design Response

Arno's work on the site began in the front garden, though its design was derived very much from the impact required at the rear. Deliberately designed to heighten the drama of the backyard unfolding upon entry to the house, the front area is subtle and reserved, using low-key plant material. Arno explains 'I didn't want any colour, no major texture really, just lots of small leaf plants and grasses'. Ironically, grasses were chosen for their relationship to the bamboo remaining throughout the property.

The renovated home's glass walls to the rear garden provided a magnificent viewing opportunity to reveal the landscape to its visitors. Arno used this to great advantage, introducing Burle Marx inspired bold and colourful foliage and rich textural interest to provide impact, contrasting with the subdued palette in the front garden.

4 The glass walls to the rear of the house provide magnificent viewing opportunities to the garden. Arno's decision to remove some of the intervening trees and garden beds and define the slope as one continuous fall from the house gives the pool greater impact.

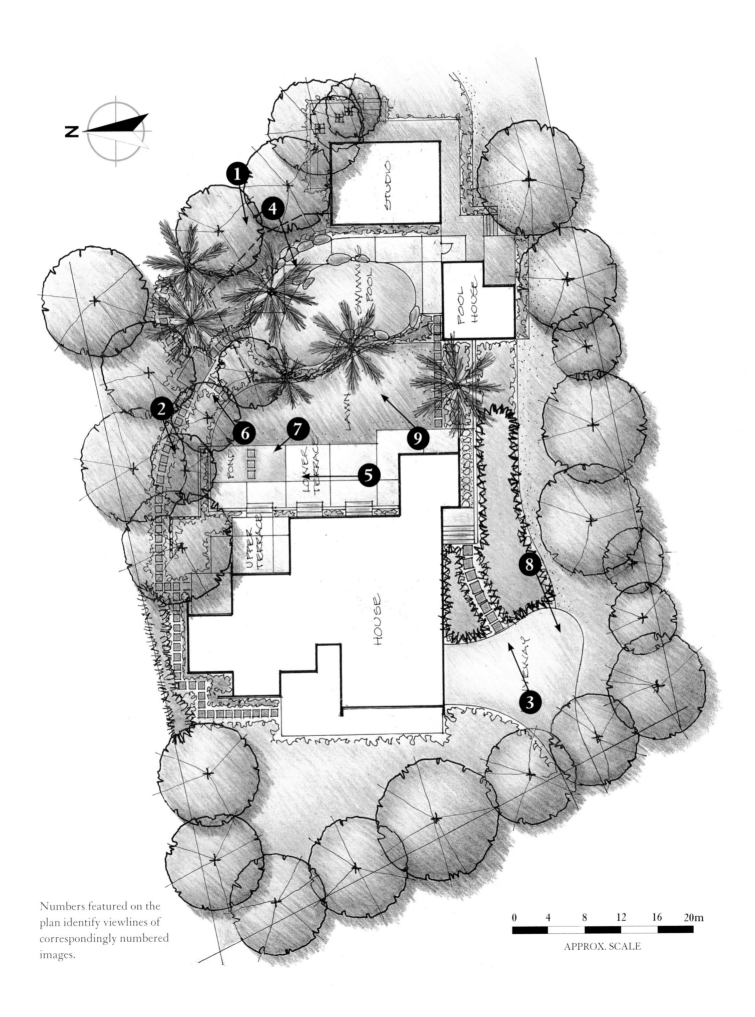

N

STUDIO

POOL
HOUSE

SWIMMING POOL

LAWN

POND

UPPER TERRACE

LOWER TERRACE

HOUSE

WALKWAY

Numbers featured on the
plan identify viewlines of
correspondingly numbered
images.

0   4   8   12   16   20m

APPROX. SCALE

5 For continuity between indoors and outdoors, a concrete surface was chosen for the terrace that used stones sourced locally as exposed aggregate within a coloured cement, chosen to match the colour of the concrete indoors.

6 This attractive bridge is an integral part of the path system through the garden. Visitors are able to enjoy the masses of foliage plants including *Philodendron* 'Xanadu' and Fish tail fern (*Nephrolepis bisserata*).

Arno believed the swimming pool and associated planting were central to the overall design so major recontouring works were also undertaken to remove existing terraced gardens in the lawn to give the pool greater prominence. With the planting of additional Royal Palms curving behind the pool, it also reinforced the effect that the pool was positioned within an amphitheatre between the palms and studio rising up to its east and the house above it to the west. The result was a sunken retreat that became the major garden focus.

Ramped timber decks were established to envelop the studio and ensure ease of access as the garden's occupants aged. Eucalypt trunks were accommodated through holes in the elevated deck, providing a feeling of integration with the surrounding forest. A bamboo circle was also designed as a focus from the studio, offering the owners a different mood and space to enjoy within the overall design.

A terrace adjoining the house was expanded to give a feeling of spaciousness to the previously constricted area. As Arno placed great importance on picking up the 1960's theme of the house in the garden, the owners' discovery of a wonderful concrete surface beneath carpets provided the perfect linking opportunity. Containing gravel and sand from the Brisbane River, it incorporated green pebbles and orange sand particles that looked spectacular when ground down as a polished surface.

Two new broad sets of steps were introduced to encourage movement between house and garden. Built to match existing steps, they appear to be part of the earlier works. Together with the addition of a large masonry planter extending along the dwelling's glass wall, they helped to ground the house within its sloping landscape.

Around the pool (again referencing the concrete prevalent in many 1960's gardens), experienced Italian and Polish contractors were engaged to cantilever a concrete deck out over the pool edge, which was later ground down to match internal finishes.

Native areas along the property's northern perimeter were provided with paths to encourage meandering. Prior to Brisbane's drought, drainage was an issue so swales were introduced to assist with directing water to the natural creek alignment. Ferns and native understorey provided wildlife habitat and low maintenance areas that contributed to the bushland feel. Left to its own devices, it now survives without irrigation and is home to abundant bird life and bush animals.

Garden lighting was a priority for the owners who wanted to enjoy the garden after their day's work. Arno designed the lighting himself and in response to the brief for the garden to 'look amazing at night', installed a wide variety of lighting, including massive spotlights in eucalyptus trees and bollards for pools of light around the swimming pool. An evening wonderland results.

Arno's final design element was a concrete pond that connects the terrace area and garden through stepping stones across the water. Initially opposed to the concept as they feared the introduction of mosquitoes and toads, his clients now favour the location to view the garden and enjoy its many sensory splendours.

Planting Design

Arno's Brisbane gardens reveal the diversity of flora that will prosper in this climate. The exciting aspect of his work is that his knowledge of plants allows him to use this extensive vocabulary in a way that is assured and effective. Here bromeliads, palms, cycads, bamboos, gingers and a fascinating range of native plants are confidently featured.

7 Below the terrace an ornamental pond provides a decorative feature and a sense of 1960's design. Arno's belief that it would provide the finishing touch to the garden was justified.

8 Arno introduced massed grasses to produce a subtle, low-key front garden, deliberately contrasting with the colours and excitement at the rear.

Empress of Brazil (*Alcantarea imperialis*) growing to 1.5m in ten years with a 2.5m flower spike covered in hundreds of fragrant white flowers and Red Bird's nest bromeliad (*Neoregelia compacta*) are featured here.

The red leaved *Cordyline fruticosa* 'John Cummins' cuts a swathe through the landscape adjacent to the studio.

Interestingly, entry to the site is made mysterious by the use of bamboos even though they had proved to be so invasive on the site in earlier times. The Giant Black Bamboo (*Gigantochloa* 'Timor Black') is a stunner, tall and with dark violet stems, it needs to be kept in check but having once experienced the potential growth of bamboos, the owners are especially vigilant.

The great advantage of bamboos is the delightful shade they create, especially the shadow pattern on paths. Many of the native trees on the site do the same and these provide a habitat where the intensity of the sun is reduced.

In the rear garden the gingers thrive; for example, the shell ginger (*Alpina zerumbet* 'Variegata'), a variegated form with yellow-green leaves effectively striped yellow. With its delicate white flowers this deserves the name porcelain lily, its common epithet. Not as tall as the non-variegated gingers, it still makes a fine landscape contribution.

There is a sense that Arno's planting carries him back to his native New Zealand for the ti's or cordylines are used simply and prosper. However, the most frequently

Thunbergia mysorensis sways in the breeze to provide a hypnotic decorative effect.

used *Cordyline fruticosa* cultivars are not Kiwis at all but native to a range of islands in the tropical areas north of Australia. So many cultivars are available but Arno selects 'Compacta'; the compact cordyline 'John Cummings', the orange cordyline with green leaves and orange edging; and 'Kiwi' and 'Negra', the form with yellow and green striped leaves, the latter particularly tall-growing.

This catalogue of plants provides a clue to the nature of the garden for foliage is uppermost. Whether it takes the form of lower planting in bold dramatic masses, for example mondo grass (*Ophiopogon japonicus*) and its dwarf form (*O.j.* 'Kyoto') or turf lilies (*Liriope* 'Evergreen Giant') or the many palms and ferns that grow taller, foliage contrasting in shape and colour makes the greatest impact.

Palms and ferns together in a garden may seem incongruous to many gardeners yet here they fit. The Fishtail Palm (*Caryota mitis*) for example forms dense multi-stemmed clumps that can grow to 8m. They fill space effectively and help to form a backdrop to other plantings. By contrast the bamboo palm (*Chamaedorea seifrzii*) from Central America fills the ground level with masses of bamboo like stems. These plants all contribute a tropical character. The tree fern (*Cyathea cooperi*) is not at first glance the outsiders' idea of a tropical plant but it has become so at home in many areas of Hawaii to be considered an aggressive weed.

Arno's clever planting scheme offers great interest and definition of different areas within the garden. Mind, this is a large garden with many wild areas that will accommodate diversity.

'Arno's vision provided us with a beautiful, calming environment to work from and live in. We love the seasonal colour changes, different patterns of ever-changing light play, and the wildlife friendly plant choices so we can co-exist with nature—a flight path for birds and abundant nests are treasured highlights.'

Garden owners

9 Native vegetation provides a complete contrast to the chaotic drama and colour of the pool area and provides a gentle softening backdrop to the garden.

DESIGN TIP

Inspiration for this garden pool house derived from the Los Angeles Case Study houses of the 1950's. The side fencing design looked directly to Californian designer, Thomas Church, and is based on one of his details. The result is an attractive back garden that perfectly fits the need for a sunny recreational space.

Borrowing ideas

No designer works in isolation, each builds upon the experience of earlier generations. Indeed designers are trained to appreciate the work of earlier artists in all media as a basis for their work. Developing an eye that appreciates the way that application of design elements can help establish moods is vital to a designer's success. Design is in many respects about communication, preparing a plan that predicts how people will respond to the setting that is created. Use of colour, form and shape, sound, texture and space all assist in conjuring up a design mood.

Arno King was fortunate in being able to visit the great Brazilian master, Roberto Burle Marx, a garden designer who is recognised, partly through his exploration of Brazil to introduce numerous plants to cultivation, as having changed approaches to garden design in tropical climes. In Arno's Brisbane design, the work of Marx was a major

influence. The effect can be seen in his massing of plants with interesting foliage textures in strong blocks and the graduation of planting so that the result is in sympathy with, and appropriate for, the style of the house.

Any home gardener has the opportunity to explore existing gardens for ideas and directions for their own garden. Reference to gardening books and magazines offers an enormous amount of material, but before ideas are borrowed, it is important to understand your site and the potential of implementing different ideas. Often gardens that ultimately give greater satisfaction combine foliage in various shapes and colours that can be sustained through time, in contrast to short-term flower displays. Photographers capture gardens in perfect light when everything is in full bloom. But gardens don't exist on this level, they change and in doing so, may lose the appeal displayed in the photograph.

A field of poppies offers a delightful scene, yet its seasonal nature needs to be considered from a design perspective.

Designers can influence our gardens in so many ways. Look firstly at plans they prepare and analyse the way they have established connections through a site and linked spaces. Assess the proportions of the site's components to see whether they are fit for purpose. While this may seem a very pragmatic approach, it is invaluable for the home garden designer who can then understand something of the sense of scale and proportion that is important to professional designers.

Visual aspects of a design can also be analysed. Assess an image to gain an understanding of the composition of a garden scene that especially attracts you. Do this by laying a sheet of tracing paper upon the image and breaking it down into its components.

Use images and visits to gardens to assist in developing your design but do remember that you need to assimilate these images and influences as part of an overall design scheme, not as a series of snapshots. Make sure your 'borrowed' design does not become a blend of several styles or ideas that lacks unity and cohesion and, of equal importance, is not an exact replica of another designer's resolution! That said, many successful garden designers have been inspired by the work of others to create responses of their own, often reinterpreting ideas to reflect their own style or specific site qualities. A significant part of this process lies in learning to both see and to analyse so that appropriate ideas can be developed that suit the style of your own home and lifestyle.

Edna Walling looked to Italian design principles when she designed her great garden at Marwarra in Victoria's Dandenong Ranges. Her use of terraces, long flights of stone steps, octagonal pond and fountain, all hark back to Renaissance Italy. Walling owned a copy of Shepherd and Jellicoe's great book *Italian Gardens of the Renaissance* and it is likely that she used this for her inspiration.

The idea of decorative hanging Japanese paper lanterns could easily be applied in a home garden.

Castle Cove Garden
Sydney

'The design of residential outdoor spaces represents both a challenge and an opportunity that should not be underestimated. Our current trend towards the construction of overscaled houses relative to their land size may present fewer options in landscape design, yet it increases the relevance of an appropriately designed garden. Though the external spaces are not huge, the impact those spaces have for the internal amenity are huge indeed.' mira martinazzo

Biography

Now balancing the dual careers of motherhood and landscape architects, Mira Martinazzo presently operates her scaled-back sole practice from her hometown of Perth, where she recently returned with her young family. Previously establishing herself as an innovative, contemporary designer while living on Australia's east coast, most of Mira's design work appears in Melbourne and Sydney. Now coming full circle, she currently limits herself to residential design in Perth on a relatively small scale, achieving maximum commitment to a minimum of projects.

Comfortable with a collaborative approach to design, Mira is prepared to allocate time to the consultative stage with clients and contractors. Lively discussion, visits to nurseries or gardens, meetings with trade experts and placing items in situ to predict their appropriateness are all part of the service.

1 The minimalist pool and surrounds perfectly complements the clean architectual lines of this Harry Seidler designed Sydney home. A paving strip provides pool access from the house. with minimal coping elsewhere to save garden space and intergrate the pool with planting.

Mira's progression to notable modern designer results from an unhurried journey from fine art in Perth to a landscape architecture course in Melbourne. Always interested in outdoor installations, and feeling limited by the cloistered world of artists, the course seemed a natural progression to Mira. It satisfied her interest in collaborating with other disciplines (engineers, architects, councils and communities), which would bring greater interaction with people and more relevance to her work. Her study, commitment and creativity were rewarded with the prestigious HASSELL Travelling Scholarship.

Mira gained graduate experience with commercial and government organisations, developing an understanding of project management and the partnership between soft and hard landscapes. A position with 'Out from the Blue', a progressive, cutting-edge pool contracting company, developed her skills in the residential field, exposing her to innovative design resolutions. Here, Mira was given free rein to design in directions that interested her, with the confidence that the second-generation pool builders she worked with could breathe life structurally into her plans. During this period, Mira tutored RMIT students of both landscape and architecture, relishing the opportunity to use her passion for art and design to inspire others.

Though a modern, hard-edged feel often pervades her work, Mira believes in responding to the specific qualities of a site rather than adhering to a predetermined style. However, she recognises there are certain materials and approaches she is attracted to. Paving laid without grouting to produce fine shadow lines and pool edges without coping are examples, as is the experimental use of simple and often stark raw materials such as blue metal as a mulching alternative. She also often features concrete in unconventional applications, admitting that, as the daughter of a crane-operating entrepreneur, she 'has concrete in her veins'.

Mira acknowledges initially focusing on the built form in her early designs, with planting merely a secondary adjunct. In direct contrast, her current philosophy places emphasis on keeping built materials low-key, with plants taking a more prominent role. Inspired by the bizarre and unique West Australian flora promoted by George Lulfitz in his Wanaroo Nursery, she uses the sculptural beauty of plants to create waterwise gardens with a strong impact.

Design brief

This house, designed by Australia's great modern architect Harry Seidler, shows the typical restraint and clean lines that characterise his work, yet the beauty of the architecture had become mired in a diverse planting scheme. Fortunately, both Mira and her client recognised this and the brief was directed to rectifying the problem. Yet, clear as this problem was, it was not the initial issue that Mira was asked to deal with. Mira's client had seen her work with pool contractors 'Out from the Blue' and saw in her contemporary design approach the type of solution he sought for his new pool. The original consultation related to pool advice, but as the client's confidence in Mira grew, so too did his willingness to accept and consider her overall design advice.

The brief, therefore, arose in stages, as different problems were identified and then a solution sought. The pool was the main focus of the design; other aspects were the creation of privacy and the establishment of views over Middle Harbour, which sits in the landscape below and is the site's most breathtaking feature. Also critical was establishing a minimalist solution sympathetic to the site's architecture, particularly when viewed from the streetscape—as this was the only public view of the house, the design had to read effectively in the landscape.

This photograph, taken during pegging out of the pool, reveals how the enclosing wall isolated the garden from potential views of Middle Harbour. The existing ground-level terrace reflects the form of the balcony above from which views were available.

The owner's enjoyment of gardening, but only within the privacy of the site, contributed to the need for minimalism in this area. Low maintenance was vital in this very public position.

Finally, one aspect of the front of the house did require protection; a large Chinese elm (*Ulmus parvifolia*) gave an exciting visual impact within the site and offered a vertical foil to the building's horizontal form.

Site analysis

For Mira, the joy of working on this project was twofold; the quality of the house designed by Seidler, and the fabulous views that were available to it. These views were most apparent from the upper floors of the house—capturing the wooded shoreline of Middle Harbour and yachting activities on the water through summer. Mira was determined to make upper floor views available to the ground floor and pool area. The wall to this north-facing garden was an engineered retaining wall, serving as a pool enclosure and safety barrier for the steep descent below.

In spite of the housing that tumbled down the slope, there was little concern about privacy due to a number of smooth-barked apple myrtles (*Angophora costata*) located along the slope. These trees had been retained where others might not have been, because their visually permeable foliage didn't compromise views. To the west, houses were apparent and did require screening.

Importantly, large windows meant garden areas were integral parts of each room in the house. This remarkable transparency gave the site a lightness that demanded a restrained solution sympathetic to the house. Restraint was also needed at the front of the site where a stunning curved wall, designed by Seidler to frame a study courtyard, was largely disguised by a range of planting. The wall of off-white bricks that matched the house consisted of tall narrow columns with fingers of space between them. These offered Mira a theme for use elsewhere, with other internal house materials, such as marble and granite, directing material selection outside.

The site sloped from the road entry point down internal steps to the rear garden. There were cross slopes, too; imperceptible at first, but becoming apparent in the rear where they were slight, but raised some difficult issues to resolve. In between, the side courtyards also sloped. Mira faced the difficult task of trying to provide greater structure and form to these spaces so they featured more prominently in internal views.

Once shrubs and other planting in the front garden were removed, it was obvious that levels in this section were confused, with the driveway sloping down to the garage and the pedestrian path falling to the house. The whole area needed resolution. As Mira explained, 'It was actually really strange to me, how the two could exist together, how you could have a house that is so bold and then a garden that was so weak.' A characteristic of the site that Mira grasped in her design response was Seidler's use of wing walls that extend from the house into the landscape.

Design response

Simplification was the key in Mira's approach to designing this garden, yet at the same time it should be observed that little work undertaken on this site was simple. Levels, spaces and materials all ensured that this design was a challenge and one that had to progress in logical stages to produce a satisfactory result.

To begin, an existing semicircular plinth extending from sliding doors was retained and converted to a pool entertaining terrace. This cleverly responds to both the architecture of the house—repeating the arc of an overhead balcony—and the constraints of the site. The garden space is so small that, had a traditional formal paved area been provided, it would have eaten into the space dramatically; so this solution extends the house and reduces the pool space without rendering it inadequate for its purpose. The paving is about 7cm above the water line of the pool which is rebated beneath the paving to give a sense of the paved area floating above the surface.

Selecting pool tiles is never an easy task. Their colour alters both as the pool fills and the light changes. Mira's

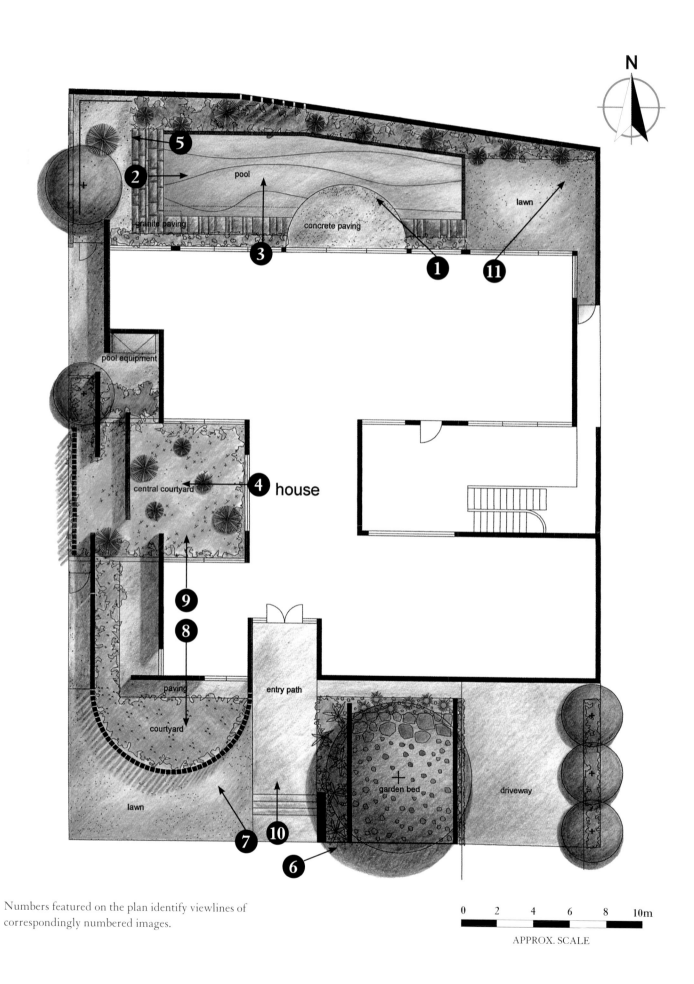

N

⑤

② → pool

granite paving

concrete paving

③

① ⑪

lawn

pool equipment

central courtyard ④ house

⑨

⑧

paving

entry path

courtyard

⑦ ⑩

lawn

⑥

garden bed

driveway

Numbers featured on the plan identify viewlines of
correspondingly numbered images.

0   2   4   6   8   10m

APPROX. SCALE

2 The pool terrace now perfectly meets a range of functional requirements; family meals, entry point to the pool, a sunbathing platform, outdoor home office working area and retreat for a cocktail in the evening. Made from sandblasted exposed aggregate concrete, it has an excellent non-slip surface.

3 Mira's decision to remove vertical slices from the boundary wall gave filtered views to Middle Harbour below. The result not only looks stunning, but creates links to marble used inside the house, and cleverly relates to the 'finger' effect of Seidler's curved front wall.

client identified a Bisazza glass tile that contained greens, blues and bronzes: a beautiful combination but extremely expensive. They considered using a cheaper tile in the pool floor and the more costly tile towards the surface. Sensibly, Mira persuaded her pool contractors to show her client a number of finished pools with different treatments and, as Mira explains, at the end of this process, 'The tiles we chose were so perfect for the colour of the water in the distance that there was no option but to use them'. The result is a dazzling success.

The concrete wall surrounding the garden was un-exciting, in fact it was downright dull. Mira's solution was to borrow from Seidler's front wall design. Vertical slices were removed from the wall so that these gave filtered views to the harbour below, without losing privacy or the functional qualities of a pool fence. The wall was then clothed in a veneer of Arabescato marble, cut so its surface pattern was mirrored in the length of the wall.

To the western end of the garden, privacy was important. An existing evergreen magnolia (*Magnolia grandiflora*) established levels and contributed to the screening, though more was needed. At the client's suggestion, the response uses a sheet metal fence, constructed not as a single vertical plane but with recesses to create shadow and depth. A further feature of the space is a tilting of

the interface of the ground plane with the fence using a thin galvanised steel sheet retaining wall that rises at a subtle angle to the west and conceals the point where the boundary fence meets the ground.

Mira attempted to create more level areas throughout the site in contrast to the slopes that consistently confronted her. This is critical in the western courtyard where the garden is an adjunct to living spaces and carries northern light into the adjacent rooms. To achieve her objectives, Mira used Seidler's 'wing wall' architectural clues, creating three parallel blade walls in a north–south direction.

Mira utilises interesting surface treatments in her work, not least in her choice of mulches. Throughout this garden, a grey, granular topping is used. This was designed to keep the ground plane clear and legible, as an appropriate contrast to the clear lines of the building, and as a setting where plants become sculptural features, contrasting with the grey mineral.

Mira extended her vision to the front of the house where, in her words, 'The existing central garden seemed at odds with the house, a random, debauched undulating mess.' All the existing plants were removed with the exception of the Chinese elm: a notable central feature. Now the presence and character of the house and the importance and subtlety of the landform all becomes clear.

4 Use of blade walls, including one 2m wall at the site boundary, achieved privacy to the west and created a level garden bed that became an attractive feature viewed from the study. Quite deliberately, it was also possible to read the flowing lines of the site contours against the blades where the land was left to fall naturally at the courtyard's outer edge.

5 By utilising sheet metal as a fence, a minimalist surface treatment was established. Painted a soothing grey, a calm and harmonious character was created for the garden, while minimizing views to adjacent properties.

6 Mira contrasted the smoothness of the ground plane of grass with the rugged railway ballast around the Chinese elm.

Using the base of the tree as her datum point, Mira set about remodelling the front garden, building retaining walls to form a level platform and then, adjacent to Seidler's curved wall of columns, reshaping the landscape to accentuate the sweeping and curving form of the brick wall. Mira's own words sum up her design intent and the results she achieved: 'The garden elements were raw, simple, unapologetic—tree, rock, rendered and unpainted walls. The voluptuous rolling ground plane [adjacent to Seidler's curved wall] was further articulated when carpeted by lawn.'

The result is a garden that offers an appropriately refined setting for an elegant house by a master architect.

Planting design

Plants play a significant role in Mira's design, yet they are remarkably low in diversity. Each was chosen for its specific quality and for its clear contribution to an overall design effect. As with other aspects of this project, selection was slow and deliberate, often the result of extended visits to nurseries to assess the opportunities and qualities that different plants provided.

In its simplest sense, the use of Sir Walter buffalo grass over the mounds at the front of the house was designed to offer refinement and elegance, enhancing the landform created by Mira. The Chinese elm retained from the earlier garden is the focus, a vertical foil to the generally

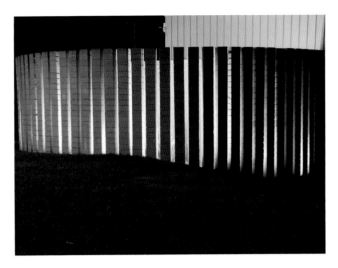

7 Removal of overgrown vegetation revealed Seidler's 'finger' wall as a dramatic architectural feature, particularly when viewed at night. A simple carpet of lawn allowed the ground contours to be clearly read against the wall.

horizontal thrust of the house. Other areas of planting in this public section of the garden offer simple but telling combinations. The broad strappy foliage of the native swamp or river crinum (*Crinum pedunculatum*) erupts from the groundcovering mass of the purple-leafed *Tradescantia purpurea*, all set in a sea of 5–15cm ballast. The simplicity of this combination is entirely appropriate for the house and far more effective than more complex schemes. River mat rush (*Lomandra*

Crinum is an extremely tough native plant, indigenous to coastal areas north of the site. With its dramatic 1m foliage and sweetly perfumed dense clusters of about 12-15 white flowers, it makes a superb contribution to the garden with little effort from the gardener.

8 Tassel rush and creeping boobialla offer a simple treatment against the curved study courtyard wall. Foliage of the latter plant forms a lush carpet over the newly formed mounding of this area allowing the effect of the vertical pillars to be savoured.

fluviatilis) provides further texture in the front garden, its attractive tussocks of foliage to about 75cm having special appeal amongst rocks.

Inside the curving front wall Mira uses mounds of the finely divided plumes of tassel rush (*Baloskion tetraphyllum*) contrasting with a sea of the bright green flat-leaf form of creeping boobialla (*Myoporum parvifolium*). This ground

cover was chosen to provide a continuum of the green of the front lawn glimpsed beyond.

A key plant located as an adjunct to the courtyard blade walls to offer increased screening to the west is the swamp banksia (*Banksia robur*). Its dramatic, large leathery foliage is a fine foil to the grass trees (*Xanthorrea johnsonii*) selected for this garden. While the swamp

9 Parrot's beak can spread over a metre or more and yet grows no taller than 15cm. Its grey-green foliage takes the appearance of a shawl cast over the grey mulch. Early pruning of the vigorous young shoots helps to maintain density.

Prostrate banksia has oblong, toothed leaves up to 40cm long with deep green fronds and a silver, hairy underside. As the leaves are held upright, they are almost as handsome as the erect yellow and light brown flower heads, up to 20cm, borne in spring and early summer. These flowers are retained by the plant so must be manually removed after maturity.

banksia was chosen for its visually impressive foliage, its greenish yellow flowers up to 15cm long are no less eyecatching and contribute to the garden for much of the year. Mira searched for an attractive groundcover for this area that would not only offset the grass trees, but also be a tonal contrast to the mulch. The selection of the parrot's beak (*Lotus berthelotii*) provided just that contrast with its fine, grey-green foliage and orange flowers.

Finally, the rear terrace garden—with the Arabescato marble giving the appearance of a mural and the spectacular views over Middle Harbour and Garigal National Park beyond—needed little planting. Plants here had only to complement textures and colours in the garden. The existing evergreen magnolia, an introduction from southeastern USA with large, superbly scented, cup-shaped creamy flowers, voluptuous in bud and bloom, creates a focus to the garden's western edge. Its drama is increased by allowing it to rise from a sea of gravel mulch with a single sculptural specimen of grass tree (*Xanthorrea glauca*) to its side. Prostrate banksia (*Banksia petiolaris*) is used nearby as a groundcover, an imposing spreading plant with hairy branches that assume a fabulous bronzy-red colouration when young.

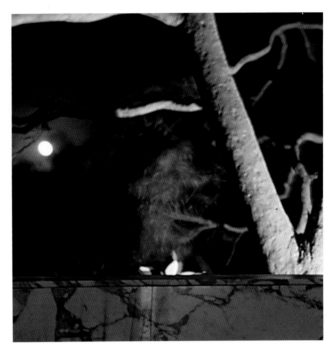

11 The effect of up-lighting an Apple Myrtle (*Angophora costata*) adjacent to the rear garden adds a distinct charm to both house and garden at night.

Importantly, the impact of plants is increased by the use of subtle and discreet lighting. Shadow patterns of plants cast against walls reinforce the viewer's experience of their form, using masonry almost as a cinema screen to bring new pictures to the garden.

'Before we started, I was particularly unhappy with the front garden and I find that we have now enhanced the area so much, simply by "nothingness". We were able to achieve a garden that works well, is low maintenance and doesn't detract from the beauty of Seidler's architecture.'

Garden Owners

10

Here, a traditional cottage-style garden is a perfect fit for the style of architecture and the broader setting in a rural English village.

Developing style

The designs throughout this book show how gardens and houses can be successfully combined to achieve an integrated living environment. Yet no two gardens are the same, just as no two houses are the same, as each is developed with its own particular character and style.

This can be appreciated in Mira's design for the garden of this Seidler house. Recognising the minimalist architecture that dominated the site, she responded by creating a garden that was also minimalist in style. It reinforced the character of the house by responding to it. Mira's repetition of Seidler's architectural elements of blade walls and individual brick piers shows how a garden can further articulate an overall style.

Successful design requires a sensitivity to the qualities of a site—a cottage or formal box-hedged garden would be clearly inappropriate in a minimalist context. While

a house will no doubt play a major role in garden style, it is not the sole determinant. Context or setting will be equally important.

In urban areas where much of the specific character of a landscape setting has been lost, architecture logically becomes the major determinant of landscape style. In more rural settings, or perhaps near the coast, other factors come into play.

Fiona Brockhoff's Flinders garden illustrates how a design response can exude a definitive coastal style, achieved through echoing plant forms and species that appear naturally in the surrounding landscape. Using locally sourced materials including gravels, timbers, paving stone options and ornamental features or objects relevant to an area also helps to reinforce styles that are based on location.

Skill is involved, however, in ensuring there is a marriage in the style of your garden and your home. Reference to gardening books and other gardens will help to identify which style best suits your home and how to achieve that look. Think carefully about your lifestyle, too, so that the design establishes an environment that encourages and supports it.

Popular styles include restrained Japanese gardens, Balinese tropical paradises, formal gardens such as French or Spanish with clipped hedges, a Santa Fe garden, redolent of hot, arid landscapes, or an English-style woodland garden. Mediterranean gardens suit coastal or warm, sunny climates. Combine terracotta pots, lemons, olives and lavender with some of our own native plants like coastal rosemary and correas, add terracotta paving and capture a gorgeous Mediterranean garden feel.

Perhaps most important is the realisation that achieving a successful interpretation of a style demands discipline. A Japanese garden, just as with any other garden style, requires a consistent palette of plants and materials. Gravels, preferably artistically raked, rocks, water, clipped plants, a deer-scarer and bamboo enclosing fence

are appropriate—terracotta pots are not. Establishing style similarly demands a recognition of the palette that contributes to a specific theme and then applying it to your garden.

There's still a need for caution. There are styles that may have considerable appeal but may not travel well. A traditional Japanese garden is appropriate in Japan or around a Japanese building, but may appear somewhat eccentric against an Australian home. That is not to say there aren't elements of a style that can serve as a design theme, to be reinterpreted with an Australian flavour, such as the use of rock placement and gravel with Australian plants and decorative features.

The argument for the use of Australian plants in rural settings is to ensure there is an appropriate integration of a garden into the broader landscape. 'Appropriate' is the key word here. Styles chosen for a garden should be appropriate. This is generally achieved through sensitive interpretation of architecture, site, locality and lifestyle. Careful consideration will help you to integrate your home, your lifestyle and your garden to achieve a harmonious overall result.

Though very clearly this is not a Japanese garden, several oriental elements have been borrowed as a basis to this John Patrick-designed garden, including bamboos and maples, mondo grass between pavers and Naturereed to provide enclosure.

Fruit trees, clipped cypress, lavender and olives all conjure up a mediterranean garden style.

Hawthorn Garden
Melbourne

'I like gardens to almost transcend time and space, giving you the feeling of having walked into another world. Gardens need to be practical and visually striking, yet they, too, must stir an inner feeling, evoke a mood, and offer opportunities for quiet contemplation. A great garden connects one to nature, feeding the spirit, stimulating the senses, and nourishing the soul.' georgina martyn

Biography

An epiphany at age fifteen began Georgina Martyn's quest to become a residential garden designer. In a surreal moment, tending the garden on her mother's farm beneath the setting sun, Georgina had a vision of her life as a landscape designer. She now runs her successful Melbourne practice, BoldSimplicity, which focuses on sustainable design that predominantly features organic forms, circular shapes, and asymmetry. An artistic and soulful style resonates through her gardens, imprinting feelings of peace, harmony and beauty on their occupants.

A profound influence on Georgina's design philosophy was an idyllic childhood association with her grandmother's stately 1-hectare garden, 'Astolat'. Georgina savours memories of enchanted walks, trails of discovery, and hide and seek. Here, her passion for voluptuous foliage gardens began, and Astolat's strong framework softened

by plants, formed the blueprint for her own style of design.

Georgina completed her horticultural science degree at Burnley in 1994, working part-time in landscape maintenance during her studies. This 'hands-on' experience, later complemented by work in a wholesale nursery, provided an opportunity to appreciate plants and understand their cultural requirements. Subsequent visits to English and European gardens inspired her greatly and she commenced her own design business on return from her travels aged 22.

Motherhood combined with her existent horticultural direction flamed her desire to follow a holistic approach to design. Acutely aware of the need for gardens to perform a nurturing role, she now employs principles of Feng Shui and biodynamic gardening in her designs. Understanding the importance of play in a child's formative years, Georgina incorporates subtle creative play opportunities where appropriate. Including organic and sustainable methods and materials in her work is part of Georgina's desire to make a positive difference in the world.

1 A curving path around the periphery of Georgina's quarter circle paving design, comprising a sawn bluestone edge filled with small black pebbles in mortar, provides a frame to the design and a bike path for the garden's resident pre-schooler. Centre: Dragon tree (*Dracaena draco*).

In the actual design process, Georgina takes cues from the site itself. She senses how to develop a garden and, preferring the creativity and softness of hand drawing, her plans simply evolve, quite intuitively, from the energy of the site. Functional requirements are also important. She carefully observes the dynamics of garden users and designs spaces that fulfil practical needs, while imbuing them with a vitality and harmony on a spiritual plane. Her greatest pleasure as a designer is in seeing her vision become a reality and observing the enjoyment derived by all who experience the garden.

Naturally drawn to quirky and artistic elements, her work often features rusted metal, sculpture, a curved seat and abundant plant material for interest through leaf, bark or berry. An early proponent of using grasses in the landscape, she remains committed to the challenge of using drought-tolerant native and exotic grasses and plants in evermore creative ways.

With Georgina's many design accolades and awards, her gardens are understandably widely sought for exposure in publications, television programs, open garden events and tours. She has regular speaking engagements, writes for horticultural publications and acts as a mentor to horticulture students at the University of Melbourne.

Design brief

Georgina used the design and construction of display gardens at exhibitions as her entry point into garden design, with her gold-medal success at the Melbourne International Flower and Garden Show in every year she exhibited translating into a constant supply of private residential design work. This garden was among them, her client simply announcing, 'I've seen your work and I just want a Gold Medal garden.' Yet, of course, there was more to it. The garden had to meet a range of functional demands; to extend the indoor living space, fulfil a need for outdoor sitting and entertaining, as well as provide a play space offering interest and adventure for the owners' young child. A mother of a young child herself, Georgina is well-attuned to the nurturing benefits a garden offers to children and designs with this in mind.

Her client had also recognised the potential to link Victoria Park beyond the boundary fence with the garden. While hoping to incorporate the wonderful park views available from upstairs, they had not quite anticipated Georgina's innovative response.

Site analysis

In such a small garden (8m x 4m), it may seem there is little to analyse. Yet nothing could be further from the truth, for by undertaking a thorough site analysis, Georgina was able to give this small space a unique character and form, distinguishable from other gardens.

This unique character derives from the site location itself as it adjoins an attractive inner-city park. Opportunities for a 'borrowed landscape' were obvious with the small garden effectively being increased in size by its visual link to the park.

The house had been designed following Feng Shui principles, so the owners were receptive to Georgina's suggestion that a Feng Shui consultant be used in the garden. The results formed an extra dimension to the site analysis. Water was required for financial success, metal in the eastern section, and an avoidance of fire and earth to the west. A significant aspect of the site was a large peppercorn (*Schinus areira* var. *molle*) to the southeast corner, just outside the boundary. It had the potential to provide root competition, removal of water and reduced plant vitality. Further, the foliage it drops can create a hydrophobic layer, resulting in poor water entry into the soil. Conversely, this fabulous specimen offered a real feature, a beautifully structured tree of a scale appropriate to the garden. Being in council property anyway, nothing could be done about it, so the garden had to work around it.

Interestingly, Georgina noted and valued the view from the laundry window to deep within the site. Aware that laundries are frequently visited rooms in most family homes, and consequently present frequent viewing opportunities, she determined that this view should extend into the design.

Finally, the last part of the site analysis only became clear as the garden was created, when buried bottles, broken clay pots and other remnants of the previously existing tip were unearthed. Understandably, the soil was poor so extensive work was required to improve it so that plants had the best opportunity to overcome competition from the adjacent tree roots.

Design response

Georgina admits to being drawn to circular shapes and organic forms with structure, so strong geometrical circles inevitably dominate her design. Pursuant to the Feng Shui requirements of the site, paving was located in the westerly position responding to the avoidance of 'earth' in this area. Preliminary sketches included a central circle, but this proved unsuitable due to the restricted area. Consideration of access from main rear doors and laundry door led her to change the full circle to a quarter circle with an asymmetric character. A curving

path, extending from the laundry effectively anchored the design and introduced a 'curved' theme that could be followed in other components. Consequently, circles now provide the overall theme to the garden. In Feng Shui, circles and the colours grey and white are manifestations of metal, so a grey and white circular repetition in the paving fitted this context.

Georgina is a great believer in feeding a child's imagination in a garden. Given a swing, it remains a swing, but given a series of garden features, a child can make of them what their imagination allows. To a child, the circles in the paving might be clouds to dream on, hopscotch to jump on or puddles to splash in.

Creation of a foreground, middle ground and background—to provide depth and perspective—is paramount in Georgina's designs. Here, paving offers foreground interest, a curved concrete seat the middle ground and the fence the background. On a larger scale,

2 The granite circle pavers were cut in a quarry in Indonesia and shipped to Melbourne. In between is a white pebble slurry, the grey and white of the paving setting a theme that was reiterated in the exterior house colours. Even the internal door fittings were matched to the metal themes of the garden.

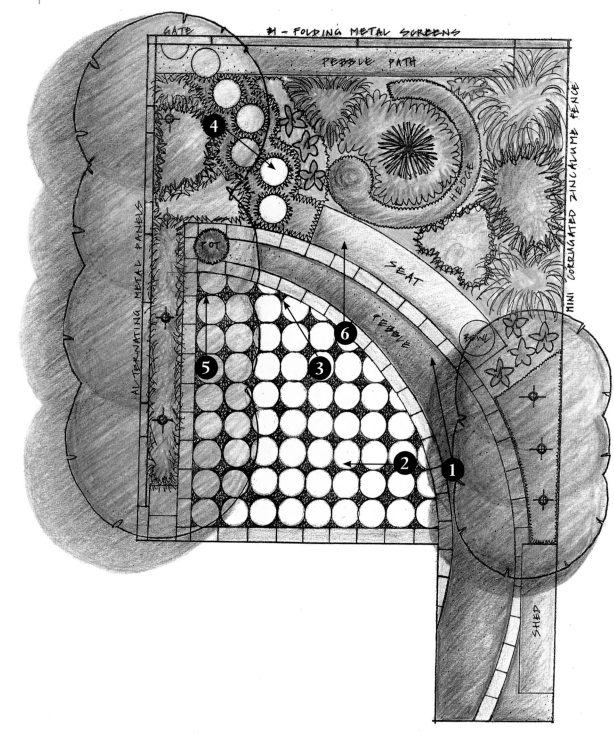

GATE

#1 – FOLDING METAL SCREENS

PEBBLE PATH

HEDGE

MINI CORRUGATED ZINCALUME FENCE

ALTERNATING METAL PANELS

POT

SEAT

PEBBLE

BOWL

SHED

Numbers featured on the plan identify viewlines of correspondingly numbered images.

0   2   4   6m

APPROX. SCALE

3 The elegant tall white pot is a perfect focus at the end of the bench.

the garden forms the foreground, the large peppercorn the middle feature, and the park beyond the distant element. One of the joys of this garden is that it reads on so many levels.

The purpose-built seat not only creates perspective in the garden, but is a functional element providing a comfortable place to sit and setting for a water bowl. Its white vertical masonry and curved bluestone capping meld with the paving theme. Metal was a demand of the Feng Shui analysis and, preferring simplicity, Georgina was attracted by a simple metal dish of still water.

To the other end of the seat, almost as a balancing feature in the asymmetrical garden, a large, elegant white pot from Milan was chosen. Traditional ceramic pots were trialled but they were too squat and jarred in the landscape. This elegant, slender contemporary pot fits perfectly. In addition, its height interrupts the view to the rear gate so that energy from the garden was contained.

Having set her garden theme, Georgina set about extending it to the boundary fencing. Use of rusty metal sheets as a garden fence represents a truly imaginative

response to the constraints placed upon a designer by bureaucracies. In this case, the Victorian Government's Residential Development Code allowed a fence height greater than 2m for a limited extent, leaving a 2m shortfall in the permitted distance and the total garden length. As a result, Georgina divided the 2m distance into four 50cm sections, alternating extension panels of sculptured Corten steel with sections of traditional fence height in between. Not only does this conform to regulations, it also has a major design advantage, for a complete fence of tall panels to the boundary would have been too enclosing and solid. It also gave a logical design cue for the southern boundary fence height to correspond with the lower sections of the northern fence. Certainly Georgina's innovative laser-cut panels featuring a champagne bubble design are a magical and beautiful solution that perfectly illustrates Georgina's belief that 'it's always about thinking creatively around constraints, and as long as you work within the rules, there's always a way to think creatively for a solution.'

4 On one hand the seat is a bench or table, on the other a stage and balance beam. It can fulfil different roles, depending upon a child's imagination.

5 The placement of the contemporary white pot effectively provides a full stop to the pebbled pathway, contains the space and allows the impression of a separate area beyond it. A clipped dome of box in this pot expresses in three dimensions the circular theme of the garden and it is a manicured foil to the looseness of other planting.

Something of this attitude can be seen in the garden's tour de force, it's rear fence. It's easy to suggest that a fence opening onto a park is an attractive solution, but not so easy to address this in a way that is both functional and imaginative. At first, the concept of a wire fence was investigated but it offered inadequate privacy. A more solid structure was needed but not one so heavy that it made opening the fence a hardship. There was one further complication—leaf litter from the peppercorn was likely to fill tracks of runners for any folding fence. The solution was to hang the fence from an upper rail rather than the bottom, which has successfully ensured trouble-free movement. An additional constraint arose from the regulation that the fence could not lay over council property, the park, when opening or closing. Cleverly designed to bi-fold internally, all issues were successfully navigated.

Georgina's resolution for the practical needs of a clothesline in this small, highly visible space again shows her ingenuity. A socket was inserted in the centre of the paving space which allows the simple erection and removal of a rotary clothesline as the need arises. A miniature, permanent line was also attached to the side wall of the

Clever design of the bi-fold rear fence to open internally ensured panels were retained within the garden, rather than trespassing on Council property. The whole effect is mesmerising, permitting the fence to be either entirely or partially opened to the park with a minimum of effort.

Sculptured dragonflies bring a whimsical element to the space, and again offer a stimulus to a child's imagination.

Lighting subtly changes the mood of the garden to a softer, more romantic space. Uplit *Acer palmatum* 'Herbstfeuer', translating to 'autumn fire' in German, will glow in the autumn night sky.

house, out of view and useful for smaller items. Storage facilities weren't overlooked either, with a slimline shed accessed by a retracting roller shutter installed close to the house on the southern boundary fence.

As a final ornamental touch, Georgina commissioned the design of metal butterflies and dragonflies, repeating the use of both rusted and matte forms of metal to reflect the use of these materials elsewhere in the garden.

The garden, though a visual treat in daylight, is totally transformed at night. Lights in the paving play up the wall of the seat, highlight the texture and colour of the side and rear fence panels, and illuminate the trunk of the peppercorn towering over the garden. Light spillage through the champagne bubbles also brings mythical imagery to park users and extends the site's sculptural effects.

Planting design

Georgina's planting imbues her gardens with a sense of drama, using unusual sustainable plant material en masse for abundance. Being particularly drawn to grasses and foliage plants, she uses them to maximise dramatic effects.

In this garden, bold foliage is offered by the dragon tree (*Dracaena draco*), a Canary Island native, located not only for the textural contrast it offers, but also as a visual focus when viewed through the house from the front door. It also provides height to the garden and will continue to do so as it matures. Near it, the spiky evergreen foliage of Chinese holly grape (*Mahonia lomariifolia*) is a contrast to two grasses, variegated maiden grass (*Miscanthus sinensis* 'Variegata') and zebra grass (*M. sinensis* 'Zebrinus'). True to her view that plants look best as drifts, Georgina has used these as large blocks.

At ground level the grass foliage form and texture is repeated in the evergreen low-growing mondo (*Ophiopogon japonicus* 'Nana'), not actually a grass but closely related to lilies. It fills pavers between the circular stepping stones to the rear gate and abuts a mass of groundcovering sedge (*Carex brunnea*), which is a fine-

Georgina comments "I tend to have a bold leaf next to a fine leaf, a round leaf next to a more spiky one." This effective planting philosophy gives her gardens striking visual impact, evident here, where cotyledons and dragon tree provide solidity as a foil to carex and a miscanthus.

leaf contrast to the form of *Agave attenuata* present at either end of the seat. Repetition within planting design helps to hold this planting scheme together, but because plant selections and placement are made with such care, they give the design a sense of cohesion. A comma-shaped box hedge echoes the curved shape of the seat in reverse, giving structure and a sense of formality within the other plant massing.

It is notable that the garden balances evergreen and deciduous plants. *Mahonia aquifolium*, frequently overlooked as a garden plant, not only offers evergreen foliage that produces occasional red leaves in autumn, but also striking yellow flowers in late winter, followed by dark blue berries.

Indeed, though this is mostly a foliage garden, there's always something happening, either from foliage, flowers, seed heads or berries. There are subtle links between plants too; the variegated leaf of *Iris japonica* 'Variegata', with charming soft blue flowers, responding

A large drift of *Miscanthus sinensis* 'Variegatus' is beautifully reflected in the water's surface. Georgina's experience with grass suggests it does better by being cut back when foliage begins to dry off. Its response is to produce lush new foliage.

An underplanting of giant mondo grass (*Ophiopogon jaburan*) softens the interface of the metal fence and paving, while white flowers in late summer respond to white pebbles. The white sculptural ball continues the theme of the circular paving, but uses colour in reverse.

to the variegation of the miscanthus. But the key feature of the garden, especially in autumn, is the maples planted along the side boundaries. To the north, the vine leaf maple (*Acer japonicum* 'Vitifolium') punctuates the rusted metal panels at each lower interval. This generally upright growing maple to 4–5m will eventually create an open canopy, thus providing the garden with more shade to the north. The leaves themselves are decorative, with 9–11 lobes; and clusters of purple/red flowers, hanging delicately from the tree in spring are far more notable

then in almost any other maple so they contribute to this ever-changing scene.

To the southern boundary, another maple, the vigorous and more rounded-growing *Acer palmatum* 'Herbstfeuer' has been chosen to screen the adjacent house, though it too offers great beauty in the brown bark of its multi-stemmed trunks, and more particularly in its strong autumn foliage, changing from bronze in late summer to bright orange in autumn.

'Our garden's connection to the park through the retractable rear fence is the real highlight. Apart from the visual and liberating appeal, it has proven to be very engaging with our neighbourhood, helping to develop a close community spirit that we value highly.'

Garden owners

6

Appropriately designed lighting can bring out new dimensions of planting as this lighting scheme by Gardens at Night shows. Lighting design is a skilled task and for the best effect consultants should be employed.

Engaging experts

In achieving the spectacular outcome in this Hawthorn courtyard garden, Georgina drew on expertise from others. Commissioning a specialist Indonesian supplier for the circular cut granite, a local metal artist and a Feng Shui expert, she successfully engaged others to ensure her vision was realised.

In one form or another, most garden owners are likely to seek some external assistance to meet design expectations. There are professionals able to meet every need of the home gardener from design, construction and maintenance to implementation of specialist features.

Engaging a professional designer is worthwhile if you lack confidence or knowledge in garden design. There are a wide range of professionals on offer, some themselves specialists in particular types or styles of garden. Many of them are members of professional organisations, either the Australian Institute of Landscape Architects or

Australian Institute of Garden Designers and Managers. Both admit members on the basis of qualifications and experience and thereby bring a guarantee of standards to their work.

There are also many well-respected designers who work outside these organisations. It is wise to view samples of a designer's work through folios and photographs or visits to finished gardens, often possible through Open Garden Schemes or charitable events. It is also a good idea to speak with past clients, to assess the designer's overall performance, ability to meet deadlines, reliability and response to requests for information.

Designers may charge differently—some a percentage of construction works, others either by the hour or a fixed fee. Clarify this and make sure you are happy. In the first case, you may need an estimate of project costs to assess what the total sum is likely to be, whereas in the

In garden construction some techniques demand specific and particular skills. Construction of stone walls, such as this one constructed by stone artist Neal Plummer, warrants the employment of an expert.

second there may be benefits in staging works to clarify the number of hours. Be sure, too, to assess exactly what your designer will provide. Review previously prepared plans to ensure they are appropriately detailed for tender and construction, otherwise results can be vague with a landscape contractor ultimately charging you for completing the designer's work or for extra works not clearly detailed on plans.

Many nurseries provide design services and this can be a useful source of design advice, but it is very often focused on plants rather than overall design quality.

Landscape contractors vary in experience and capability. Many will be members of the Landscape Industry Association in your State and this provides a good starting point. Always get prices from two or three contractors, visit previous work sites to assess the quality of their work, and ask for references, assessing issues such as punctuality, willingness to right mistakes, site tidiness and overall performance.

Many contractors are also designers; however, by combining roles they often avoid the process of competitive tendering with the benefits of price reductions that this can bring. It is likely that your designer can provide names of experienced contractors, but always check their performance for yourself to ensure you are comfortable with them.

Consider the benefits of engaging appropriate experts to undertake specific elements of garden construction. While irrigation, garden lighting, installation of water features and arboricultural works are all possible to undertake yourself, professionals working specifically in these fields will undoubtedly contribute expertise and knowledge, and, more often than not, actually save you money in the process.

Maintenance is another area where professional services can be worthwhile, particularly for a new garden. It is a good idea to employ your contractor to implement maintenance for an initial establishment period as part of the original contract to ensure the garden grows satisfactorily. Material that dies during this period should be replaced free of charge. Liaison between designer and maintenance contractor is sensible to ensure the design vision is understood and ultimately realised. Do recognise too that conditions change in gardens, so you may need to get your designer back periodically to direct changes in planting, for example, as shade develops over the garden in place of sun.

There are many other professionals who can help you with the implementation of your garden. Your designer is likely to know of artists with specific skills, for example trompe l'oeil, mosaic, sculpture or stone wall specialists. By engaging various experts—just as Georgina employed a metal artist to construct her design for the corten steel laser-cut panels and retractable fence for her Hawthorn courtyard—you too can add style and originality to your garden.

For a high quality and long-lasting result in paved areas, the employment of qualified tradesmen can be both a time and cost saving process in the long run.

Gippsland Garden
Victoria

'Garden design today is heavily influenced by maintenance, often resulting in stark, 'season-less' gardens. I love the idea of using plants in a romantic, textural and seasonal way without blowing out the issues of maintenance. By using a carefully selected, limited palette of plants, I can create a garden that is plant-driven, stimulating and with exaggerated seasonal change that I am confident is within the capabilities of my clients to manage.' michael mccoy

Biography

Michael McCoy established his landscape design business in 1997, quickly gaining a reputation for having an artist's and horticulturist's eye for designing with plants. Now practising from Woodend, Victoria, Michael is one of Australia's foremost plantsmen. Having built a design platform from this intimate plant knowledge, he designs spaces that skilfully showcase the bold and striking plant combinations he loves.

Michael's interest in gardening began in early adulthood, when he was confined to a summer holiday at home with his ailing father. Born of sheer boredom, his fascination for plants was ignited by the discovery of propagation. 'This curious idea that you could actually break a bit of something off and stick it in the ground and it would reproduce itself' he comments was the beginning of Michael's obsession with the craftsmanship of gardening.

After a Botany degree, Michael completed a gardening apprenticeship under the expert tutelage of Oliver Frost at Ripponlea, a National Trust property in Victoria. A concurrent design course at the Melbourne School of Art affirmed to him the importance of the underlying principles of design, applicable in any form of artistic expression. He became Head Gardener at 'Hascombe', a notable privately owned Mt Macedon garden and, during this role, worked in England at 'Great Dixter' with Christopher Lloyd. Lloyd's influence helped to liberate Michael's approach to design, encouraging him to 'have more fun' in the garden, take risks and experiment with plant combinations. Visits to Sissinghurst and Powis Castle were inspirational and remain unsurpassed memories of excitement.

Emerging from the challenge to reconcile his love of plant diversity with the need to create gardens that are manageable for clients, Michael has developed a pared-down approach to design. Inspired by the work of American designers, van Sweden and Oehme, he believes a limited palette of plants may be used without

---

Colours and materials of both house and garden elements blend sympathetically to form a perfectly integrated landscape. Prostrate *Juniperus horizontalis* 'Wiltonii' (blue rug juniper) and *Beschorneria bracteata* provide a dramatic planting combination.

sacrificing the seasons. Definition of spaces, scale and proportion become even more crucial to design, as does specific plant selection. Paradoxically, this simplicity of planting requires an extensive knowledge of thousands of plants.

Michael's portfolio includes commissions for Leo Schofield at Bronte House, Sydney and Yering Station in Victoria's Yarra Valley. Apart from his successful design career, he has conducted garden tours, has regular public speaking engagements, and, as an accomplished photographer and writer, is the author of *Michael McCoy's Garden*. He contributes regularly to newspapers and gardening publications, currently writing for *Gardens Illustrated* and *Your Garden*.

Michael is passionate about rekindling in people joy and pleasure in the processes of gardening. Just as the appreciation of 'slow' food over 'fast' is gathering momentum, he is intent on reversing the current 'fast' gardening trends. Though some would see a contradiction in Michael's celebrated success at bringing his own Woodend garden to maturity in just two seasons, Michael points out that even in this short time frame, many hours of 'hands on' gardening were passionately invested. It's this 'hands on', human intervention that he advocates over the detached process of 'instant' garden installations. Recognising the power of nature, nothing delights Michael more than seeing clients fully interacting with their gardens.

Design brief

'I don't know whether I have really ever formally sat down for this whole sort of "briefing" process that so many designers talk about,' says Michael. The design of this garden was no exception, being an ongoing affair over a decade, developed from an overriding philosophy rather than a specific brief.

Michael, the third designer to work on the project, was selected by his client, Barbara, from an article he had written about a romantic garden. Barbara's opening words were, 'I saw those photos and I knew I didn't want any of that, but I can see in that a quality that I am assuming you will be able to translate to other things.' That his new client had been able to view a very different garden and extrapolate Michael's potential to work with her and meet her expectations impressed him. The key words of her brief were, 'I want something bare and barren and beautiful.' It is that which they have jointly strived for over the ten years of the project.

Any design work had to respond to the grand scale of the rammed-earth and timber house designed by West Australian architect, Kim Stirling. Barbara did not want a romantic or countrified garden despite its rural setting so maintaining an urban sophistication was a vital part of the design. Her love of strong, geometric shapes, symmetry and the bright, childish colours of the art deco movement also influenced the garden's development.

An open-ended brief of this nature is certainly unusual. Michael says, 'If anything, I was called in to have a look at the garden, see what I thought of where they currently were, see whether I could make something of the stage they had reached and improve on it.' Blessed with an enthusiastic and committed client actively engaged in both the design and construction of the garden, Michael embarked on the project with equal enthusiasm and yet admits, 'Neither of us had any idea or could have envisaged this end result at the start.'

Site analysis

Michael was impressed when he arrived at the picturesque rural Gippsland setting for this garden, taking in the angular geometry of the rammed-earth house poised above a short cleared valley amid native bushland. The garden surrounding the house was laid out by a previous designer and included separate Japanese, Greek and Australian areas. Michael faced the challenge of integrating spaces and developing the garden as a unified whole.

Fortunately, an appropriate scale for the garden had been established, particularly in the form of a unique field of lavender. This expansive area provided a benchmark for the scale of other components, and conformed with Michael's

The location of the house maximized the benefit of rural views. **Foreground:** *Miscanthus* 'Sarabande'.

opinion that an appropriately scaled response between house and garden was the key design consideration. This would ensure the imposing home would not overpower its surroundings and address Barbara's desire for a 'bare, barren and beautiful' landscape.

An existing timber deck was surrounded by a large swathe of tussock grass (*Poa labillardierei*). Michael's experience told him this plant dies out from the middle, despite being considered an evergreen grass, and he was determined to replace it.

The topography of the land was also a consideration with slopes falling away from the house. The valley sloped from the deck to pasture and a substantial farm dam, forming the focus of stunning views from living rooms and deck. An existing swimming pool appeared cramped in relation to the scale of other site components so Michael resolved to visually enlarge the area it occupied and connect it more appropriately to the garden.

He observed that additional trees were not required within the garden because of the enclosing nature of the valley. The vertical plane existed through the surrounding hills and towering eucalypt forests at its fringe. Any new trees would interrupt the flow of the inner garden and compete with its broader setting.

Design response

Michael and Barbara designed together as they walked the site, allowing both an opportunity to recognise the impact of their ideas and to refine them as they went. Barbara was adamant that Michael should not waste time at the drawing board—preferring his presence on-site where they could discuss ideas, evaluate options and resolve issues immediately, rather than prolong the process with sketches and plans. Michael does concede that without an overall master plan, mistakes have been made but re-doing sections of the garden was never a problem with Barbara's pragmatic philosophy—'When in doubt, rip it out!'

Rammed earth, the main construction element of the house, used as paving, retaining walls, pool surrounds and steps helped to establish a link between garden and house. Horizontal timber posts link to timber laid horizontally in the courtyard paving.

The deck now measures 25m x 9m and is constructed on piers to counteract the slope. Lengths of treated pine, 14cm wide by 4.5cm deep were used and allowed to weather naturally to relate to its surroundings. A 20,000 gallon tanklies beneath the deck.

Each section of the garden evolved as an individual area, though linked to the one before it. This relationship extended to the house itself, with Michael acutely aware that for the garden to succeed it had to marry in scale and materials to the house.

Michael began by extending the outdoor entertaining deck adjoining the family room, sited to capture stunning views of farmland and the lagoon below. He increased it to relate it in scale to the house and to address the 'bare and barren' nature of the brief.

Continuing the garden's grand scale, Michael mass-planted hundreds of *Miscanthus* 'Sarabande' in a huge wave surrounding the deck to form an ephemeral sea that rises like a tide each spring, receding in late winter when cut to the ground. The grasses' whimsical, feathery flowerheads form a shimmering ocean lapping against the deck. This simple, block planting provides a perfect foil for the stark beauty of the house and also a low maintenance solution to a large garden area. The generous planting also magnifies the delicate changes in colour of the grasses and the hypnotic qualities of their gentle movement in the breeze. To contrast with the fluidity of the *Miscanthus*, Michael planted *Agave americana* 'Blue Form' in nearby swathes. This particularly blue agave has broad, fleshy leaves that offer a contrasting rigidity.

The swimming pool adjoining the deck is enclosed by rammed-earth walls and bordered by the house on one side. It is set in an established lawn, and neither Michael nor Barbara was satisfied with the lack-lustre pool surrounds. Determined to do more, they introduced the modernist design style of Martha Schwartz who they both admired. They commissioned square grids of 80–140cm rusted iron and laid them across the lawn, some overlapping, to form geometric outlines on the lawn's surface. Further grids were mounted on the house wall, extending the pattern vertically.

Looking from the hub of the kitchen/meals area across the swimming pool, the land falls sharply to paddocks beyond. Clinging to the hillside and hidden behind rammed-earth retaining walls is a French-inspired potager. The parterre-

The blue form of *Agave americana* looks remarkable against the colour of the rammed earth walls and autumnal bronze hues of the grasses *Miscanthus* 'Sarabande'.

style garden spills over two terraces carved from the slope. Its grand scale continues the site's overriding theme and provides a workable area to produce family supplies using biodynamic principles employed throughout the farm.

At the entrance to the property, arrived at from a meandering farm track, an imposing archway leads the visitor to the rear of the house into a large courtyard. An octagonal pond is the centrepiece to the expansive rammed-earth paved area, broken up using 10cm-posts of red gum laid horizontally in a geometric grid. This breaks the monotony of using one material over such a large area and provides an interesting pattern from the upper storeys of the house. Michael concedes he would never have thought

Ficus pumila (Creeping Fig) was planted carefully to grow through holes in the rammed earth walls so that, in time, the iron grids will form flat green squares on the wall's face to echo the expanse of lawn and effectively enlarge the pool area. The addition of randomly placed concrete spheres and spherically clipped box introduced a dynamic quality previously missing.

Meeting his client's needs for order and symmetry, the terraced potager perched on the hillside beyond the pool uses clipped box (*Buxus sempervirens*) to enclose the infill of more loosely planted seasonal vegetables.

An octagonal pond provides the centerpiece to the rear courtyard which uses red gum posts in a grid pattern within gravel paving. By laying the gravel on a bitumen base and heat sealing it, an appearance of loose gravel was achieved yet avoiding problems associated with its tracking around the garden or into the house.

Arrival at the house is at the end of a meadering gravel driveway. The house is revealed slowly, screened by mass *Miscanthus*.

of using rammed earth as paving, but credits the previous designer, Stan Smith, with the spectacular result.

Planting against the house was avoided to emphasise the austerity and continue the theme of 'bare, barren and beautiful'. Instead, the courtyard is punctuated with formally clipped bay trees in ceramic pots that originally contained olive trees. Michael substituted bay trees (*Laurus nobilis*) to introduce a design strength through their dark colour and tight clipping. Red marbles are used as a potting mulch to give a touch of pizzazz to the otherwise barren courtyard—Barbara eventually sourcing 1-in diameter, tomato-red marbles from Mexico!

Lutyens-style semicircular steps of rammed earth link the rear courtyard and a breathtaking zone that is essentially a field of lavender, planted out in straight rows on mounds of gravel with a central aisle that leads to a stage at its focal point. The individual lavenders give the feel of a 'full house', with all eyes appearing to focus on clipped bay hedging forming the stage wings— a veritable outdoor auditorium. The sentinel forms of *Cupressus sempervirens* 'Glauca' form the backdrop and, with its magical theatrical setting, even the Melbourne Symphony Orchestra has considered using it for concert performances.

Michael and Barbara faced the challenge of selecting an appropriate feature to provide the central focal point between the bay tree wings. This important axis required a special treatment that would complement the expansive amphitheatre feel and be an appropriate focus to terminate the view. Both Michael and Barbara felt nervous about the use of sculpture in this position and were delighted when they discovered three 2m-tall gourd-shaped palm tree bases.

An exuberant array of perennials rise up in an engulfing mass of foliage and flowers beyond the lavender field. Delineated by crisp clipped English box (*Buxus sempervirens*) to maintain sophistication and order, the classic McCoy-style border is a touch of chaos in a sea of calm. This lavish border peaks in mid to late summer when Michael believes gardens should be looking their best. With long, balmy evenings and time to relax or entertain, this, Michael says, is when gardens are most often on show. He insists that a garden can still look good at the end of a long hot Australian summer if appropriate plant choices are made. Proving the point, Michael used his encyclopaedic plant knowledge in this garden to select a palette of plants that perform on cue during the garden's most prominent 'show time'.

An unexpected delight at the end of the perennial border is an intricate knot garden. Across from the knot garden is a large Roman terracotta pot almost 1.5m high dating from 400–700 BCE. It acts as a dual focal point, terminating views from both the knot garden and swimming pool. Michael and Barbara felt confident in its earthen qualities, having been collected originally from Turkey where it stored grain. In Michael's view, 'There is something lovely and functional about it which makes it less self-conscious than a piece of pure statuary.'

With swollen bellies and blackened trunks, three gourd shaped palm tree bases now stand centre stage, their organic shape and form giving a wonderfully unselfconscious aura.

Fashioned from clipped English box, the spiralling pattern of the knot garden is clipped at varying heights to give an illusion of movement as it dips and weaves over a bed of polished black pebbles.

Lighting is a deliberate exclusion from the garden, with both Michael and Barbara content for the garden to be dark at night, just as nature intended. Barbara also sees this as an opportunity to be flexible in the installation of temporary function lighting to cater for a specific celebration or style of outdoor entertaining.

Michael and Barbara's collaborative design for the garden creates a large and dramatic setting for outdoor living that epitomises the Australian lifestyle, and yet confidently incorporates contemporary influences from designers across the globe, most notably van Sweden and Schwartz—with a Charles Jenks-style pond in Barbara's plans!

Planting design

Though renowned for his exceptional skill in designing with a diverse range of plants, Michael acknowledges that in this garden, plant diversity was deliberately minimised, partly to address his client's desire for simplicity and partly for the opportunity to create bold effects from mass plantings of individual species. In such a large garden, the overall structure was paramount, with plants forming a purely decorative role once the framework was successfully established. Michael claims that if a garden possesses strong bones, with spaces appropriately defined and linked, it maintains an elegance and beauty even without flowers. To achieve this strength, Michael uses hedging and repetition of species within the design to provide separation of spaces, yet an overall continuity. The use of bay trees as a hedging plant provides a dense, evergreen curtain to the stage area of the lavender field, and is specifically chosen for its uniformity of growth, ability to be tightly clipped, its tough, drought tolerance and its moderate growth rate which minimises the frequency of clipping. Repetition of the bay trees appears in a circular hedge defining the knot garden and as clipped topiary specimens in pots in the rear courtyard of the house. The use of English box, hedged to delineate spaces and as sculptural spheres in the pool area, again reinforces the structure of the garden and provides a year-round framework to rest upon.

Adjoining the deck, *Miscanthus* 'Sarabande' growing to 1.5m in a season, forms a substantial mass, yet is not too tall to restrict views to the valley below. Michael finds the easiest way to maintain this grass is to tie it in large bunches in winter, cut it at the base with hedge trimmers then drag the whole sheaf away.

The use of different varieties of *Miscanthus*, in vast block plantings around the garden, has multiple purposes. Firstly, the decision to replace the existing mass-planted evergreen tussock grass around the deck with a deciduous grass addressed Michael's penchant for highlighting seasonal change in a garden. The pronounced changing hues and size of the *Miscanthus* signals the progression of time, with its cutting back at the end of winter bringing anticipation of spring. Its forced regeneration each year also overcomes the issue of unsightly and continuous die back associated with evergreen grasses and in Michael's view, the advantages in form and flowerhead, as well as in its attractive seed head left to age over autumn, result in a far superior impact in the garden. Repetition of the *Miscanthus* on a hillside at the rear of the house provides continuity and a link between sections of the garden.

Michael's extensive plant knowledge also led him to replace the lavender cultivar in the existing field. As 'plant perfectionists', both Michael and Barbara agreed that the newly available (at that time) *Lavandula* 'Egerton Blue' was a more consistent performer than the previously planted English lavender variety and would provide a much stronger blue to accentuate the area. Similarly, he replaced the Italian cypress species that formed the backdrop to this area with the far superior *Cupressus sempervirens* 'Glauca', to bring a reliability of form and an absence of unsightly cones.

In the herbaceous border, plants have been carefully selected to fulfil a specific role within the space. Mexican sunflower (*Tithonia rotundifolia*) is used for its long display of orange flowers; Brazilian sage (*Salvia guaranitica*) for its delicious lime-green foliage and midnight-blue spires; and *Plumbago auriculata* 'Royal Cape' for its rich blue flower and cascading form. The addition of Ceanothus 'Trewithen Blue', *Sedum* 'Autumn Joy', the sunflowers *Helianthus* 'Lemon Queen', and red hot pokers (*Kniphofia* cvs) not only addresses Barbara's love of strong, vibrant colours but also offers a progression of flowering through the season and a palette of tough, sun-loving performers that are happy in their exposed position.

Featured plants include (*rear*) *Miscanthus sinensis* 'Giganteus' which reaches up to 5m in a season and *Canna* 'Wyoming' for its striking burgundy foliage and orange flower colour

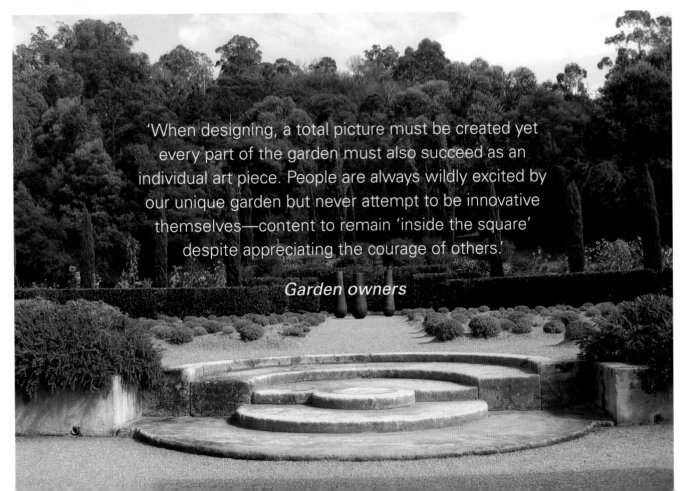

'When designing, a total picture must be created yet every part of the garden must also succeed as an individual art piece. People are always wildly excited by our unique garden but never attempt to be innovative themselves—content to remain 'inside the square' despite appreciating the courage of others.'

Garden owners

DESIGN TIP

While limited to a seasonal floral display, a band of brightly coloured sunflowers, combined here with the complementary colour tones of blue globe thistle (*Echinops ritro*), are certainly a breathtaking site.

Designing with plants

Even for an experienced garden designer, planting design is difficult. For home gardeners, the large diversity of plants available and the inevitable changes that result to their character and form as they grow can cause considerable angst. Maintenance requirements also change plant forms, often leaving disappointing and unexpected gaps or downtimes in our gardens.

As a renowned plantsman, Michael places great importance on the selection of appropriate individual plants in developing a successful overall scheme, noting that even in schemes with low plant diversity, the selection is critical to ensure those few plants offer appropriate impact and functionality.

To begin with, he considers the overall garden effect he wants to achieve. He may want one short dramatic display such as summer colour for a beach house, or alternatively a year-round effect in a suburban home. He may want a

design based on flower or foliage colour or texture; have emergent trees growing out of massed groundcovers, or follow traditional lines, low at the front getting taller towards the rear.

Once the desired effect is identified, to establish a planting scheme that achieves the objectives Michael suggests preparing a plan that breaks up each particular garden bed into separate planting areas, initially highlighting the mass or style of planting required for each area. It's important to consider the three-dimensional nature of plants.

By plotting your planting beds on graph paper where 1cm^2 is 1sqm on the ground, you have a clear guide to the area your planting is taking up. Plants can then be plotted referring to their eventual size and spread.

During this process, identify the form and style of plants you need to fill in your areas, be they broad or fastigiate

This predominantly silver plant palette, designed by Emma Plowright, features euphorbias, correa, yuccas, New Zealand flax, olive, cotyledon, aloes, aeonium and eucalypts. It combines natives and exotics in a low water scheme that perfectly complements the soft grey tones of the house.

trees, rounded or recumbent shrubs, clumping or climbing specimens, either in multiples for effect or as a single highlight. Next, identify specific plants to perform those roles within the scheme, considering, of course, the growing conditions available in each position. For each plant role, Michael suggests identifying three or four plant options that meet both the cultural conditions and physical attributes sought. For example, if a tall, purple-flowering, evergreen shrub is required for an open position in a temperate zone, options might include *Iochroma cyaneum*, *Eupatorium megalophyllum*, *Hibiscus syriacus*, *Wigandia caracasana* or *Buddleja davidii*. Then, depending on garden style, preferred flowering time, colour or textural complements and contrasts with other plants, and your capacity for maintenance, choose the best plant to perform the specific role and contribute to the overall scheme.

There are some rules to follow when developing a planting palette. Start with the major structural plants. Being the largest and making the biggest contribution, they may be used as individual specimens. As you move from larger to smaller plants, do realise you will need multiples of them to achieve a balancing mass. You don't necessarily want all plants to have exactly the same visual impact. You might choose a yellow foliage plant to

create interest. Too many would destroy the effect, but a single specimen can offer strong contrast. Similarly, a well-placed plant with bold or dramatic foliage has great impact; a mass of them would be less effective. As you move from taller to lower plants remember the value in repeating blocks of plants so there is continuity and rhythm in your scheme.

To guarantee success, put together a plant materials sheet in the same way you might develop a colour board for an interior design. Consider which of the plants will flower together, checking that the wonderful contrasts of colour that you see in your mind's eye will actually happen!

Inevitably, you will make mistakes but at least with plants you can move them around or pot them up for friends. In herbaceous schemes, consider using bulbs or seasonal bedders like pansies or violas to cover gaps, particularly in winter. Seek a second opinion on plant choices from your local nursery but don't be persuaded to change selections because they're not in stock. Most can be ordered and it's worth waiting for exactly the right option.

Most importantly, enjoy playing with plants. They offer so much excitement and pleasure, though success with them can be hard earned. Once a good planting scheme is achieved, the results are to be savoured and shared!

The use of coppers, bronzes and golds gives a stronger more autumnal character than the silver palette above. Cannas, crocosmia, cordyline, dahlias and daylilies contribute to the scheme.

North Beach Garden

Perth

'With many gardens today consisting of small courtyards adjoining internal living areas, they must look good for twelve months of the year. Permanently on show, almost like a painting forming a backdrop to everyday life, a strong design framework and reliable plant palette, with as little down-time as possible, is essential to ensure the garden offers constant interest and beauty in its high-profile position.' janine mendel

Biography

Janine Mendel, Perth garden designer, has a penchant for practical and innovative residential design. Known for her contemporary courtyards, her passion is for the designing small spaces so that they provide maximum impact and useable space in confined areas. Often using angles to make spaces seem larger, Janine is attracted by geometry in design, believing strong architectural lines and shapes form the basis of stylish and eye-catching gardens.

Using bright colours in walls and built features, Janine adds interest using her hard landscaping elements for year-round appeal, rather than relying on seasonal flowering for colour. Similarly, creative use of water for aural, reflective or visual interest is a regular feature, again providing a focus for permanent enjoyment.

Initially trained as a cartographer, Janine's affinity with survey maps and land contours has given her an edge in the presentation of plans and an understanding of levels in the landscape. Her practice, Cultivart Landscape Design, was fleetingly contemplated in her 20s, but it was a decade later, as a single mother in her 30s intent on a more creative career, that her practice developed into a means of survival. Through an advertisement in a local newspaper and an 'underwhelming' initial response, her first paid commission arose. Janine recalls, with amusement, that it was a resounding creative success but a financial failure, having paid a horticultural consultant more to plant the garden than she received in design fees! It inspired her, however, to study horticulture and fully launch her new career.

Janine realised that, with her limited portfolio, to attract her preferred style of work she needed to produce a prototype garden to prove her ability. Convincing her bank manager to fund the design of her own garden—to attract client attention and a flow-on of design commissions and income—was a risky business, but ultimately proved rewarding. Winning a sweep of awards, Janine's garden generated huge media interest,

1 Well known for her use of geometric design, here Janine's strong clean garden lines complement the linear architecture. The pink flowered frangipani (*centre*) was specifically selected from nursery stock for its high branching asymmetrical form to suit the contricted space.

exposing her talents and opening up opportunities for daring and big budget designs.

Despite using innovative products in her work, Janine insists it is inappropriate to be governed solely by fashion or to use new materials unless they are proven to be durable and environmentally sustainable. Similarly, she acknowledges a striking, contemporary garden is not right for every client or site. She works with owners and the existing architecture of their homes to satisfy individual requirements, achieving sympathetic gardens that, particularly at the interface of front garden and streetscape, relate to their surroundings. She believes 'site analysis' is where 'garden design' begins, with a view to achieving her goal 'that a house should look as if it's been planted in a garden.'

Janine cites Luis Barragan as a source of inspiration. Barragan works with a similar stark light and hostile climate in his native Mexico, and Janine says that 'his use of vibrant colour and water in the landscape' and 'his simple geometric abstract designs' have often inspired her work.

Publishing her first book in 2006, *Quintessentially Oz*, which profiles her gardens, Janine offers clients willing to be adventurous an opportunity to procure a stylish and functional garden of unique beauty and striking design.

Design brief

The owners of a newly built two-storey residence in the Perth suburb of North Beach always knew they wanted a Janine Mendel-designed garden. Exposed to Janine's innovative work through magazine and newspaper articles, they were confident that with her passionate and creative approach, Janine's involvement would realise their vision for an 'elegant, tastefully luxurious and low-maintenance garden'.

The relatively straightforward brief was for a crisp, clean design to complement the simple contemporary-style architecture of the house. Specific requirements included a timber-decked outdoor entertaining space for 6–8 people to seamlessly integrate with internal timber flooring. Permanent shelter over the area wasn't required, with the

intention that shade sails could be installed at a later date if necessary. Considering their two small children and a golden retriever, the clients sought Janine's advice about including a rear play area of lawn, as they were unsure whether the aspect in the rear garden would provide a suitable growing environment.

Wind protection and a tough, coast-tolerant plant palette were priorities, especially as the owners were not gardeners themselves, yet they did seek an interesting array of plants that would provide textural interest in keeping with the modern theme of their home. A quiet trickle-style water feature to provide a focus to both indoor and outdoor living areas was also requested.

Resolution of an awkward slope between the footpah and front door of the house was perhaps the most critical aspect of the brief. Seeking a sharper looking, functional alternative to the existing sloped entry area, they left the ultimate design response to Janine, confident that she would resolve the issue appropriately.

Site analysis

The square-shaped 450sqm site was largely occupied by the centrally located contemporary home. Glass family room walls on the ground level provided high visibility and a connectedness to the site's western garden areas, which comprised a north-facing front courtyard and a south-facing rear garden. These areas would logically become the focus of any design for the garden, fortunately they were larger in area than the remaining peripheral garden spaces around the home.

Proximity to the coast, however, and the combination of 40-degree temperatures in summer and shade cast from the northern courtyard wall in winter imposed great constraints on plant choices for the high-profile northern area. On the positive side, Janine noted that an imposing western boundary wall between the clients' and a neighbouring home would provide an impressive backdrop for a proposed water feature.

Entry to the house was made difficult by a short, relatively steep slope from the footpath, with a need for access to an existing letterbox within a front fence pillar causing further complications to the front garden design. The clients' agreement to allow Janine to relocate the letterbox greatly increased her design options.

Janine's analysis of the site also uncovered the potential to incorporate strong geometric shapes and angles in her design—not only would this approach fit with site architecture, but would also offer visual interest and pattern in the garden when viewed from the upper storey.

As with most Perth landscapes, the soil on this site comprised impoverished sand with little water-holding capacity or nutrient content. Major soil improvements were necessary to give plants the best opportunity for growth.

Design response

Janine's process of design involves a site visit to ask numerous questions, and listen very carefully to her clients. She then prepares a design based on her gathered information, as though she was in fact the client, calling on her own experiences as a home owner, mother and entertainer, as well as a designer—often becoming very attached to the design in the process. In this way, she manages to realise her clients' vision as though it were her own and, as is usually the case, her initial design for this garden was exactly to her clients' liking.

To begin, Janine used the proportions of the house to divide the residual garden spaces into four distinct areas; the entry, the northern courtyard, the rear grassed area for children and the service area to the east. Within these separate areas, continuity is achieved through the repetition of well-proportioned layered squares and rectangles.

To address the clients' wish for a stylish and functional point of entry, Janine created a series of three floating plinths that safely guide the visitor down the awkward entry slope from the footpath above. The impressive steps were individually formed up by the landscape contractor. A fourth step in oiled batu timber offers contrast to the

2 A sloped driveway of in situ limestone, constructed from crushed limestone (a natural product in Western Australia) and concrete additives ground back and marked as required after pouring, provides direct access to the garage. A rendered cement retaining wall to match the house incorporates the relocated letter box and separates vehicle and pedestrian access.

3 The beautifully detailed front entry steps were constructed with a special aggregate concrete hand washed to gain the desired surface effect.

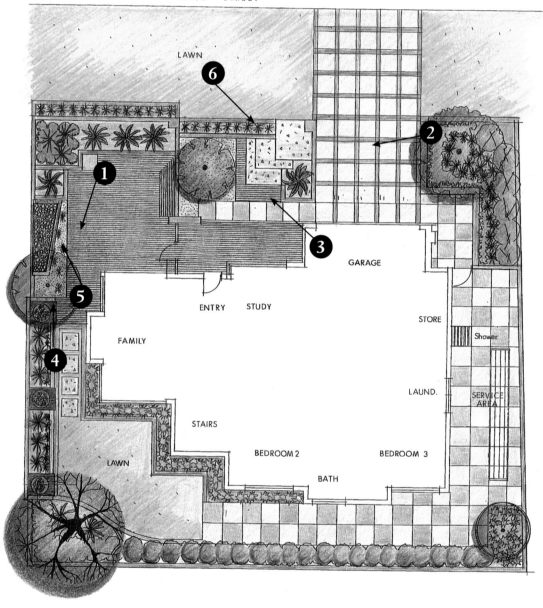

HALE STREET

LAWN

6

2

1

3

GARAGE

ENTRY   STUDY

STORE

Shower

FAMILY

5

LAUND.

SERVICE
AREA

4

STAIRS

LAWN

BEDROOM 2   BEDROOM 3

BATH

N

Numbers featured on the plan identify viewlines of
correspondingly numbered images.

0   2   4   6   8   10m

APPROX. SCALE

limestone and links with both the timber entry porch and the entertaining deck in the northern courtyard. The remainder of the front garden is deliberately simple in its design, comprising a gravel-mulched area of rainbow stone (over a geotextile fabric to suppress weeds) with a centrally located frangipani tree for sculptural impact and summer fragrance. A raised rendered planter box offers enclosure from the street along the northern boundary.

The clients' request for a relatively small entertaining area for 6–8 people was accommodated in Janine's cleverly designed north-facing courtyard. The compact 7m x 7m area appears deceptively spacious thanks to the repetition of timber as the surface both indoors and out, creating the illusion of a single, larger integrated space. Built-in timber seating and a timber daybed within the masonry retaining walls of the raised beds provide permanent seating while leaving the deck open and uncluttered from traditional, cumbersome outdoor furniture. The raised planters also increase the impact of plant material, softening the hardscape elements and acting as an enticement to venture outdoors into the garden.

Located on the western boundary and designed as the focus from within the glass walls of the family room and in the outdoor entertaining area is a 3m x 2m cleft-face granite water wall, ordered pre-cut from China. The gentle trickling effect of the water provides a soothing backdrop without interfering with conversation. The reservoir, designed at an acute angle to create interest particularly from first floor viewing, is constructed from marine-grade stainless steel, with a stainless steel grill as a holding frame for the decorative Australian washed river stones.

Limestone steppers allow passage from the northern courtyard through to the rear garden area. The turfed play area was created with a waterwise variety of lawn that is an appropriate and reliable surface for both the clients' children and their golden retriever. Janine then designed a series of raised garden beds around the lawn, with a feature tree in the garden's southwest corner. The use of timber is repeated in three evenly spaced individual

timber platforms within the raised beds, upon which imported Italian 'Serralunga' fibreglass pots of succulents provide colourful highlights to the rear garden.

Sub-surface irrigation to garden beds and the lawn prevents water loss from the high winds frequently experienced in the area. Durable Hunza low-voltage marine-grade stainless steel lighting has also been implemented throughout the garden to account for the coastal location.

The eastern section of the garden is a paved service area, again utilising poured limestone used elsewhere in the garden for unity and its appropriateness to Perth landscapes. Paving continues from this area through a security gate to connect with the front driveway and permits easy manoeuvring of bins, as well as quick access to the service area's outdoor shower after returning from the beach just 200m away.

Janine's use of natural design elements creates a contemporary landscape appropriate for an Australian beach house. The bleached colours reminiscent of Perth summers are represented here in her use of timber, gravel, river stones, washed aggregate concrete, poured

Use of timber for deck and seating links to internal timber finishes. Janine's introduction of the raised garden beds at different heights and angles around the courtyard perimeter provides depth and perspective to the confined area.

4 The gentle trickling effect of the water on the granite water wall provides a soothing backdrop without interfering with conversation.

limestone and soft-coloured rendered walls, ensuring both house and garden fit perfectly into the broader Western Australian landscape.

Planting design

Renowned for her colourful and innovative use of hard landscaping elements, it is still plants, in Janine's view, 'that change an outdoor space into a garden'. Critical to this garden's success was the selection of a palette of low maintenance plants (remembering her clients were not gardeners) that would withstand the harsh coastal environment, as well as provide the desired contemporary, architectural style to complement the property. To achieve this, Janine used a blend of hardy Australian natives and proven exotics that perform well in Perth conditions.

For the high profile positions at the front entry and northern courtyard, Janine had two super-advanced frangipani trees (*Plumeria acutifolia*) craned in to achieve instant sculptural impact. The pink-flowered variety in the courtyard was selected specifically for its high branching, narrow form, making it suitable for its intended position close to the boundary. A more evenly branched white-flowering specimen was chosen for the entrance and in time will provide a glorious fragrant canopy to be enjoyed from beneath and above via the upstairs balcony. A honey locust (*Gleditsia triacanthos* 'Shademaster') was planted in the rear garden to provide shade for the lawned play area and, because 'everyone should have a lemon tree', one was included as a balancing element in the opposite corner of the rear garden. In the exposed northeastern corner, Janine introduced an olive tree (*Olea europaea*), a proven performer in Perth coastal areas.

The sago palm (*Cycas revoluta*) with its elegant finely toothed evergreen fronds is used repeatedly, to add year-round architectural foliage—as an accent at the entrance, a border in the raised courtyard beds and an understorey beneath the honey locust at the rear. Mass plantings of the drought- and wind-tolerant grass-like native mat rush (*Lomandra longifolia* 'Tanika') provide a contrasting looseness to the architectural form of other plants, such as the red-leaved *Cordyline australis* 'Red Sensation' along the western rear boundary and the sculptural dragon tree (*Draceana draco*), a corner feature of the courtyard.

To provide a splash of colour to the east of the driveway, and an eventual screen from wind and neighbours, native kangaroo paw (*Anigozanthos manglesii*) is mass-planted against the successful frontline coastal shrub *Coprosma repens*. A groundcover planting of the emu bush (*Eremophylla glabra* 'Kalbarri Carpet') provides impact at ground level.

Janine's restrained use of a limited palette of reliable, visually appealing textural plants has without doubt achieved the required transformation of outdoor space to 'garden', with the added assurance that the resultant landscape will withstand the rigours of time and its coastal environment.

5 Subtle lighting washes the water wall and branches of trees ensuring the garden remains useful and interesting well into the night.

Italian 'Serralunga' pots of *crassula* spp. interspersed with *Cordyline australis* 'Red Sensation' bring coloured texture to the rear gardens.

'Janine's crisp, contemporary garden realised our vision and provides a low maintenance, functional space for both adults and children to enjoy. It perfectly complements our modern seaside home—evidenced by the number of strangers who come knocking on the door for the name of our landscape designer!'

6

Garden owners

DESIGN TIP

This garden, designed by Steve Taylor, Creative Outdoor Solutions, is based on strong angles to provide an attractive scheme that responds to the form of the house and defines separate spaces within the unusual front garden shape. **Centre:** Coral bark maple (*Acer palmatum* 'Sango Kaku')

Geometry and angles in design

In the design of this small Northbeach garden, Janine used simple geometries to good effect. This approach particularly suits small gardens because lines based on strong shapes, circles, squares and rectangles are economical in terms of use of space, but also relate well generally to the geometries created by architects when they design houses.

A good starting point, therefore, is to use the angles of a house as a source of geometries for a design. For the home gardener, it is a good idea to undertake this work overlaid on a sheet of graph paper, where each 1cm square equals 1sqm of garden. Plotting the garden areas is then a relatively simple exercise and provides an opportunity to not only create interesting geometric shapes, but also to assess the relative size of each portion of the garden as it's

designed. It also allows you to estimate approximate areas such as paving, lawn or deck to make simple calculations about project costs.

Designing your garden from this starting point doesn't mean that the garden's components have to be at 90 degrees to the house. By turning your lines 45 degrees, you can work with diagonal lines. Longer than direct 90-degree lines, they help give a sense of greater space. Angles of 30 or 60 degrees are also useful. This is especially relevant to narrow garden areas where long, skinny rectangles are often all that remain after house construction. Designing spaces that intersect the rectangle on an angle breaks the elongated form of the original space and gives an impression of greater depth.

In this garden, Janine has used strong geometric lines to create a series of linked garden beds and open spaces of varying sizes based on a repetition of squares and rectangles that relate to the built form of the house.

The crisp, clean lines reinforce the minimalist site character and ensure the areas surrounding the home combine efficient use of space with structural design strength. An acute angle at the base of the water feature creates visual interest, especially when viewed from above.

Too frequently, small courtyards include a narrow ribbon of planting that extends around the edge of the garden. This actually increases the sense of a long narrow garden, whereas the use of angles can minimise the narrow effect, and simultaneously create planting areas that are wider than a simple boundary strip. Angled areas not only affect perceived width, but also assist in breaking up the length of a garden, giving a sense of separate spaces and zones within a site.

While the concept of using geometries to design gardens may sound hard-edged, this approach merely provides a framework for planting. Once structure and form have been established, planting can be selected to soften the lines, though the structural skeleton remains within the design. Climbers and trailing plants to clothe walls, and shrubs that have a broad, rounded form rather than vertical growth all make a valuable contribution as will tufting plants along edges to straight lines. To increase softness, leave gaps in gravel or paving to plant into, for these can create a delightful nuance, giving a soft and natural feeling to a structured garden.

For success with angles and shapes, the use of a set-square and compass helps with the creation of angles, lines and circles to produce neat and visually striking spaces with a strong structural framework. Of course, geometric elements need not be purely horizontal, with three-dimensional effects achieved by raising planting areas, building decks and by use of vegetation.

In the garden of designer, Carey Cavanagh, the circle is a relaxing and softer geometric form that still provides strength of design. Iris and Korean box surround a circle of mini mondo grass.

Using angled lines to shape garden beds in narrow spaces creates planting areas that are wider than a simple boundary strip. The resultant angled beds provide ideal spaces to create multi-layered plantings, including trees with space appropriate for trunk and root development.

Clendon Road Garden
Melbourne

'The important elements of successful garden design are sensitivity to site architecture and setting, and the generous apportionment of spaces within a garden to allow the practical needs of different components to be met. Too often, gardens are over-designed with a complexity of materials and features that contribute little to the charm or efficiency of a design. Simplicity and restraint, and a sustainable, complementary plant palette, ensures the creation of an inviting and functional garden that won't fall victim to fashion or difficult maintenance regimes.' **john patrick**

Biography

John Patrick came to Australia from England in 1980 and spent eight years lecturing in landscape design at Burnley College, Melbourne. He established his landscape architectural practice in 1988 and now specialises in heritage-based conservation studies, park masterplans, and commercial and residential design. The creation of functional gardens, with innovative use of traditional styles and materials, is characteristic of the practice's work throughout Australia.

Raised in the English countryside, not surprisingly John developed an affinity with plants and the landscape from an early age. He was drawn to the outdoors, ultimately gaining qualifications in ecology, landscape design and landscape management. His gardens reflect his love of plants and he is a great advocate of involving the property owner in plant selection, believing this connects the garden occupants to the garden, ensuring a sense of ownership and engagement.

John has a passion for life that has brought a rich tapestry of experience to his landscape design, resulting in an ability to produce a wide-ranging style of gardens. Indeed, it is his personal philosophy that every design should be an interpretation of individual client and site-specific characteristics, ensuring a unique outcome on every occasion.

Awarded a Churchill Fellowship in 1996, John has studied and travelled extensively throughout Europe, North America and Japan. Since 1998 he has led unique international garden tours, combining his love of gardens, history, art, architecture, people and travel.

Major influences on his work have been John Brookes, Tom Wright and Tony du Gard Pasley. Christopher Tunnard's book *Gardens in the Modern Landscape* and Thomas Church's *Gardens are for People*, focusing on simple functional gardens and outdoor lifestyle, have been increasingly influential in his Australian career.

1 The gently winding woodland path invites indolent passage at a speed permitting full appreciation of groundcovers. A close integration between path and woodland was achieved through the massed informal plantings and overhanging branches, while the three dimensional nature of the trunks, layer upon layer, disguise the depth of the garden and distance to the boundary.

John is prominently involved in gardening and design in Australia. He lectures widely, often presents on radio and appears regularly on ABC's *Gardening Australia*. He has written several books, was series editor for Lothian's gardening series and presently writes for *Gardening Australia* magazine. He was involved in the establishment of Australia's Open Garden Scheme and wrote its first two guidebooks. He also chairs the biennial national Landscape Conference in Australia and New Zealand.

A passionate supporter of the horticultural industry, he often works in a charitable capacity to promote and support the design profession, nursery sector, garden clubs, history societies and the general gardening public. He is a friend of the Royal Botanic Gardens Melbourne, a mentor for university students, and regularly donates his time and knowledge to forge links with the new generation of designers. Through his Rotary run 'Garden DesignFest' concept, he has helped to raise substantial funds for charity while also raising the profile of the landscape profession.

Design brief

The brief for this garden was remarkably open. The client, having spent many years in England, was enthusiastic about the idea of having gardens of diverse styles that recaptured the plant diversity and richness of English gardens. Yet, at the same time, he wanted to respect his Chinese origins by establishing a carp pond close to the house where he could enjoy quiet contemplation. Passive recreation of this nature, including strolling through the garden or simply sitting and reading, was important to the owner. The removal of the existing tennis court and swimming pool was consequently a high priority to maximise garden areas.

2 The 1920's character of the heritage listed house was important, for the garden design needed to respond to its style and character by providing a complementary setting, in terms of scale, planting style and historic layout. An 'in-out' U shaped driveway was retained as its symmetry was appropriate to the symmetry of the house. **Rear left:** Mauve spring flowering Foxglove Tree (*Paulownia tomentosa*) **Centre:** White flowering 'Mt Fuji' cherry trees **Right:** Lilly Pilly (*Syzygium* sp.)

3 A large golden elm (*Ulmus procera* 'Lutescens') and a lilly pilly (*Syzygium* sp.) dominate the front garden. They provide a sense of maturity for the site, appropriate to the scale of the house and the garden space but their shade and roots restrict the growth of surrounding lawn. Canopy reduction improved light entry and encouraged greater density of grass.

The size of the garden meant privacy wasn't a major issue; however, there was a need for screening to the street, without changing the historic form of the low masonry boundary wall from the 1920s. Recognition had to be given to the proposed rear extension to the house, with a softening to the building form and façade required.

The final aspect of the brief required a sketch design to be prepared within 48 hours for presentation to the client! In a further unusual twist, a three-dimensional model was constructed and transported to Hong Kong, with the designer, for final approval.

Site analysis

With the house located towards the centre of the large, generally level, rectangular site, the design approach was to accommodate the house within a garden setting. An 'in-out' U-shaped driveway was retained as its symmetry was appropriate to the symmetry of the house.

The site contained mature trees, though a number of over-mature, weedy specimens needed removing. In the front garden at least, existing vegetation established an attractive setting for the house. The mature trees though, being taller than the house, were contrary to the requirements of Feng Shui. Some were slated for removal but were protected within the local planning scheme.

Fortunately, the introduction of a water feature with moving water satisfactorily addressed the issue and the trees were retained.

The considerably larger rear garden was more complex. The presence of a swimming pool and tennis court had meant that much of the site was quite open, yet to the south there was a dense planting of conifers. They formed a green thicket that gave privacy to the pool from adjacent houses but offered little other value. They were removed.

The site had been part of a large nineteenth-century garden before its subdivision in the 1920s. Existing vegetation, including a mature holly oak (*Quercus ilex*) along the northern boundary, gave the site maturity but together with large trees on neighbouring properties such as the Queensland kauri (*Agathis robusta*) they cast shade and brought root competition that restricted the plant palette for the garden.

The relationship between the house and surrounding gardens was important. To the south of the house were service areas, garages and a work courtyard which could be isolated from the garden. To the north, the house's major reception and sitting rooms led out onto areas of the garden that were quite narrow and very clearly related to the adjacent house spaces. Further into the garden, the influence of the house diminished; the garden was of such a length that the distant areas had little relationship to the house at all.

The small internal courtyard to be converted into a caretaker's private garden was completely enclosed, giving it a specific microclimate with a lot of reflected heat from surrounding walls. This was also an issue to the northwest of the house. A new library extension to

4 Creating shade, the robinia court is a simple elegant paved space planted with four symmetrically located mop top robinias that arise from formal sandstone paving. Architectural details of walls and pillars maintained the 1920's architectural vocabulary.

5 Steps from the formal terraces lead to an intersecting path running the full width of the garden and offering a cross link for the site. **Left:** (centre) *Stipa giganten* (front) *Sedum* 'Autumn Joy' **Right:** (centre) *Penstemon* (front) *Salvia leucantha* (Mexican sage).

the south, combined with the original wall to the rear of the house, caused substantial reflected light and heat, creating an area that required protection.

While the site was reasonably level, there was a fall of 2.2m from east to west. Over the length of the garden, the change was gradual, but sufficient to give the option of terracing and steps to establish different spaces.

Design response

Construction of a house extension resulted in a substantial area between the building and the northern boundary that extended the house into the garden. It provided the obvious setting for a series of terraces that met functional demands, including sitting terraces and a carp pond site, as well as the source of design links through the garden in the form of axial view lines and paths. Resolution of this upper garden area into a series of simple linked courtyards created paved terraces that bridged the house and the more extensive garden space. However, the use of shading trees and climbers were essential to soften the spaces and provide shelter to mitigate the effects of exposure.

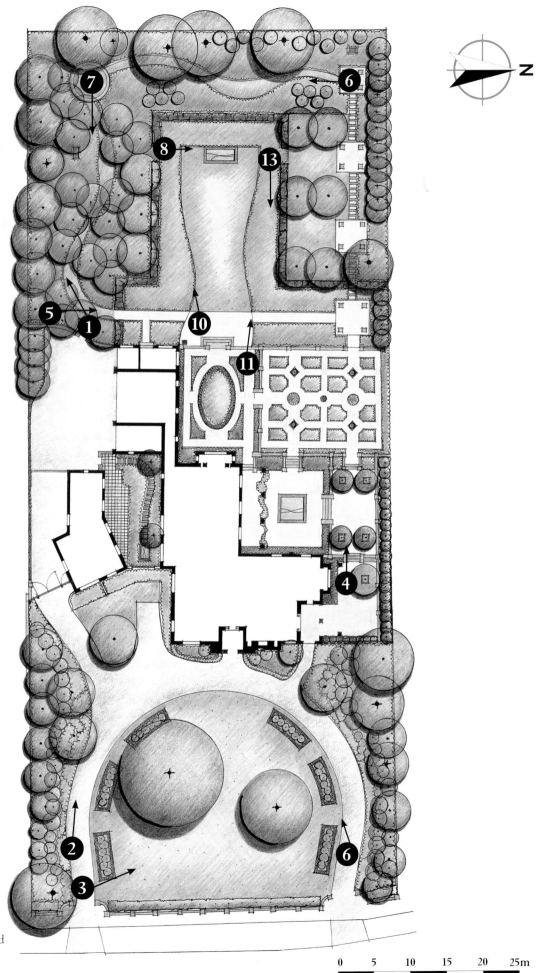

Numbers featured on the
plan identify viewlines of
correspondingly numbered
images.

0   5   10   15   20   25m

APPROX. SCALE

6 The contrast between the massed groundcovers and birch of the woodland and the planting of the American borders is intentionally obvious. Throughout the garden, the objective was to reinforce differences between various garden spaces. The dark-eyed cone flower provides a feature to the foreground with massed miscanthus behind.

Beyond these terraces, the broader landscape is divided into a series of 'habitats'. A U-shaped hedge of myrtle separates the central part of the garden from the encircling peripheral areas. The garden has a simple form; the cross link beneath the terrace, a path to either side, and the central formal garden enclosed in its hedge. This combination of spaces gave the garden a simple and natural progression for strolling and sitting, responding to the client's brief.

The central garden contains traditional English-style mixed borders. Shrubs provide scale and masses of herbaceous plants, many with rich foliage texture, offer contrast to them.

A formal lawn is necked at the centre to lead the eye to a formal rectangular pond as its focus. This central garden is effectively contained, with its own character, colour scheme and style, yet intentionally the height of the enclosing hedge was established to allow the planting schemes beyond to be appreciated. It is only the canopies of the trees beyond that are visible so that they cradle the

7 As an informal garden area, it was important that the path through the birch woodland reflected this character. This was achieved not only by curving the path but by varying its width. Further informality was achieved by using gravel as the path surface.

internal space, providing enclosure and containment to the broader view, ensuring the complex enclosed planting is fully appreciated.

The side paths allow movement around the outer part of the site To the south, a birch woodland was established to secure privacy to the boundary. As an informal garden area, it was important that the path through the birch woodland reflected this character. This was achieved not only by curving the path but by varying its width. Further informality was achieved by using gravel as the path surface.

The informal woodland path extends the full length of the southern edge, then turns 90 degrees to follow the garden's western boundary, outside of the central hedge and running parallel to the house itself. At the junction point, the curving path enters a stone-edged circular sitting area. From here, views extend back the length of the woodland and across the site to the north, the width of the view contained all the time by the central hedge.

8 The rectangular pond forms the focus to the central garden. Richness of planting here demanded simpler schemes closer to the house. **Centre left:** *Pennisetum alopecuroides*, red flowering *Dahlia* 'Bishop of Wandaff', mauve flowering ground cover and (*rear*) rose coloured *Sedum* 'Autumn Joy'.

9 Planting to the boundaries of the front garden created an informal style that reaffirmed its 1920's heritage. The existing severely cracked concrete driveway was replaced by exposed aggregate concrete with a brick edge and drainage channel. This was sympathetic to the period of the house, while simultaneously offering a functional and safe surface. Massed white *Azalea* 'Alba magnifica' are a spring feature.

A paved circle provides a switching point not only in direction but also in garden style, from a birch woodland to an American prairie-style garden modelled on the rich designs of Oehme and van Sweden.

Here, the gravel path changes, sweeping in broad curves of consistent width appropriate to the massed plant groupings, reflecting the more narrow space available between the rear fence and the central hedge.

Approaching the northern fence line, the path turns again, this time in a square of sandstone. With a view towards the courtyards around the house, the path comprises a number of sandstone-paved squares with a sandstone path that links these squares through a verdant lawn containing an orchard of citrus, apples, plums and pears.

A sense of mystery was provided by two gaps cut in the central hedge that offer cross-site views, firstly to the pond in the central garden then ultimately to the woodland. Although a contemporary sculpture was originally proposed, at present the effect of a visual focus is achieved by the massed silver trunks of the birches.

10 The traditional English-style mixed borders of the central garden are set against the small foliage size of a hedge of myrtle—a perfect plain contrast to the diverse foliage of the planting. To the south, the canopies of standard cherries hang over the hedge into the central garden, softening the line of the hedge and linking the central garden with the birch woodland.

Adjacent to the house, sandstone terraces were created on a series of levels, each with a distinct character. To the north, extending a quiet internal sitting room was a sitting space intended to offer a serene, shaded courtyard where a meal could be enjoyed or the garden occupants could read. The third courtyard, the rose garden, is broader than the other courtyards and far more intricately planted. It extends across from the northern boundary to the square carp pond courtyard that occupies the area directly to the west of the house. The final courtyard, the lavender garden, is located axially from the library and provides the formal axis through the centre of the garden—an axis which crosses the formal lawn and ultimately focuses upon the ornamental pond as the garden's main feature.

The front garden is formal to meet the architectural and heritage demands of the site. The presence of the in-out driveway isolated a central, approximately semicircular lawn with garden beds to its corners. Planting was limited to a series of island beds that lined the driveway, reinforcing its alignment while also sympathetic to heritage forms.

By contrast, the areas to the northwest and southwest were completely planted out using layered shrubs, tallest to the rear and shorter to the front, and emerging trees. The overall effect was one of framing the house and softening it, setting it into the garden in a way that reaffirmed its 1920s heritage.

The small courtyard garden attached to the caretaker's residence is a completely separate and isolated space and could have been designed in any way. Yet there was much to be said for retaining established design directions and materials. The use of a formal pond and sandstone paving gives a charming character and functionality to the outdoor entertaining area.

Planting design

Planting within this garden follows a few principles. The use of a largely exotic palette reflects the heritage nature of the site and respects the owner's wishes for the diverse characters of English gardens, yet it caused problems—

the planting appropriate for English climates was not entirely suited to Melbourne's hot, dry summers.

Planting followed principles of massing and colour scheming to create gardens of specific visual character. Ultimately, the rear garden comprised different ecologies and planting themes: a birch woodland dominated by white trunks and massed shade-tolerant groundcovers; an American-style garden with massed grasses and perennials; an orchard; a rose garden; a lavender garden; and, as the main feature of the rear garden, a mixed shrub and perennial garden based on purples and mauves set against silver foliage.

Trunks and their bark were to be a major attraction of the woodland garden. To achieve a 'woodland' effect, random placement of trees was essential. Edna Walling used potatoes tossed across the garden to achieve positions with a random effect. Here, a more calculated response was achieved by random placement in a drawing. Lillypilly (*Syzygium smithii*) forms enclose boundary planting so the birch woodland is within clearly defined bounds.

The birch trunks form a major visual feature so groundcover massing is simply a range of low-growing plants that retain the woodland effect, including perennial geraniums such as *Geranium* 'Johnsons Blue', *G. macrorrhizum* 'Ingwersen's Variety', and for height *G. maderense*. More traditional massings of Japanese windflower (*Anemone japonica*) and hellebores (*Helleborus orientalis* and *H. argutifolius*) corsicus are also included.

American prairie-style planting provided inspiration for the extensive garden extending east–west across the site. Among the bold plantings are Russian sage (*Perovskia atriplicifolia*), the dark-eyed coneflower (*Rudbeckia* 'Goldstrum'), the grasses *Miscanthus* 'Flamingo' and *M. sinensis*, *Helictotrichon sempervirens* and, edging the path,

11 An English style garden was created, though not with a typical English plant palette. With careful plant selection and drip irrigation, appropriate visual effects and satisfactory growth was achieved. **Front:** English lavender, penstemons, sedums. **Centre:** *Yucca gloriosa*, yellow *Rudbeckia* and *Miscanthus* form a part of this rich planting scheme.

Wisteria floribunda 'Macrobotrys alba' was planted along the rear of the library extension to create shade and soften the imposing building.

Bergenia cultivars including 'Silberlicht' and 'Alberglut'. This planting is set against the inner hedge to the east and a mixed shrub planting against the western boundary. Sweet viburnum (*Viburnum odoratissimum*) dominates this planting, though for contrast, groups of the roughly textured *V. rhytidiphyllum* were introduced.

The central garden features mauve, purple, blue and silver, and planting was selected to provide an extended display. Long-flowering perennials like society garlic (*Tulbaghia violacea*) and sea lavender (*Limonium latifolium*) are planted adjacent to tiny, evergreen *Artemisia canescens* with its dazzling silver foliage. The giant, dark blue agapanthus 'Loch Hope' has elegant, tall flowering stems that provide significant summer colour. Of the shrubby plants, *Lavatera* 'Barnsley' offers striking masses of silver-pink flowers over an extended summer period. It is a notable contrast to the deep purple *Iochroma cyaneum*, and the buddleias 'Clear Pink' and

12 A complex planting scheme gives a sense of greenery to the small courtyard garden in an area that otherwise could have appeared harsh. Today it offers a charming green space open to excellent winter sun while also enjoying summer shade from small deciduous canopy trees including Japanese Maple (*Acer palmatum*).

silver-foliaged *Buddleia crispa*, with soft pink spring flowers. Native plants can be mixed into traditional planting schemes and here, cushion bush (*Leucophyta brownii*) and coastal rosemary (*Westringia fruticosa*) add their silver and grey hues.

The lavender garden utilises two lavender cultivars interplanted with the South African fairy's fishing rod (*Dierama pulcherrima*) and edged by the intensely blue *Salvia* 'Ostfriesland'. The salvia's repeat-pruning ensures ongoing flowering over extended summer periods.

The pond court and robinia court were other spaces where a simple planting scheme was implemented; such as two libertias (*Libertia pulchella* and *L. paniculata*) providing contrasting evergreen foliage and massed white spring flowers.

By contrast the front garden is relatively simple. Massed camellias as background planting, oak-leaf hydrangeas (*Hydrangea quercifolia*) and blocks of azaleas, clivias, rhododendrons, camellias, hellebores and Japanese anemones ensure a low-maintenance scheme appropriate to the site's period character.

The internal courtyard adjacent to the garage required a more intimate solution, being a smaller space designed as an adjunct to a private residential area. Smaller-leaved plants were selected including dwarf tobira (*Pittosporum tobira* 'Wheelers Dwarf'), its perfume of orange blossom lingering over spring. *Corydalis* 'Panda Blue' with iridescent blue flowers set against delicate ferny foliage contrasts with *Sedum* 'Ruby Glow', *Epimedium versicolor*, *Alchemilla mollis* and *Geranium endressii*. Larger material was required to the rear, so sacred bamboo (*Nandina domestica*) and mop-top hydrangea (*Hydrangea macrophylla* 'Geoffrey Chadbund') were included.

Bluebells provide a traditional ground carpet style in the European woodland garden.

'Our garden provides opportunities for quiet contemplation as well as a world of garden rooms to retreat to. The English-style borders and woodland provide comforting memories of our time living in England and it is always a pleasure to return to the garden to enjoy its beauty and be surrounded by nature.'

Garden owners

DESIGN TIP

With an expansive view to enjoy, Jim Fogarty cleverly combined a garden path with broad circular lawn terraces to provide both movement and resting points via the turfed viewing platforms.

Movement through a garden

In all but its smallest form, passage through a garden adds pleasure, allowing the garden visitor to fully experience a site. There are both functional issues and aesthetics to consider in design.

Thinking practically to start with, garden paths should be safe, non-slip and appropriately drained. Path width will vary depending upon its purpose. Broad inviting paths 1.5m wide encourage visitors to walk side by side and compare thoughts about a garden. A 1.2m-wide path is more appropriate for most home gardens, but paths can be narrower and still provide an effective surface. Stepping stones hardly provide a path at all, just a suggestion to be followed, but in a subtle way they direct the eye and encourage discovery and exploration. Suit your path width and type to purpose. In an informal garden, gravel mulch can extend to become a path. In this

situation there are no formal edges between planting and path, and casual wandering or lingering among plants may be more likely to result.

Design is a communication process and successful design helps visitors to a garden decide how to respond to it. Paths play a major role in communicating intended movement through, and discovery of, a garden. They can entice—as mentioned, stepping stones suggest there is something to be seen just around the corner and cry out to be followed. Alternatively, a broad paved plinth suggests a viewing point, somewhere to slow and halt, enjoying a significant view or perhaps changing direction. Subtle effects can be achieved through change of surface material. Broad, smooth pavers give a relaxed character, whereas the use of cobbles or smaller paving materials is more hectic and tends to hurry the visitor through.

In this case gates left invitingly ajar, a sundial and a pear tree all attract. Their impact is reinforced by the framing of a pergola.

Paths alone do not influence movement through the garden. Features attract the eye and also entice visitors to move towards them. This can be reinforced by framing planting or a pergola, so views and spaces are revealed in the best way.

Steps, too, provide a valuable role in movement. Broad semicircular steps, popularised by Edwin Lutyens, promote movement in varied directions, while narrow,

Broad semicircular steps, popularised by Edwin Lutyens, promote movement in varied directions, while narrow, straight steps suggest one directional movement from or to a particular area in the garden.

straight steps suggest one directional movement from or to a particular area in the garden and not only make passage possible but can also dictate views to be enjoyed. Employed in John's Toorak garden, the use of cut outs in enclosing hedges also encourages transition through a garden by offering glimpses of spaces to entice further exploration.

Placement of a seat invites the garden visitor to halt and to admire a view. You can also strengthen impact by placing pots or other features nearby to intensify a sense of place as a resting point within a garden.

Cairns Garden
Queensland

'I don't think a designer should ever take total credit for a garden— particularly in the volatile and intriguing environment of the tropics where plants grow so rapidly and change is such a constant, either through early maturation or total wipe-out from a cyclone. I simply provide the bones for a garden, structuring the components in an organised fashion after interpreting exactly what the client is looking for. It's a very involved and demanding process for everyone, so working and relating well with your clients is critical. You see it through their eyes, not your own, and in that way every garden is refreshingly different.'   suzan quigg

Biography

Suzan Quigg began life, and ostensibly her career, in a sleepy Sussex village in England. In her early years, her bedroom was given over to a burgeoning cacti collection and resembled more of a greenhouse than a child's bedroom.

Suzan's school teachers eventually 'took pity' on the eccentric teenage conservationist and collector, taking her to England's famous Kew Gardens when she was fifteen. Suitably impressed and spontaneously mapping out her career path, Suzan wrote immediately to Kew, directing them to accept her to undertake horticultural studies. She wrote simultaneously to the Royal Horticultural Society at Wisley, being an equally impressive institution, for a place to complete her compulsory practical year, having automatically assumed that, of the twenty esteemed Kew positions available to students worldwide, she would be selected!

As comical as her own naïvety now seems to Suzan, incredibly Kew staff saw a future for this confident and presumptuous teenager and her plans materialised

as she foresaw them. However, upon conclusion of her studies, she realised her career map hadn't extended beyond her blissful immersion in all things botanical at her prestigious training ground. Unsure of her next direction, she enrolled in a secretarial course on her parents' suggestion and, though a failure in terms of a career option, it succeeded in establishing a contact with a fellow student's architect husband, leading her to her first design commission.

Suzan looks back and laughs at her youthful arrogance and supreme confidence that, as a distinguished Kew graduate, any horticultural task was within her capacity. She does concede, however, that this 'can do' attitude resulted in a variety of job opportunities and horticultural experience, ranging from decorating an Israeli embassy with 9000 roses for a party, to a landscape design role with English Woodlands, an established British forestry company, where she created elaborate country gardens for the wealthy.

In 1983, following her heart and eventual husband to Hervey Bay, a then-undeveloped paradise two hours

---

1 This tranquil evening view of a tropical Cairns garden is complemented by the cooling effects of a waterfall.

north of Brisbane, Suzan was so entranced by the glorious surroundings and exotic lifestyle, her plan to return home to complete Landscape Architecture Studies was abandoned. Eternally optimistic, Suzan found diverse employment, ranging from children's book illustrations, botanical drawings and painting, to horticultural work pushing barrows, laying paths and digging holes. It wasn't until settling in Cairns in 1986 that she established her own garden design business; recalling her unfamiliarity with tropical plants and growing conditions, she admits to initially encountering a steep learning curve. Twenty years on, with her frenetic energy and signature 'can do' approach, she now single-handedly produces up to 70 commercial and residential landscape designs a year.

Suzan confesses, 'I sort of eat, breathe and sleep it' when she is designing a garden, walking around the spaces in her head before she uses her artistic talents to create beautiful plans of her three-dimensional visions.

With landscape design only recently becoming a mainstream profession in Cairns, Suzan sees herself and her few local colleagues as pioneers, inventing their own style and taking inspiration directly from clients. This opportunity for originality is refreshing and, in Suzan's view, makes working in the region wonderful.

Design brief

Coincidences can often be the source of work for designers. In this case Suzan had left drawings for an earlier project at her printers where they were seen by a man with an office in the next building. Impressed by their artistry, and aware of Suzan's work through a friend's garden he hired Suzan as his landscape designer. She soon realised her clients had an existing knowledge and enthusiasm for tropical plants that thrived so readily in the Cairns area. What they needed was a professional designer able to put them into a landscape context and, in doing so, achieve a setting for their family's tropical lifestyle.

The brief for this project typifies the Cairns lifestyle; a large free-form swimming pool for outdoor recreation, a thatched gazebo for lazy outdoor living and eating, and

the opportunity to view these elements as a focus from the house and move effortlessly from house to pool to pavilion to encourage al fresco dining.

Appropriate siting of plants was crucial to secure privacy but also to permit strong links from house to garden. Such was the nature of the house with broad, shading eaves and large windows, oriented to view the landscape beyond, that the garden needed to provide a splendid visual focus; after all, it was effectively the background to the family's daily life.

Site analysis

The site was the rear portion of a 2-hectare Cairns property where the clients' efforts had resulted in the lawn being enclosed in a mass of 2m-tall vegetation approximately two years old. This planting formed an attractive, artistically and carefully planned backdrop, but it left the central part of the garden as a sloping lawn that fell across the site and accordingly across the view from the house.

As mentioned large windows to the rear of the house meant the rear yard was effectively a backdrop to the house, yet there was one especially important view— on opening the front door of the house the whole of the garden was revealed — a patch of bright tropical sunlight beyond the shade and darkness within the house itself. There was an opportunity to create a distinct and impressive showpiece both during the daytime and, if lighting could be appropriately designed, at night.

The fall that crossed the lawn was part of a more extensive slope that extended to other back gardens higher up the hill. In times of heavy rainfall, and that is not infrequent in Cairns' tropical climate, surface water flowed across the site resulting in the garden being a quagmire. Suzan lost count of the shoes she ruined making site visits prior to implementing her design, so intractable was the wet, heavy soil.

Fortunately, the garden was located in a setting that allowed the surrounding landscape to be included in any design. Rising land clad in lush tropical forest allowed

2 Extensive perimeter planting by the owners had ensured enclosure for the rear garden and created a lush backdrop for Suzan to work with.

the occupants to have a sense of being part of a much larger landscape environment.

Design response

Suzan's design solution for this garden fulfils the intentions of its brief in a spectacular way. For the first-time visitor, the moment of entry into the house and the vision of the garden is simply breathtaking. Yet the design solution is deceptively simple and is built around a few powerful and dramatic visual elements—a large informal swimming pool, a thatched gazebo designed to accommodate a tropical lifestyle, a dramatic waterfall, and open grassed areas that permit full appreciation of wonderfully rich and diverse planting.

Remarkably, in achieving this design solution Suzan was also able to resolve the major issue, that of deflecting the surface water that caused so many problems prior to the construction of the garden. This was achieved, not by expensive in-ground drainage but by the use of much simpler, open surface drains that collected water and led

it away along the site perimeter. In a further practical response, costs were also reduced by retaining much of the soil excavated for the pool on the site in the form of a large mound. Effectively, this acted as a barrier to the surface flow of water that was then collected in an open swale and led along the site margin to the rear of the designed garden.

The mound also formed the setting for a large waterfall constructed of local rock. Waterfalls are frequently included in Cairns swimming pools yet are often badly handled. Suzan looked to her Wisley training about appropriate use of strata in rock to create a natural form of rock embankment that fits the site context. The mound also disguises the waterfall's pump and deadens its noise for it is set within the soil and rocks.

The large informal pool is the true heart of the garden and home. It fills much of the open space close to the house and offers the setting for the pavilion, the focus of the view. Suzan designed the pavilion as a broad, low

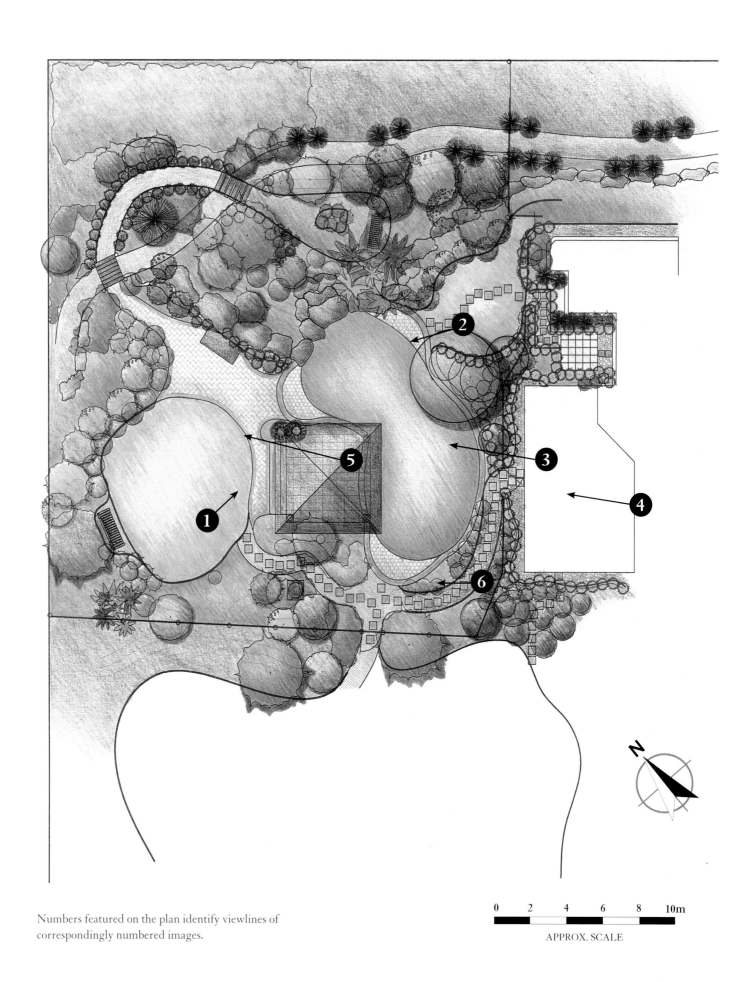

Numbers featured on the plan identify viewlines of
correspondingly numbered images.

3 The image of tropical paradise, revealed as you open the front door, is made the more exciting by the contrast between the bright, intense Cairns sunshine that illuminates the dazzling pool and multi-coloured tropical foliage and the cool shade of the house itself.

4 The pool and pavilion are lit. Not only does this provide for evening use of the pool, for outdoor entertaining and parties, it also means that the garden becomes a focus for views from the house at all times.

5 Safe and clear paths cut through the enclosing vegetation but their presence is generally functional rather than aesthetic, a secondary element to the beauty of the tropical vegetation that envelopes the whole garden.

element in the landscape, its squat form allowing it to be accommodated within the surrounding planting. So often gazebos are built as rather fragile structures with long thin posts and a roof so high as to offer little shade, but this example—raised a little off the ground and perched invitingly above the surface of the pool—provides a really effective outdoor room. By bringing the edge of the pavilion over the pool edge, the two elements appear integrated within the design. Outdoor lighting ensures the area continues as a functional space and a stunning feature after dark.

Informality is the guiding spirit of the tropical lifestyle and so too with this garden. Here, the combination of concrete pavers with pebble in pathways offers a balance between practicality and informality, and function and appearance, that is entirely appropriate.

Though Australia's own sense of a tropical garden style might still be evolving, borrowings from other tropical design traditions help to decorate the garden. These include voluptuously carved Balinese-style pots, a clever foil to the exciting colours of the surrounding plants,

containing either dramatic foliage plants or tropical water plants, and oriental sculpture pieces in the form of stylised heads, appropriate to the context of the design.

The design process that created the garden was time-consuming. Plans evolved slowly. So close was the relationship that developed between Suzan and her clients that she felt no concern at returning regularly to walk through it in order to understand the implications of her design decisions and the opportunities they opened up.

In some respects these repeat visits provided the experience of living in the garden and understanding the daily and seasonal changes within it. Though in truth, the Cairns environment is remarkably consistent through twelve months. Having finally established a successful design, Suzan arrived at the most exciting portion of the project, preparing her planting plan.

Planting design

In the owners of this garden, Suzan found, in many respects, perfect clients. Both she and her clients loved the opportunities in Cairns for flamboyant flora and were keen to seek out interesting and unusual material. Their combined efforts have produced a unique garden of great beauty and stunning plant diversity.

Since the nursery industry in Far North Queensland was not as well developed as in other parts of Australia, in the conceptual stage of the design Suzan often reviewed plants on Hawaiian web sites. She is surprised by how many plants are actually available in Australia when she seeks them out, all that is needed is for a demand to be created to stimulate the local nursery industry to produce them on a commercial basis. In this way, Suzan and her designer colleagues have greatly increased the range of plants readily available in the area.

For vertical elements in the garden, Suzan looks predominantly to Heliconias, including the pendulous *H.* 'Sexy Pink' as well as *H. bihai*, *H. rostata* and *H. psittacorum* varieties such as 'Holiday', 'Golden Torch' and 'Daintree' rather than traditionally used palm species. These are better suited to the scale of the garden

The silver Bismark palm (*right*) grows to 6 or more metres across and up to 25m tall, so it does need space. Grown here with the red coleus (*Solenostemon* 'Big Red'), in summer when at their best, a red glow is reflected into the garden. Mauritius Hemp (*Furcraea foetida* 'Mediopicta') (*left*) in a beautiful variegated form with cream foliage also features, providing a dramatic effect that fits perfectly into the garden's tropical style.

and avoid the problems associated with the rapid growth rate and potential size of many tropical palms, such as the native Foxtail Palm (*Wodyetia bifurcata*). Used sparingly though, and located where their eventual size can be accommodated, palms do feature to provide the characteristic tropical feel to the garden, including the collectors' palms, Arenga and Lipstick varieties. While palms do identify a quintessential tropical garden, their sheer bulk and effect on nutrient level in soils create headaches for designers in residential projects. Suzan's decision to introduce a plant palette that did not rely on palms, though an unusual approach at the time, has proven ultimately rewarding, ensuring maintenance is manageable and avoiding the need to replace overscaled palm specimens within a short time frame.

The blue form of bismarck palm (*Bismarckia nobilis*), native to Madagascar, is one of Suzan's feature palms that does provide an eye-catching display in the garden. The broad, silver pleated and deeply cut leaves of this exquisite palm provide a foil for selected material to be planted for

The lipstick palm (*Cyrtostachys renda*) is one of the loveliest things about living in the tropics. Its stunning red stems are much prized and specimens of any size fetch considerable sums of money.

Use of low cost metal fencing allowed Suzan to incorporate a large area of the garden within the pool fence but vegetation is quickly disguising it so that it remains functional but is visually less intrusive.

Gingers include the true gingers, such as Beehive Ginger (*Zingiber spectabilis*) with yellow and white waxy curled bracts that look beehive like, the showy torch gingers (*Etlingera* spp.) as well as the costus identified from the true ginger by their spiralling stems. Crepe Ginger (*Costus speciosus*) is one of the largest with pale pink, crepe-like flowers on top of red bracts and broad, elegant leaves; in this garden Suzan has selected a variegated form. Red tower ginger (*C. barbatus*) is one of the best known, growing to 2 metres with a glossy red head of bracts contrasting with bright yellow, edible flowers. Bamboo ginger (*C. stenophyllus*) is nearly extinct in its native habitat in Costa Rica. While its red bracts with small bright yellow flowers are attractive, much of its appeal lies in the bamboo-like stems with alternating sections of brown and light tan.

contrast. Unusual feature plants add a special touch to this garden, yet it is more common plants, the crotons, acalyphas, cordylines, heleconias and gingers that inevitably form the bulk of the planting. Reliable and decorative, they give the garden a rich, tropical character.

With over one hundred varieties of plants specified in the garden, there is always something spectacular to delight the garden occupants and its many visitors. Such is the extraordinary diversity and density of planting in this garden, such the vigour and health with which plants grow, that it achieves a wonderful flamboyance, as might be expected in a tropical garden.

Left: The dwarf clumping Heliconia angusta 'Red Holiday' produces beautiful long lasting flowers, perfect for indoor arrangements, through winter and spring. **Centre:** *Gustavia superba* **Right:** The torch gingers (*Etlingera elatior*) feature widely in the garden, including pale pink, red and white varieties.

'Despite being keen gardeners, engaging a designer was paramount to reducing our initial stress as we felt daunted by our "blank canvas". As well as being fun to work with, Suzy excelled in combining our ideas with her own to create an artistic, tropical paradise. Her amazing plant palette of more than 100 species tapped into our passion for unusual plants and inspired us to continue the challenge to acquire rare and unique tropical species. Exceeding our original expectations, its practicality and beauty means we're outside more than we're in and it genuinely enriches our lives.'

Garden owners

DESIGN TIP

The concept of the glass pool fence can be taken to extremes as in this design by 'Out of the Blue', where it provides the rear window to the house and a link between pool and living space.

Pool fences

Designing a swimming pool so that it is fully integrated with its garden setting can be challenging, but this process is made more difficult by the legal requirement to enclose a pool as a safety precaution.

Key issues to be considered are the pool fence alignment, fence materials and the possibility of isolating a pool without a fence at all. In the latter case it must be possible to secure the area the pool occupies through the use of perimeter fences, built form and self-closing doors with latches at least 1.2m above floor level. Self-closing doors must open into the house and windows opening onto the pool area must be restricted to an opening of 10cm by use of window latches. These features can easily be retrofitted into a home or incorporated during house construction.

Greater difficulty may result from the need to isolate the pool from neighbours because fence rails may provide climbing access to the pool from an adjacent property. There may be a need to provide sheer vertical fencing to both sides of a fence. Overhanging tree limbs offer a source of entry, too, and these should not protrude over a pool area. Side access ways also need to be fenced with pool-safe gates. It is advisable to consult a building surveyor, who will know whether options proposed will achieve the required isolation. An unfenced pool offers the obvious benefit that the pool can be effectively integrated into the overall garden design. The fence, both a costly and visually intrusive element, is no longer an issue. Practically though, care needs to be taken to ensure house doors are closed—it can be very tempting to keep them open!

With imagination and flair, pool fences can be made from unorthodox materials. In this Portsea garden, Fiona Brockhoff used the timber from a Portland abbatoir, linked with horizontal copper pipes that are sufficiently malleable to allow construction of a curved fence. Its informality suits the site where planting spills through the fence between pool and garden.

Designing a pool fence into a garden is never easy. Where independent pool fencing is necessary, options available to gardeners include traditional metal fences, glass fences and actually constructing the pool so that its edge becomes the fence.

Metal fences come in a range of styles and colours. There may be exceptional circumstances where pool fencing can be decorative, but generally it is best kept simple, though it can provide opportunities to link architecture or other structures within a site. Dark colours that blend or recede into a garden, such as black or dark green, are advisable. Feature gates, rather than a complete feature fence, are often more appropriate as a design highlight.

Use of glass is even less intrusive, though approximately twice the price. Glass fences do show dirt and splash, requiring constant cleaning, but their visual permeability allows for surveillance and provides a strong sense that spaces flow through them. They can be supported by elegant, minimal framework to maintain structure or, as a more expensive option, can be completely frameless. Panels are simply located within channels in paving and offer a virtually seamless integration of pool and garden.

As with Suzan's design, there is no reason why fence types cannot be mixed in certain situations. Suzan chose to use the more expensive glass fencing adjacent to the house so that uninterrupted views and linkage to the pool were maintained, but low-cost metal fencing was used elsewhere, eventually disguised within planting.

Having chosen your fence type, it is important to consider its alignment. In Suzan's case, she chose to enclose the greater part of the garden within the pool fence so that, once inside it, there was lawn, sitting areas and plenty of planting to enjoy. This solution works well in larger gardens, but, on smaller sites, the fence is likely to have to relate more closely and formally to the pool. Do ensure you allow sufficient space around the pool for children's play, social gatherings, furniture and cleaning. Informal pools that attempt to integrate with the garden need more space.

Complications arise with sophisticated pool design elements, such as a wet edge. A glass fence may be needed across the face of the wall to secure the 1.2m isolation. Consulting a specialist pool contractor is worthwhile to ensure unobtrusive, legally compliant enclosure is achieved.

It is possible to use the wall of a pool itself as fencing, providing access at one end only as revealed in this Portsea, Victoria garden designed by Georgina Martyn. For this to work, the pool must be a minimum of 1.2m above ground level but the result, swimming out into open space, is breathtaking.

Woodbridge Garden
D'Entrecastaux Channel, Tasmania

'Garden design for me is the result of a unique three-way connection between myself, the client and the site—the greater the connection, the more successful the garden. I see my role as reconnecting people to their wider landscape, designing gardens with meaning and a direct relationship to the land itself. By using materials, textures and colours that have a tangible link to the natural environment or hark back to its historical use, a garden and its users will be comfortable in their surroundings.' catherine shields

Biography

Catherine Shields is a landscape designer with an English heritage, who now weaves a deliberately 'Australian' thread through her residential designs. As an immigrant herself, and conscious of Tasmania's relatively short period of settlement, she feels strongly about exploring through her work the notion of 'belonging'. She particularly wants for the many recent arrivals to Tasmania, to feel at home. Catherine is passionate about the uniqueness of her new surroundings and endeavours to preserve this natural beauty in her designs.

Catherine traces her respect for the broader landscape to her English childhood when family holidays to remote country areas incorporated an understanding of ecology and the interconnectedness of life. Her passion for nature, though, seemed far removed from the sterile suburban gardens of the time and she initially didn't consider a gardening career. A physics degree was, however, uninspiring so she returned to nature for fulfilment. A

'Design a wildlife garden' course inspired her to study horticulture then landscape achitecture.

A combination of employment in urban landscape design practices and extensive world travel, including work in Australia, offered her vast experience in many facets of design, yet often made her face internal conflicts. Disillusioned with intruding on the natural landscape rather than working with it, she broke away from landscape architecture to head up a residential design office for a nursery and design firm in Devon in the UK. Two years on, faced with the expiry of her Australian visa, Catherine migrated to Tasmania, seeking a more relaxed lifestyle. In Hobart, she combined commercial landscape architectural work with the gradual establishment of her own practice. Her business, 'The Alchemy of Gardens', looks to combine the essential elements of a site: character of land and vegetation, past and present occupants, and site architecture to produce something rare and precious.

Catherine designs with awareness of her environmental responsibilities. The isolation and unspoiled character

---

1 Catherine recognised the potential of the view down D'Entrecastaux Channel as a basis for design. Plants that are currently still in their infancy will eventually be clipped to shape that echo the local landforms.

of the Tasmanian landscape reaffirms her desire to use simple, unpretentious materials, preferably with low embodied energy. Where planting is concerned, she draws on a palette of water-efficient plants that relate to, rather than jar with, the surrounding native vegetation.

The design process itself involves a careful survey of the site and detailed discussion with the clients. Catherine then takes time to filter through the brief, the site's physical attributes and her own intuitive responses. She generally establishes one underpinning idea that is then teased in various directions to create a garden of unity and strength. Though her roots are in the English gardens of Hidcote and Sissinghurst, she recognises the inappropriateness of this style in Australia and strives to give a local Tasmanian identity to her designs. Believing design can become too contrived, she deliberately relies on simplicity and subtle interpretations of nature to create a harmonious blend between a garden and its broader setting.

Design brief

The brief for this garden was informal and loose but Catherine perceived a need to respect the site and its history. While farmed for more than a hundred years and continuing to graze stock, it was previously bushland, inhabited by indigenous people. This provided an opportunity to explore the quality of the land and to respect traditions. At the same time Catherine was aware that she had to work with contemporary architecture and owners, and the design needed to accommodate current lifestyles.

In part, key issues were determined by the nature of the site and its constraints. Rabbits were present in enormous numbers and brought huge challenges to plant establishment. Equally damaging were the southwesterly winds, 'a great problem because you can hardly stand up here sometimes'.

The retention of views was essential as was the creation of appropriate living spaces for outdoor use. These included traditional outdoor eating and entertaining areas but also

a fire pit where informal recreation and enjoyment of the night sky could occur.

Creating a connection between the house and its setting was important, with Catherine immediately struck on arrival by the sense that the house was separate from the landscape. Integration was required, not simply in terms of vegetation, but by gently establishing horizontal elements around the house to provide unity.

A guest cottage some distance from the house needed to be linked to the main dwelling by a pathway. A parking bay for four cars was also required, external to the main garden.

Finally, two aspects of plant selection arose. This was not the place for strong colour but rather for a garden that built upon its natural character and themes so that, rather than jarring, the garden should complement its setting. Given its remote location and that its owners often travelled, the garden also had to be low maintenance.

Site analysis

This 12-hectare site is located on a peninsula south of Hobart, jutting into the D'Entrecasteaux Channel. Despite its coastal position, it is sheltered from salt sea winds. However, wind exposure was still an issue, with extremely strong and damaging land-based winds making outdoor sitting an unpleasant experience at times.

However, other aspects of climate were advantageous. The site received good rainfall and a similar level of sunlight to Hobart. The soil, though, was of considerable concern, being an extremely shallow, nutrient-deficient sand over a thick white clay. Catherine recognised early in the design process the value of using successful indigenous species and that any exotic plant species would require imported soil.

Looking down D'Entrecasteaux Sound, the distant landform had a distinct shape that provided a dramatic silhouette against the sun. The presence of the grey-blue sea, the colour of which varied according to the light, and local rock exposed on the coastal headlands were other features that directed elements of Catherine's response.

2 A spiral of native tussock grass (*Poalaillarteires*) gently encircles an outdoor fire pit, a place for gathering, conversation and keeping warm on chilly Tasmanian evenings. The paved fire pit area incorporates stone pitching around a steel spiral; the former a reference to old bush tracks where stones were 'pitched' on the ground to form a rough cobbled effect, and the latter continuing the underpinning 'spiral' theme of the site.

The location of the site was exciting and magical, yet at the same time it was challanging and demanded sensitivity.

A dense woodland of eucalypts, almost impenetrable in parts, but fortunately effective at reducing some wind impact, bordered the garden. Among the dominant vegetation was the Tasmanian endemic black peppermint (*Eucalyptus amygdalina*) and the more widely distributed stringybark (*E. obliqua*) with shrub massing of tea tree (*Leptospermum* spp.). On the hillsides the planting masses appeared dark and foreboding, suggesting to Catherine that her planting palette should be sympathetic to this, though not without patches of colour close to the house to offer seasonal interest.

Design response

To Catherine, design is almost intuitive. While clearly informed about the site's qualities and constraints and aware of her clients' wishes, she develops her schemes on a small scale on tracing paper first, then begins to rough out a broad conceptual design. In this case, perhaps in response to contours that ran along the promontory, both

3 The ha-ha fills a key function within the garden, providing a reasonably flat lawn that overcomes the sense that the house is sliding down the slope. It permits views over the distant landscape and also helps to prevent entry of rabbits and wallabies.

Catherine and her client felt curving lines suited the site. While a preconceived 'look' wasn't identified, Catherine was fortunate that her preliminary sketch resulted in a scheme that delighted her client.

Curving lines in the form of spirals, initiated here by a swirling stone ha-ha, provide a key element of the vocabulary, separating the domestic area from the remaining bush and pasture. A further spiral threaded through the design arises at the front door (the indoor/outdoor threshold) and terminates further along the peninsula at a hearth (an outdoor fire pit), a powerful cultural symbol of home. At the opposite end of the garden, where the guest cottage is situated , another stone sitting area completes the spiral. Catherine sees the spiral as an ancient cultural symbol present in her own Celtic origins where it symbolises growth, seasonal change and a journey through cyclical rotations of time, as well as representing a campsite in Australian aboriginal culture. In this design the spiral, travelling through the garden

and changing materials several times (a reference to the changing nature of time and growth), allows energy to flow through the garden and onto the peninsula. The dynamic connection between house and garden is an effective practical response to the prevailing elongated landform.

Spirals also feature in the site's most dramatic element, three large vertical mild-steel plates standing in a staggered formation. They are the first element of the garden visible on arrival and fill three functions; screening cars from within the garden, providing wind protection from the strong southerlies (with holes drilled through them filtering the wind), and creating a visual key for visitors, directing them to the location of the front door which is not immediately apparent.

By staggering the screens, external views are available to the garden. The holes, hand-drilled by local boat-builder David Goulding to Catherine's design, create

4 Walls are made of local stone, comprising a hidden mortar technique that uses the minimum amount of mortar to the rear of wall for stability yet allowing water to move through it. They also have a low embodied energy compared to other options such as concrete.

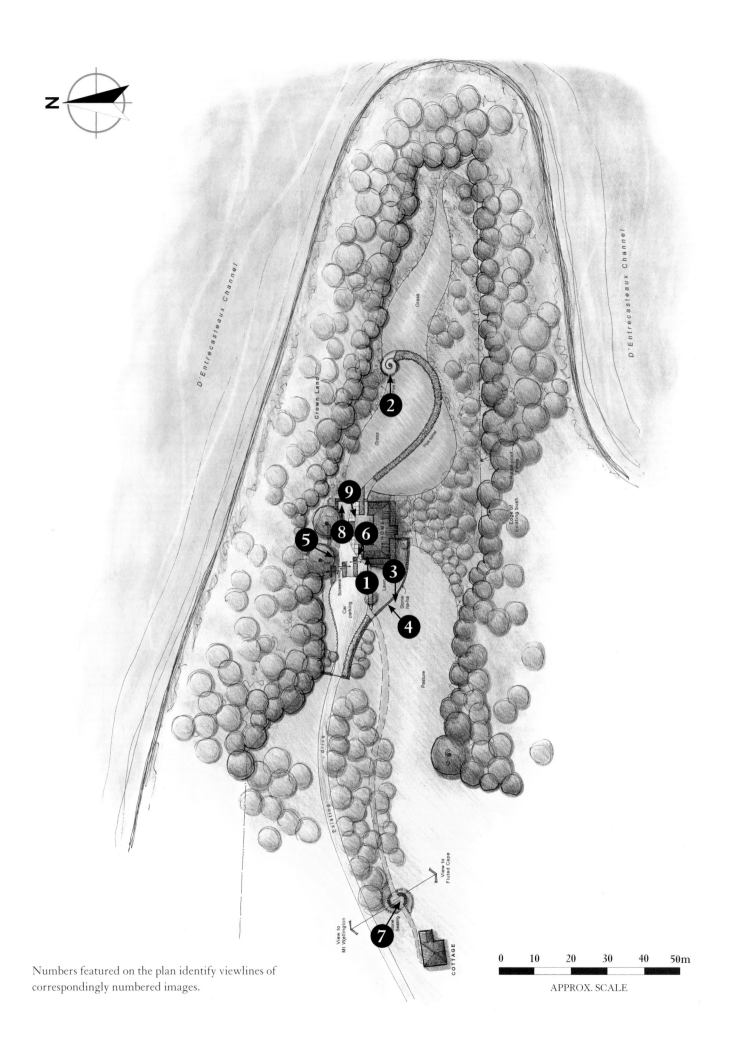

N

D'Entrecasteaux Channel

D'Entrecasteaux Channel

Crown Land

Grass

Grass

Grass

Dog gate

Dog proof

Rabbit-proof Fence

Edge of Existing bush

HOME

Car parking

Screens

Lawn

Stone ha-ha

Pasture

Existing drive

View to Fluted Cape

View to Mt Wellington

Stone Seating

COTTAGE

Numbers featured on the plan identify viewlines of
correspondingly numbered images.

0   10   20   30   40   50m

APPROX. SCALE

5 Responding to the underpinning spirals of the garden design and referencing swirling movements of nearby water, the hand-drilled rusted steel screens look magical in their settings. The staggered siting allows extended views into the broader landscape..

6 A seat at the northern end of the terrace defines the boundary of garden near the house, draws people from the deck to the water and balances the screens to the east end of the garden.

7 The stone sitting area at the Guest Cottage is designed for social gatherings or solo contemplation. It focuses on Mt Wellington in one direction and looks to Bruny Island's Fluted Cape in the other.

spirals intended to give a joyous and dynamic feeling. The planter boxes that double as seats on the terrace also incorporate the spiral motif, here cut into grey-painted timber with a rusting metal plate behind.

One of the main 'carriers' of the site's spiral motif is the ha-ha that extends to the south of the house before rising out of the ground to the west to become a garden wall as it nears the entry gate.

Designs for the garden gates are based upon traditional farm gates and match those created for pedestrians to access the wood pile and cottage. Solid steel lower sections were specifically designed to exclude grazing animals.

Catherine's sensitivity to the site is typified in the appropriate nature of her materials. Stone was used for the way it ties with the garden's setting and needs no maintenance. Steel is utilised for its relationship, when rusted, to the colours of the local mudstone. It also symbolises the use of metal in the original agricultural landscape. Finally, hardwood is featured as a reference

to the surrounding vegetation, in planter boxes, supports for the metal screens and in the decking.

The creation and use of seats is a deliberate design element, for this is a garden of views. Seats not only function to allow visitors to explore views, they assist in definition of spaces and enclosure for the garden. For example, an L-shaped stone corner seat delineates the inner garden and the stone seats created at the east and west outer edges define the extended garden against its broader setting. In addition, seats built in the form of a spiral around the fire pit allow users to sit closer to or further from the fire as required.

Planting design

Sensibility to setting are the key words in Catherine's approach to planting design. Needless to say her scheme is low water demanding, but she also sought 'a simplicity and lightness that would not detract from the surrounding environment and yet provide enough interest and seasonal change to engage the senses close to home'. While much of the site's drama is the changing moods of the skies,

8 In general terms, ornamental planting was focused around the house while natives were established in the broader setting. The ornamental plantings provide a little more flower colour to mark seasonal change.

expanse of water and the distant views, the planting can provide not only a connection to that drama but also a degree of comfort as a counterbalance to it.

Catherine involves her clients in plant selection. By putting together plant image sheets, she gives her clients an insight into the final appearance of the garden. In this case, plants were chosen for site and soil appropriateness and for texture and foliage colour in preference to flowers, though still permitting a changing palette through the seasons. Ornamental planting was focused around the house, while natives were established in the broader landscape.

Interpreting the distant view of rolling mountains within the garden, Catherine used undulating hedges of native coastal rosemary (*Westringia rigida*) planted as overlapping layers. Still at a formative stage, they will be clipped to echo the shape of the distant mountain groups. Grey woolly thyme (*Thymus pseudolanuginosus*) grows beneath, planted amongst pebbles to eventually carpet the ground

plane, its colour perfectly mirroring the adjacent coastal shallows. Other foliage in the garden also responds to the hues of the sea and the ever-changing sky.

Close to the steel screens the elegant Mediterranean grass *Stipa gigantea* is planted with native cushion bush (*Leucophyta brownii*). The stipa stems are retained as they dry, their fine, straw-coloured heads relating perfectly to the rust-coloured screens. By contrast, their grey-blue foliage links to the greys of the cushion bush which, clipped into strong blocks of foliage emerging from a sea of pebble, provides a fascinating textural and colour combination at the site entry. On the house side of the exquisite screens, elegant foliage of she-oak (*Allocasuarina verticillata*) provides contrast in form and colour and wind protection for the inner garden.

Closer to the house, planting is more detailed. Seasonal herbs and vegetables grow in tubs on the deck while more permanent planting fills surrounding beds. Catherine is restricted to selecting plants grown in Tasmanian

Cotinus coggygria 'Grace', a burgundy smoke bush was specially selected to echo the colour of thundery skies. On long, arching stems, this shrub produces round, purple leaves that turn magnificent autumnal tones. Also featured; red flowering *Anigozantho* w., tufting blue oat grass (*Helichtotrichon sempervirens*) and foreground Clary Sage (*Salvia sclarea*).

The eastern Mediterranean native rusty foxglove (*Digitalis ferruginea*) is well suited to the shallow, rocky soils and, though short lived, its large creamy flowers provide an eye catching display.

nurseries, yet this has not compromised her palette which includes many superb plants rarely encountered in Australian gardens. The stout form of the eastern Mediterranean rusty foxglove (*Digitalis ferruginea*) contrasts with the more elegant native kangaroo paws (*Anigozanthos* spp.) which provide masses of colour and delight local birds with their nectar. By using new improved cultivars, Catherine has avoided previous problems of ink spot fungus.

Many grasses are used throughout. Native grasses feature extensively in the broader landscape, such as common tussock grass (*Poa labillardierei*), its beautiful heads picking up every nuance of breeze. Growing locally in dry sclerophyll, it performs well in the acidic soils and dryness of this site.

Blending of exotics and natives continues with the silver groundcover Stachys 'Cotton Ball' linking well to scale-leaf bush everlasting (*Ozothamnus scutelifolius*), a

Tasmanian endemic wide spread in dry locations. With regular pruning, it offers rewarding dense silver foliage, especially as a contrast with the lax growth of Russian sage (*Perovskia atriplicifolia*). The openness of the sage allows its delightful blue spires to sway in the breeze. While the silver-leafed *Eleagnus angustifolia* 'Quicksilver', a selected form of the Russian olive with brilliantly silver foliage, makes a perfect foil for the burgundy smoke bush *Cotinus coggygria* 'Grace' specially selected to echo the colour of thundery skies. On long, arching stems, the round, purple leaves of this shrub turn magnificent autumnal reds. Cut back each year, it contributes to the garden permanently.

An avenue of she-oaks has recently been established by the garden owners, as they so loved Catherine's planting of them adjacent to the screens. For Catherine, this says, 'The garden owners are starting to own it back and to develop it in their way too', producing a successful triangle between designer, owner and the site itself.

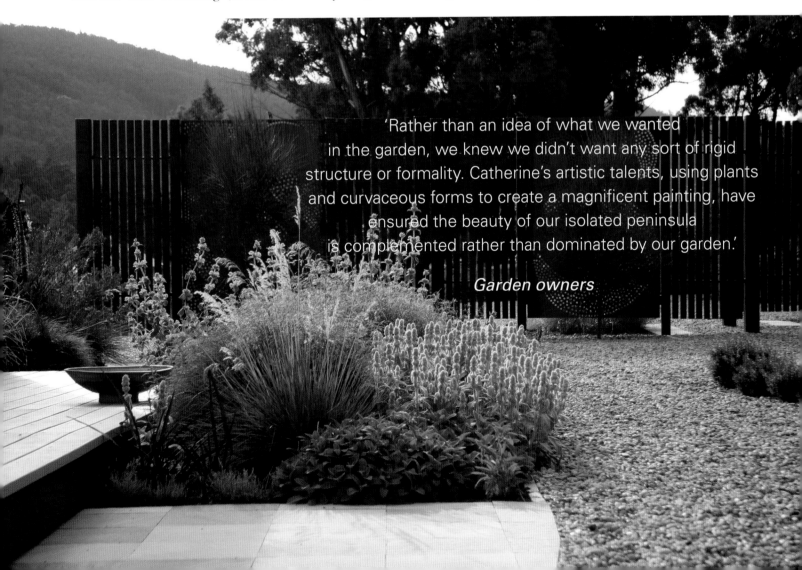

'Rather than an idea of what we wanted in the garden, we knew we didn't want any sort of rigid structure or formality. Catherine's artistic talents, using plants and curvaceous forms to create a magnificent painting, have ensured the beauty of our isolated peninsula is complemented rather than dominated by our garden.'

Garden owners

DESIGN TIP

Robert Boyle's design for this Mornington Peninsula garden uses low foreground planting to maintain distant views, blurring the boundaries between the garden and its surroundings.

The borrowed view

How fortunate Catherine was in her work at 'Woodbridge'! While she was responsible for creating the charming garden surrounding the house, she had nothing to do with the garden's magnificent broader setting. Her role was to ensure it became part of the garden and that the benefits accruing from it were maximised.

Appreciating a site's context is critically important in the development of a garden design. Borrowing a view can add a new dimension, especially to smaller gardens. It permits apparent increase in size that can effectively blur boundaries and give an illusion of more space than actually exists.

Within urban landscapes, boundaries are often tight and enclosed. Those fortunate enough to border a reserve or park gain a backdrop that gives access to sky, trees, and often expansive grass that can be used to effectively extend a garden. Fences could be hinged at the centre, or retractable as in Georgina Martyn's design, to allow views from the garden that break down barriers. Where privacy is not important, an open wire fence can allow continuity. Alternatively, removal of boundary fences completely enables garden and perhaps adjoining bushland to blend and permit subtle integration.

While borrowed view opportunities may be limited in the smaller town garden, they can still be valuable. Tall-growing trees and shrubs in a neighbouring block might offer a backdrop to your garden that can be planted up to and integrated into your planting scheme. It may be that

With Australia's spectacular harbour views, detail in the garden's design is pointless, the view becomes all.

there is only a single tree to borrow. Repetition of that species within your own garden will create perspective. You may also plant to frame views of church steeples, Victorian towers, impressive neighbouring architecture or distant city lights. These options both extend the garden and increase its impact.

A trompe l'oeil, a painted garden backdrop, can also provide a dramatic borrowed view, carrying the eye out of the garden into a distant, entirely contrived landscape. Planting within your garden to link to its theme is a great way of achieving extended space. But use evergreen plants, as seasonal change will give the game away!

Coastal properties, too, may borrow a view, although some are quite distant and only observed over intervening house roofs. The borrowed view can be improved with appropriate coastal planting that screens the lower view of buildings while maintaining the feature view of water or headlands.

Catherine had great borrowed landscape opportunities. To one side, the sea and D'Entrecastaux Sound's promontories and headlands offered a fabulous series of focuses. Such a situation is fortunate, for long sea views without a frame can be beautiful but lack drama. The retention of vegetation that frames such a view and keeps the eye down to the sea and the horizon is invaluable. Where a broad sea view exists without such a feature, consider introducing a frame—it could be a simple metal shape that helps establish confines to the view. A pergola may do a similar job when viewed from inside a house.

On occasions when views are especially wide, there is much to be said for screening a portion of a view to allow it to be broken up. While a 180-degree view can be dramatic, sometimes it is wasted by revealing it all at once. By limiting it with trees or shrubs, a section of the view can be framed and highlighted while a second broader viewing experience is revealed beyond the planting, with perhaps a seat for added enjoyment.

To further capitalise on borrowed views, Catherine used an invaluable tool at 'Woodbridge'—the ha-ha. The traditional ha-ha is a sunken wall, historically often combined with a ditch that presents a barrier to stock entry as they cannot climb it from below, but allows for extended views from the garden. For eighteenth-century gentry, it offered a sense of grandeur, suggesting that their land ownership was limitless.

Iris Origo created her own borrowed landscape at La Foca, Tuscany, by planting Italian cypresses as a focus to her garden view. The repetition of cypresses as a perimeter garden planting provides a linking element to the landscape beyond.

Port Douglas Garden
Queensland

'As a passionate designer of tropical landscapes, I am excited by the possibilities we have in Australia to forge ahead in design for the tropics. Most climatically similar regions are in developing countries, without the resources for discretionary spending on gardens. Here, we have the means and opportunity to develop our own style of 'Australian' tropical design, honouring the incredible natural beauty and flora of the region, the innovative vernacular architecture, the individual personalities of our people and, most importantly, our own unique 'sense of place'.' **john sullivan**

Biography

Entranced by the alluring climate and lifestyle of the tropics during student work experience in Cairns in the late 1980s, John Sullivan has now lived and worked in far north Queensland for more than a decade. His design business Hortulus, began in 1997 and specialises in designing residential and commercial landscapes with an Australian tropical feel, as well as providing construction and maintenance services. Distinguishing himself by the use of unusual and high quality plant material, John's business also incorporates a nursery to avoid reliance on local supply.

John began life in the eastern suburbs of Melbourne, a boy scout surrounded by gum trees with 'nature boy' tendencies. Succumbing to parental persuasion, he relinquished his intention to undertake a nursery production apprenticeship and completed formal studies instead. Imbued with an intrinsic understanding of the design process from design history lectures, he credits this awareness of the past with his confidence to design for today.

Conscious of Australia's position as a young nation in global terms, he believes 'Australian' design is still evolving, grounded in the English landscape movement of the eighteenth century but increasingly influenced by the philosophies of our Asian neighbours. He is aware of a link between the stark beauty of the Australian landscape and the simple, pared-back approach of Japanese gardens—in his view, this was alluded to in early Australian design by Ellis Stones and Edna Walling in their restrained treatment of rock and vegetation in its natural state.

Sense of place is also critical to John. He strongly believes in recognising the special qualities of his immediate environment, adamant that a garden should reflect the identity of its location. He deliberately incorporates elements that highlight and manage seasonal change in the tropics, celebrating the ability of nature to transform a purpose-built dry creek bed into a raging torrent when the wet season erupts.

Inspired by the commitment of the world's few remaining intrepid plant collectors, John senses the urgency of

1 Natural-styled ponds, designed to manage and retain site water, are a feature of this Port Douglas garden.

preserving the world's threatened flora, hoping one day to personally join the plant-collecting crusade. Meanwhile, he believes educating his clients to understand and manage their own gardens is the first step in environmental awareness, as well as an essential element in delivering an appropriately designed garden. To John this is the essence of good garden design. In the tropics the issue of maintenance often controls the design as the growth rate of plants is extraordinary. Attention to the owner's capacity either physically or financially to maintain a design is therefore critical, avoiding the inevitable alternative of a neglected, non-functional space.

Actively involved in his profession, John writes for gardening magazines, and has chaired and participated in many influential horticultural bodies. He identifies a need for the education of gardeners in design and maintenance of tropical landscapes, noting the disparity between reference material available for garden design in Mediterranean climates compared to the tropics. While lack of historical precedent encourages originality, a need still exists for the training of horticulturists to appreciate the opportunities and restraints of tropical landscapes. Armed with an enthusiasm and understanding of the possibilities within his environment, John brings a vibrant optimism to Australian tropical landscape design.

Design brief

Construction of a new house in Port Douglas presented John with an ideal project that allowed him to exercise his love for Australia's native plants, particularly unusual varieties not the subject of breeding and selection programs. Fortunately, his clients shared his vision, noting that despite most local gardens being designed for wet tropics, Port Douglas vegetation was scrubby and coastal. They sought a garden that responded to the individual micro-climates of their property, which included wet tropical responses in heavily shaded or moist areas and dry tropical elsewhere.

Also influential in producing the brief was architect, Angus Crowe, who had clear views about the garden setting. The form of the house with its many pavilions, dramatically roofed and deeply incised by the landscape allowed views into intimate garden spaces. These spaces were to be developed to appear as informal creeks typical of the north Queensland landscape. Roof runoff water was to be retained on site to flush the purpose built creek system and then soak into the ground to top up the water table. With heavy rainfall a common occurrence (two to three metres in a season) flushing could take place regularly to clean through the system.

A free-form pond enveloping the buildings was an integral aspect of the architect's design and the garden was to be designed around it. Recreational space was important. A pool, outdoor eating area, quiet space for contemplation and an atmosphere of welcome were all part of the initial brief. Acquistion of adjoining land for a tennis court extended the brief, as did the owners' request for a garden that would attract birds and butterflies.

Service, too, could not be forgotten, so a garage area and drying space were required in the front area of the site where they could be isolated. As the house was a holiday home, there was the usual need for low maintenance, but realistically this was difficult to achieve, given the plant-growth rate in the tropics.

Site analysis

The site is part of a new development approximately 50m from the renowned Five Mile Beach. Originally, the area was covered by a mixed coastal woodland of paperbarks (*Melaleuca* spp.), together with the beautiful bird-attracting golden bouquet tree (*Deplanchea tetraphylla*) and red beach tree (*Dillenia alata*). As part of the original Mirage development, African oil palms (*Elaeis guineensis*) were planted as an avenue to the access road. While not native, these do contribute to the character of the site and have become a major landscape element through this part of Port Douglas.

The site itself is relatively flat, and no vegetation was retained on the site during the development. To the south is the Port Douglas Golf Course with extensive areas of mown grassland and feature trees. The tennis court on the adjacent block to the north gave this site the luxury of

The architect proposed a pond system beneath the elevated buildings as a means of handling heavy rainfall and allowing maximum soakage into the soil. This provided John with a theme to expand upon in his design. The presence of native *Lepironia articulata* fits well as an emergent aquatic species.

uninterrupted space on all sides and, given that the house was well set back on the block and from the road, the opportunity to create a private tropical setting was real.

By locating the house to the south of the site, the architect achieved two objectives; leaving an extensive tract of land available for the tennis court and removing the house from a public path to the beach. The house location also avoided the need for extensive screen planting which would have been necessary to provide privacy not only from the footpath but also from an adjacent house on a neighbouring block.

Design response

As with any site, the house itself established much of the design response. With its high roof form, separate but linked components, and considerable building mass, it was critical to John that he integrate the house with its landscape setting. His work began outside the site where he introduced native planting to soften the access from the road.

Responding to the architect's pond system, John introduced water to the garden at the site entry through

2 Inside the entry the building was dominant. Selection of plants that allowed the scale of the built form to be humanized and integrated into the site was important. John achieved this by using advanced native palms to create impact and to link with those in adjoining landscapes.

3 Capitalising on the anticipated Port Douglas rainfall and to reinforce a sense of place, John created small creeks to feed an overflow lined with geofabric and pebbles and, during heavy rain, water floods into the adjacent golf course where it can puddle before soaking away.

an informal pond; water then became a recurrent theme through the site. John's view about the heavy rainfall of the area is interesting. He sees it as perhaps the single most defining element of Port Douglas. A sense of place in Sydney may derive from coastal views, in rural Victoria from misty winter vistas, but at Port Douglas a 2- or 3-hour downpour contributes to the character and mood of the place.

For many with gardens in northern Queensland, even temporary flooding is seen as unacceptable, but for John it is a valuable recognition of place. In his view, residents need to review their attitudes and recognise that flooding is only temporary but vital in the way it recharges ground water and flushes through natural systems.

The adjacent golf course offers an invaluable setting for the garden and a magnificent borrowed landscape. Fortunately, native Alexandra palms (*Archontophoenix alexandrae*) dominated the course so their repetition within the garden was an appropriate plant choice and

4 Planting at the golf course edge assimilated the house into the landscape. Within the shade of the house and planting its occupants are well hidden, yet they benefit from the light from the course itself. Around the pool, use of screening planting was employed where privacy was more crucial.

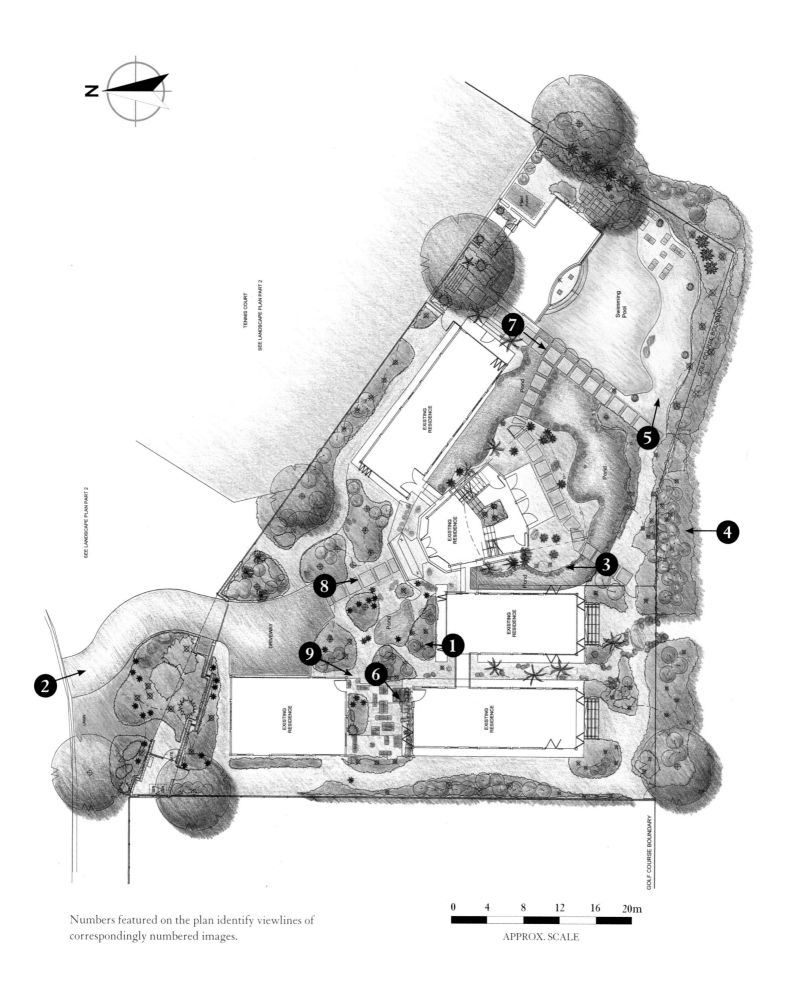

Numbers featured on the plan identify viewlines of
correspondingly numbered images.

0   4   8   12   16   20m

APPROX. SCALE

5 Shrub planting (*right*) provides privacy screening to the site from the golf course to the pool area. However, by keeping planting relatively low, shade is minimized and the pleasures of a sunny pool area are maximized.

6 John's desire to embed secret retreats within the garden saw the creation of a zen-style garden where open space, burgundy coloured walls, golden stem bamboo, gravel floor and seating, provide space for contemplation.

a unifying element between the garden and its broader setting.

John makes an interesting observation about the garden's relationship to the golf course that explains why he did not provide a significant and dense privacy screen at the site interface. Views from the light of the course into the shade of the house are very limited. In contrast, views from the shade into the light are more telling and these are available to the owner's great advantage.

Having set a theme of informal native planting reinforced by paving surfaces in the form of raked sands and gravels, John extended the informal theme to the large free-form swimming pool with its adjacent outdoor eating area. Constraints to design in northern Queensland do result from its distance from manufacturing areas, (not that many residents would wish to change things), and this tends to reduce the available palette of materials. For example, paving materials must be available in assured supply otherwise there can be delays in completion of projects.

By utilising permeable paving wherever possible, John has also maximised water entry into the soil. Stone available for paving may be restricted in the region, but the local Daintree gravel is excellent and provides a real sense of character and place. It is used to surface informal paths which wind their way around the perimeter of the site, ensuring that an attractive low-key character is dominant.

Designers in far north Queensland do have a significant advantage in that plant growth is so rapid gardens mature almost overnight. Yet this can also be a disadvantage as on-going maintenance is needed. Unlike in similar climatic regions, such as Bali, where high maintenance requirements are met with low cost labour, maintenance expenses can surprise owners. Recognising this, John plants immature stock and low maintenance plants to try and overcome this problem. His choice of dryland native species also contributes to more manageable growth rates, compared to wet tropical varieties.

There is a strong sense here of a garden and house set within a tropical paradise and John was happy to

7 The presence of the swimming pool and overflow ponds adjacent to each other suggested to John that a visual link should be established. Water jets suggest movement of water from the swimming pool into the floodway, enhancing the role of water in the design.

encourage this within his design. But he also sees value in the contrast between being enveloped between abundant tropical vegetation and the availability of open space. Consequently, there is a balance of different garden areas that cater to varying moods and lifestyle needs.

Planting design

Being an enthusiastic plant lover, John's unusual plant suggestions inspired and excited his clients. They often researched plant options on the internet and became actively involved in creating the garden. John's planting work in this garden was ultimately completed in two stages; the tennis court area only eventuating as the planting for the main house garden was complete.

Hearing of a large garden at Jullaten that had plants for sale, John purchased some of the mature plants for re-use in this garden, to secure the setting of the house in its landscape and accommodate the scale of the built form. Weeping cabbage palms (*Livistona decipiens*), for example, were placed close to the house where they established

8 Mature planting was used to secure the setting of the house in its landscape and accommodate the scale of the built form. Among these was screw pine (*Pandanus solms-laubachii*), **Right:** one of the most characteristic plants of the dry tropics which spreads from eastern Cape York Peninsula to Cairns. **Left:** *Macrozamia moorei*

scale. A springsure zamia (*Macrozamia moorei*) was also relocated and, as one of the most ornamental of cycads, provided the perfect low level companion to the palms; indeed, it looks like a small palm tree.

While John's gardening philosophy sees the use of fascinating flora that have hardly been explored for their horticultural value, others are well-known; for example pink phyllanthus (*Phyllanthus cuscutiflorus*), native to lowland rainforest in the Cooktown area, has been used widely as a screening plant, a replacement for the lillypillies that John has used previously. It grows fast yet maintains low foliage, and this gives it special value.

However, though functional, it provides little garden glamour so John was keen to include some of the more ornamental natives that bring flower and colour to the garden and with them native birds and insects.

Along the site's southern boundary against the golf course, he has used the golden-flowered *Grevillea* 'Golden Lyre' a hybrid of *G. formosa* that is native to the Kakadu area. In spite of its narrow linear foliage, it provides a dense screen to a height of approximately 2m. Other grevilleas in the garden also capture the eye: *G.* 'Cooroora Cascade', a groundcover that spreads to 2.5m wide and is covered by glorious golden flowers; *G.* 'Billy Bonkers', a shrub to

Left: The little known *Fagraea berteriana* is native to stream banks in the lowland rainforests of north–eastern Queensland. Only recently introduced into cultivation, its attractive flowers, glossy evergreen foliage and heavy scent suggest it will become increasingly popular. **Middle:** John utilises gardenias familiar to most gardeners where there is some moisture and humidity. While the dwarf gardenia is used for massed effect here, a new introduced cultivar *Gardenia tubifera* 'Soleil D'Or' is used as a specimen. Its cream flowers age to gold in three to four days. **Right:** In any plant selection, the white bat plant (*Tacca integrifolia*) is one of the most dramatic. It has been described as one of the world's weirdest plants with flower heads of up to 30 blooms that look like bat faces.

2m wide with a terrible name but glorious red flowers that last on the plant for most of the year and are superb bird-attractants; Maytown grevillea (*G. dryandri*) native to the western Tablelands with pink to orange flowers; and *G.* 'Peaches and Cream' which reaches 1.5m and has bicoloured flowers, cream and soft pink. John has found that many of these only grow in the wet tropics if grafted on appropriate rootstocks, otherwise local soils are simply too poorly drained for them.

John also delights in using flamboyant tropical plants, such as his signature heliconias including 'Hot Rio Night', which grows to 4m and has inflorescences of 6–10 red bracts; 'Sexy Pink', perhaps more beautiful if less flamboyant, with pendulous inflorescences of up to 28 soft pink bracts that look even more spectacular hanging from a plant that can grow to 5m; and for complete contrast, *Heleconia stricta* 'Dwarf Jamaica', growing only to .5m and with smaller flowerheads of 3–5 bracts but useful for lower, infill planting.

John returned to native plants for the northern boundary screening and privacy and shade from western sun. As his dominant plant, he repeated the native palm *Ptychosperma macarthurii* that enjoys a limited natural distribution from northeastern Cape York Peninsula through to the Torres Strait Islands. Generally regarded as benefiting from protection from full sun, it has prospered in a sunny location in this garden to provide an effective screen.

Finally, mention should be made that much of John's knowledge of plant performance in the Cairns area has come about through experience. For example, in the beginning he used a wide range of native grasses in his work, but experience taught him that he lost those unless all thatch was removed from within the plant. Fungal attack in the humidity seems to have caused the problems. However his recent experience that the native kangaroo grass (*Themeda australis* 'Mingo') performs well even in the humidity if given a sandy soil reflects one of John's joys in gardening in Port Douglas—he never finishes learning.

'John's open approach and enthusiasm for our initial ideas gave us great confidence in the design process. While his overall design is cohesive and flows well between spaces, we love all the different nooks and crannies that offer their own special feel. There's always something to delight in every season though as the garden has been planted specifically with butterfly-attracting plants; butterfly season is truly spectacular.'

Garden owners

9

DESIGN TIP

Jim Fogarty's design for this Melbourne garden uses simple gravel-lined swales to bring interest close to the house, encourage wildlife and hold water to allow it to slowly percolate. Once dry, it takes on the appearance of a dry creek, not unlikely in an Australian landscape.

Using site water

With global warming demanding greater attention, there is increasing pressure on garden designers to respond by creating gardens that are water sensitive. One approach has been to utilise plants that have a lower water demand or which are more appropriate ecologically to a garden location.

An equally valid approach is to retain water on-site to ensure that, rather than draining away through drainage systems, it benefits the garden and local water table. This approach is evident in John's garden where the management of periodic tropical rainfall and water run-off makes a valuable contribution to site ecology as well as interesting visual impact.

Within any garden, numerous procedures can help reduce run-off. As a fundamental, collection of water from roofs

into tanks makes a positive contribution. Undertaken on a large number of residential lots, it greatly decreases discharge during maximum rainfall and risks of flooding. As well as reducing run-off, it supplies water for gardens that can either drain through the soil or be transpired into the atmosphere, recharging the natural water cycle.

For this to work, it is important that water in tanks is used so that when rainfall occurs they are able to collect further water. Use of a grey water system provides a useful adjunct to tanks as it allows irrigation to take place while tanks await refilling from rain.

Minimisation of paving in gardens is also beneficial. Paved areas collect heat and re-radiate it at night as temperatures fall, further contributing to dehydration. Or if pavers are light-coloured, they reflect heat into the

The use of large cobbled paving provides effective protection of tree roots in this Eckersley Stafford design and, being permeable, permits water to soak into adjacent soils to enhance tree health. Adjacent grasses intercept rainfall, allowing it to slowly percolate into the water table.

atmosphere during the day. Limit these areas to reduce such effects, simultaneously leaving increased soft landscape available to take up moisture.

Permeable paving is preferable since it allows for water penetration. Gravels are good but even unit paving can be designed to have gravel-filled gaps between them for water percolation, or fall towards garden beds. There are also permeable unit paving options available. A gravel strip in the centre of a driveway provides an attractive soakaway. Drainage pits may be located at levels where collected water can slowly soak into soil, with only excess water draining away to prevent flooding.

By utilising extensive masses of foliage, the rate at which water enters drainage systems is also slowed. Foliage of trees, shrubs and grasses captures large volumes of rainfall, holding it in the leaves and plant structure. Tall grasses like Miscanthus species are especially effective at reducing runoff at times of maximum flow, releasing it later to percolate into the ground water.

In this garden the most valuable mechanism to capture water lies in the rain-garden and ponds fed by the link drains that lead from the house gutters to the ponds beneath. These take water and hold it during periods of rainfall, replicating natural processes that would have happened on the site prior to development.

There are advantages in this approach apart from the obvious aesthetic ones of introducing water into a garden and reducing flow into engineered drainage systems. Water collected can evaporate, cooling the atmosphere as well as slowly and naturally soaking into the groundwater system.

While John's design has extensive pond areas—the result of a decision, made by the project's architect to hold water on-site—the same can be achieved by the construction of simple swales within planted areas. These dished areas hold water in the landscape in the short-term and become integrated in the garden as they dry. With imagination, these can be developed as gravelled beds which look like seasonal water flows and bring a natural effect to a garden.

Wherever water is stored, issues of safety must be considered. Your local council is a good place to start for safety information. Where decks provide a pond/water interface, appropriate safety barriers should be in place.

The combination of a waterwise planting scheme, sensible irrigation that takes account of wind, rain and individual plant needs and consideration of site water retention will ensure sustainability and success in the garden.

While water storage ponds and their associated wildlife provide great intrigue for children as in this Greenmark Landscape garden, they should be located where adult supervision can be provided.

Adelaide Garden
South Australia

'As designers of landscapes we are interested in the creation of gardens in the context of community and environment both locally and globally. We view design as an artistic pursuit, literally, as well as a social art interwoven with people's lives. We are interested in the power of the central narrative, but also of the smallest detail—and ultimately how public and private space represents and shapes who we are. We want people to experience these interests in our work, to feel both the serious intensity and simple joy that landscape design can bring.' kevin taylor & kate cullity

Biography

Kevin Taylor and Kate Cullity, founding directors of the landscape architectural practice, Taylor Cullity Lethlean, enjoy both a personal and professional partnership. Both studied landscape architecture and with complementary backgrounds—Kate's in botany and art, and Kevin's in architecture and social planning—their renowned poetic expression of landscape and culture through garden design evolves harmoniously from a multi-disciplined base. Committed to sensitive and sustainable development, their celebrated work spanning public and private spheres exhibits strong cultural, social and environmental awareness.

Kevin was raised in Adelaide and his relationship to landscape was shaped by many childhood hours spent fishing in remote elemental landscapes along the Southern Ocean. Kate reflects on the shaping of her character and career as a child of the west, romantically recalling hometown memories of Perth's vast blue skies

and piercing light. The view of writer Robert Drewe that 'all West Australians are ... inheritors of the myth of landscape' rings true for her.

A child of the 60s, she remembers dreaming, not only of gardens, but of modernist, rectilinear houses, often constructing models out of moss and beautiful timber samples salvaged from her father's work. Modernist influences resonate through the combined work of Kate and Kevin today, where contemporary sculpture and artistic collaborations are often defining elements of their gardens. They strive to imbue designed spaces with an interpretive and layered quality. Their garden designs are also influenced by the extensive work done in national parks, often using patterns inspired by the shapes and textures of arid and elemental Australia.

Though much of their work exhibits innovative design, Kate's strong personal interest and affinity with plants guarantees the role of vegetation. She sees plants as food for the soul and pivotal to emotional wellbeing, as well as providing all important modulation of light and atmosphere. Her knowledge of native and exotic flora is

1 The Desert Space recalls the experience of Australia's desert heart and is augmented by 20 squares of sculpture edged with rusted steel representing various elements of the Australian landscape.

Detail of sculptural square featured in the Desert Space.

invaluable in establishing striking planting schemes to meet specific requirements for beauty, sustainability or wildlife habitat.

Both Kate and Kevin recognise the power of landscape in empowering people. They actively engage in wider conversations with colleagues, communities and collaborative professionals such as architects, artists, historians, horticulturalists and scientists through conferences, seminars and journal articles. They hope their interrelated approach results in a layering of skills that positively contributes to the social, artistic, emotional and economic lives of others. Kevin also particularly fosters an emphasis on socially responsible design through extensive community consultation.

Winning more than 60 local and international awards, Kate and Kevin, in association with Perry Lethlean, are responsible for inspired landscapes including the North Terrace Redevelopment, Adelaide; the Australian Garden in the Royal Botanic Gardens at Cranbourne, Victoria; and the Uluru Aboriginal Cultural Centre. With more

than 25 years experience and a deep understanding of, and passion for, interpreting Australian culture through designed landscapes, they continue to create ecologically sound, innovative living tributes that both celebrate and define who we are.

Design brief

As professional landscape architects, Kate and Kevin see their home as a place to experiment. The broad breadth of projects they have undertaken in their practice sees them utilising ideas formulated, implemented and assessed in their own garden. These are not only landscape ideas but also sculptural concepts, for their work is about the poetry, spirit and sustainability of the Australian landscape and its interpretation in installation as much as it is about landscape design.

Kate's desire in this site was to create a garden appropriate to the Adelaide climate which can be very tough with low rainfall. This was not to be a garden of perennials like she had created in her earlier Melbourne gardens, but one where she could assess the performance of plants with potential for use in her broader landscape schemes.

Kate and Kevin also saw their garden as a quiet retreat where friends were welcomed. They have different ideas about relaxation—Kate enjoying the act of gardening, weeding, clipping and experimenting, while Kevin tends to stroll, linger and think. Despite her willingness to garden, Kate stresses that the garden must be able to survive neglect on occasions when she isn't able to tend it.

Use of native plants was important, not only for their toughness and ability to tolerate Adelaide's climate but also to attract birds into the garden for the life, movement and colour they bring.

Finally, and perhaps most importantly, the garden had to be visible from different parts of the house. It also had to provide an extension to the house, an outdoor area that extended living spaces, flowing from them into the garden setting.

Site analysis

The site is approximately 1000sqm located 10 minutes south of Adelaide city centre. It is a corner block and this was important in the early stages of the development of the garden since it provided two access points, one to the west-facing house and one to the rear studio, originally the office for their landscape architectural practice via its northern street frontage.

In many respects the site was unremarkable—flat, with the house centrally located while the studio occupied about a third of the back garden. As a result, there was limited space all around the house; however, this was to provide appropriate areas for creation of their series of garden rooms.

The original front garden consisted of lawn skirted with narrow garden beds. The 1970's low and open besser block fence was ineffective in screening views of a neighbouring school and hospital and bore no relationship to the century-old sandstone house. The side fence to the north also needed replacing to provide enclosure from the street and maximise the opportunity for northern exposure for outdoor entertaining adjacent to the living area.

Existing vegetation included an apple tree, large lillypilly and a double flowering plum (*Prunus* x *bliereana*), retained for its fabulous burgundy foliage that contrasts so beautifully with surrounding green vegetation.

Design response

The garden has developed over almost seven years as funding and time have permitted, using not only Kate and Kevin's skills but those of contractors and landscape architectural students. True to its purpose, the garden has changed as different design experiments take place. However, there is consistency in the garden, too, notably in the way that it comprises different compositions revealed within different rooms. In some respects the overriding theme that extends through the design is Kate and Kevin's desire to introduce elements of non-urban Australia to their urban environment. They have

The garden is an experimental place and often changes. Originally formed as an oval lawn at the front of the house featuring stacked sandstone tiles, this area has been remodelled as an oval of desert sand.

2 'Woven Walls' creates a sitting area at the edge of the outdoor living space extending indoor space and benefitting from northern sun. Moss clothes the walls, exploiting the shade created by surrounding vegetation.

3 Sculptural pieces within the garden can be transient as in 'Red Squares' created by artist Ryan Sims in the 'Still Waters' garden courtyard.

4 Seasonal leaves and fruit are floated on the water's surface to create changing interest in the 'Still Waters' garden room.

distilled the essence of Australia's bushland character and interpreted it in the distinct spaces around their home.

Fiercely red and burning, the pivotal 'Desert Space' recalls the nature of Australia's inland heart, a character that is enhanced by the presence of twenty squares of sculpture edged with rusting steel. Their positioning through the space recalls the character of the desert, the visitor carefully moving between spinifex and the detritus of the dry, arid landscape.

The appearance of the plots within the garden may change, but their character and scale remains consistent on the flat background of red sand. The containment of the landscape features within their metal frames heightens the visitor's awareness of the different elements. A microcosm of the Australian bush exists within each, using native plants such as kangaroo paws (*Anigozanthos* sp.) or cushion bush (*Leucophyta brownii*), against different coloured pebbles, gravels, sands, timbers, seed pods, stems and dried leaves.

Stepping stones separate the 'Desert Space' from the 'Woven Walls' and allow for a change in mood and character. In 'Woven Walls', curving walls interlock to

provide sitting areas at the edge of the outdoor living area.

Again, this is a garden of experimentation, the walls being built of a local sand and gravel mix to give an aged appearance. On the floor of the space, random sandstone pavers are laid with round black pebbles forming lines through the garden and extending across the entire rear of the house. Along with sandstone paving, these create structure as well as a sense of spaciousness in a garden area that is, in fact, relatively small.

Extending through the garden, the pebbles and sandstone lead to the next courtyard, providing a link to 'Still Waters'. Three parallel rectilinear walls separate the house from the studio. In one of these, water is captured and provides a counterpoint to the dry desert landscape of the front garden. Seeds or leaves float on the surface of the water that also reflects winter light into this garden space.

Kate's training as an artist shines through in this unique garden. It is a constant feast for all the senses and references to the Australian landscape are challenging and enthralling. What's more, there are delightful and subtle changes. 'Twisted Limbs' is a garden to the north

Numbers featured on the plan identify viewlines
of correspondingly numbered images.

APPROX. SCALE

0   1.5   3   4.5   6   7.5m

5 'Twisted Limbs' utilises eucalypts and blue fescues for dramatic effect. A bedspring bench by artist Julie Pieda is a focus located beneath an old apple tree.

'Snake in the Grass' offers a meditative space for visitors and occupants of the garden and is setting for the sculptural piece 'Spine'.

of the studio. Accessed from the street, this garden utilises blue-grey foliages from dwarf South Australian gums (*Eucalyptus leucoxylon rosea* 'Eucy Dwarf') and the dwarf, mounding grass *Festuca glauca*. The twisting trunks of the eucalypts are an exquisite foil to the grass and to the random natural stone paving that offers access to the space.

South of the house is the 'Ripple Lawn', where stepping stones provide an outer arc that contrasts with mown areas of grass, a play on the traditional dwarf hedge. The form of the grass is underlined by a curving natural stone wall that helps to define its elliptical shape. A bright red gate at the end of the path is the entry to the service area of the home, which is carefully enclosed and separated from other garden rooms.

Finally, 'Snake in the Grass' looks to Zen gardens of Kyoto for inspiration. Swaying grasses form a serpentine-shaped

A corten-steel gate at the site entrance displays a form based upon the microscopic structure of plant cell walls.

calligraphic sweep through the garden, a contrast to the texture, colour and raked surface of the gravel.

What is remarkable about this award-winning garden is the way it works on so many levels and captures the character of the Australian landscape. While it may be viewed as a garden, it is equally justifiable to consider it a work of sculpture in its own right, one that interprets the vastness of the Australian landscape in small scale. It is a place of vision and a place of dreaming.

Planting design

Plants may be thought to be secondary elements of this garden given its sculptural character, yet it is in planting design that the garden's experimental nature shines through, for Kate and Kevin like to assess the performance of plants before using them in broader landscape settings. In their own garden, they can discern every characteristic of a plant, their response to drought and to irrigation, to shade and to the levels of maintenance.

6 Matt Rush (*Lomandra longifolia* 'Tanika') replaces the original use of turf in 'Snake in the Grass' for its greater drought tolerance. Laurustinus (*Viburnum tinus*) and ornamental pears (*Pyrus calleryana* cv.) form a backdrop.

7 The Ripple Lawn provides a sculptural element as well as constant fascination and subtle play opportunities for children.

Both recognise that well-selected planting can positivly contribute to a designed landscape, by screening or shading, establishing depth or creating the illusion of increased size in a small space.

In the north-facing area where a high fence creates enclosure, the Japanese sacred bamboo (*Nandina domestica*) has been utilised to offer a sense of depth and shadow with its numerous vertical stems and delightful light foliage. At the ground level, massed clivias (*Clivia miniata*) enjoy the protection of shade. Where cypresses once screened the adjacent house to the south, a new generation of screening trees has been selected, all of Australian origin. Chenille honey myrtle (*Melaleuca huegelii*) is familiar to Australian gardeners, especially those seeking reliably drought-tolerant performers. In this case it has been pruned to a small screening tree, allowing its foliage to be appreciated and to disguise its internal woodiness, which can be a drawback if not maintained. It is enhanced by forest oak (*Allocasuarina torulosa*) with deeply furrowed, cinnamon-coloured fibrous bark and finely textured weeping foliage that is especially delightful following rain; the pink-flowered cultivar of blueberry ash (*Elaeocarpus reticulatus* 'Prima Donna'), with long, glossy evergreen foliage and dark shiny blue fruit, which responds well to pruning; and the richly rewarding and extremely floriferous native hibiscus *Alyogyne huegelii*. Both this and the melaleuca commemorate the nineteenth-century Austrian botanist, Karl von Hugel.

The 'Snake in the Grass' garden no longer, in fact, features a grass, but a selected form of mat rush (*Lomandra longifolia* 'Tanika') clipped to give it exquisite elegant shape and dense growth. The evergreen native climber wonga wonga vine (*Pandorea pandorana*) is used on the fence. The use of the garden as a laboratory is reflected in Kate's comment: 'I probably wouldn't use this plant as a background creeper again as it bolts up the screen and becomes bare lower down and is too vigorous.' This comment is echoed by so many gardeners frustrated by the tendency of climbers to grow towards the light.

As already described, the 'Twisted Limbs' garden is dominated by dwarf yellow gum and the blue grass *Festuca Glauca*. Part of its value lies in its thatch of blue-grey foliage that fits well with woolybush (*Adenanthos serica*), flax lilies (*Dianella brevicaulis* and *D*. 'Little Rev'), mat rush (*Lomandra* 'Wingara'), and especially bearded iris (*Iris germanica*).

As the focus to the front garden, the 'Desert Space' is vitally important. Cushion bush is a first choice for this type of space especially since it has also been used by Kate to form balls of foliage that act as sculptures in the garden. The flax lilies, increasingly recognised for their value as garden plants, feature large here, too, with *Dianella caerulea* 'Breeze' surrounding the central feature and the dwarf cultivar *D*. 'Cassa Blue' introducing exquisite blue foliage on a plant reminiscent of a dwarf New Zealand flax. Kangaroo paws are also featured, though they are subject to black spot fungus in the garden's clay soils.

The dwarf form of river wattle (*Acacia cognata* 'Green Mist') brings yellow flowers in spring but for a really bright display Kate has introduced red lechenaultia (*Lechenaultia formosa*), which actually flowers in a range of colours from cream through yellow to orange and occasionally scarlet.

While Kate has found that her selected native plants offer immense success in the garden's sunny areas, she points out that they are less accommodating in shade; she has discovered that in these conditions South African iris (*Dietes* sp.), clivias (*Clivia miniata*), the silver-foliaged *Helichrysum petiolare*, and St Patrick's cabbage (*Saxifraga spathulata*) have all proved better performers. Inclusion of this last plant that is so often overlooked by gardeners shows how widely Kate and Kevin have searched for appropriate material for their garden, and its experimental nature means this is an ongoing process.

'Our garden is many things; a quiet retreat, a place to experiment and explore new concepts and materials, an outlet to indulge in a love of gardening (yet also be forgiving of neglect) and foremost, a place to encourage a love of being at home with family and friends.'

Garden owners

The structure of a pergola defines a loose garden room appropriate for outdoor dining in this Melbourne garden designed by Eckersley Stafford Design. The use of draping Boston ivy (*Parthenocissus tricuspidata*) increases the sense of enclosure.

Garden rooms

Kate and Kevin accommodate the different elements that make up their garden within distinct spaces around their home and studio. By doing so, they do more than separate the garden's contents, they add intrigue, anticipation and a sense of excitement to their design. This approach has potential for most gardens and even within small gardens, a sense of subtle separation, perhaps between areas of sun and shade, can provide substantial impact.

In order to create garden rooms, it is important to develop an effective site plan that organises the garden into appropriate spaces. Some of these may meet functional needs, such as service areas for clotheslines or compost, while others will allow you to explore your garden's potential for pleasure and recreation.

The size of garden rooms should be appropriate to support their purpose. Spaces that allow for activities at different times of the day can be developed; for example, a space that suits family use may contain a pool, lawn and dining terrace comprising the greater part of the garden. Separate outdoor rooms may be developed adjacent to the house for evening use, such as sitting areas adjoining bedrooms, where private space meets the needs of different occupants—relaxed, subtly lit with silver foliage for parents, more vibrant and exciting with dramatic plants for younger family members.

Spatial separation is especially useful for long, narrow gardens. Breaking a garden of this type into a series of smaller spaces changes the proportions of the garden completely from a long, narrow area into a series of better proportioned garden courts.

Vital to successful garden rooms is effective division of the garden, yet in creating separate spaces, a sense

At Chateau de Brecy in Normandy a glimpse through a gate gives a delicious sense of anticipation. Such effects can be achieved even in small gardens if carefully planned.

of continuity between them is all important. While a different theme can be designed for each 'room', the containing element—be it walls, fences or hedges—can provide the continuity. Paving surfaces, too, may provide a link, even if only one component of the paving extends through; for example, brick might act as a paved frame to gravel, natural stone and concrete pavers in three different garden courts, establishing a recurrent theme.

If spaces are to be effective, then the height of the separating elements is important. A 1.8m enclosure will be above eye-level for most, ensuring spaces are discrete. A circular opening in a wall offers a glimpse, drawing a visitor inwards, whereas a completely closed garden that only becomes apparent at the opening of a gate has a dramatic, entirely surprising impact.

By establishing a range of spaces, different themes can be pursued. This was famously implemented at Sissinghurst where Vita Sackville-West and Harold Nicholson established a white garden, a herb garden, a rose garden, and a yellow, orange and red cottage garden among others within the walls of an old castle in Kent, England.

In Canberra, Polly Park famously designed her garden to capture different international styles including Japan, Italy and Brazil within a series of separate courtyards.

At Cruden Farm, Dame Elisabeth Murdoch separates her fabulous herbaceous borders within a walled garden to be enjoyed at their summer peak.

Creating smaller, separate rooms within a larger area offers the opportunity to capture attention without competition from broader views. It facilitates the development of different moods and sensory awareness on a more intimate scale, where enclosure and containment heightens the experience. Spatial division can also highlight and provide a setting for garden features such as sculpture or text as is achieved in Karina Harris and Neil Hobbs Canberra garden.

For Kate and Kevin, spaces have allowed them to experiment in their garden, assessing different design approaches and artistic installations before implementing them elsewhere. To this extent their garden of spaces is a labratory for innovation and assessment. This possibility exists for other home gardeners, too; a broader range of opportunities can be developed, leading to a more exciting garden.

Sissinghurst is the classic garden of rooms. A glimpse through a hedge from one room to another creates a sense of anticipation and excitement, drawing the visitor on.

Illustration credits

All garden plans drawn by individual designers, except Fiona Brockhoff's Flinders garden plan, redrawn for publishing purposes by Leanne Dowey.
Plans were coloured by Jenny Wade.

Preliminary pages

Endpaper image: Leaves in John Patrick garden by Bridget Laird
Title page images: Suzan Quigg gazebo by Paul Phibbs
Imprint page images: Bridget Laird except *centre* Simon Griffiths
Page v images: Bridget Laird except *left* Simon Griffiths
Page vi images: *left* Bridget Laird, *centre* Simon Griffiths, right Paul Phibbs
Introduction: Fiona Brockhoff's garden gate image by Bridget Laird

Paul Bangay

All photography by Simon Griffiths except formal garden design (p 10), allees of trees (p 14), and flowering privet hedge (p 15) by Jenny Wade; *Alchemilla mollis* (p 16), steps to pool (p 19), 'Eryignac', France (p 19), Paul Bangay's Elwood courtyard (p 19) by John Patrick; and Edna Walling garden plan (p 18) by Brian Stonier

Fiona Brockhoff

All photography by Bridget Laird except clipped she-oak (p 30) and clipped box (p 31) by John Patrick; and coastal rosemary under lemon-scented gums (p 31) by Jenny Wade

Jamie Durie

All photography by Jason Busch (copyright Jamie Durie Publishing, garden designed by PATIO Landscape Architecture and Design, styling by Nadine Bush, props supplied by Twig on Burton) except Phil Johnson's timber boardwalk (p 41) by Greenmark Landscapes; Thomas Church deck (p 40) by Steve Mullany; and

Thomas Church deck around mature trees (p 41) and John Patrick deck (p 41) by John Patrick

Rick Eckersley

All photography by Eckersley Stafford Design except oak-leaf hydrangea (p 49), Chinese star jasmine (p 50) by Brigid Laird; and Phil Stray path, Crafted Landscapes (p 53) by Jenny Wade

Jeremy Ferrier

Photos of the entire garden (p 54 and p 63), vertical distance between house and garden (p 57), a large orb (p 60), planting at the forest's edge (p 61), golden bamboo (p 61), single butterfly (p 62), Royal Botanic Gardens, Cranbourne (p 64) by Jenny Wade; hole in the ground (p 56) by Jeremy Ferrier; existing bamboo (p 58), spiralling sandstone blocks (p 58) by Imago Photography Pty Ltd; Annie Coney's Garden, NZ (p 65); and Kate Cullity (p 65) by Kevin Taylor

Marisa Fontes

All photography by Bridget Laird except the breezeway before redesign (p 69) and the pool fence (p 70) by Marisa Fontes; and the Eckersley Stafford Design pathway (p 76) and the front entrance path (p 77) by John Patrick

Peter Fudge

All photography by Bridget Laird except plant groups (p 87), Pride of Madeira, (p 88) and Emma Plowright design (p 91) by Jenny Wade; David Kirkpatrick's design for a sloping site (p 90) by John Patrick; and Susan Small's steps (p 91) by Martin Bicevskis

Karina Harris & Neil Hobbs

All photography by Ben Wrigley except house access (p 95), rectangle hedges (p 96), patterned paving (p 97), sweet 16 (p 99), turf cubes (p 100) and dianella (p 102) by

Bridget Laird; Normandy girl (p 105) by John Patrick; painted poles (p 104) by Jay Vee Landscaping; metal screen (p 105) by Andy Rasheed and metal shoes and handbag by Bridget Laird

Dean Healy & Matt Huxtable
All photography by David J. Adams except paving fingers (p 109), Crinum pedunculatum (p 114), diverse planting (p 114), Sinatra Murphy design (p 116) by John Patrick; Paul Bangay symmetrical pond (p 117) by Peter Clarke, Latitude Photo (lighting designed by Light on Landscape); Phil Johnson's Olinda garden (p 117) by Greenmark Landscapes; and natural billabong (p 117) by Adam Humphrey

Dean Herald
All photography by Danny Kildare (copyright Rolling Stone Landscapes) except free-form pool (p 128) by Steven Mullany, Paul Bangay lit pool by Peter Clarke, Latitude Photo and natural swimming hole (p 129) by Greenmark Landscapes

Arno King
All photography by HS Photography except existing vegetation (p 133), garden pool house (p 140), Japanese lanterns (p 141) and Edna Walling garden (p 141) by John Patrick; pond (p 137) and *Thunbergia mysorensis* (p 138) by Jenny Wade; and poppy field (p 141) by Jay Vee Landscaping

Mira Martinazzo
All photography by Bridget Laird except pegging out the pool (p 144) and courtyard (p 148 and p 150) by Mira Martinazzo, Mediterranean-style garden (p 153) and oriental garden (p 153) by John Patrick; and cottage-style garden (p 152) by Lorraine Nadebaum

Georgina Martyn
All photography by Bridget Laird except dragonflies (p 161) by Simon Griffiths; stone wall (p 165) by Hugh Anderson; and paving (p 165) by Jenny Wade

Michael McCoy
All photography by Simon Griffiths except house window view (p 169), auditorium garden (p 175) knot garden (p 173) and Emma Plowright's silver plants (p 177) by Jenny Wade; rammed earth steps (p 166), creeping fig (p 171), terraced potager (p 171), swimming pool (p 170), octagonal pond (p 172), and driveway (p 172) by John Patrick; and sunflowers (p 175), and autumnal flowers (p 175) by Lorraine Nadebaum

Janine Mendel
All photography by Ron Tan except angle garden by Steve Taylor, Creative Outdoor Solutions (p 186) and Carey Cavanagh garden (p 187) by John Patrick

John Patrick
All photography by Bridget Laird except front garden with flowering cherries (p 190), garden seat (p 201), pergola (p 201) and semi-circular steps (p 201) by John Patrick; and path (p 192), pond (p 195) an rear borders (p 199) by Gary Chowanetz

Suzan Quigg
All photography by Paul Phibbs except daytime garden view (p 207) by Jenny Wade; Georgina Martyn garden (p 213) by Georgina Martyn; perimeter planting (p 205) and Fiona Brockhoff's curved fence (p 213) by John Patrick; and glass pool fence (p 212) by Out from the Blue

Catherine Shields
All photography by Bridget Laird except Robert Boyle's garden (p 224) by Heather at Seawind Studios, Tuscan garden (p 225) and Sydney harbour view (p 225) by John Patrick

John Sullivan
All photography by Hortulus except small creek (p 230) by Jenny Wade; view from back path (p 230); water jets (p 233), zen-style space (p 232), door of Bak (p 235) and front garden mature planting (p 234) by Racheal Isolde Samuels; Rick Eckersley cobbled paving (p 237) by

Eckersley Stafford Design; water storage pond (p 237) by Adam Humphrey (copyright Greenmark Landscapes); and gravel-lined swales (p 236) by Jim Fogarty

Kevin Taylor and Kate Cullity

Photos of red squares (p 242) twisted limbs (p 245), snake in the grass and spine (p 245), and mat rush (p 246) by Edward James; desert space (p 239) by Trevor Fox; woven walls (p 241), still waters leaves (p 242), corten-steel gate (p 245), matt rush (p 246) by Andy Rasheed; sculptural square detail (p 240), ripple lawn (p 246) by Kate Cullity; Sissinghurst (p 249) and Chateau de Brecy (p 249) by John Patrick; and Melbourne garden pergola (p 248) by Eckersley Stafford Design

Contributor images: Paul Bangay by Simon Griffiths, Fiona Brockhoff by Bridget Laird, Jamie Durie by Jason Busch, Rick Eckersley by Eckersley Stafford Design, Jeremy Ferrier by Jeremy Ferrier Landscape Architects, Marisa Fontes by Bridget Laird, Peter Fudge by David Matheson, Karina Harris and Neil Hobbs by Bridget Laird, Dean Herald by Danny Kildare, Arno King by Annette Irish, Georgina Martyn by Bridget Laird, Michael McCoy by Tim Lane, Janine Mendel by Denise Williams, John Patrick by Bridget Laird, Suzan Quigg by Hannah Quigg, Catherine Shields by Bridget Laird, Kate Cullity and Kevin Taylor by Taylor Cullity Lethlean

Final photo of Michael McCoy garden by Simon Griffiths

Contributors

Paul Bangay
PRB Design

Fiona Brockhoff
Fiona Brockhoff Landscape Design

Jamie Durie
PATIO Landscape Architecture
& Design

Rick Eckersley
Eckersley Stafford Design

Jeremy Ferrier
Jeremy Ferrier Landscape Architects

Marisa Fontes
Outsidesign

Peter Fudge
Peter Fudge Gardens

**Ryan Healy &
Matt Huxtable**
Newforms Landscape Architecture
Pty Ltd

**Karina Harris
& Neil Hobbs**
Harris Hobbs Landscapes

Dean Herald
Rolling Stone Landscapes

Arno King

Mira Martinazzo
Modern Urban Design (M.U.D.)

Georgina Martyn
BoldSimplicity Pty Ltd

Michael McCoy

Janine Mendel
Cultivart Landscape Design

John Patrick
John Patrick Pty Ltd

Suzan Quigg
Suzan J Quigg Landscape Design

Catherine Shields
The Alchemy of Gardens

John Sullivan
Hortulus Landscape Design
& Management

**Kevin Taylor
& Kate Cullity**
Taylor Cullity Lethlean

Acknowledgements

The production of a book of this type involves an enormous cast who each contribute a vital portion of the overall package. Each designer included in the book — and frequently members of their design team — was consistently helpful and attentive to our demands for continual scraps of information. We hope they enjoy their gardens in our final accounts. It was they who contacted garden owners to seek approval for each garden's inclusion in the book. Fortunately all of the owners happily agreed and were endlessly helpful in providing their thoughts and opinions about the outcome of the design work. It speaks volumes for landscape designers that every client was abundantly satisfied with the outcome and happy to have their property on show. To each we express our gratitude.

ABC Books has been wonderful to work with. From Brigitta Doyle who bravely commissioned the book (after consultation with Daffy the Staffy!), to Jo Mackay who tolerantly and gently guided us through the hoops that authors face, Susin Chow who edited the script and Nada Backovic and Jude Rowe who designed the final product, each has been unfailingly supportive and helpful.

Photographs are vital in capturing the spirit of gardens. Bridget Laird worked with us from the start, taking images of gardens around the country, a tiring task with early starts and late nights. Ben Wrigley and Simon Griffiths characteristically provided perfect images and cheerful support, while Lorraine Nadebaum, Gary Chowanetz and Steve Mullany also allowed us to use their images. We are also indebted to Barry Stonier who allowed us to reproduce a previously unpublished Edna Walling plan.

Colleagues at *Gardening Australia* are a fount of knowledge and Colin Campbell and Jerry Coleby-Williams gave special help in finding gardens in Queensland. Susan Small in Tasmania, Lorna Barnett from Haughty Culture and Josh Byrne in Perth provided guidance in their respective states.

Leanne Dowey, Andrea Proctor, Tim Bungey, Ngaire Hudson and Simon Howe together with the rest of the team at John Patrick Landscape Architects, offered every imaginable type of support from assisting with computer glitches, plan drawing, finding John's lost manuscripts and notes and simply tolerating John's periodic pre-occupation with the book (by contrast Jenny Wade deserves special thanks for tolerating John's lack of pre-occupation with the book).

This project grew out of Kew Rotary Club's Garden DesignFest event, a project opening Melbourne designed gardens to raise money for charity. We thank the members who became involved in the success of that project and Ian Dalton, who always gives support when required. Fiona Langley, Gardens at Night, Light on Landscapes, John Rayner of Melbourne University's Burnley horticultural campus and Phil Johnson of Greenmark Landscapes went out of their way to provide help and support, as did many other designers and supporters in the garden design industry.

We would also like to particularly acknowledge and thank Peter Nixon, Jim Fogarty, Jenny and Neil Delmage, Phil O'Malley, Myles Baldwin and Steven Clegg, and respective clients, for their generous commitment of time and support for the project.

Finally, to Professor Jim Sinatra who has been a great friend to many of us in the landscape architectural profession in Australia and who has inspired many students who have passed through his hands in over twenty years in Melbourne, thank you for the foreword.

JOHN PATRICK AND JENNY WADE

The writing and coordination of a book such as this is an enormous job. Only those who have been involved in such an exercise appreciate how many hours of often tedious work are involved. I wish to acknowledge the extraordinary efforts that Jenny has put into completing this book, chasing up designers, photographers and owners but above all, me, to ensure a satisfactory conclusion to our work. I trust that she feels it was all worthwhile, for the result is a tribute to her efforts and very much her book.

I must also thank my family who are well aware of my love for books and who are only too used to my either reading or writing them. Now it's done, I will no doubt dismay them by finding another project.

JOHN PATRICK

Apart from all of the wonderful aforementioned contributors, I would also like to thank you John for the opportunity to be involved in this project and many others. I am forever in awe of your knowledge and understanding of design, architecture and all things horticultural and have learnt so much from your willingness to teach.

To my much loved and adored family, Grae, Ruby, Eliza and Nelson, how can I ever thank you for your unwavering support? Your self-sufficiency in my absences, unconditional love and understanding, reassurance, approval and assistance in so many ways from housework to hugs has meant the world to me. Likewise, heartfelt thanks to my magnificent extended family and friends who have helped in no small way with everything from child minding, home duties to base colouring and proof reading and most of all, by your forgiveness for being constantly ignored while I've had my head in a good book! I sincerely hope you all now share in a sense of achievement and find the finished product worthy of your varied and much appreciated contributions.

JENNY WADE

Index